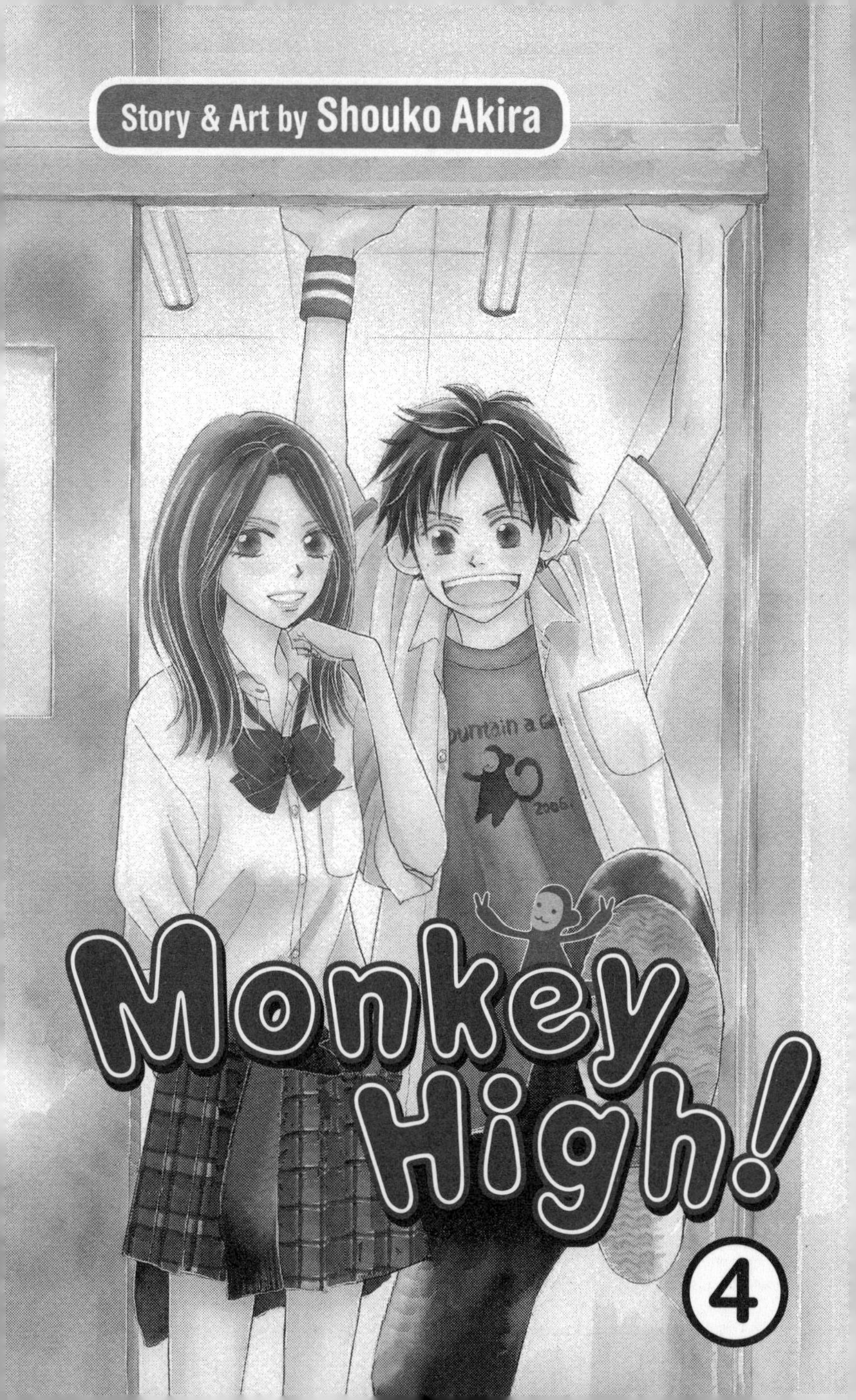
Story & Art by Shouko Akira
Monkey High!
4

Monkey High!

4

CONTENTS

10th Monkey: Summer's About to Begin
5

11th Monkey: Even a Scary Dare Can't Cool Down the Summer Heat!!
51

12th Monkey: Who Wants to Do Homework in the Summer?!
93

13th Monkey: Finish Your Homework Before the New Semester! (Hopefully)
139

Postscript
184

Story Thus Far

Masaru Yamashita
(Nickname: Macharu)

Haruna starts going out with Macharu (often teased and called a baby monkey) at her new school. Every day is like a carnival with her rowdy classmates. So many events and happenings... Haruna and Macharu seem to have safely reached the summer, but...?!

Haruna Aizawa

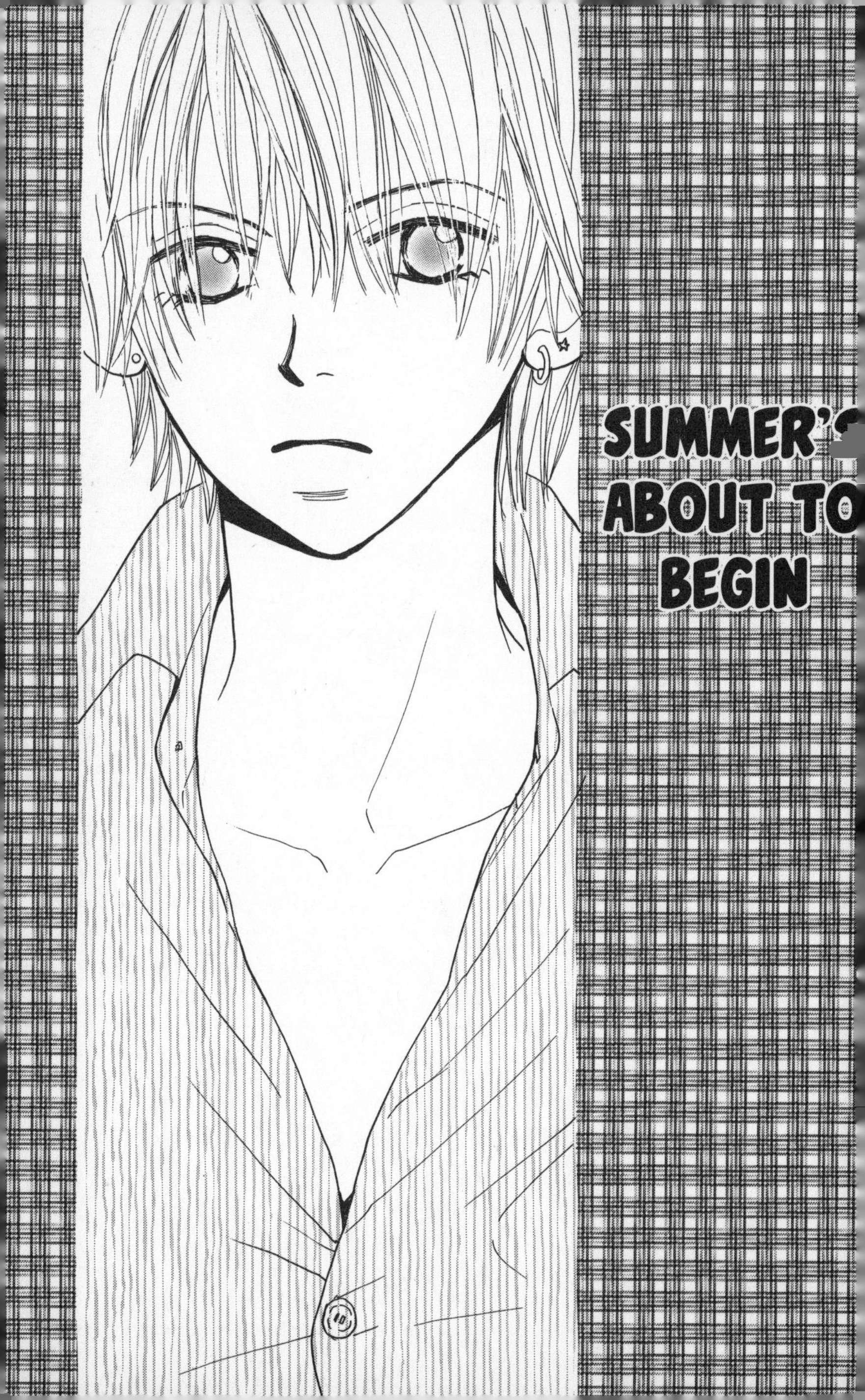
SUMMER'S ABOUT TO BEGIN

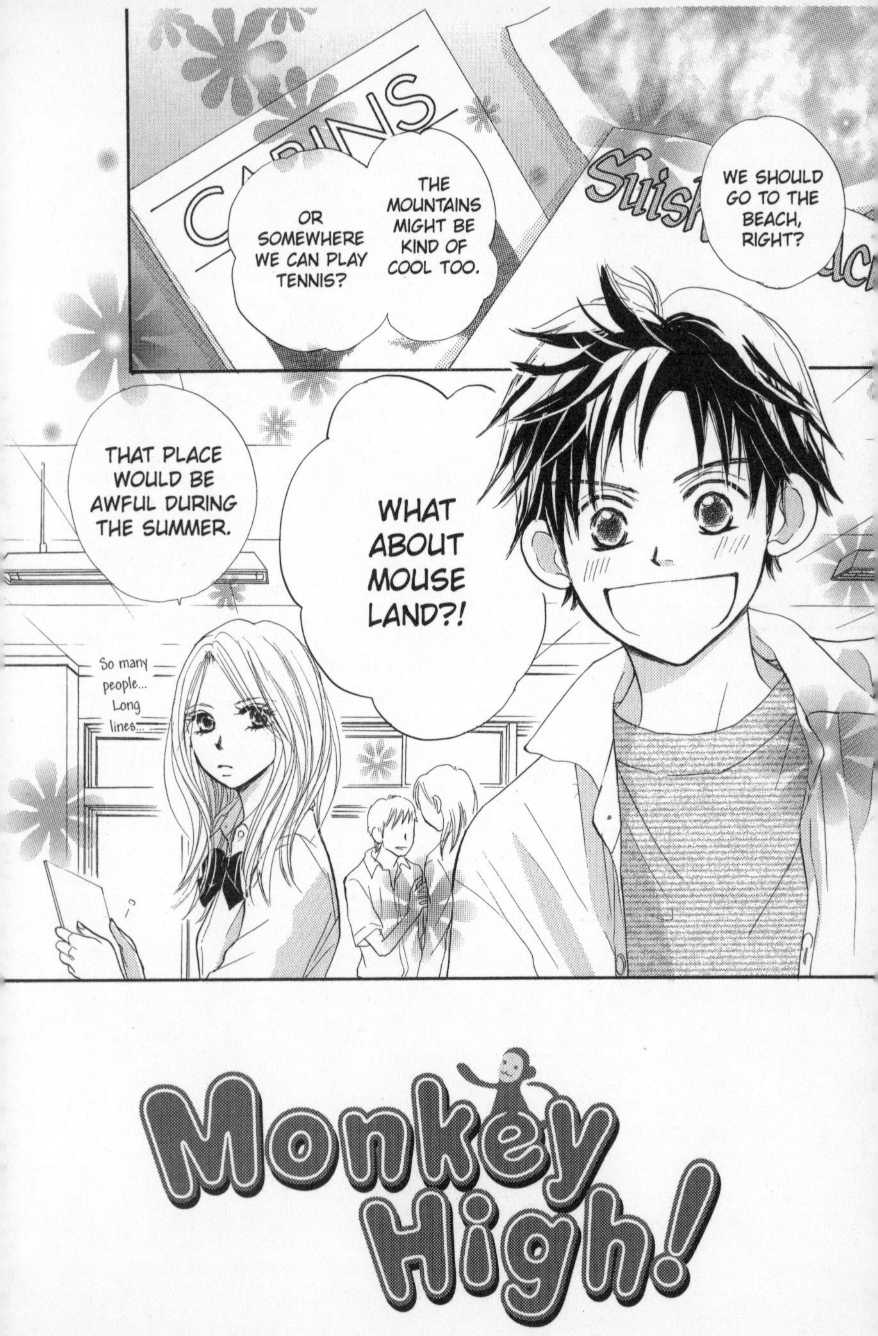
WE SHOULD GO TO THE BEACH, RIGHT?
THE MOUNTAINS MIGHT BE KIND OF COOL TOO.
OR SOMEWHERE WE CAN PLAY TENNIS?
WHAT ABOUT MOUSE LAND?!
THAT PLACE WOULD BE AWFUL DURING THE SUMMER.
So many people... Long lines...

Monkey High!

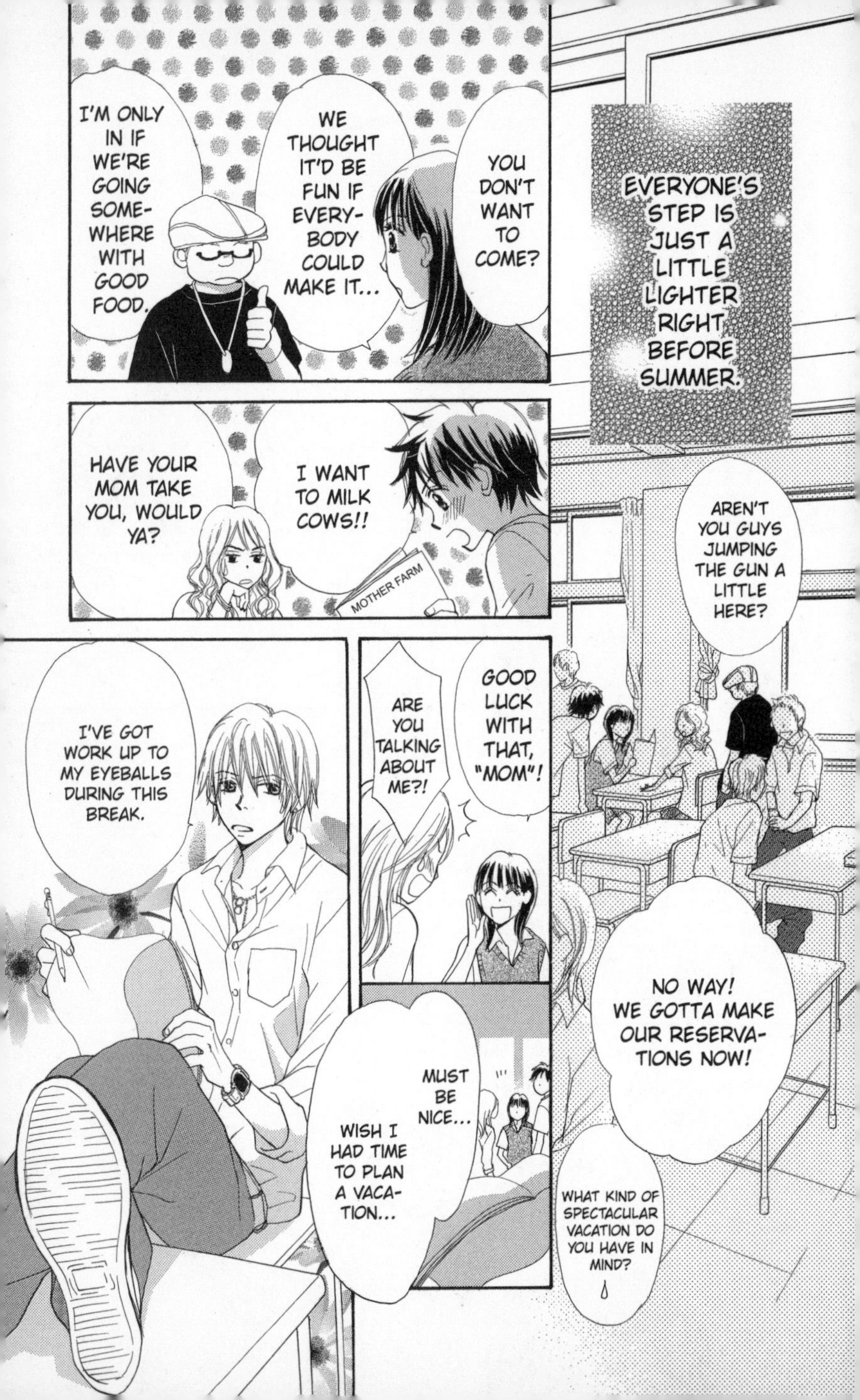
EVERYONE'S STEP IS JUST A LITTLE LIGHTER RIGHT BEFORE SUMMER.
AREN'T YOU GUYS JUMPING THE GUN A LITTLE HERE?
NO WAY! WE GOTTA MAKE OUR RESERVA-TIONS NOW!
WHAT KIND OF SPECTACULAR VACATION DO YOU HAVE IN MIND?
YOU DON'T WANT TO COME?
WE THOUGHT IT'D BE FUN IF EVERY-BODY COULD MAKE IT...
I'M ONLY IN IF WE'RE GOING SOME-WHERE WITH GOOD FOOD.
I WANT TO MILK COWS!!
MOTHER FARM
HAVE YOUR MOM TAKE YOU, WOULD YA?
GOOD LUCK WITH THAT, "MOM"!
ARE YOU TALKING ABOUT ME?!
MUST BE NICE...
WISH I HAD TIME TO PLAN A VACA-TION...
I'VE GOT WORK UP TO MY EYEBALLS DURING THIS BREAK.

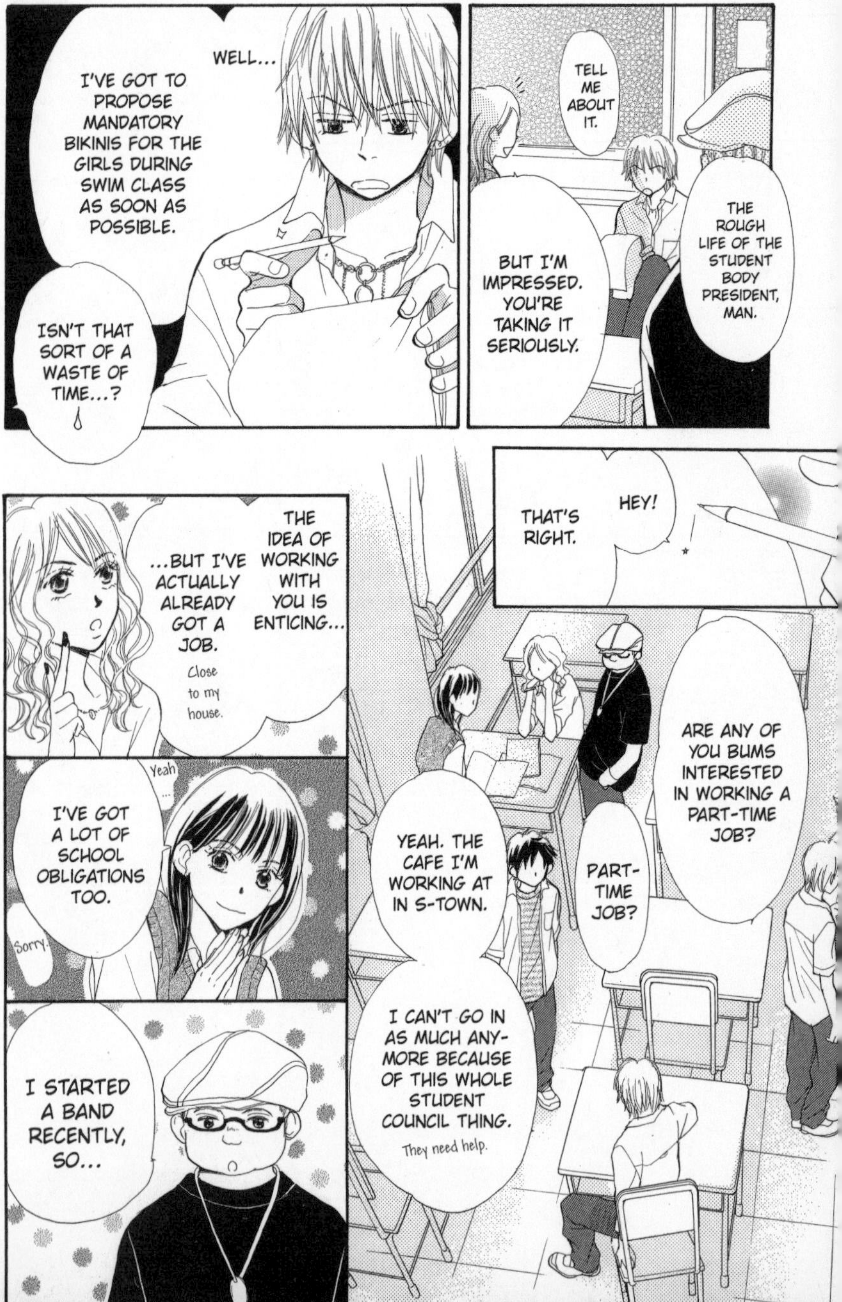
TELL ME ABOUT IT.
THE ROUGH LIFE OF THE STUDENT BODY PRESIDENT, MAN.
BUT I'M IMPRESSED. YOU'RE TAKING IT SERIOUSLY.
WELL...
I'VE GOT TO PROPOSE MANDATORY BIKINIS FOR THE GIRLS DURING SWIM CLASS AS SOON AS POSSIBLE.
ISN'T THAT SORT OF A WASTE OF TIME...?
HEY!
THAT'S RIGHT.
ARE ANY OF YOU BUMS INTERESTED IN WORKING A PART-TIME JOB?
PART-TIME JOB?
YEAH. THE CAFE I'M WORKING AT IN S-TOWN.
I CAN'T GO IN AS MUCH ANY-MORE BECAUSE OF THIS WHOLE STUDENT COUNCIL THING.
They need help.
THE IDEA OF WORKING WITH YOU IS ENTICING...
...BUT I'VE ACTUALLY ALREADY GOT A JOB.
Close to my house.
Yeah...
I'VE GOT A LOT OF SCHOOL OBLIGATIONS TOO.
Sorry.
I STARTED A BAND RECENTLY, SO...

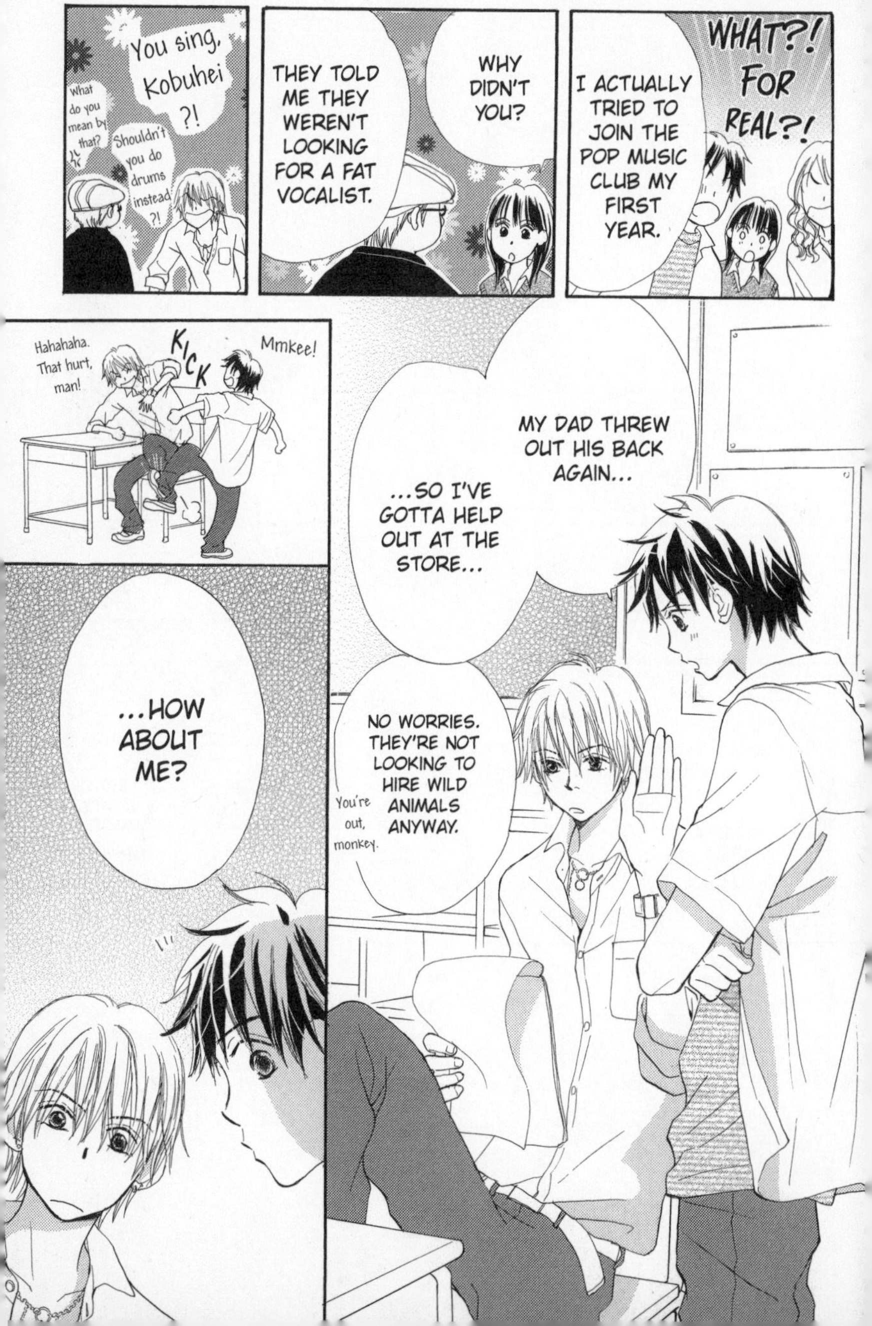
WHAT?! FOR REAL?!
I ACTUALLY TRIED TO JOIN THE POP MUSIC CLUB MY FIRST YEAR.
WHY DIDN'T YOU?
THEY TOLD ME THEY WEREN'T LOOKING FOR A FAT VOCALIST.
You sing, Kobuhei ?!
Shouldn't you do drums instead ?!
What do you mean by that?
MY DAD THREW OUT HIS BACK AGAIN...
...SO I'VE GOTTA HELP OUT AT THE STORE...
NO WORRIES. THEY'RE NOT LOOKING TO HIRE WILD ANIMALS ANYWAY.
You're out, monkey.
Mmkee!
KICK
Hahahaha. That hurt, man!
...HOW ABOUT ME?

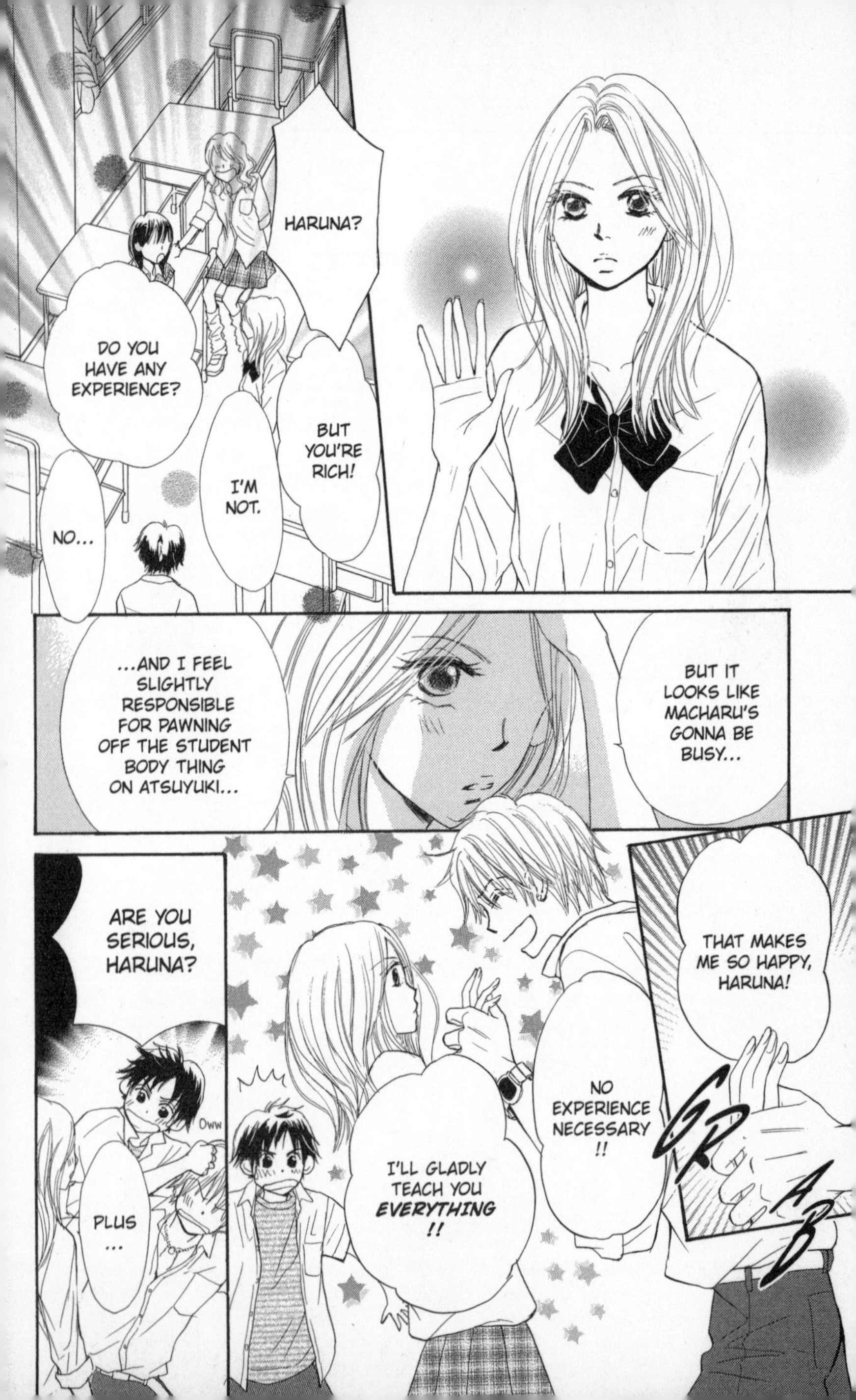
HARUNA?
DO YOU HAVE ANY EXPERIENCE?
BUT YOU'RE RICH!
I'M NOT.
NO...
BUT IT LOOKS LIKE MACHARU'S GONNA BE BUSY...
...AND I FEEL SLIGHTLY RESPONSIBLE FOR PAWNING OFF THE STUDENT BODY THING ON ATSUYUKI...
THAT MAKES ME SO HAPPY, HARUNA!
GRAB
NO EXPERIENCE NECESSARY!!
I'LL GLADLY TEACH YOU *EVERYTHING*!!
ARE YOU SERIOUS, HARUNA?
OWW
PLUS...

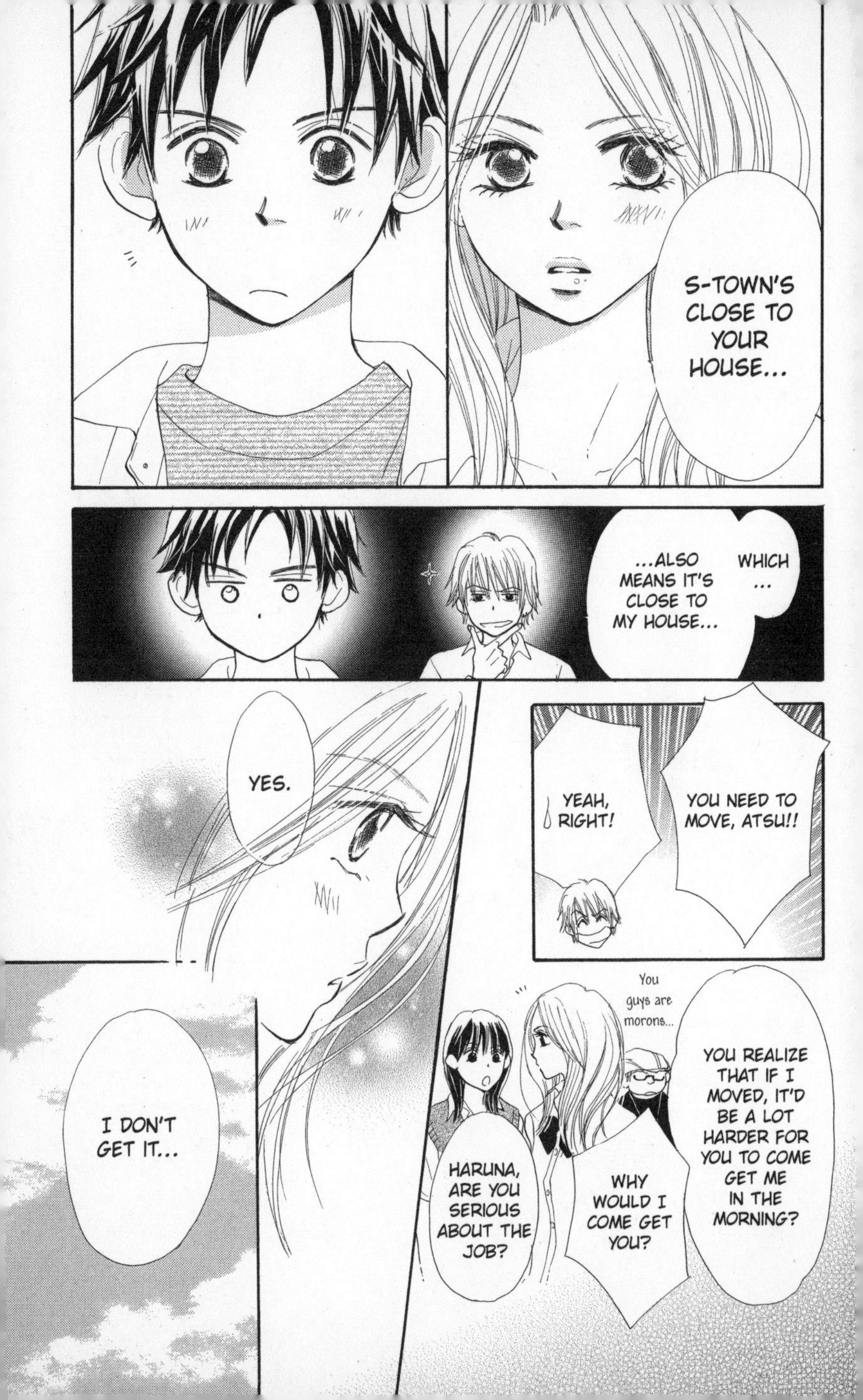
S-TOWN'S CLOSE TO YOUR HOUSE...
WHICH ...
...ALSO MEANS IT'S CLOSE TO MY HOUSE...
YOU NEED TO MOVE, ATSU!!
YEAH, RIGHT!
YES.
You guys are morons...
YOU REALIZE THAT IF I MOVED, IT'D BE A LOT HARDER FOR YOU TO COME GET ME IN THE MORNING?
WHY WOULD I COME GET YOU?
HARUNA, ARE YOU SERIOUS ABOUT THE JOB?
I DON'T GET IT...

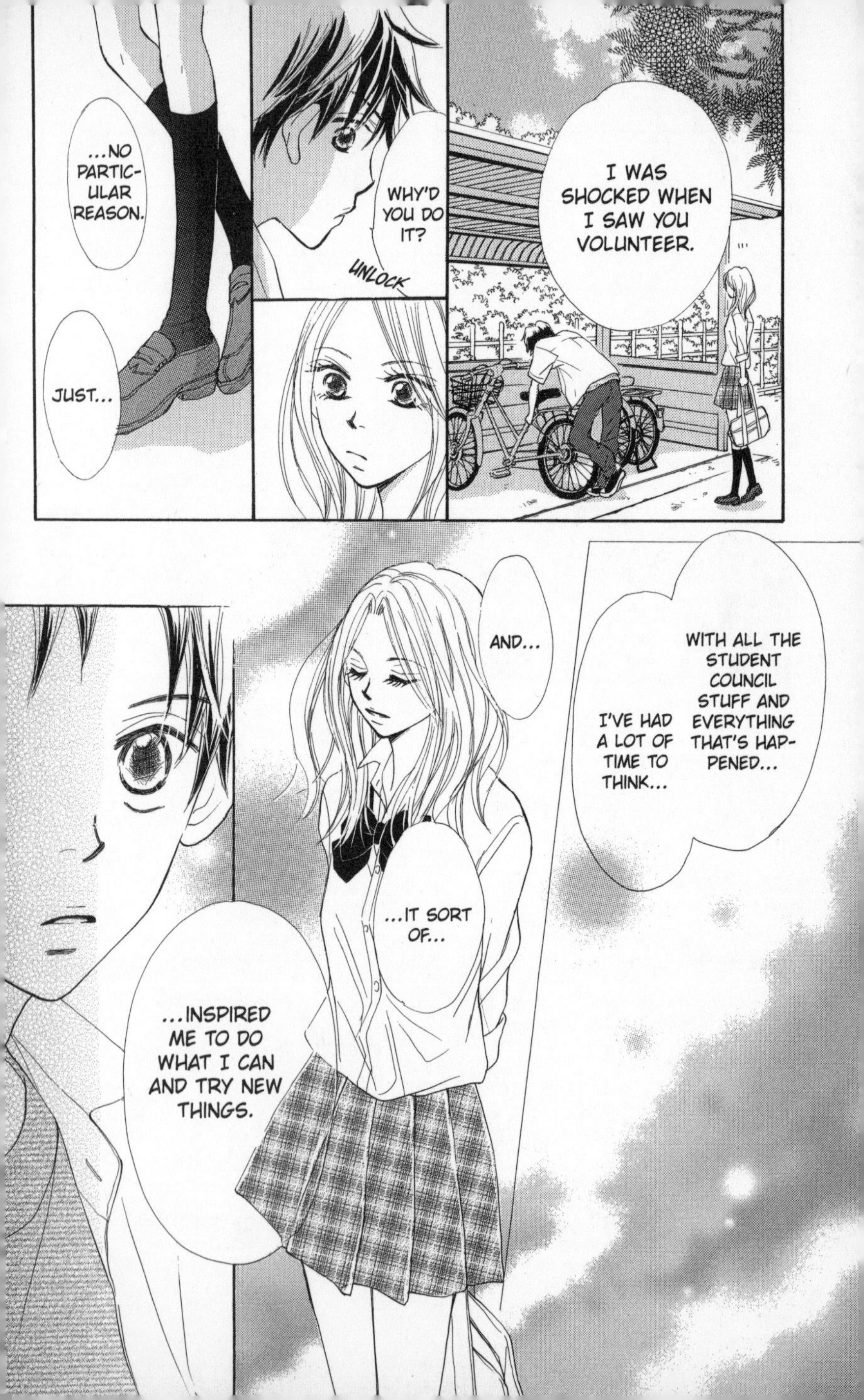
I WAS SHOCKED WHEN I SAW YOU VOLUNTEER.
WHY'D YOU DO IT?
UNLOCK
...NO PARTICULAR REASON.
JUST...
WITH ALL THE STUDENT COUNCIL STUFF AND EVERYTHING THAT'S HAPPENED...
I'VE HAD A LOT OF TIME TO THINK...
AND...
...IT SORT OF...
...INSPIRED ME TO DO WHAT I CAN AND TRY NEW THINGS.

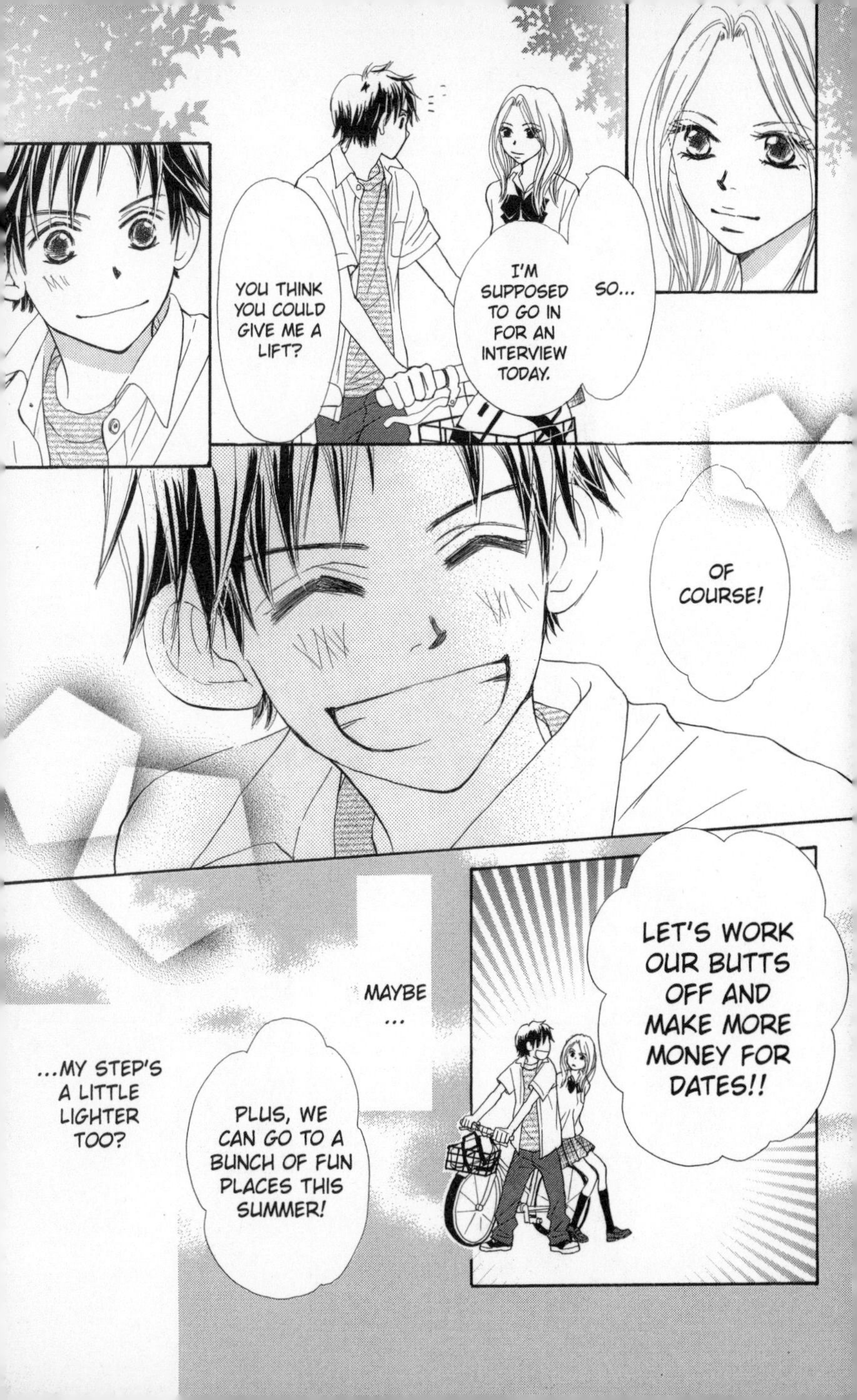
SO...
I'M SUPPOSED TO GO IN FOR AN INTERVIEW TODAY.
YOU THINK YOU COULD GIVE ME A LIFT?
OF COURSE!
LET'S WORK OUR BUTTS OFF AND MAKE MORE MONEY FOR DATES!!
PLUS, WE CAN GO TO A BUNCH OF FUN PLACES THIS SUMMER!
MAYBE ...
...MY STEP'S A LITTLE LIGHTER TOO?

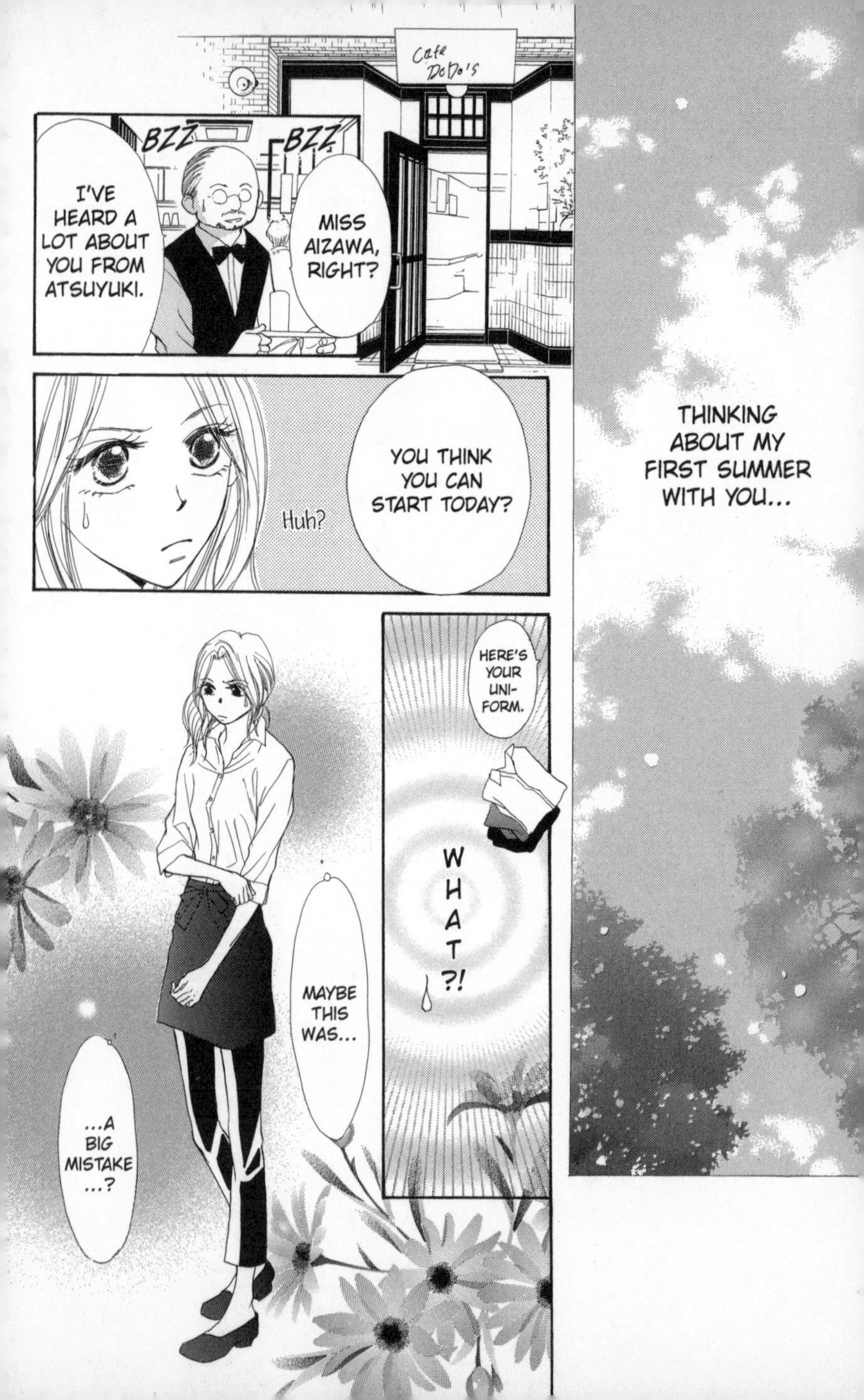
THINKING ABOUT MY FIRST SUMMER WITH YOU...
Cafe DeDo's
BZZ
BZZ
MISS AIZAWA, RIGHT?
I'VE HEARD A LOT ABOUT YOU FROM ATSUYUKI.
YOU THINK YOU CAN START TODAY?
Huh?
HERE'S YOUR UNI-FORM.
WHAT?!
MAYBE THIS WAS...
...A BIG MISTAKE ...?

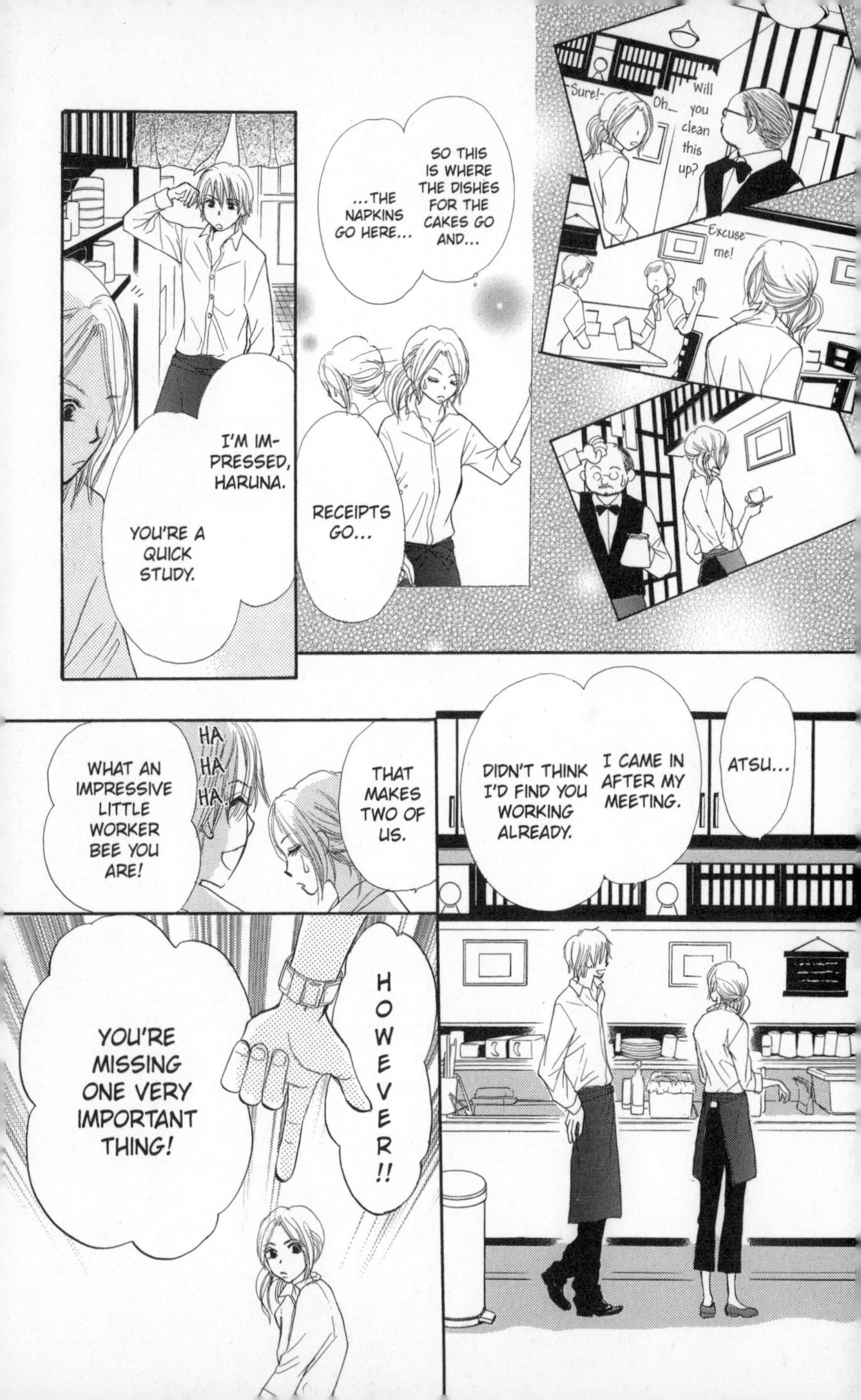
Will you clean this up?
Oh_
Sure!-
Excuse me!
SO THIS IS WHERE THE DISHES FOR THE CAKES GO AND...
...THE NAPKINS GO HERE...
RECEIPTS GO...
I'M IM-PRESSED, HARUNA.
YOU'RE A QUICK STUDY.
ATSU...
I CAME IN AFTER MY MEETING.
DIDN'T THINK I'D FIND YOU WORKING ALREADY.
THAT MAKES TWO OF US.
HA HA HA.
WHAT AN IMPRESSIVE LITTLE WORKER BEE YOU ARE!
HOWEVER!!
YOU'RE MISSING ONE VERY IMPORTANT THING!

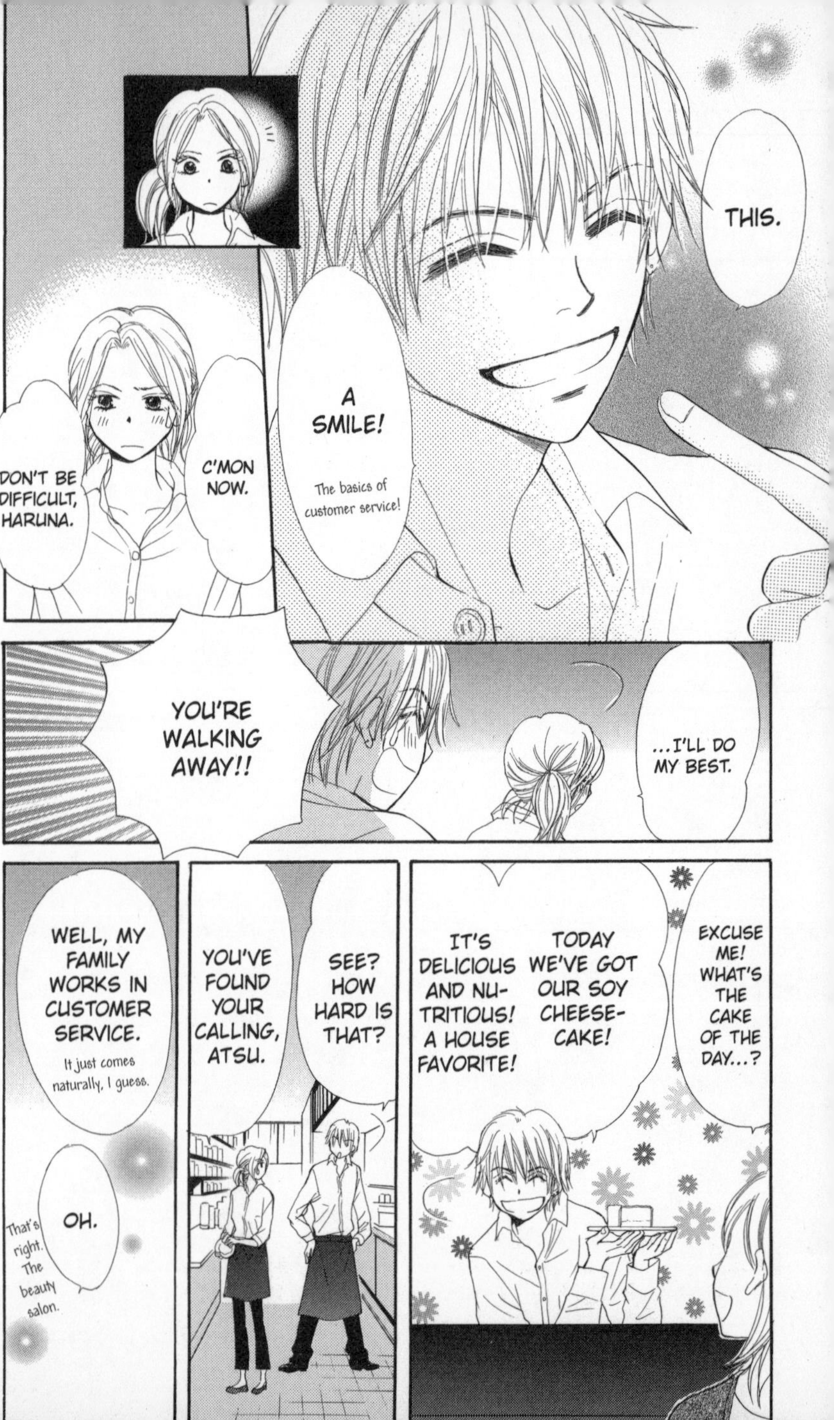
THIS.
A SMILE!
The basics of customer service!
C'MON NOW.
DON'T BE DIFFICULT, HARUNA.
...I'LL DO MY BEST.
YOU'RE WALKING AWAY!!
EXCUSE ME! WHAT'S THE CAKE OF THE DAY...?
TODAY WE'VE GOT OUR SOY CHEESE-CAKE!
IT'S DELICIOUS AND NU-TRITIOUS! A HOUSE FAVORITE!
SEE? HOW HARD IS THAT?
YOU'VE FOUND YOUR CALLING, ATSU.
WELL, MY FAMILY WORKS IN CUSTOMER SERVICE.
It just comes naturally, I guess.
OH.
That's right. The beauty salon.

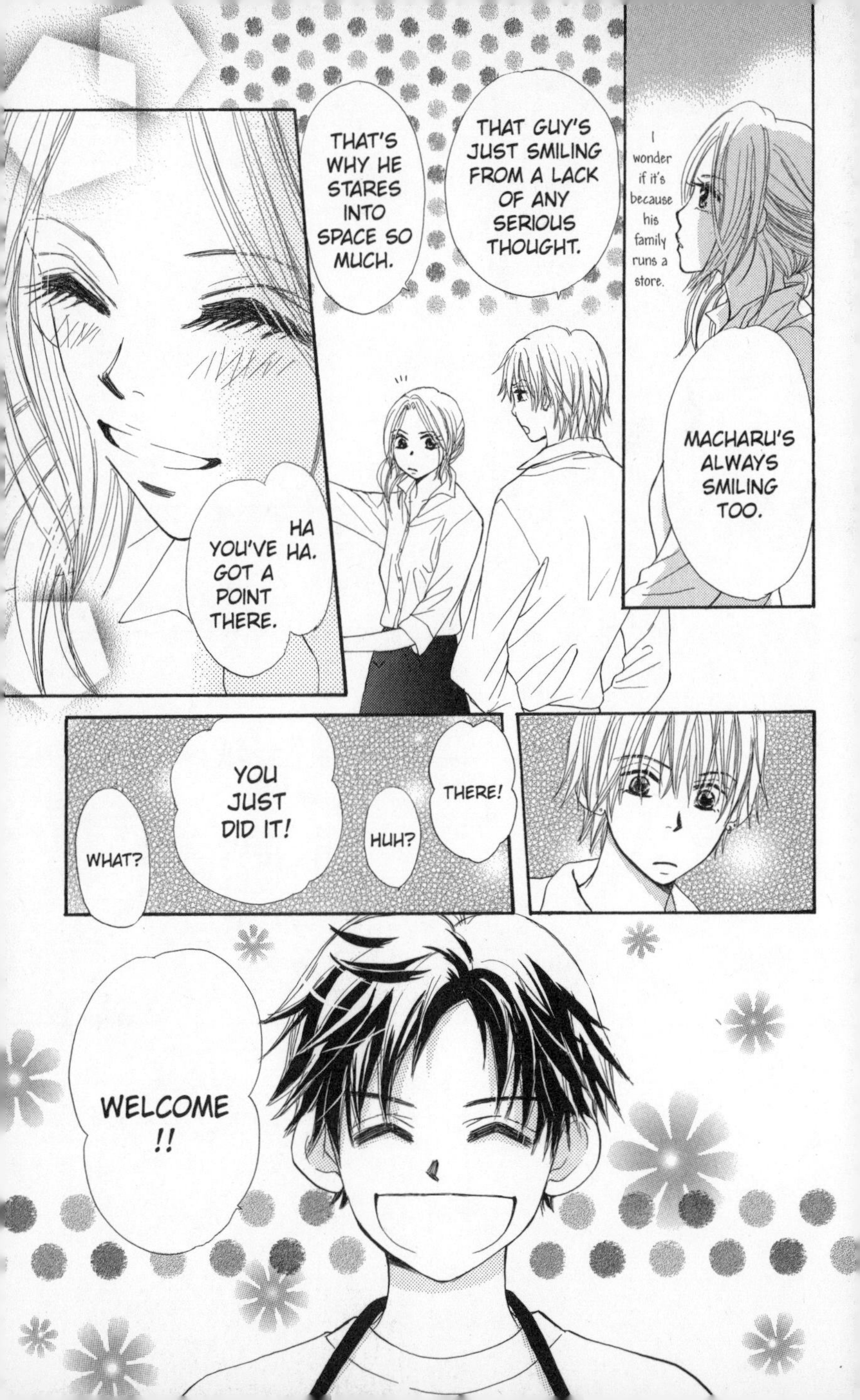
I wonder if it's because his family runs a store.
MACHARU'S ALWAYS SMILING TOO.
THAT GUY'S JUST SMILING FROM A LACK OF ANY SERIOUS THOUGHT.
THAT'S WHY HE STARES INTO SPACE SO MUCH.
HA HA.
YOU'VE GOT A POINT THERE.
THERE!
HUH?
YOU JUST DID IT!
WHAT?
WELCOME !!

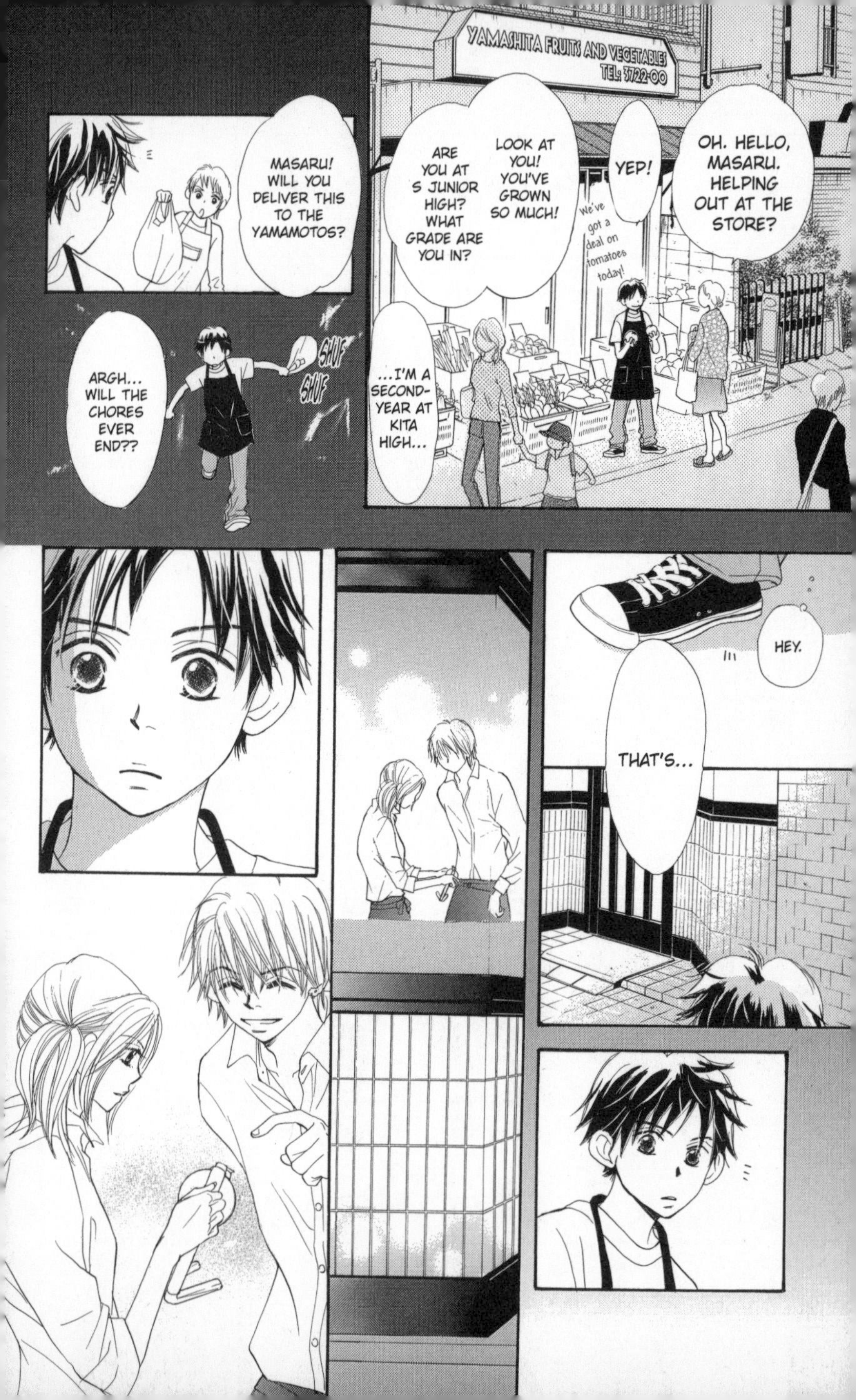
YAMASHITA FRUITS AND VEGETABLES
TEL: 3722-00
OH. HELLO, MASARU. HELPING OUT AT THE STORE?
YEP!
We've got a deal on tomatoes today!
LOOK AT YOU! YOU'VE GROWN SO MUCH!
ARE YOU AT S JUNIOR HIGH? WHAT GRADE ARE YOU IN?
...I'M A SECOND-YEAR AT KITA HIGH...
MASARU! WILL YOU DELIVER THIS TO THE YAMAMOTOS?
SHUF
SHUF
ARGH... WILL THE CHORES EVER END??
HEY.
THAT'S...

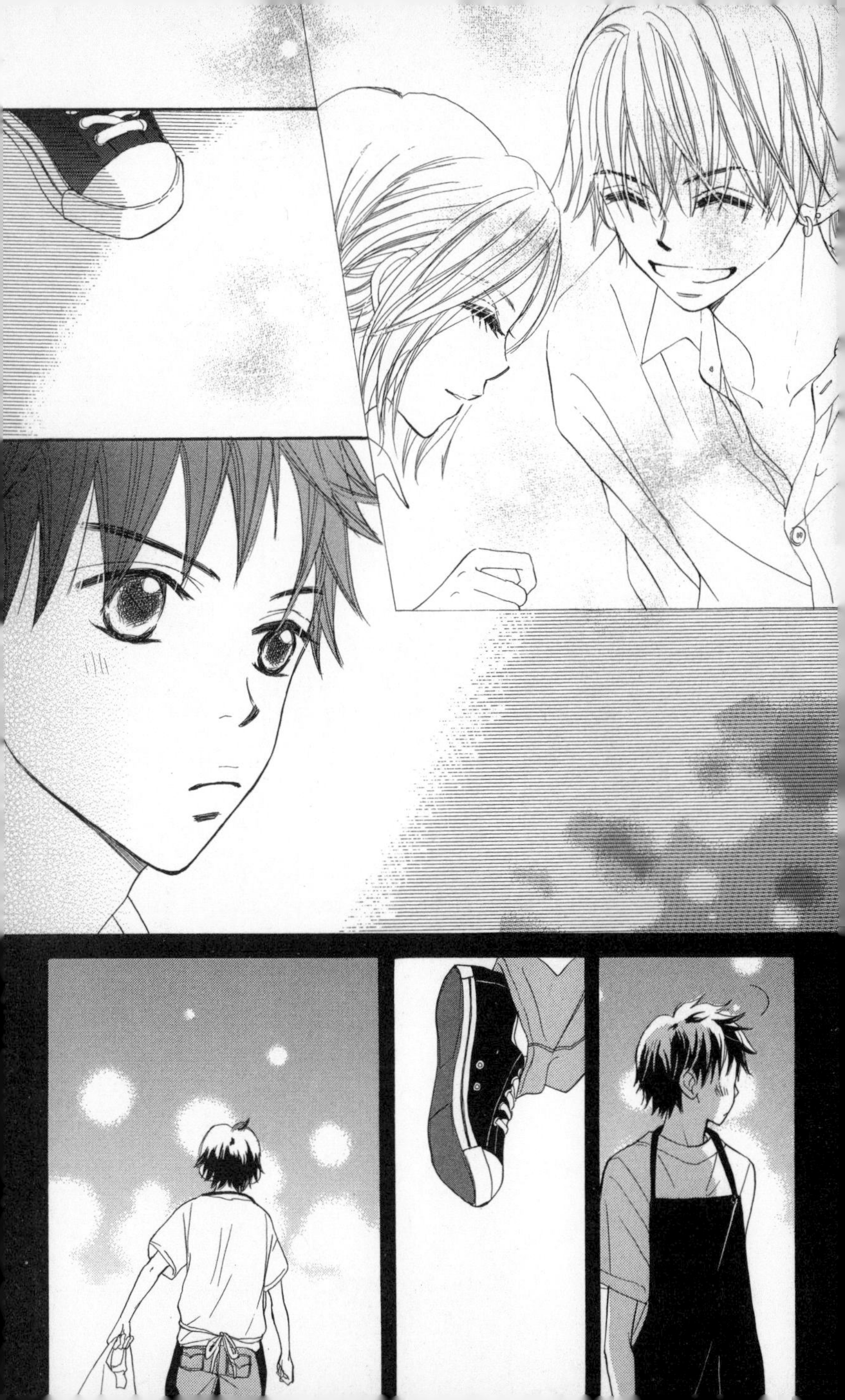

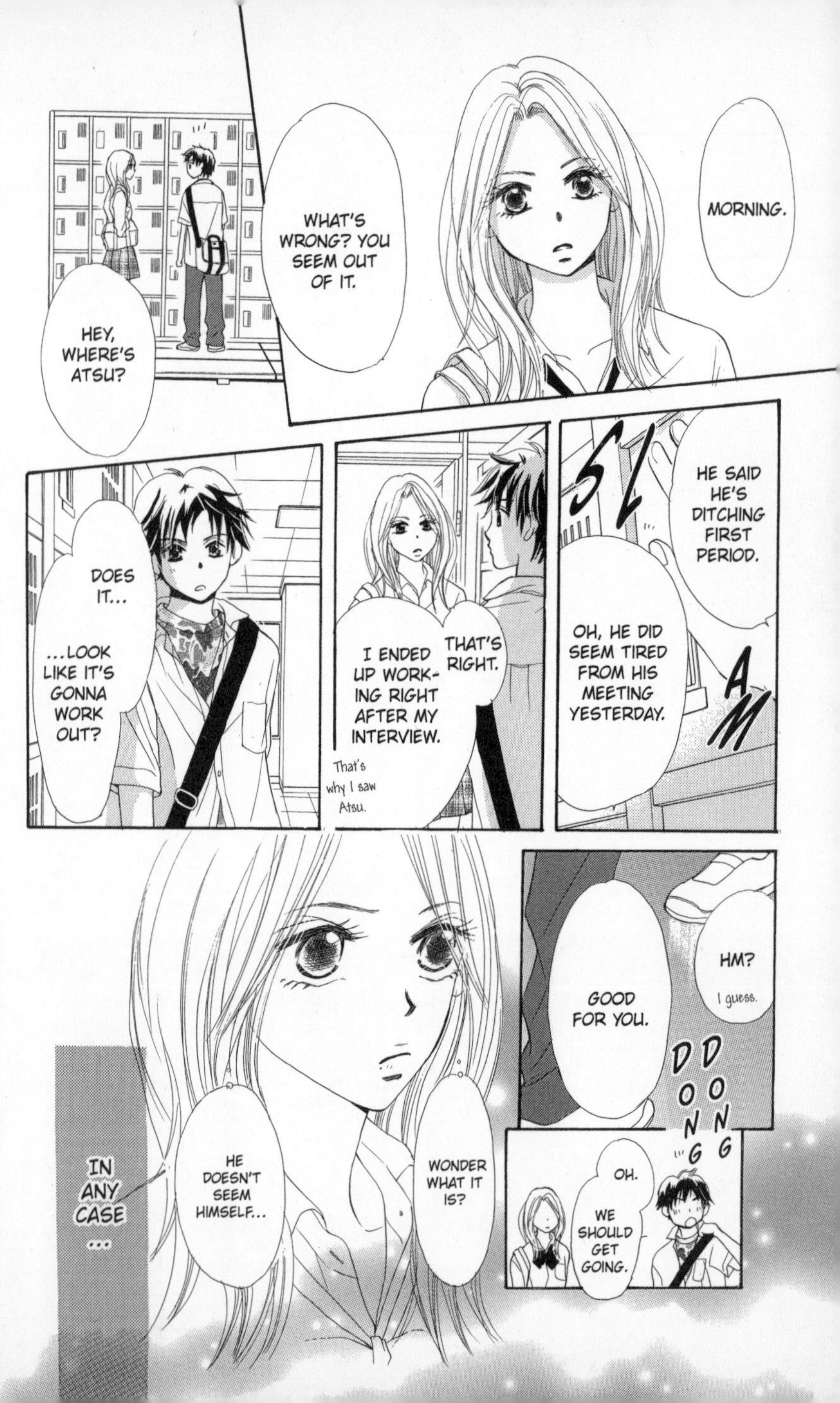
MORNING.
WHAT'S WRONG? YOU SEEM OUT OF IT.
HEY, WHERE'S ATSU?
HE SAID HE'S DITCHING FIRST PERIOD.
SLAM
OH, HE DID SEEM TIRED FROM HIS MEETING YESTERDAY.
THAT'S RIGHT.
I ENDED UP WORKING RIGHT AFTER MY INTERVIEW.
That's why I saw Atsu.
DOES IT...
...LOOK LIKE IT'S GONNA WORK OUT?
HM?
I guess.
GOOD FOR YOU.
DONG DONG
OH.
WE SHOULD GET GOING.
WONDER WHAT IT IS?
HE DOESN'T SEEM HIMSELF...
IN ANY CASE...

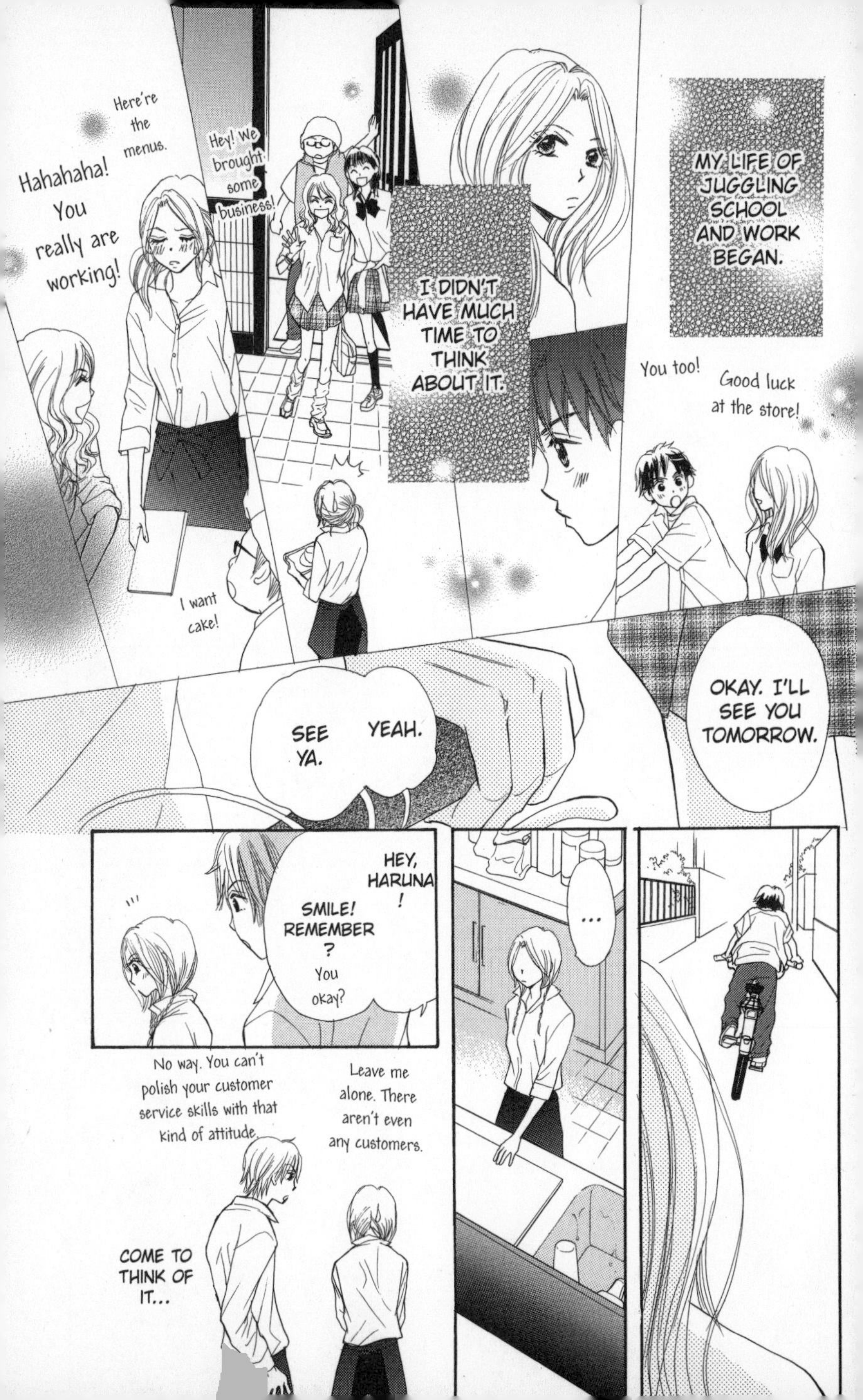
MY LIFE OF JUGGLING SCHOOL AND WORK BEGAN.
Good luck at the store!
You too!
I DIDN'T HAVE MUCH TIME TO THINK ABOUT IT.
Hey! We brought some business!
Here're the menus.
Hahahaha! You really are working!
I want cake!
OKAY. I'LL SEE YOU TOMORROW.
YEAH.
SEE YA.
...
HEY, HARUNA!
SMILE! REMEMBER?
You okay?
Leave me alone. There aren't even any customers.
No way. You can't polish your customer service skills with that kind of attitude.
COME TO THINK OF IT...

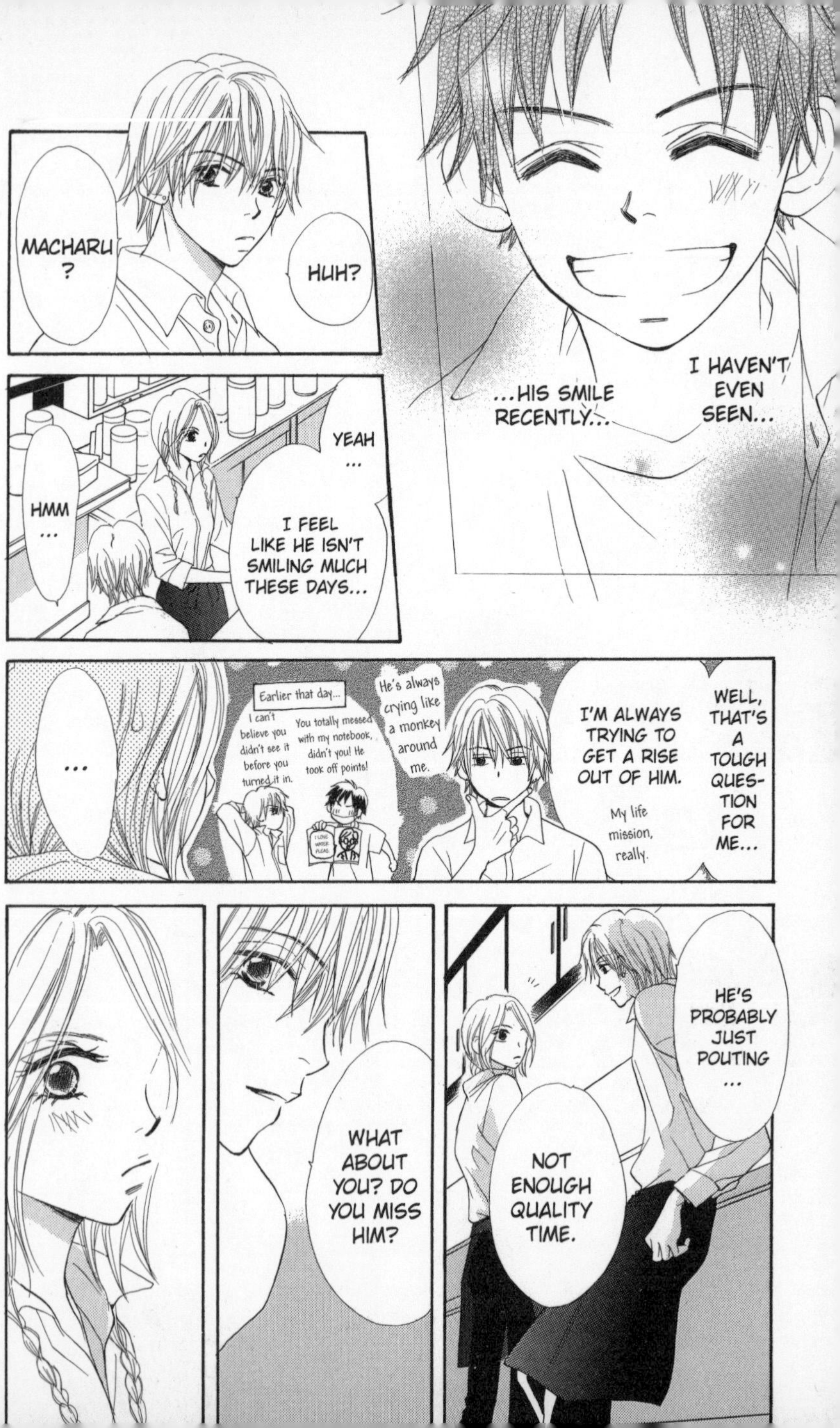
I HAVEN'T EVEN SEEN...
...HIS SMILE RECENTLY...
MACHARU ?
HUH?
YEAH ...
I FEEL LIKE HE ISN'T SMILING MUCH THESE DAYS...
HMM ...
WELL, THAT'S A TOUGH QUES-TION FOR ME...
I'M ALWAYS TRYING TO GET A RISE OUT OF HIM.
My life mission, really.
He's always crying like a monkey around me.
Earlier that day...
You totally messed with my notebook, didn't you! He took off points!
I can't believe you didn't see it before you turned it in.
...
HE'S PROBABLY JUST POUTING ...
NOT ENOUGH QUALITY TIME.
WHAT ABOUT YOU? DO YOU MISS HIM?

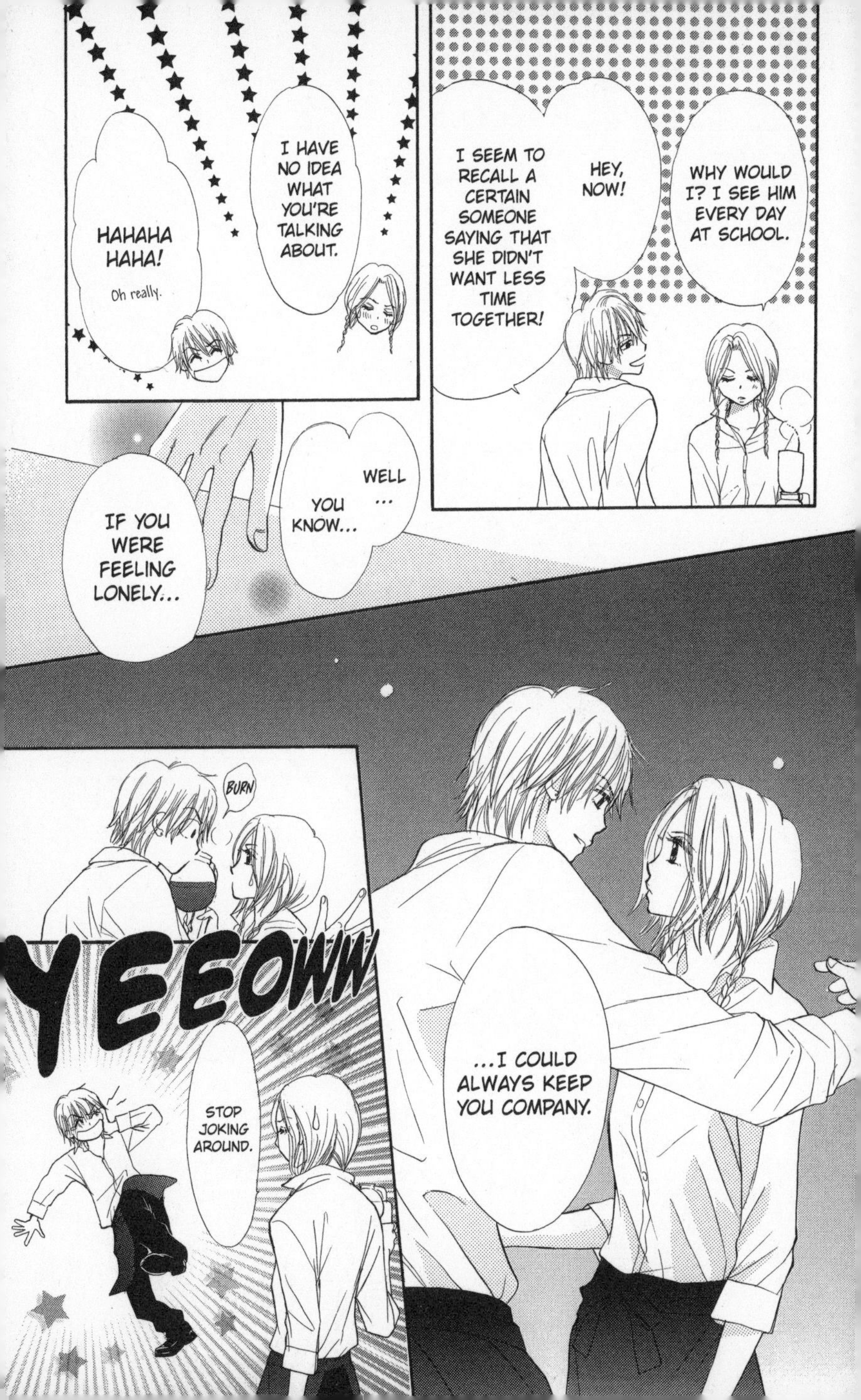
WHY WOULD I? I SEE HIM EVERY DAY AT SCHOOL.
HEY, NOW!
I SEEM TO RECALL A CERTAIN SOMEONE SAYING THAT SHE DIDN'T WANT LESS TIME TOGETHER!
I HAVE NO IDEA WHAT YOU'RE TALKING ABOUT.
HAHAHA HAHA!
Oh really.
WELL...
YOU KNOW...
IF YOU WERE FEELING LONELY...
...I COULD ALWAYS KEEP YOU COMPANY.
BURN
YEEOWW
STOP JOKING AROUND.

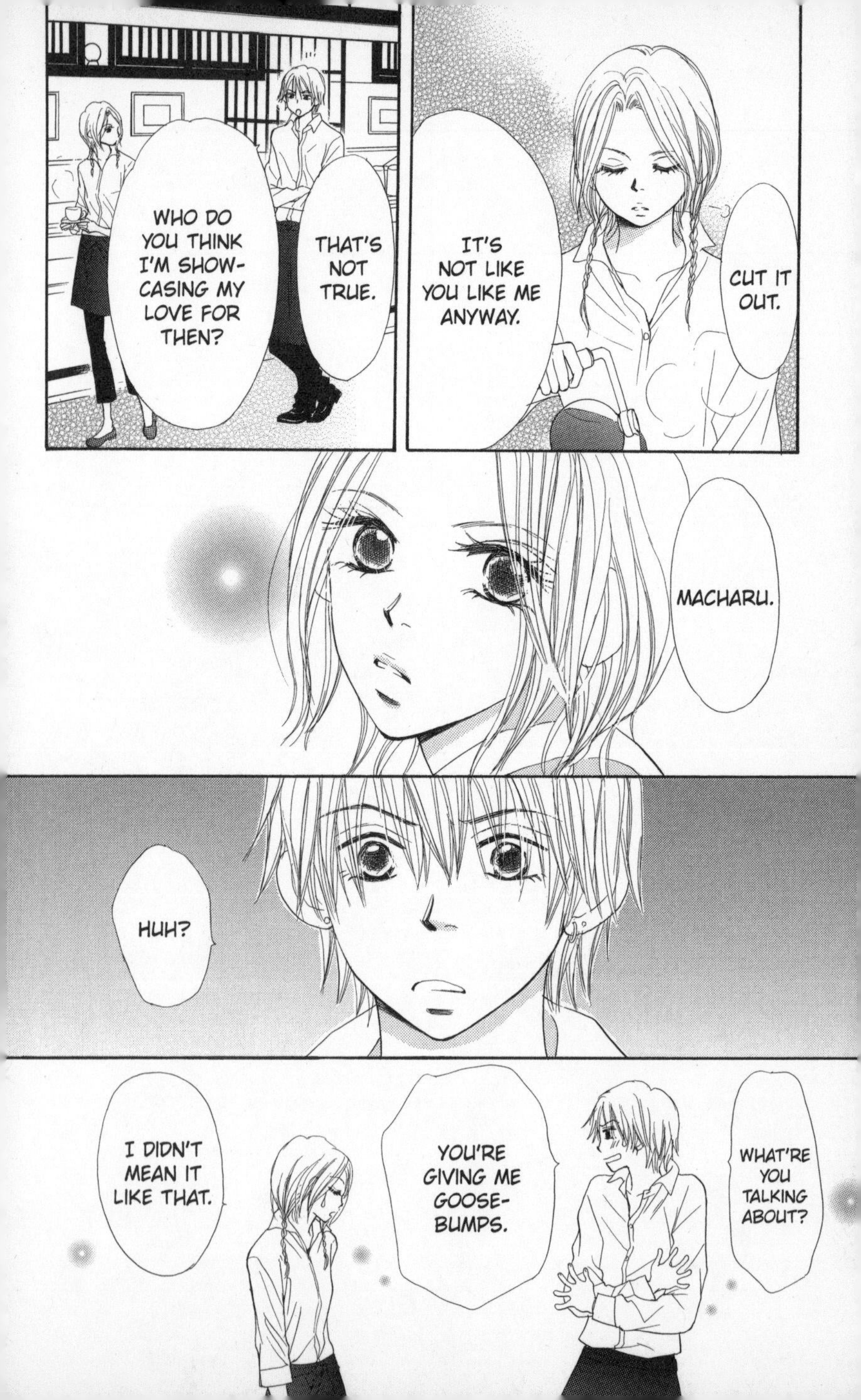
CUT IT OUT.
IT'S NOT LIKE YOU LIKE ME ANYWAY.
THAT'S NOT TRUE.
WHO DO YOU THINK I'M SHOW-CASING MY LOVE FOR THEN?
MACHARU.
HUH?
WHAT'RE YOU TALKING ABOUT?
YOU'RE GIVING ME GOOSE-BUMPS.
I DIDN'T MEAN IT LIKE THAT.

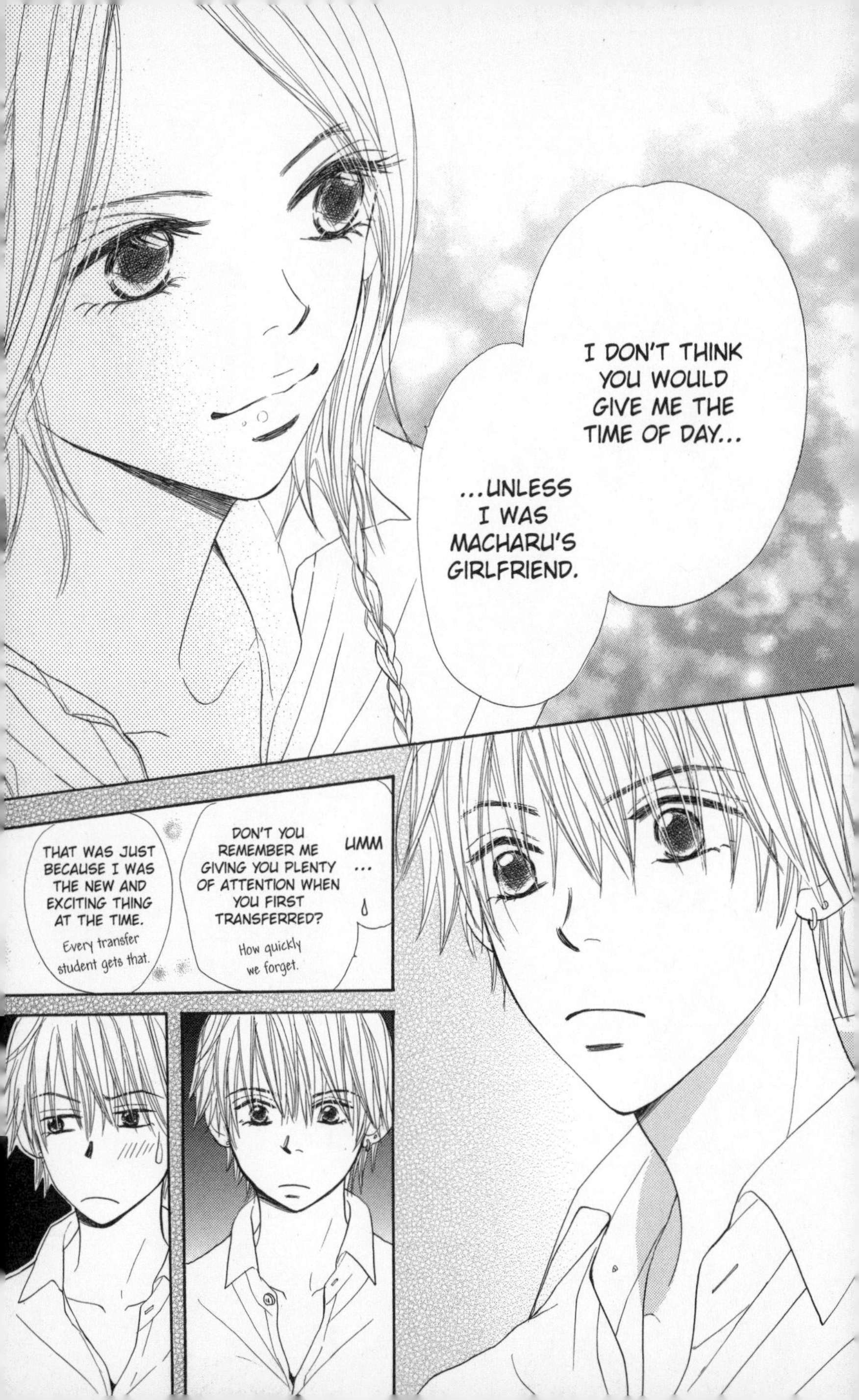
I DON'T THINK YOU WOULD GIVE ME THE TIME OF DAY...
...UNLESS I WAS MACHARU'S GIRLFRIEND.
UMM ...
DON'T YOU REMEMBER ME GIVING YOU PLENTY OF ATTENTION WHEN YOU FIRST TRANSFERRED?
How quickly we forget.
THAT WAS JUST BECAUSE I WAS THE NEW AND EXCITING THING AT THE TIME.
Every transfer student gets that.

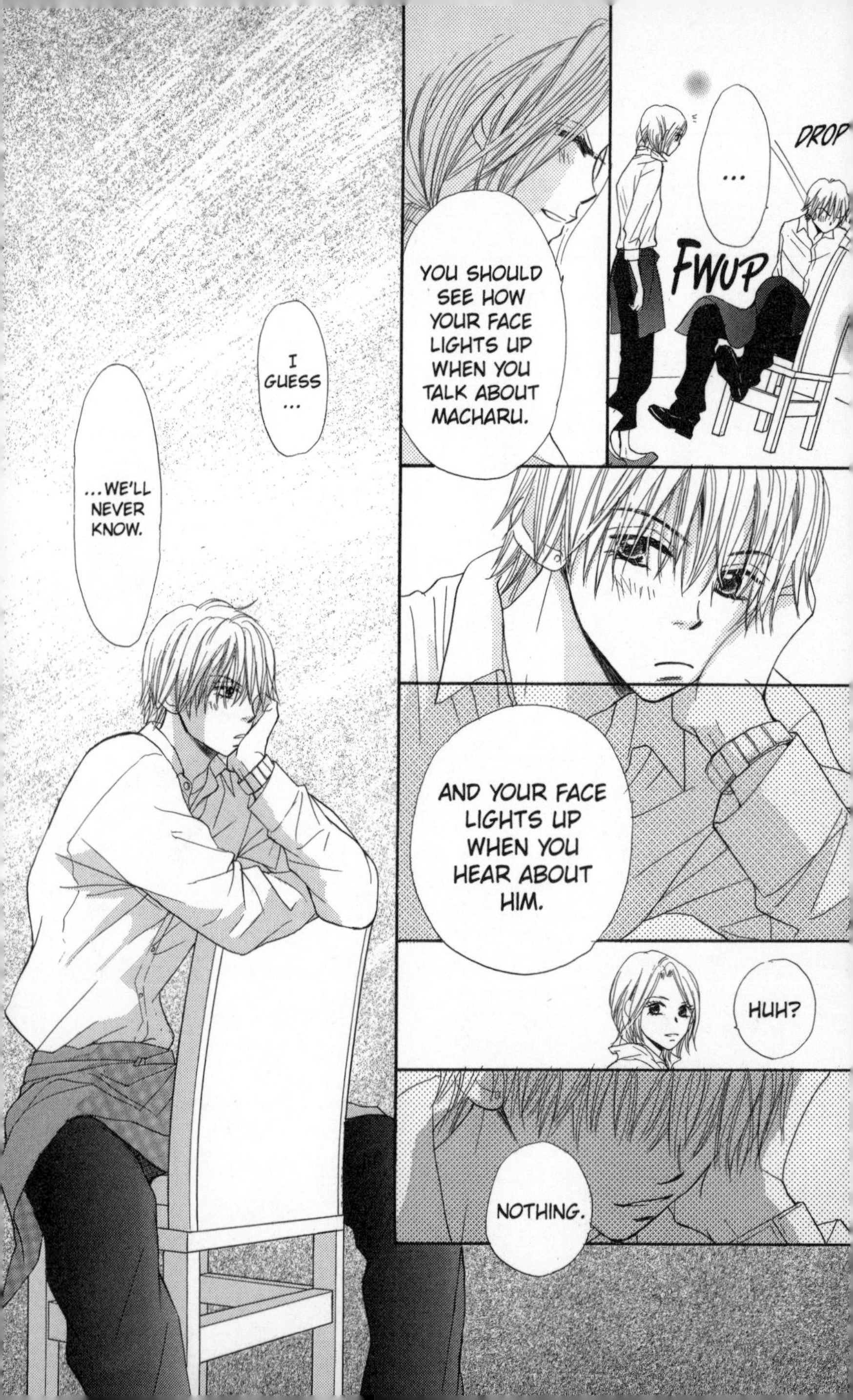
DROP
...
FWUP
YOU SHOULD SEE HOW YOUR FACE LIGHTS UP WHEN YOU TALK ABOUT MACHARU.
AND YOUR FACE LIGHTS UP WHEN YOU HEAR ABOUT HIM.
HUH?
NOTHING.
I GUESS...
...WE'LL NEVER KNOW.

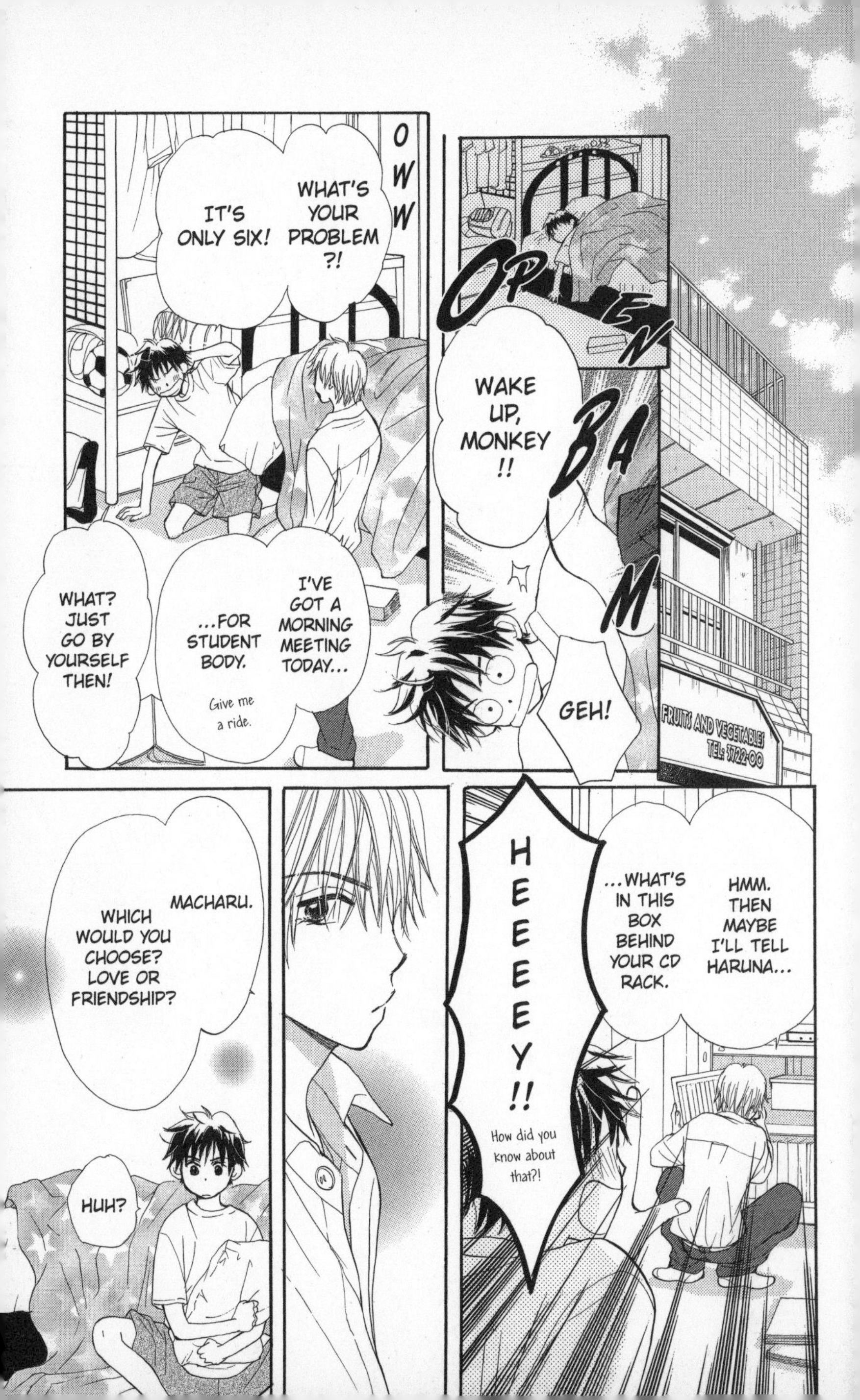
OPEN
WAKE UP, MONKEY!!
BAM
GEH!
FRUITS AND VEGETABLES
TEL: 3722-00
OWW
WHAT'S YOUR PROBLEM?!
IT'S ONLY SIX!
I'VE GOT A MORNING MEETING TODAY...
...FOR STUDENT BODY.
Give me a ride.
WHAT? JUST GO BY YOURSELF THEN!
HMM. THEN MAYBE I'LL TELL HARUNA...
...WHAT'S IN THIS BOX BEHIND YOUR CD RACK.
HEEEEEY!!
How did you know about that?!
MACHARU.
WHICH WOULD YOU CHOOSE? LOVE OR FRIENDSHIP?
HUH?

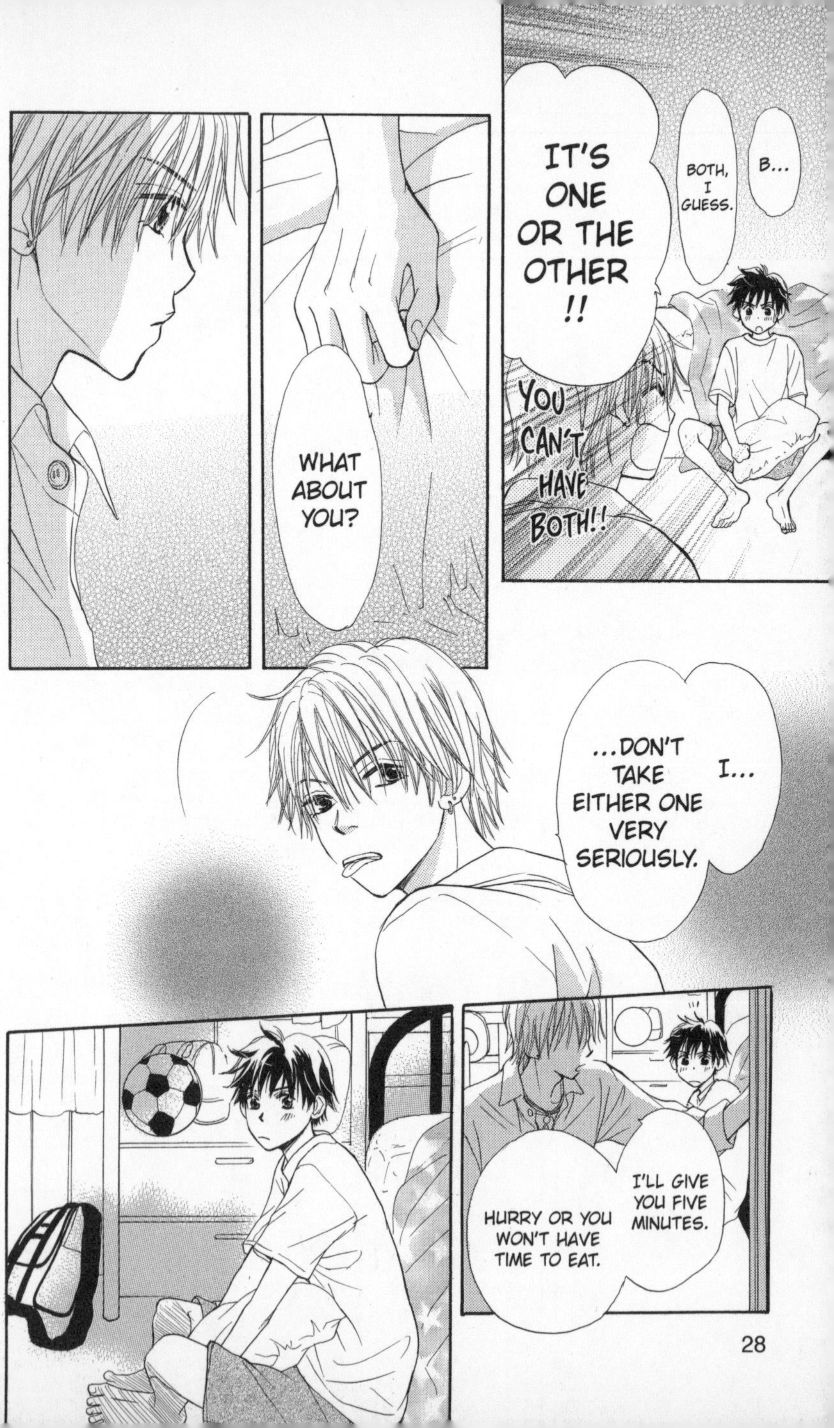
B...
BOTH, I GUESS.
IT'S ONE OR THE OTHER!!
YOU CAN'T HAVE BOTH!!
WHAT ABOUT YOU?
I...
...DON'T TAKE EITHER ONE VERY SERIOUSLY.
I'LL GIVE YOU FIVE MINUTES.
HURRY OR YOU WON'T HAVE TIME TO EAT.

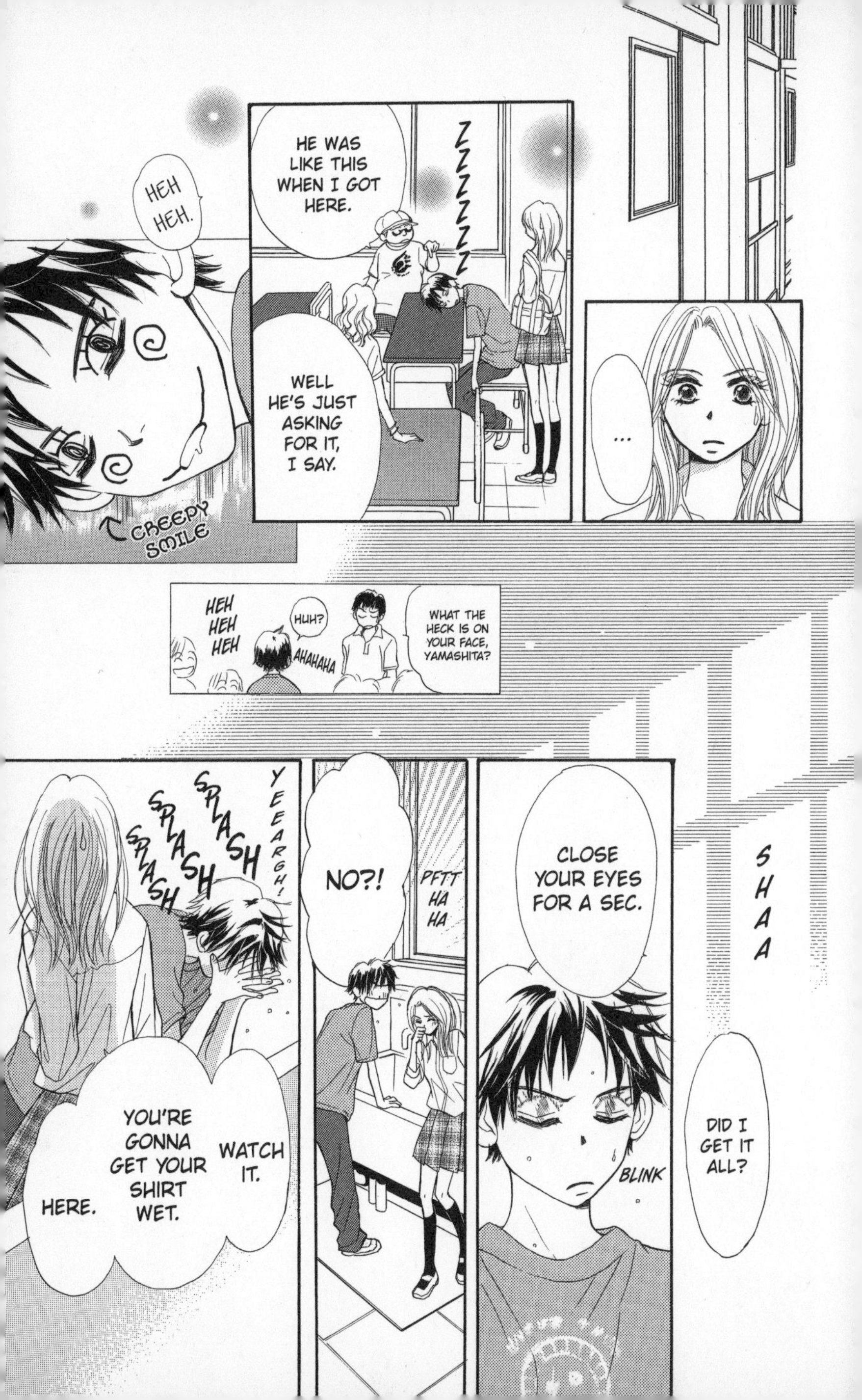
...
HE WAS LIKE THIS WHEN I GOT HERE.
ZZZZZZZ
WELL HE'S JUST ASKING FOR IT, I SAY.
HEH HEH.
CREEPY SMILE
WHAT THE HECK IS ON YOUR FACE, YAMASHITA?
HUH?
AHAHAHA
HEH HEH HEH
SHAA
CLOSE YOUR EYES FOR A SEC.
DID I GET IT ALL?
BLINK
NO?!
PFTT HA HA
YEEARGH!
SPLASH SPLASH SPLASH
WATCH IT.
YOU'RE GONNA GET YOUR SHIRT WET.
HERE.

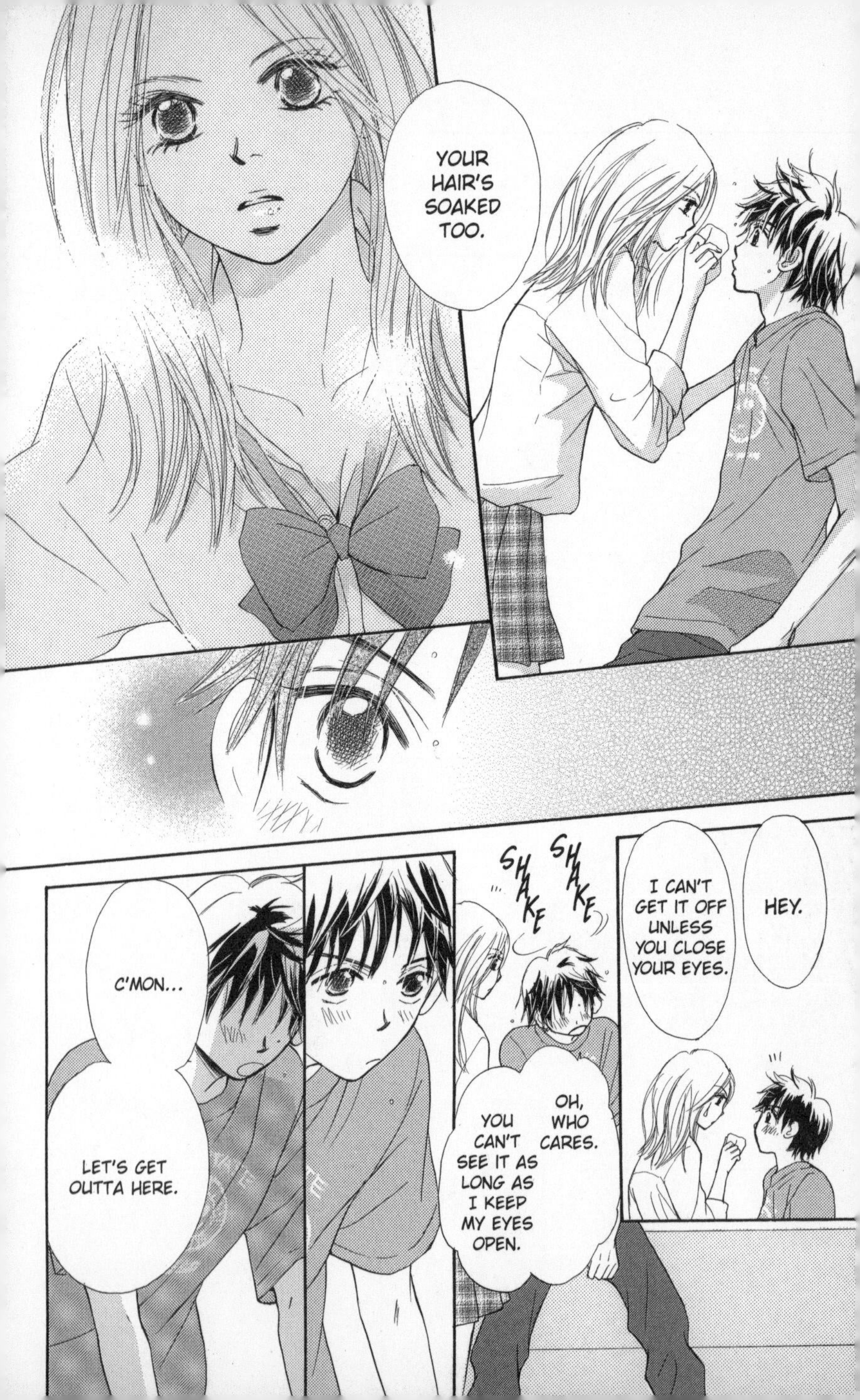
YOUR HAIR'S SOAKED TOO.
HEY.
I CAN'T GET IT OFF UNLESS YOU CLOSE YOUR EYES.
SHAKE
SHAKE
OH, WHO CARES.
YOU CAN'T SEE IT AS LONG AS I KEEP MY EYES OPEN.
C'MON...
LET'S GET OUTTA HERE.

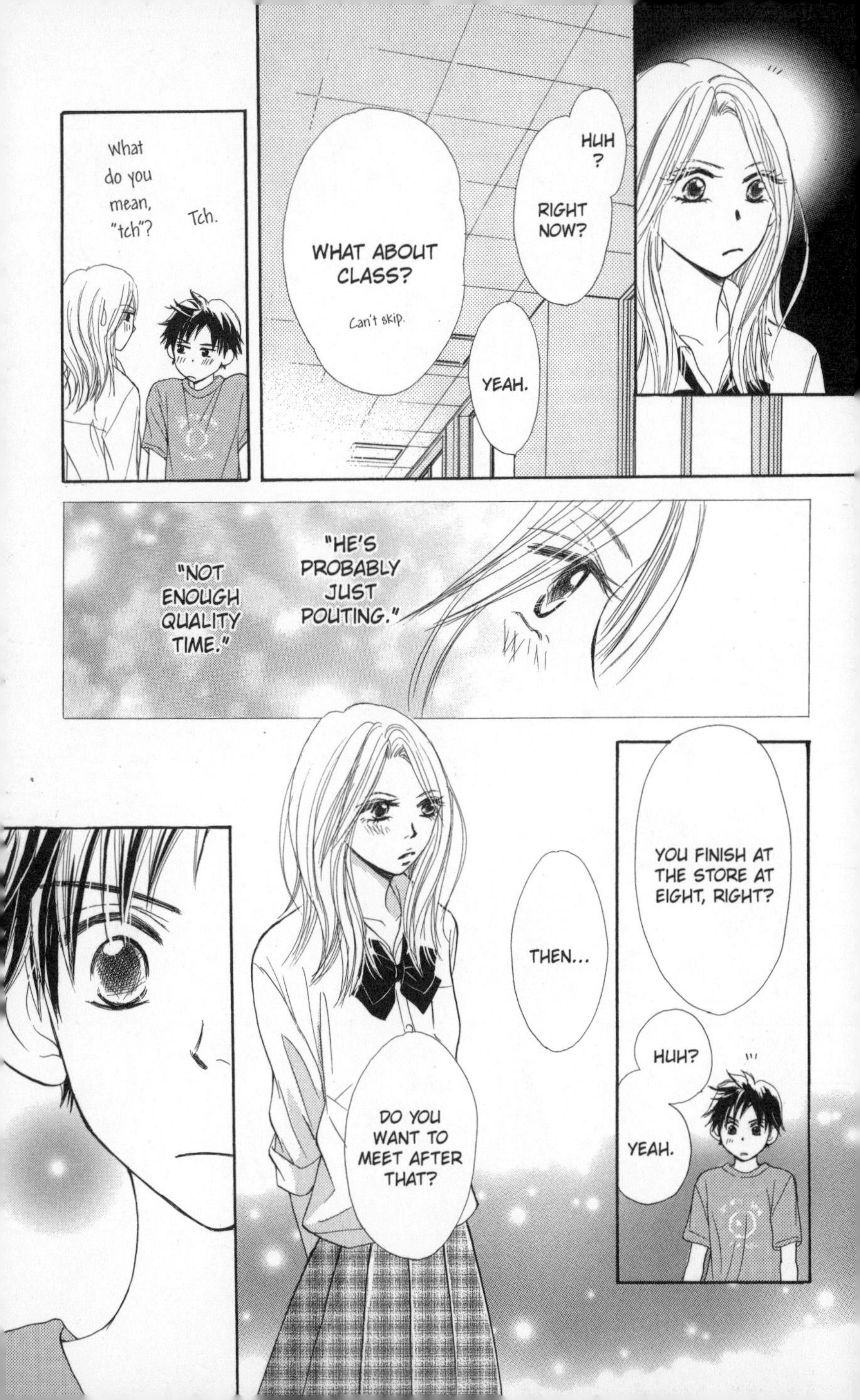
HUH? RIGHT NOW?
YEAH.
WHAT ABOUT CLASS?
Can't skip.
Tch.
What do you mean, "tch"?
"HE'S PROBABLY JUST POUTING."
"NOT ENOUGH QUALITY TIME."
YOU FINISH AT THE STORE AT EIGHT, RIGHT?
HUH?
YEAH.
THEN...
DO YOU WANT TO MEET AFTER THAT?

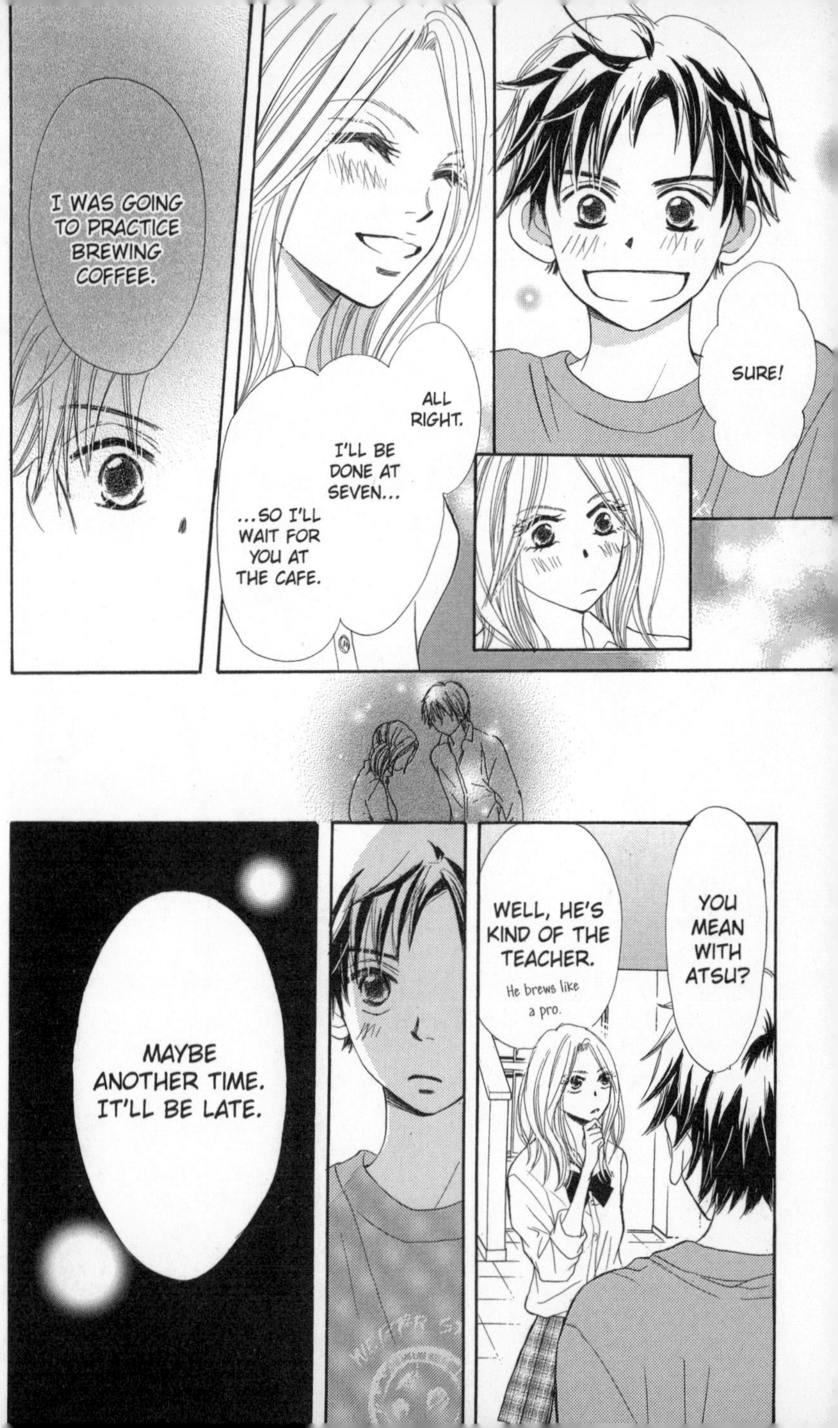
SURE!
ALL RIGHT.
I'LL BE DONE AT SEVEN...
...SO I'LL WAIT FOR YOU AT THE CAFE.
I WAS GOING TO PRACTICE BREWING COFFEE.
YOU MEAN WITH ATSU?
WELL, HE'S KIND OF THE TEACHER.
He brews like a pro.
MAYBE ANOTHER TIME. IT'LL BE LATE.

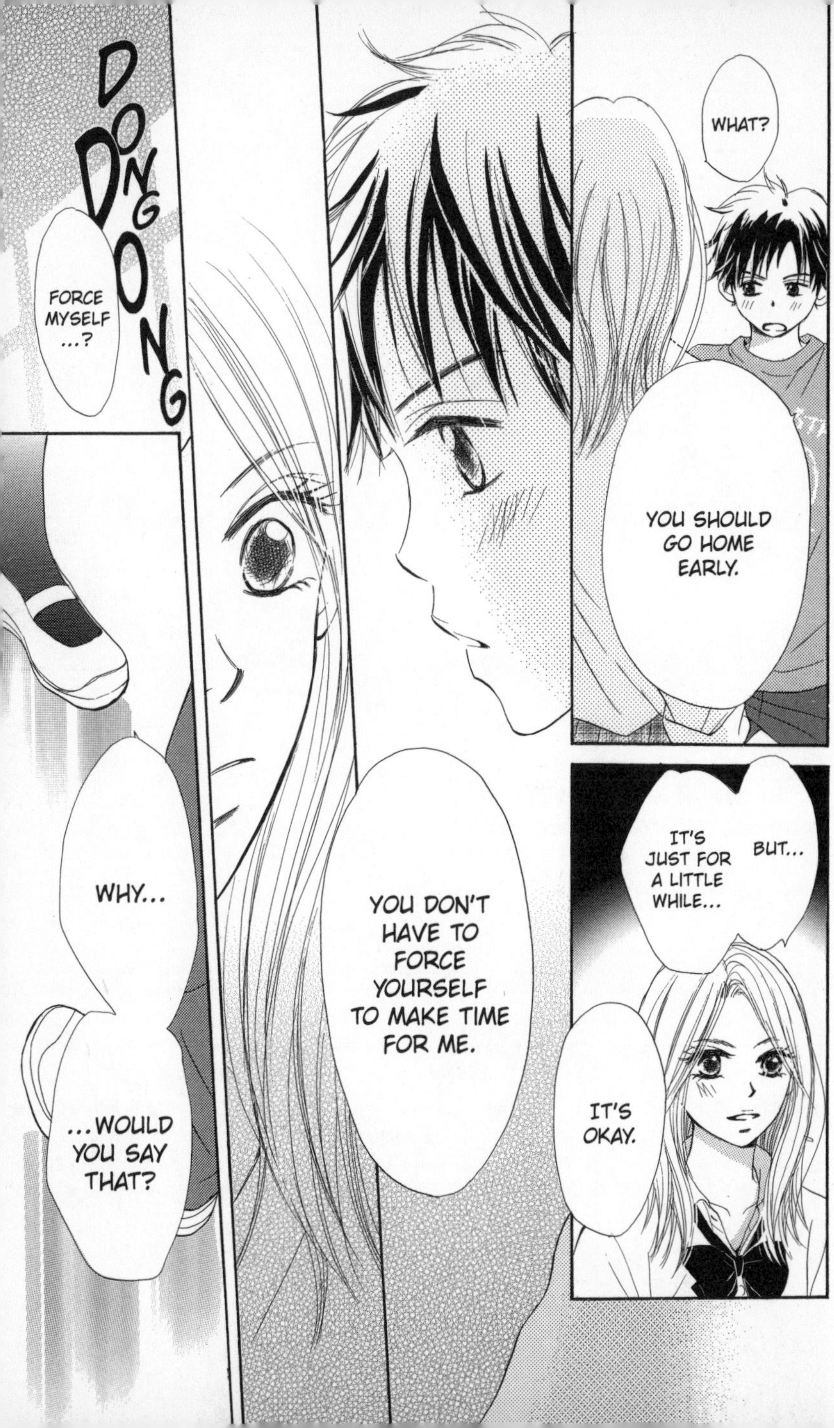
WHAT?
YOU SHOULD GO HOME EARLY.
BUT...
IT'S JUST FOR A LITTLE WHILE...
IT'S OKAY.
YOU DON'T HAVE TO FORCE YOURSELF TO MAKE TIME FOR ME.
DONG DONG
FORCE MYSELF ...?
WHY...
...WOULD YOU SAY THAT?

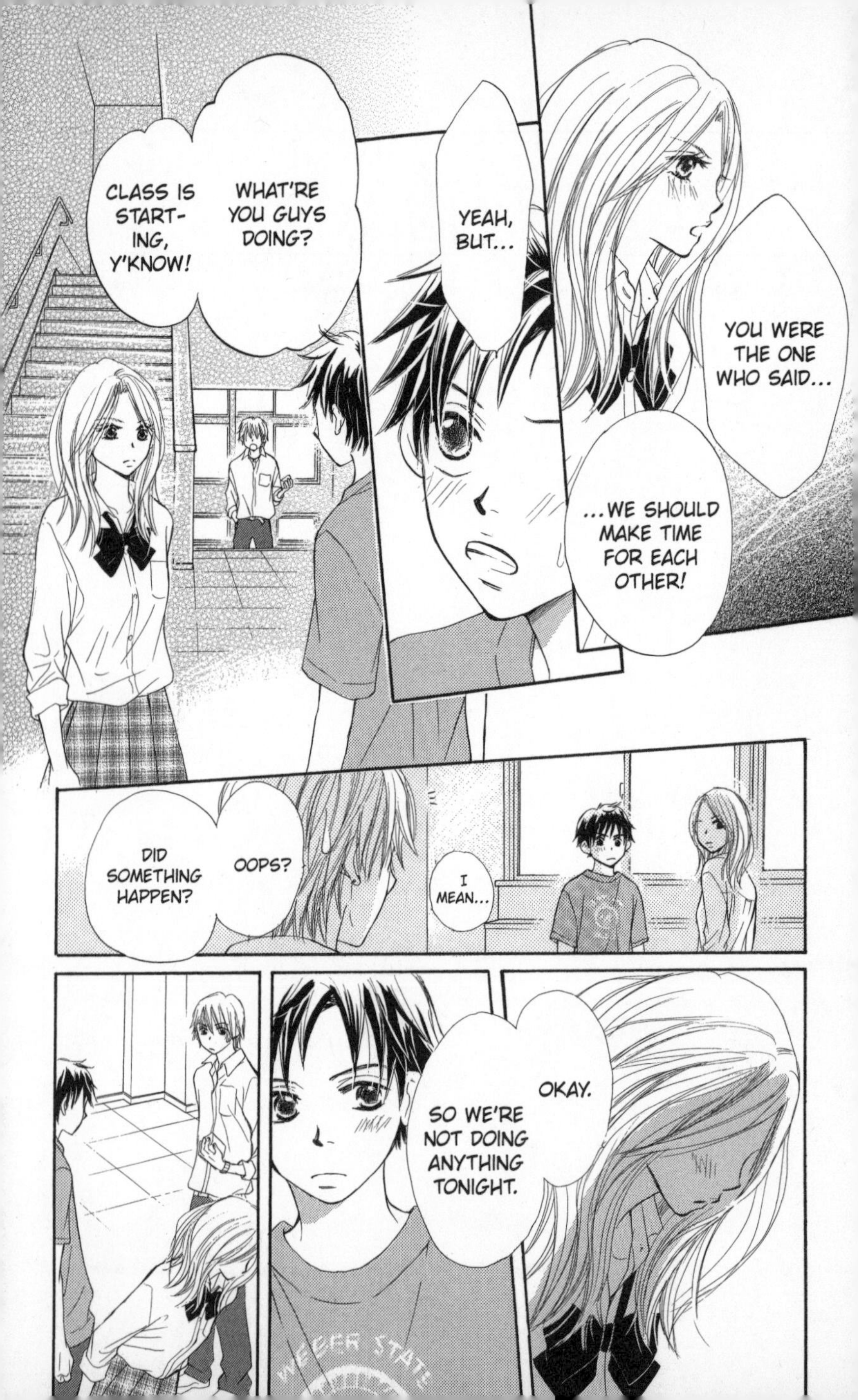
YOU WERE THE ONE WHO SAID...
...WE SHOULD MAKE TIME FOR EACH OTHER!
YEAH, BUT...
WHAT'RE YOU GUYS DOING?
CLASS IS START-ING, Y'KNOW!
I MEAN...
OOPS?
DID SOMETHING HAPPEN?
OKAY.
SO WE'RE NOT DOING ANYTHING TONIGHT.

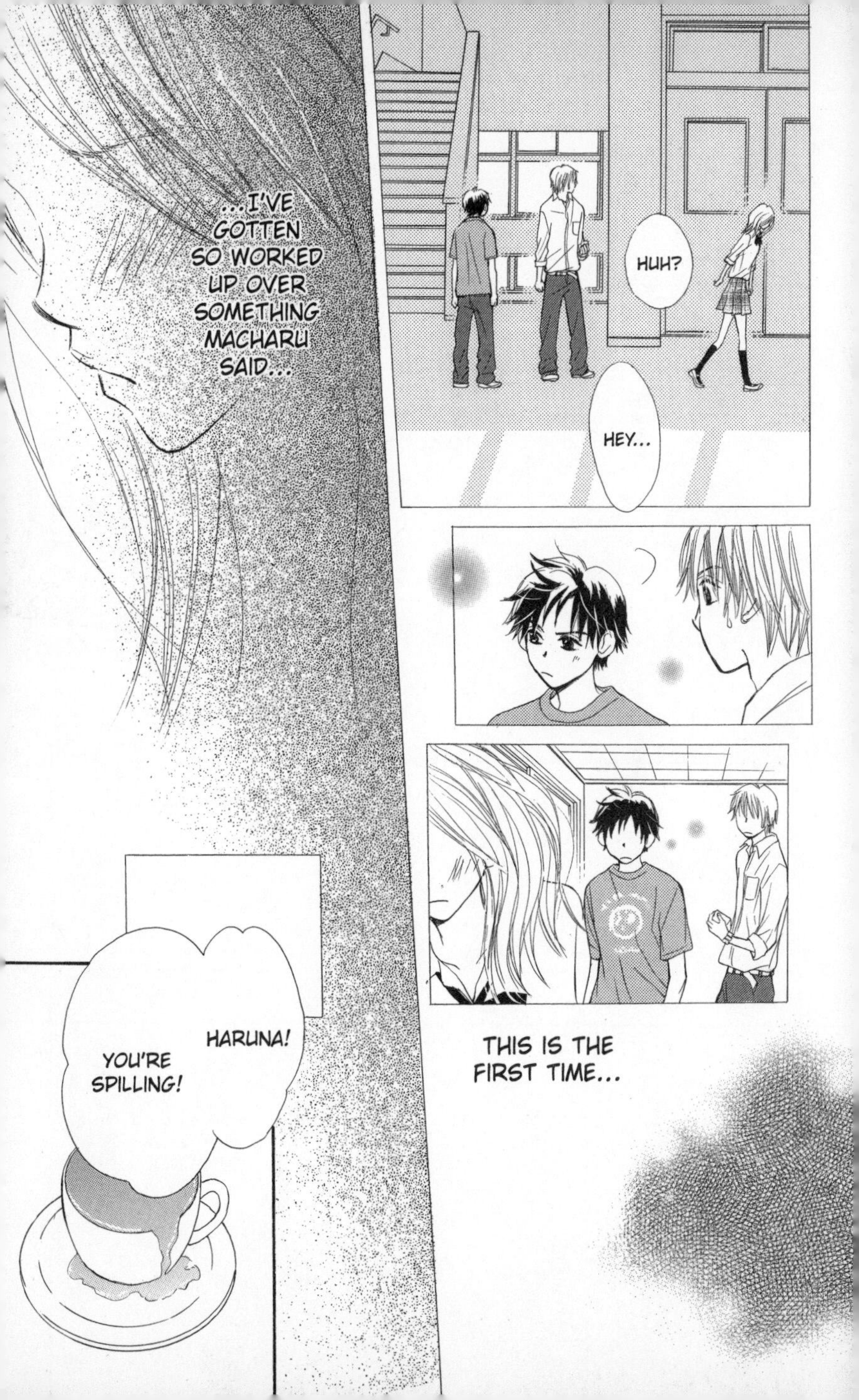
HUH?
HEY...
THIS IS THE FIRST TIME...
...I'VE GOTTEN SO WORKED UP OVER SOMETHING MACHARU SAID...
HARUNA!
YOU'RE SPILLING!

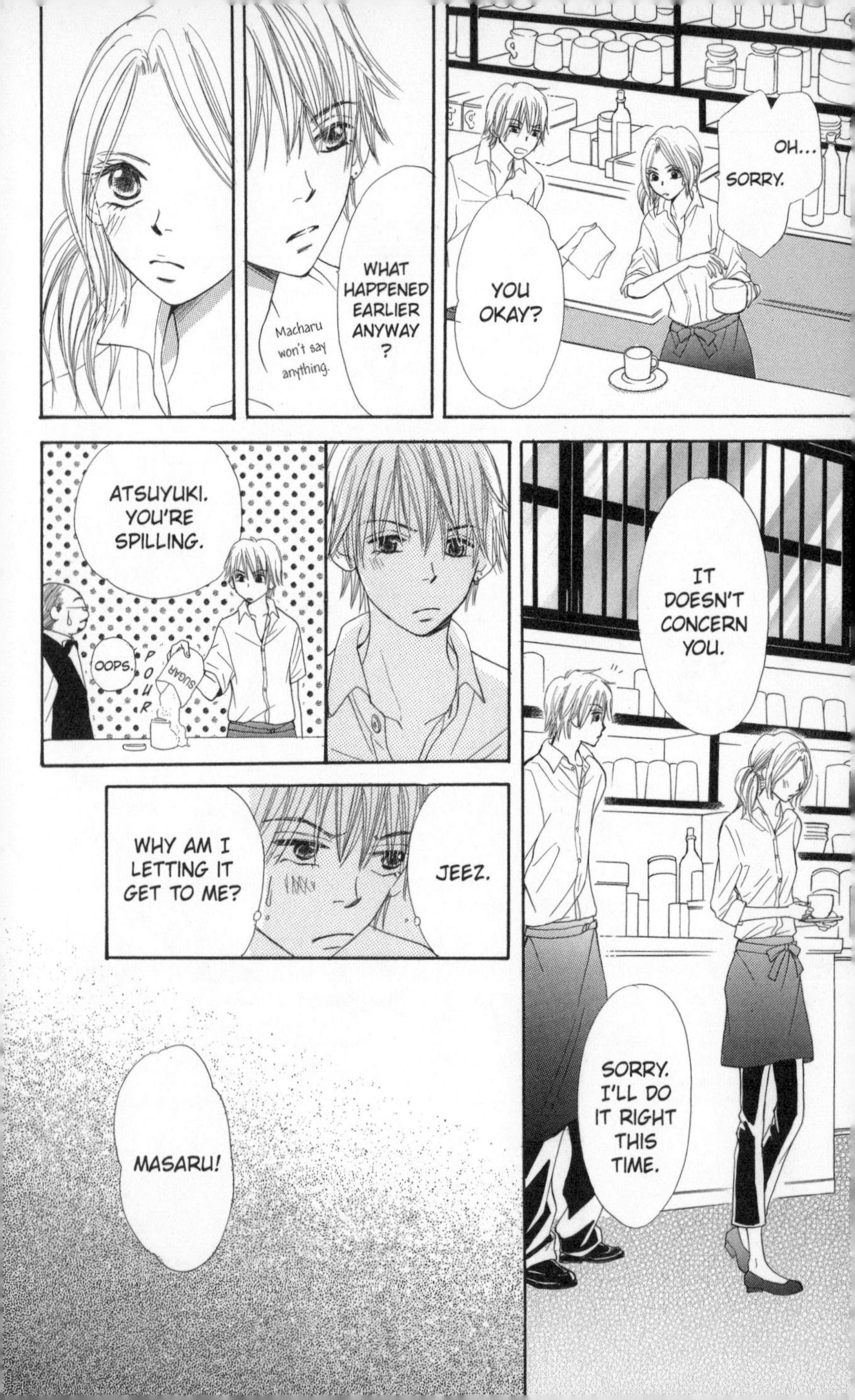
OH...
SORRY.
YOU OKAY?
WHAT HAPPENED EARLIER ANYWAY?
Macharu won't say anything.
IT DOESN'T CONCERN YOU.
SORRY. I'LL DO IT RIGHT THIS TIME.
ATSUYUKI. YOU'RE SPILLING.
SUGAR
POUR
OOPS.
JEEZ.
WHY AM I LETTING IT GET TO ME?
MASARU!

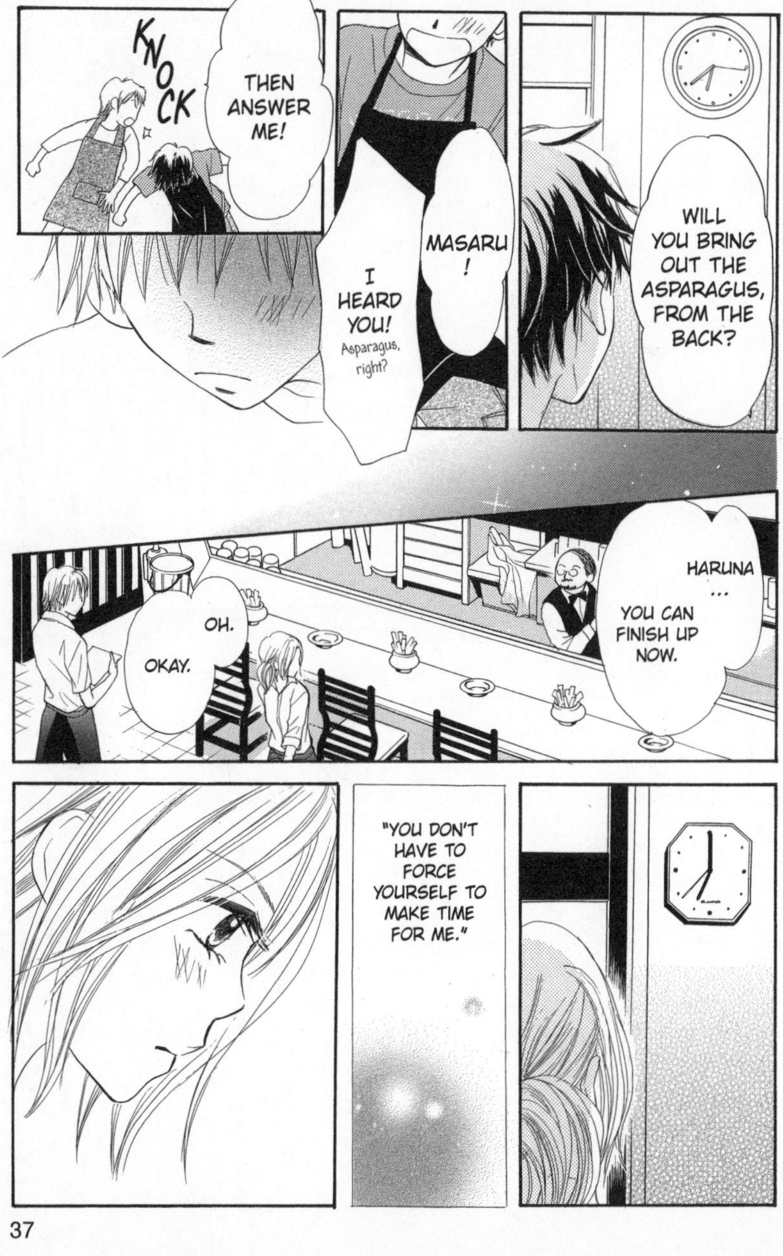
WILL YOU BRING OUT THE ASPARAGUS, FROM THE BACK?
MASARU!
I HEARD YOU! Asparagus, right?
KNOCK
THEN ANSWER ME!
HARUNA... YOU CAN FINISH UP NOW.
OH. OKAY.
"YOU DON'T HAVE TO FORCE YOURSELF TO MAKE TIME FOR ME."

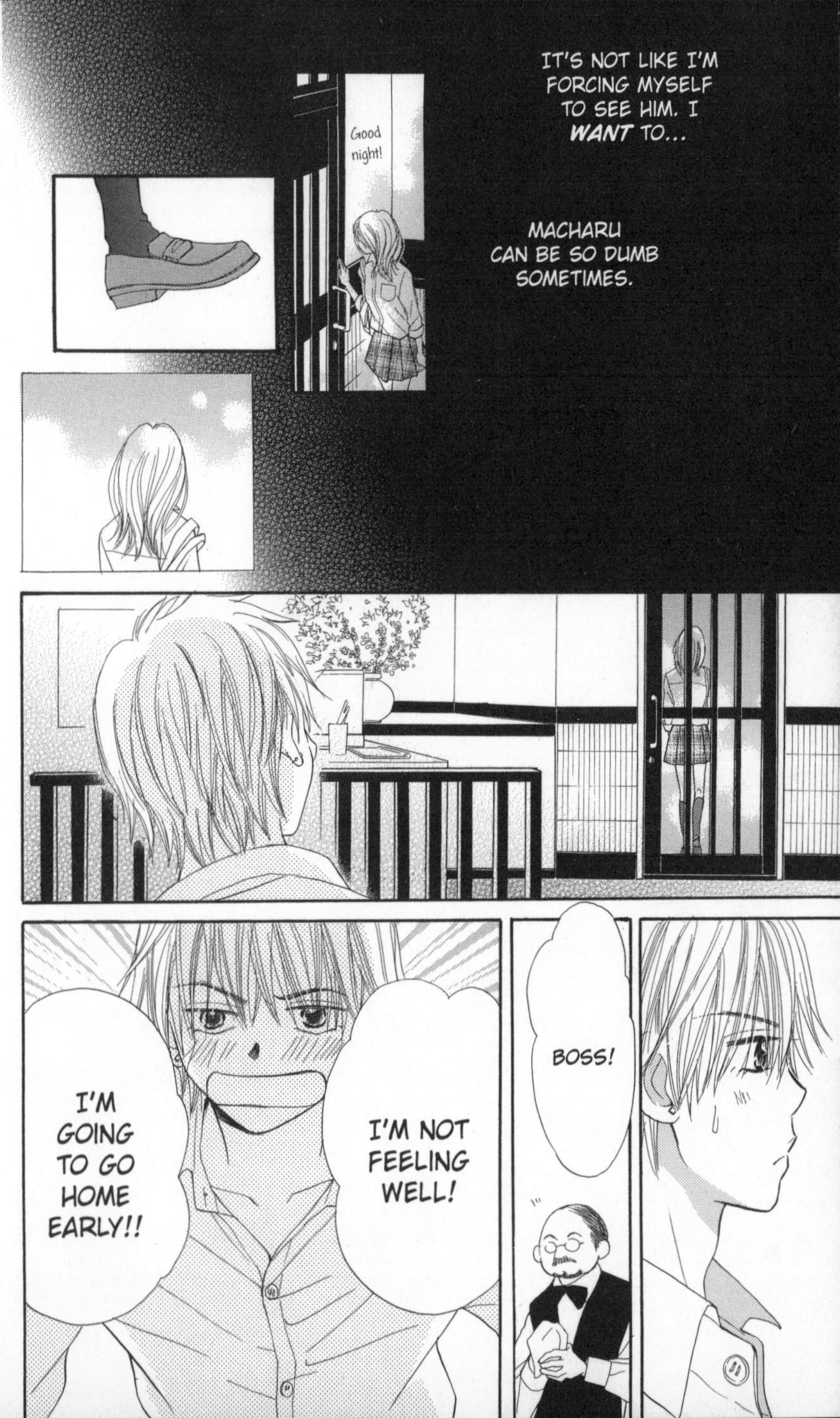

IT'S NOT LIKE I'M FORCING MYSELF TO SEE HIM. I *WANT* TO...
Good night!
MACHARU CAN BE SO DUMB SOMETIMES.
BOSS!
I'M NOT FEELING WELL!
I'M GOING TO GO HOME EARLY!!

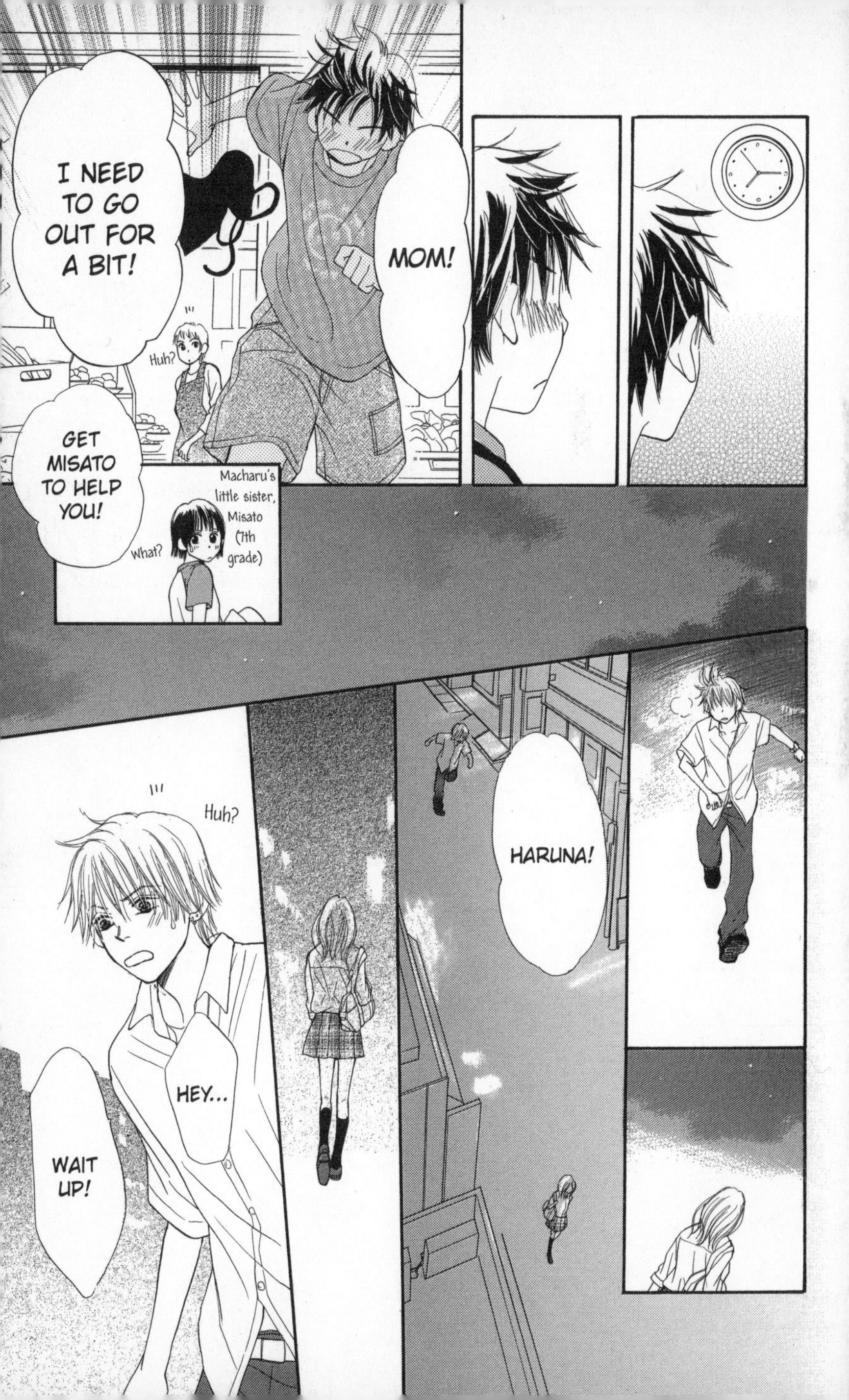
MOM!
I NEED TO GO OUT FOR A BIT!
Huh?
GET MISATO TO HELP YOU!
Macharu's little sister, Misato (7th grade)
What?
HARUNA!
Huh?
HEY...
WAIT UP!

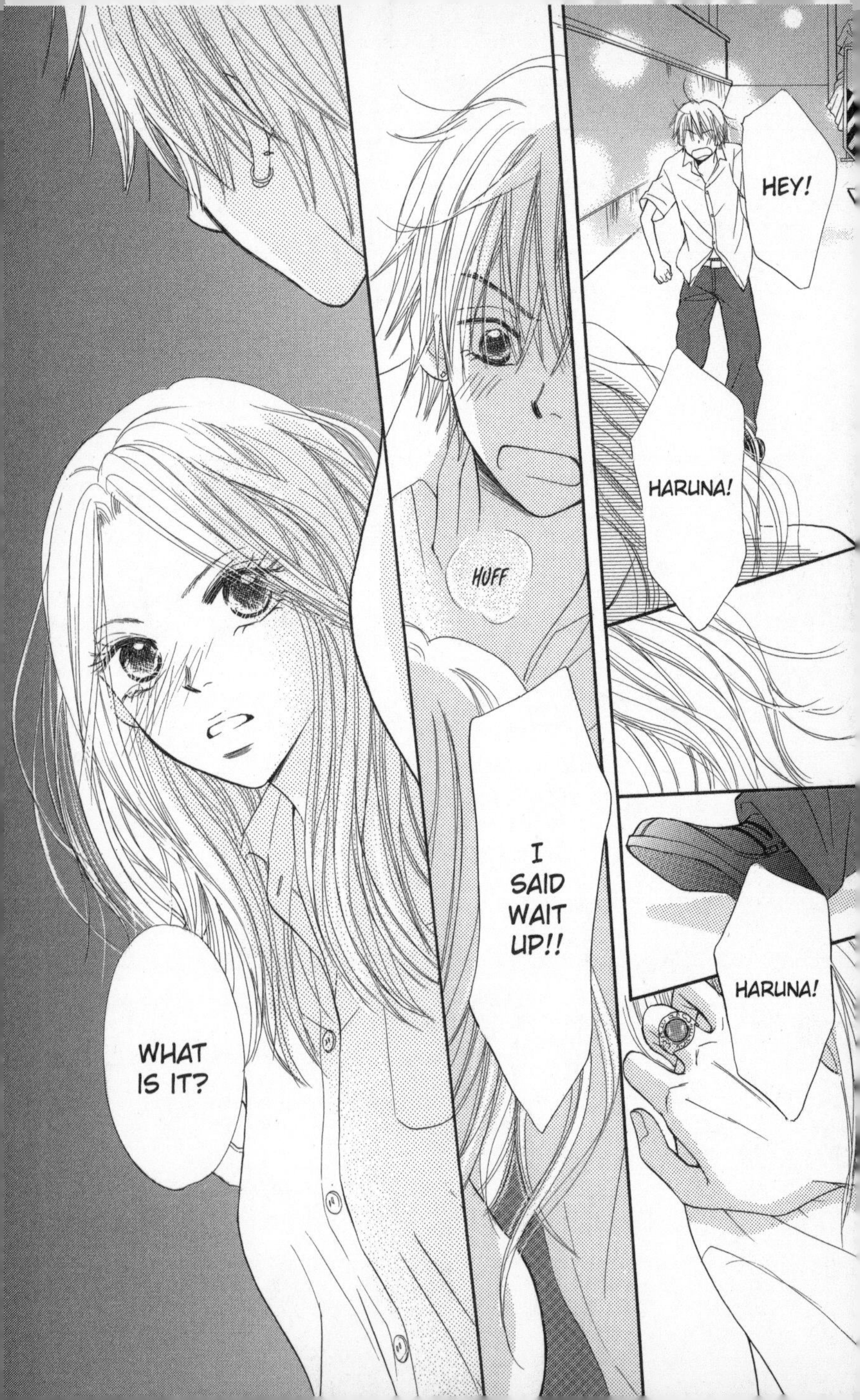
HEY!
HARUNA!
HARUNA!
HUFF
I SAID WAIT UP!!
WHAT IS IT?

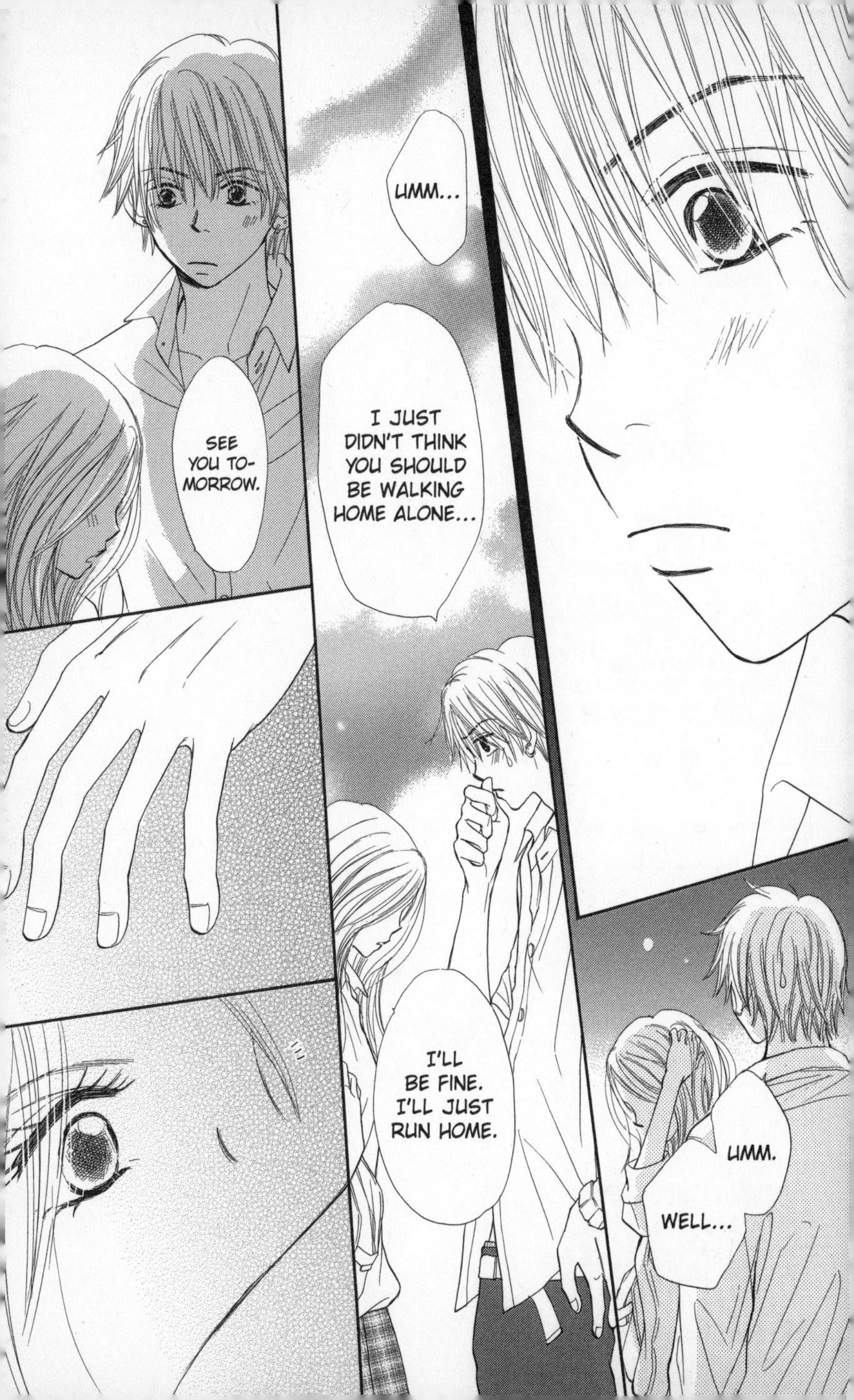
UMM.
WELL...
UMM...
I JUST DIDN'T THINK YOU SHOULD BE WALKING HOME ALONE...
I'LL BE FINE. I'LL JUST RUN HOME.
SEE YOU TO-MORROW.

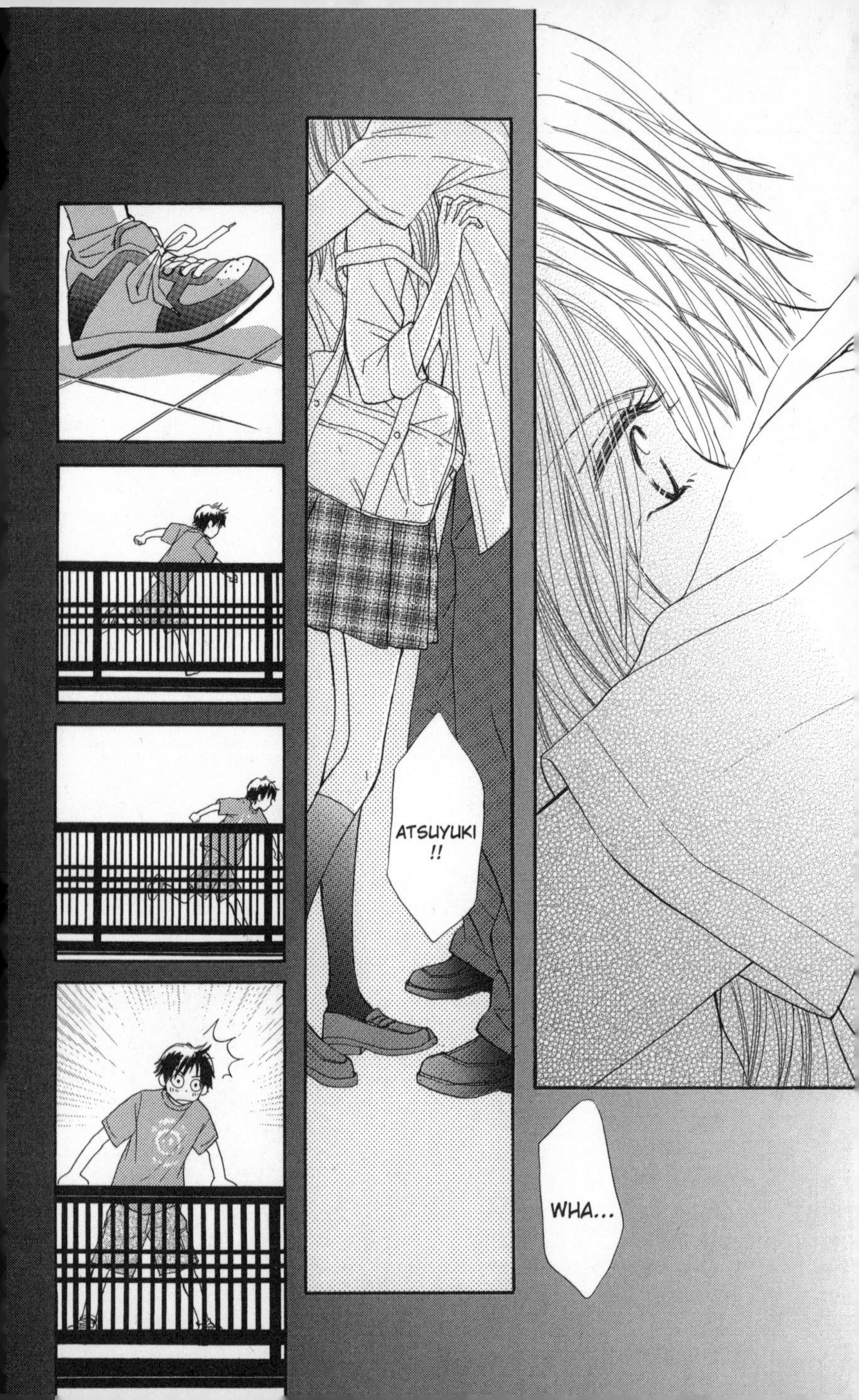
WHA...
ATSUYUKI !!

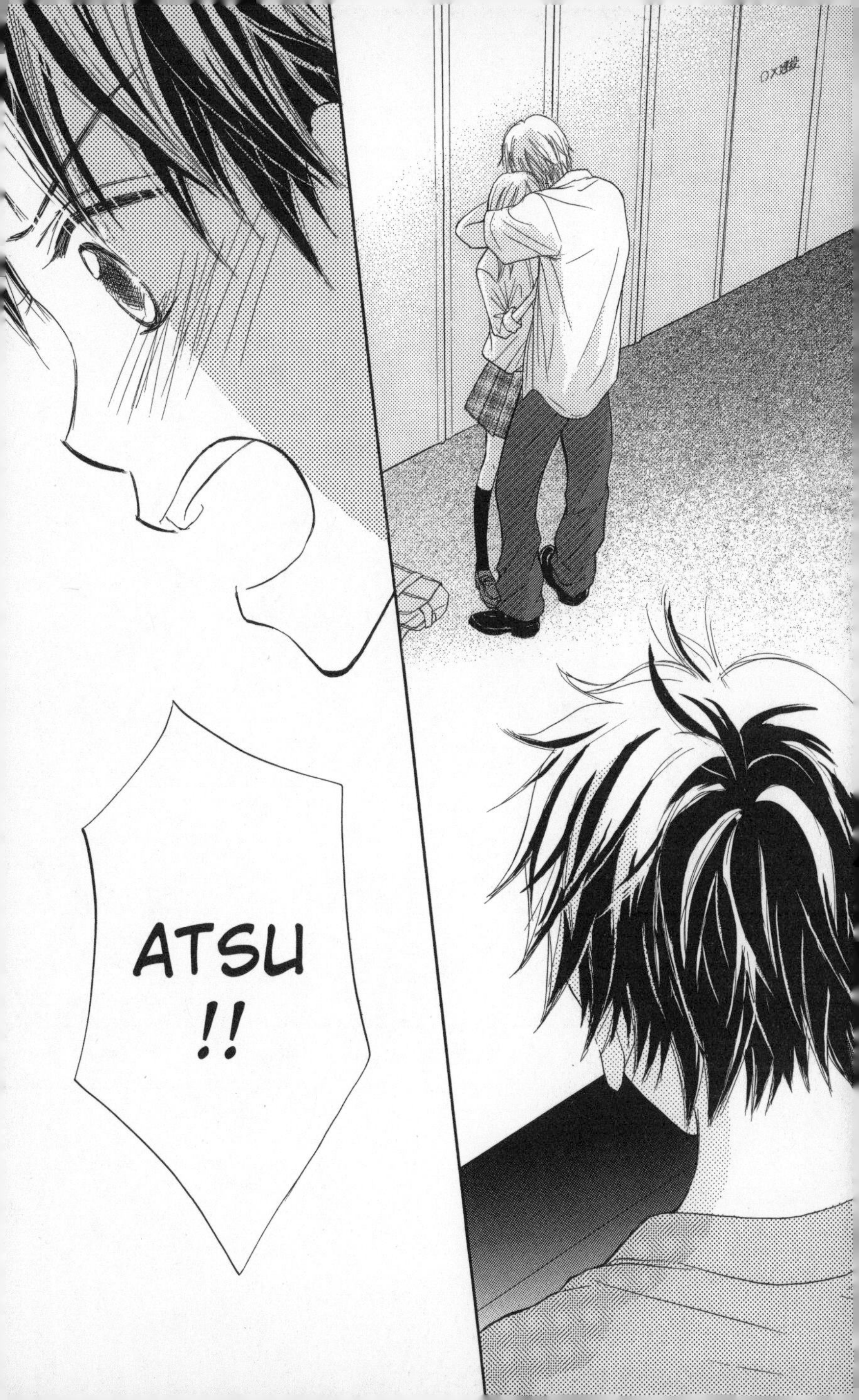
ATSU !!

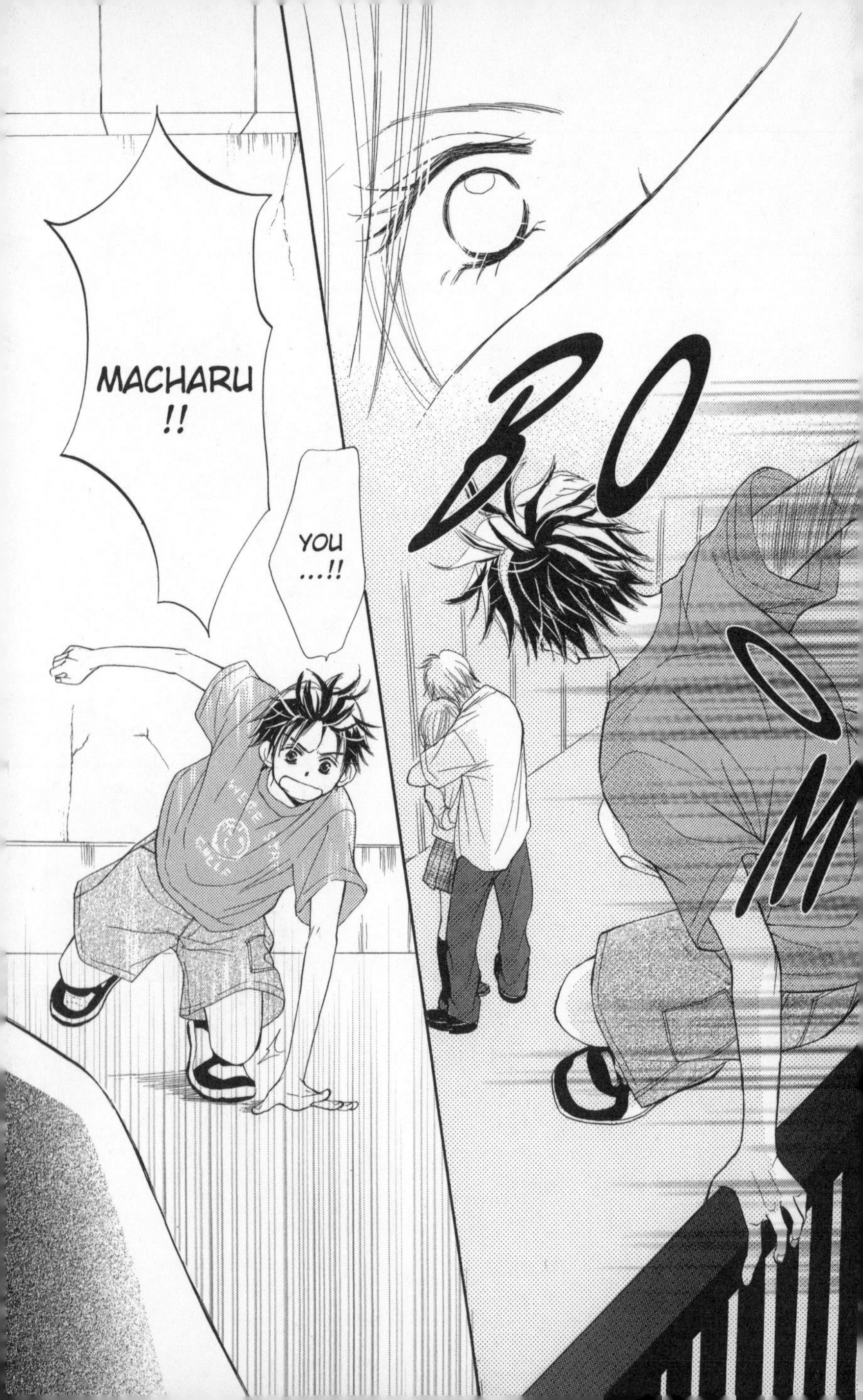
BOOM
MACHARU!!
YOU...!!

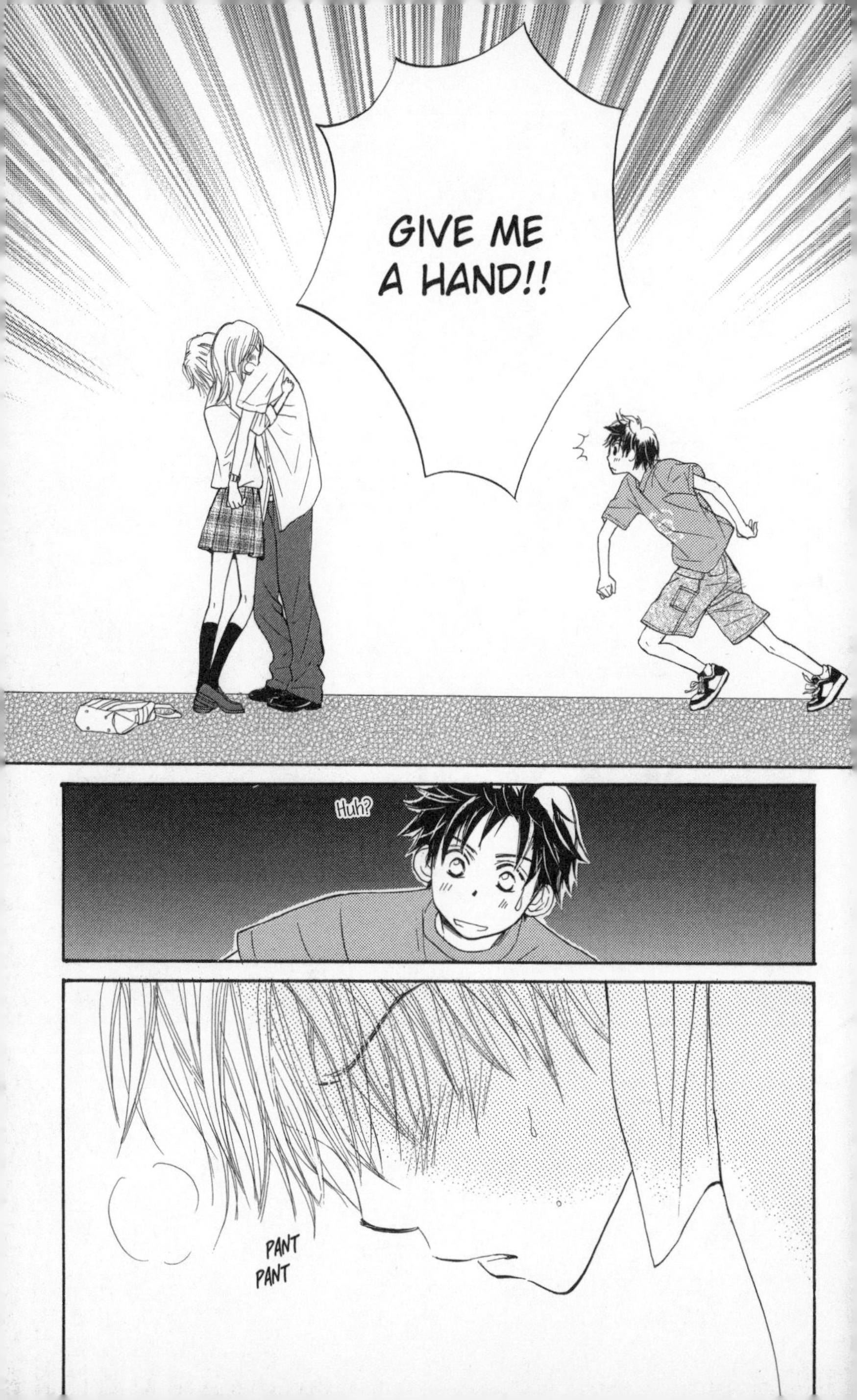
GIVE ME A HAND!!
Huh?
PANT PANT

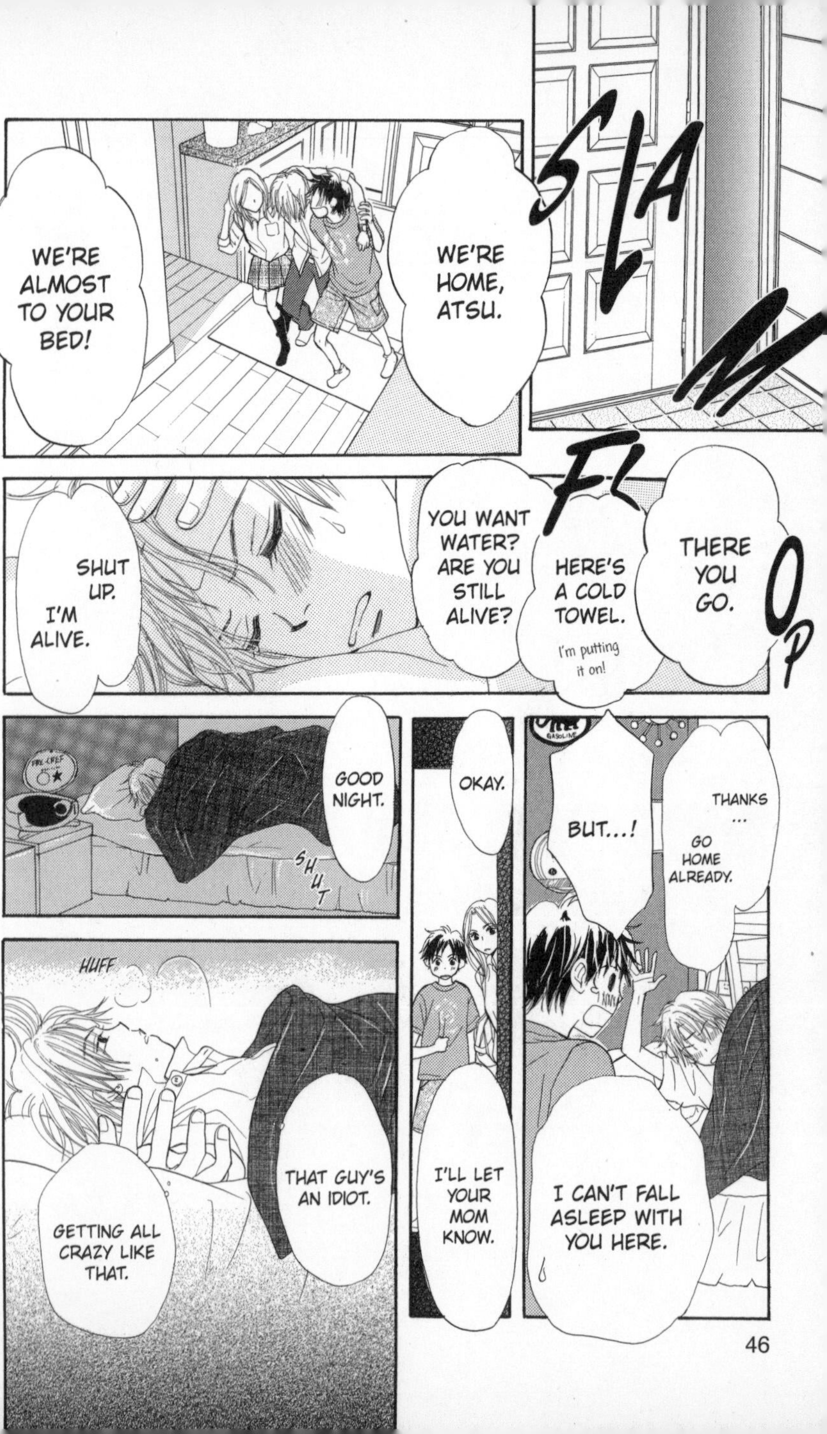
SLAM
WE'RE HOME, ATSU.
WE'RE ALMOST TO YOUR BED!
THERE YOU GO.
FLOP
HERE'S A COLD TOWEL.
I'm putting it on!
YOU WANT WATER? ARE YOU STILL ALIVE?
SHUT UP. I'M ALIVE.
THANKS... GO HOME ALREADY.
BUT...!
I CAN'T FALL ASLEEP WITH YOU HERE.
OKAY.
I'LL LET YOUR MOM KNOW.
GOOD NIGHT.
SHUT
HUFF
THAT GUY'S AN IDIOT.
GETTING ALL CRAZY LIKE THAT.

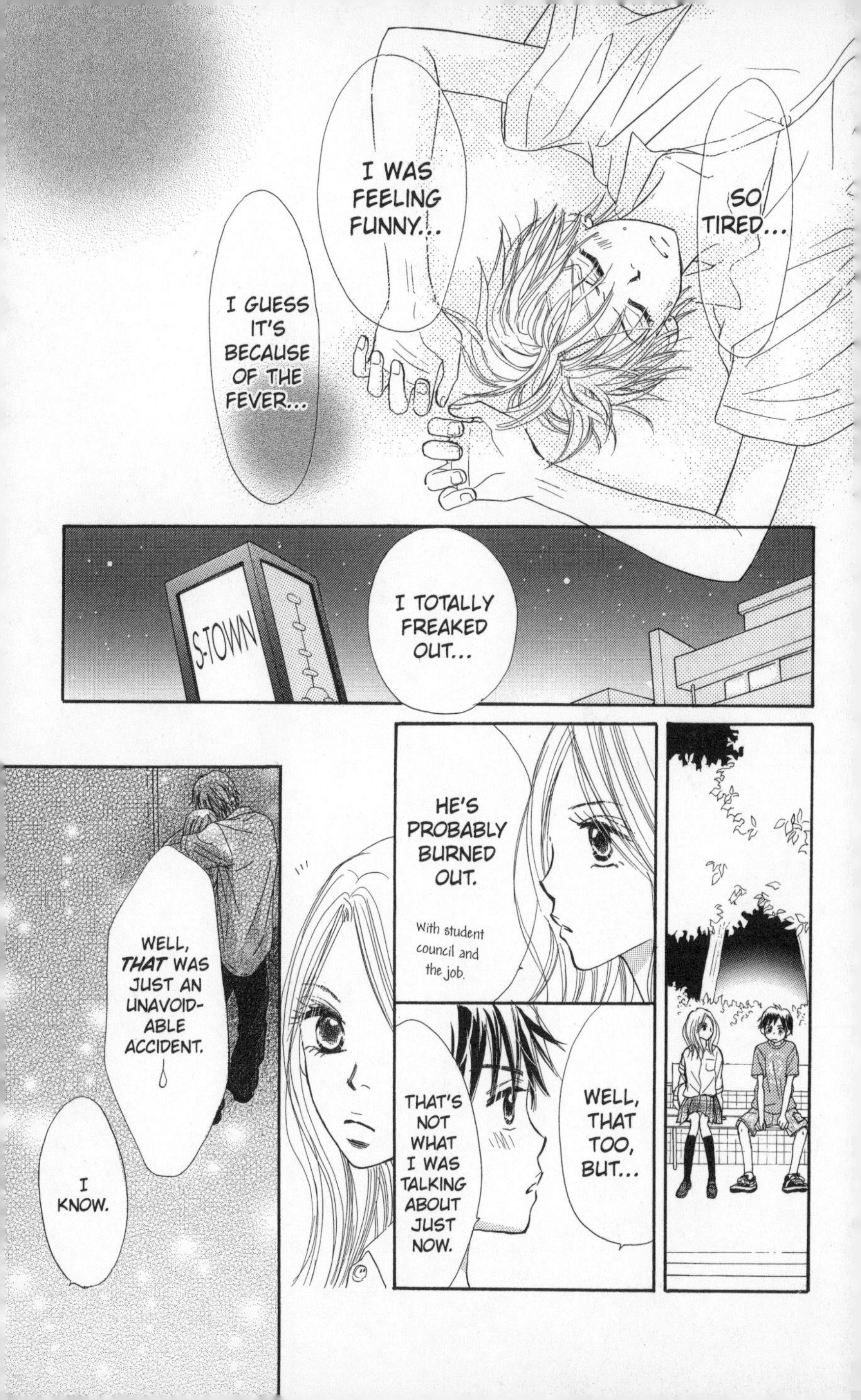

SO TIRED...
I WAS FEELING FUNNY...
I GUESS IT'S BECAUSE OF THE FEVER...
S-TOWN
I TOTALLY FREAKED OUT...
HE'S PROBABLY BURNED OUT.
With student council and the job.
WELL, THAT TOO, BUT...
THAT'S NOT WHAT I WAS TALKING ABOUT JUST NOW.
WELL, *THAT* WAS JUST AN UNAVOIDABLE ACCIDENT.
I KNOW.

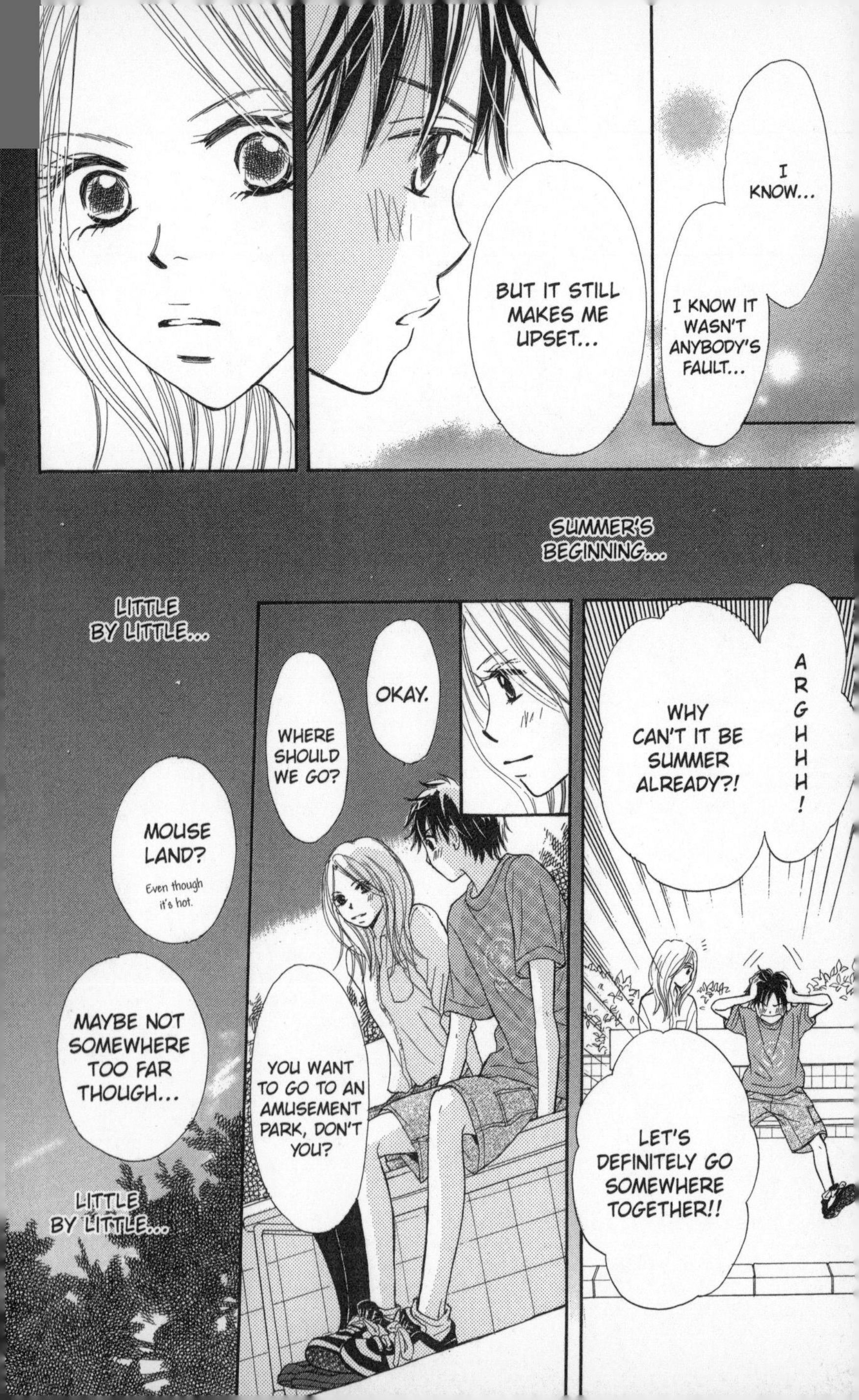
I KNOW...
I KNOW IT WASN'T ANYBODY'S FAULT...
BUT IT STILL MAKES ME UPSET...
SUMMER'S BEGINNING...
ARGHHH!
WHY CAN'T IT BE SUMMER ALREADY?!
LET'S DEFINITELY GO SOMEWHERE TOGETHER!!
OKAY.
WHERE SHOULD WE GO?
YOU WANT TO GO TO AN AMUSEMENT PARK, DON'T YOU?
LITTLE BY LITTLE...
MOUSE LAND?
Even though it's hot.
MAYBE NOT SOMEWHERE TOO FAR THOUGH...
LITTLE BY LITTLE...

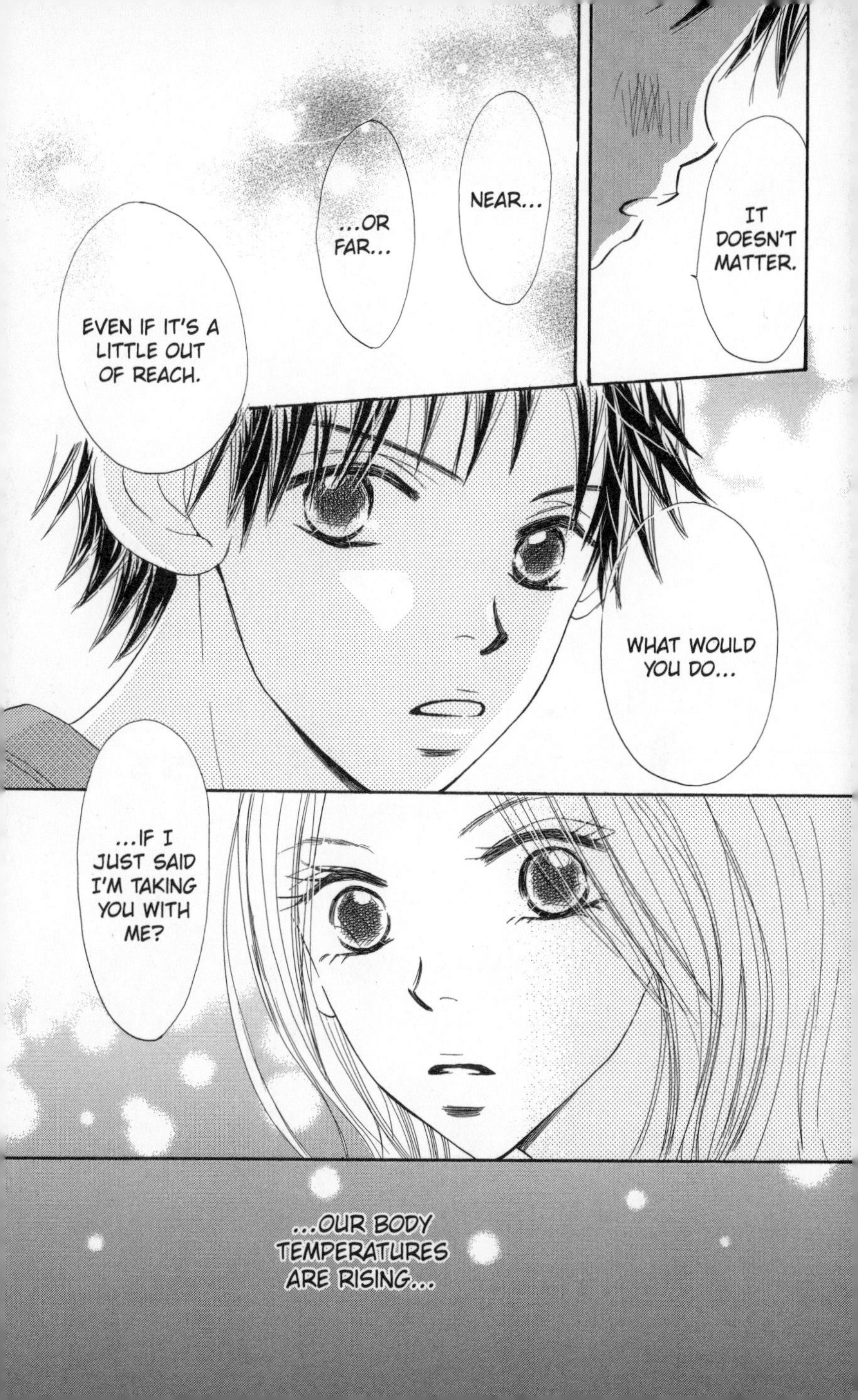
IT DOESN'T MATTER.
NEAR...
...OR FAR...
EVEN IF IT'S A LITTLE OUT OF REACH.
WHAT WOULD YOU DO...
...IF I JUST SAID I'M TAKING YOU WITH ME?
...OUR BODY TEMPERATURES ARE RISING...

KOBU
(NOT "FATTY")

GOD   MONKEY

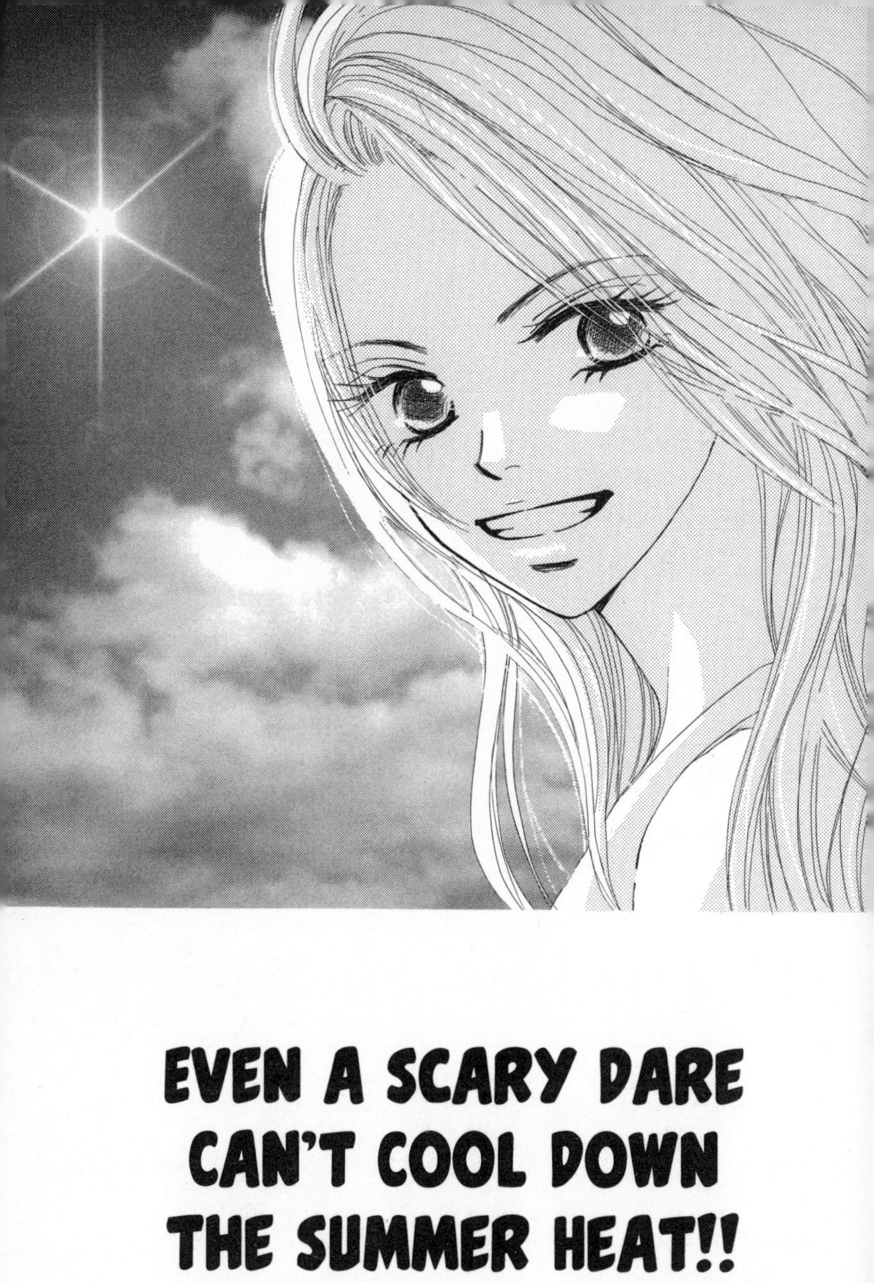

EVEN A SCARY DARE
CAN'T COOL DOWN
THE SUMMER HEAT!!

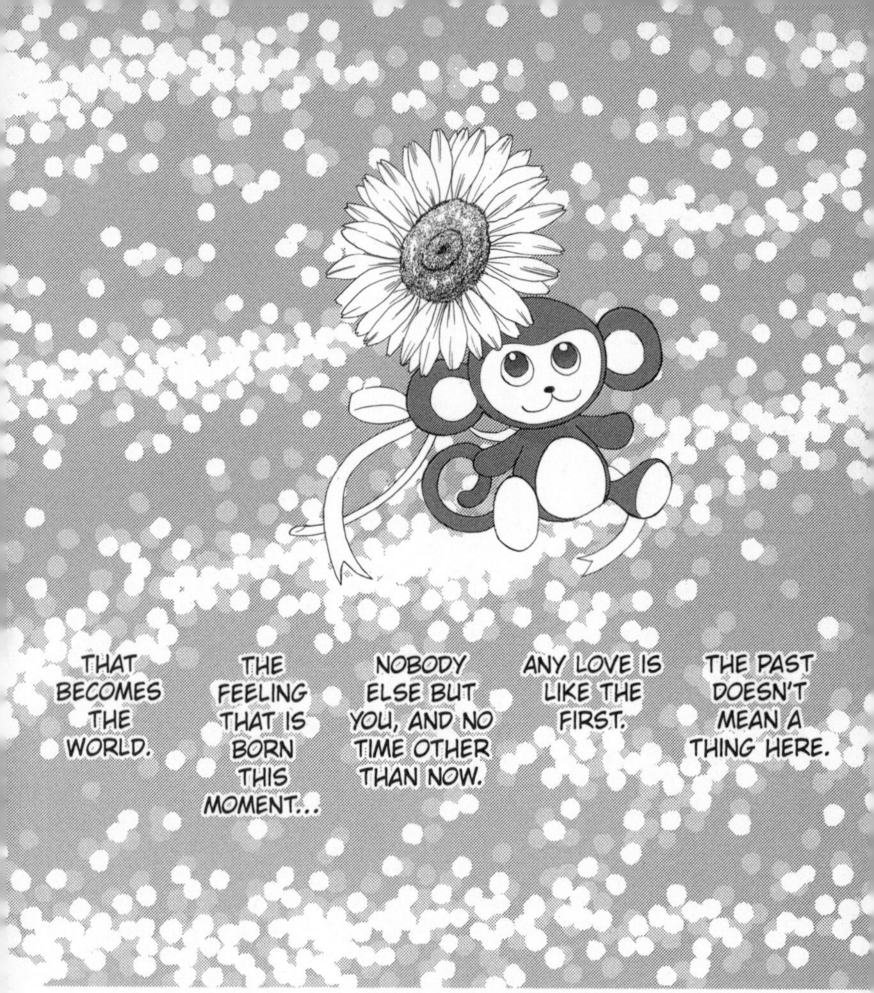
THE PAST DOESN'T MEAN A THING HERE.
ANY LOVE IS LIKE THE FIRST.
NOBODY ELSE BUT YOU, AND NO TIME OTHER THAN NOW.
THE FEELING THAT IS BORN THIS MOMENT...
THAT BECOMES THE WORLD.

Monkey High!

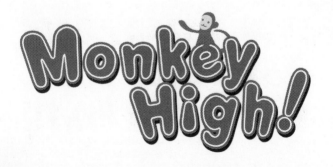

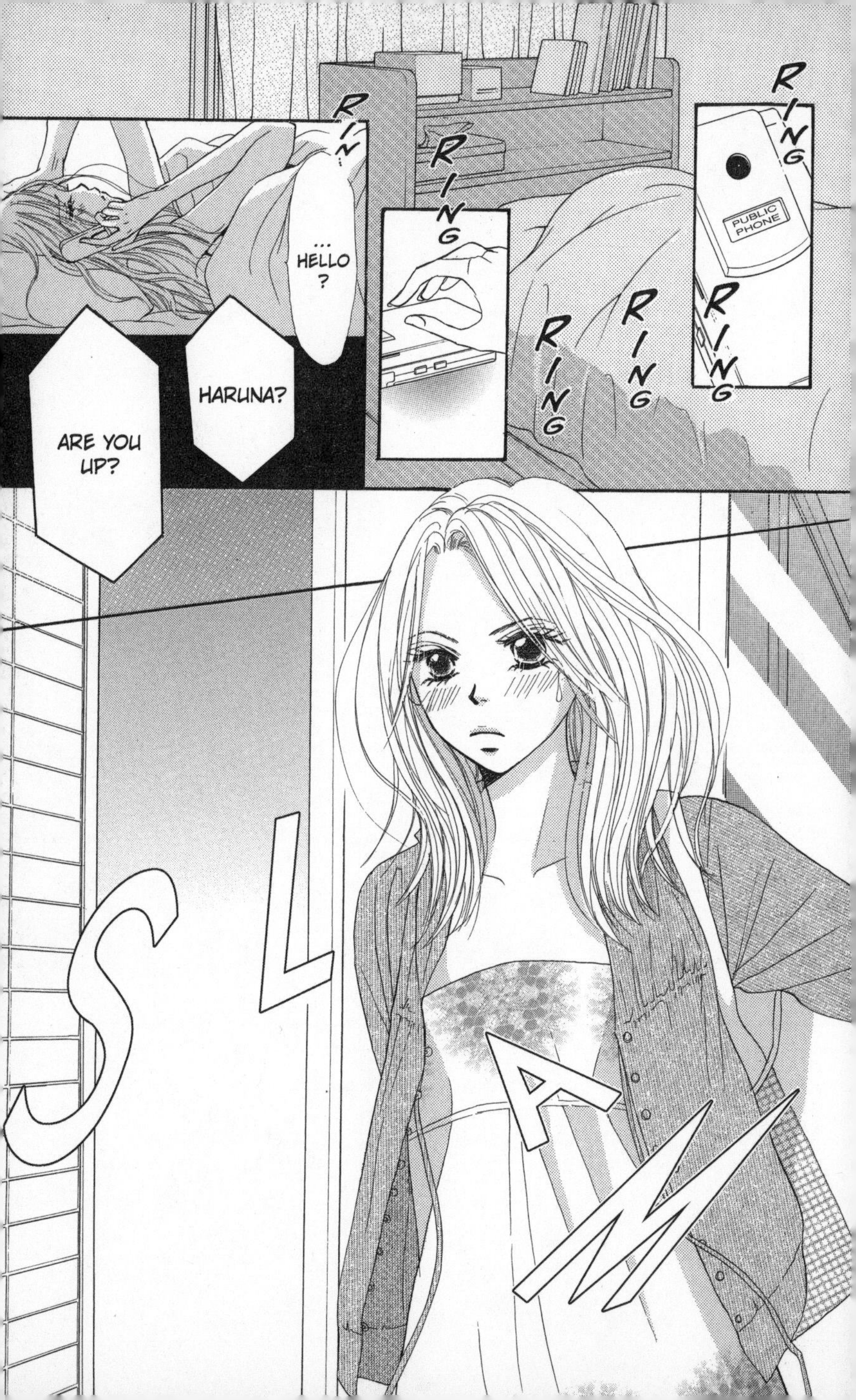
RING
PUBLIC PHONE
RING
RING
RING
RING
RING
RIN...
...HELLO?
HARUNA?
ARE YOU UP?
SLAM

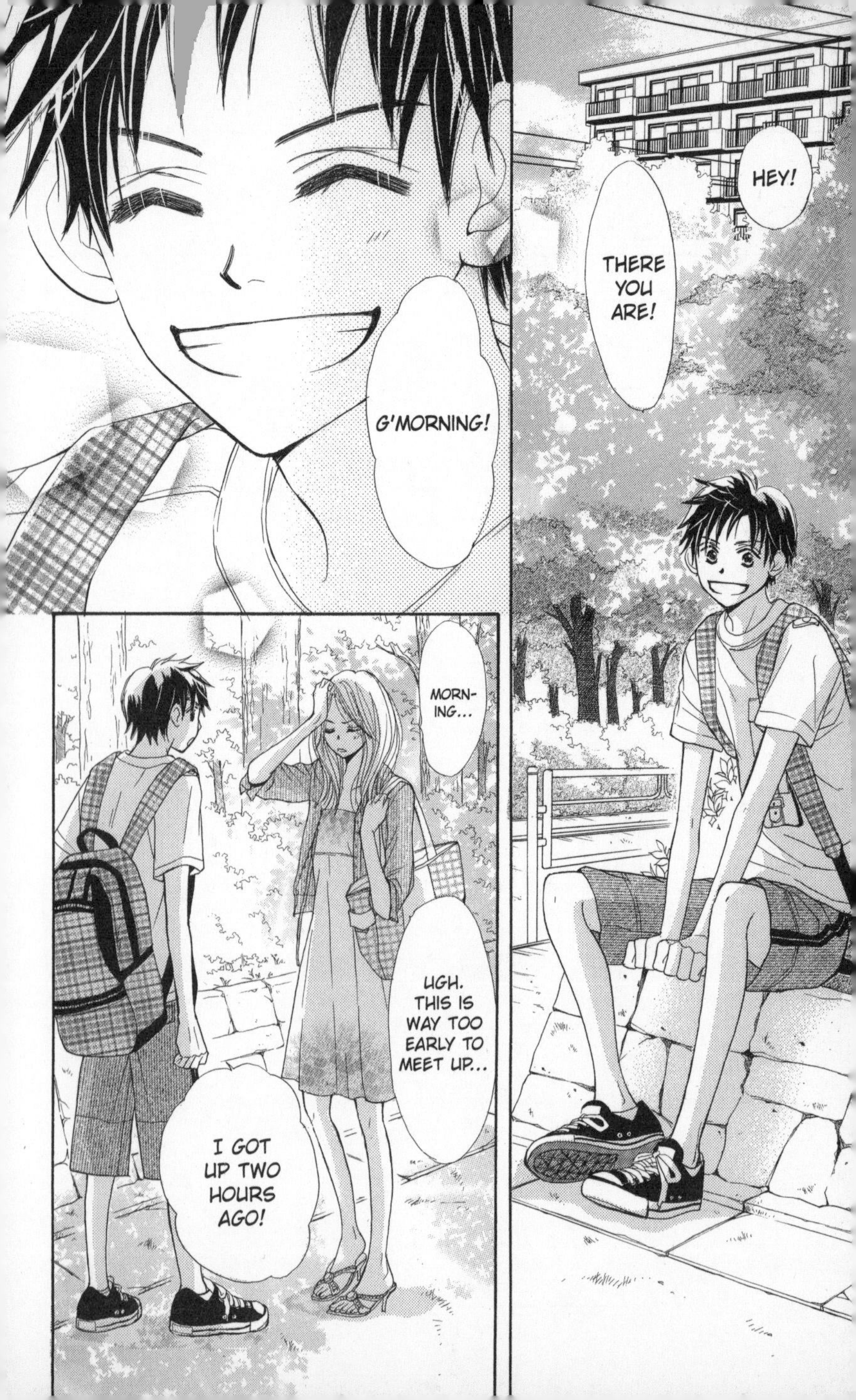
HEY!
THERE YOU ARE!
G'MORNING!
MORNING...
UGH. THIS IS WAY TOO EARLY TO MEET UP...
I GOT UP TWO HOURS AGO!

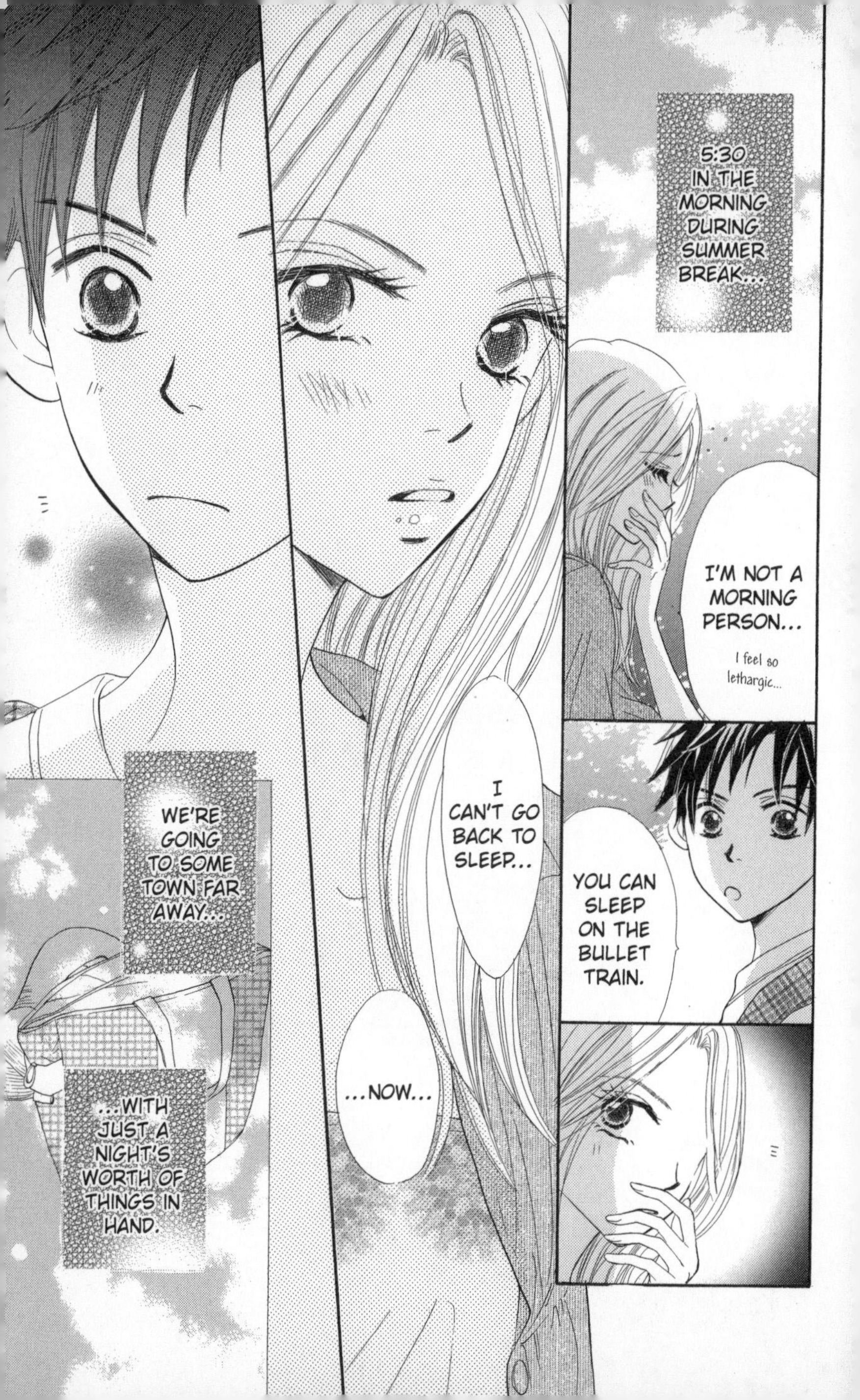
5:30 IN THE MORNING DURING SUMMER BREAK...
I'M NOT A MORNING PERSON...
I feel so lethargic...
YOU CAN SLEEP ON THE BULLET TRAIN.
I CAN'T GO BACK TO SLEEP...
...NOW...
WE'RE GOING TO SOME TOWN FAR AWAY...
...WITH JUST A NIGHT'S WORTH OF THINGS IN HAND.

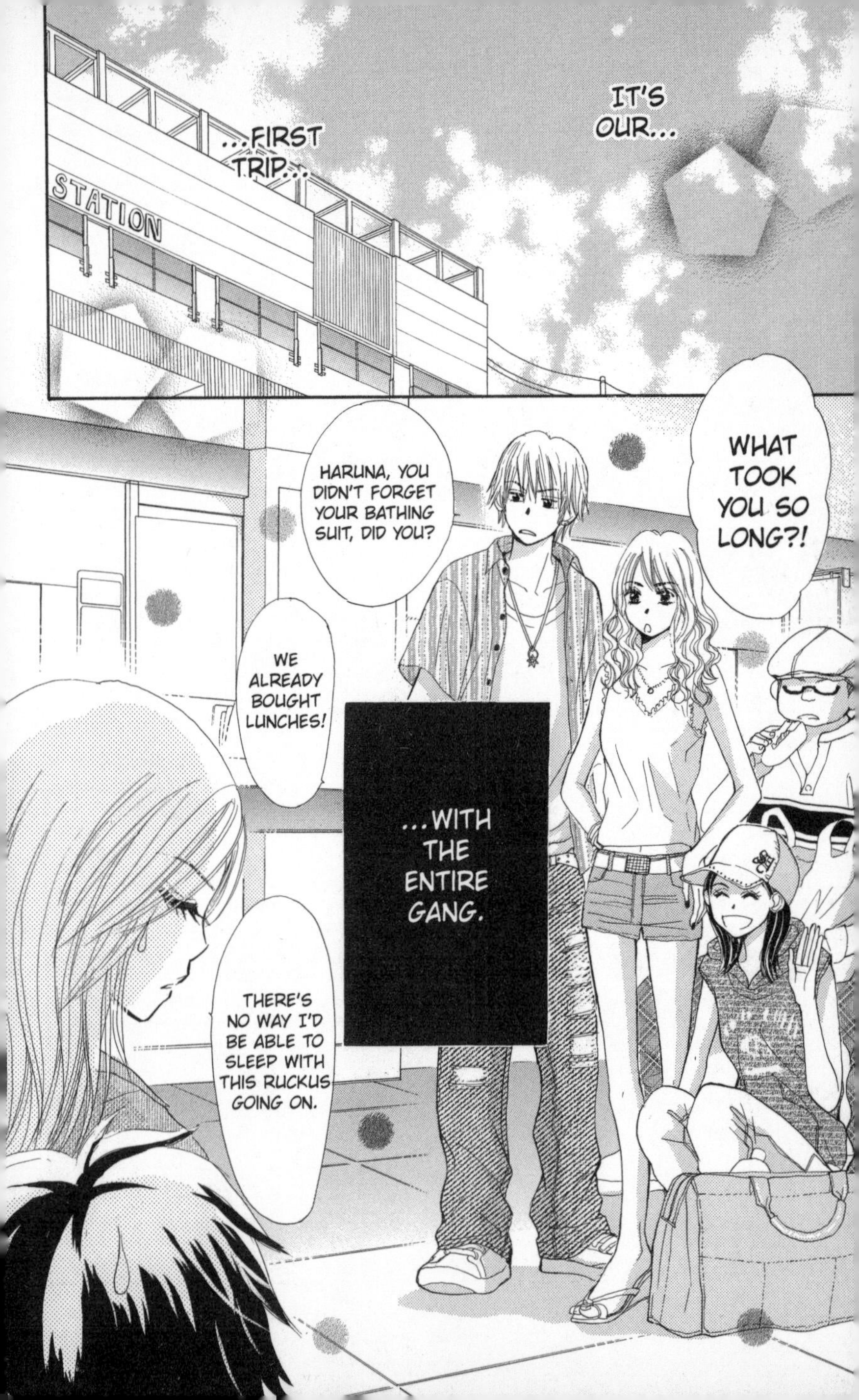
IT'S OUR...
...FIRST TRIP...
STATION
WHAT TOOK YOU SO LONG?!
HARUNA, YOU DIDN'T FORGET YOUR BATHING SUIT, DID YOU?
WE ALREADY BOUGHT LUNCHES!
...WITH THE ENTIRE GANG.
THERE'S NO WAY I'D BE ABLE TO SLEEP WITH THIS RUCKUS GOING ON.

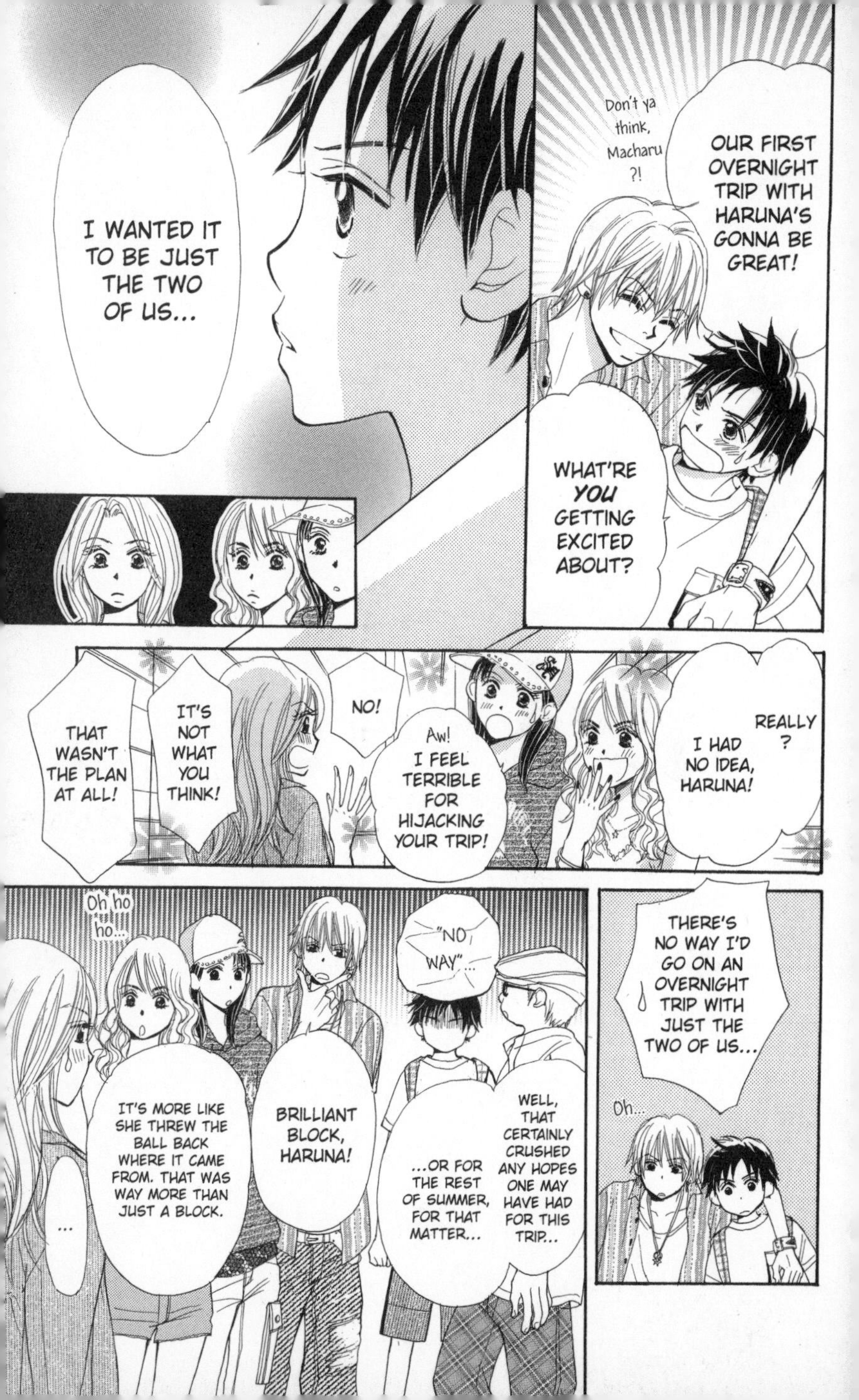

OUR FIRST OVERNIGHT TRIP WITH HARUNA'S GONNA BE GREAT!
Don't ya think, Macharu ?!
WHAT'RE YOU GETTING EXCITED ABOUT?
I WANTED IT TO BE JUST THE TWO OF US...
REALLY ?
I HAD NO IDEA, HARUNA!
Aw! I FEEL TERRIBLE FOR HIJACKING YOUR TRIP!
NO!
IT'S NOT WHAT YOU THINK!
THAT WASN'T THE PLAN AT ALL!
THERE'S NO WAY I'D GO ON AN OVERNIGHT TRIP WITH JUST THE TWO OF US...
Oh...
WELL, THAT CERTAINLY CRUSHED ANY HOPES ONE MAY HAVE HAD FOR THIS TRIP...
...OR FOR THE REST OF SUMMER, FOR THAT MATTER...
"NO WAY"...
BRILLIANT BLOCK, HARUNA!
IT'S MORE LIKE SHE THREW THE BALL BACK WHERE IT CAME FROM. THAT WAS WAY MORE THAN JUST A BLOCK.
Oh ho ho...
...

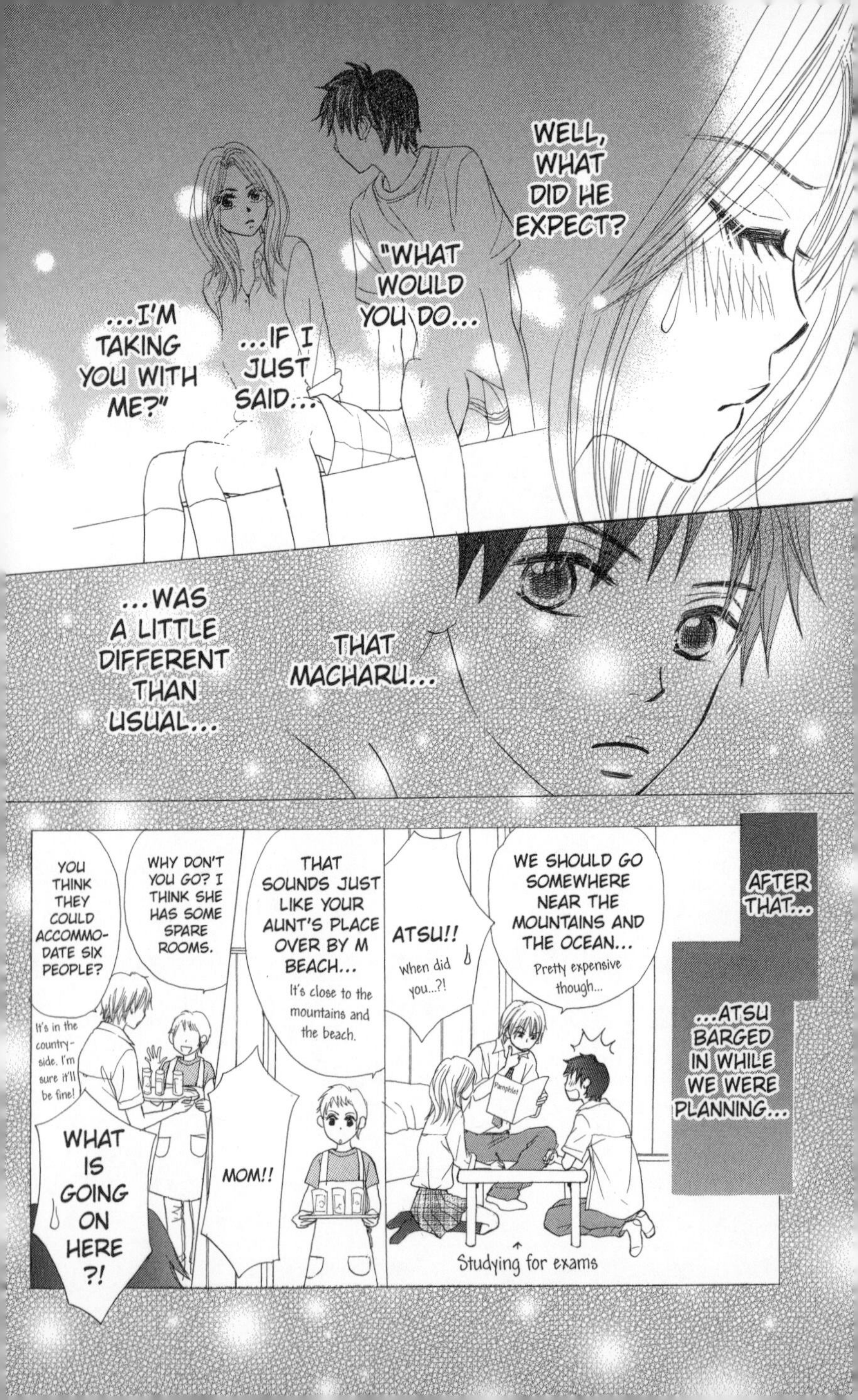
WELL, WHAT DID HE EXPECT?
"WHAT WOULD YOU DO...
...IF I JUST SAID...
...I'M TAKING YOU WITH ME?"
THAT MACHARU...
...WAS A LITTLE DIFFERENT THAN USUAL...
AFTER THAT...
...ATSU BARGED IN WHILE WE WERE PLANNING...
WE SHOULD GO SOMEWHERE NEAR THE MOUNTAINS AND THE OCEAN...
Pretty expensive though...
ATSU!!
When did you...?!
Pamphlet
Studying for exams
THAT SOUNDS JUST LIKE YOUR AUNT'S PLACE OVER BY M BEACH...
It's close to the mountains and the beach.
MOM!!
WHY DON'T YOU GO? I THINK SHE HAS SOME SPARE ROOMS.
YOU THINK THEY COULD ACCOMMODATE SIX PEOPLE?
It's in the countryside. I'm sure it'll be fine!
WHAT IS GOING ON HERE?!

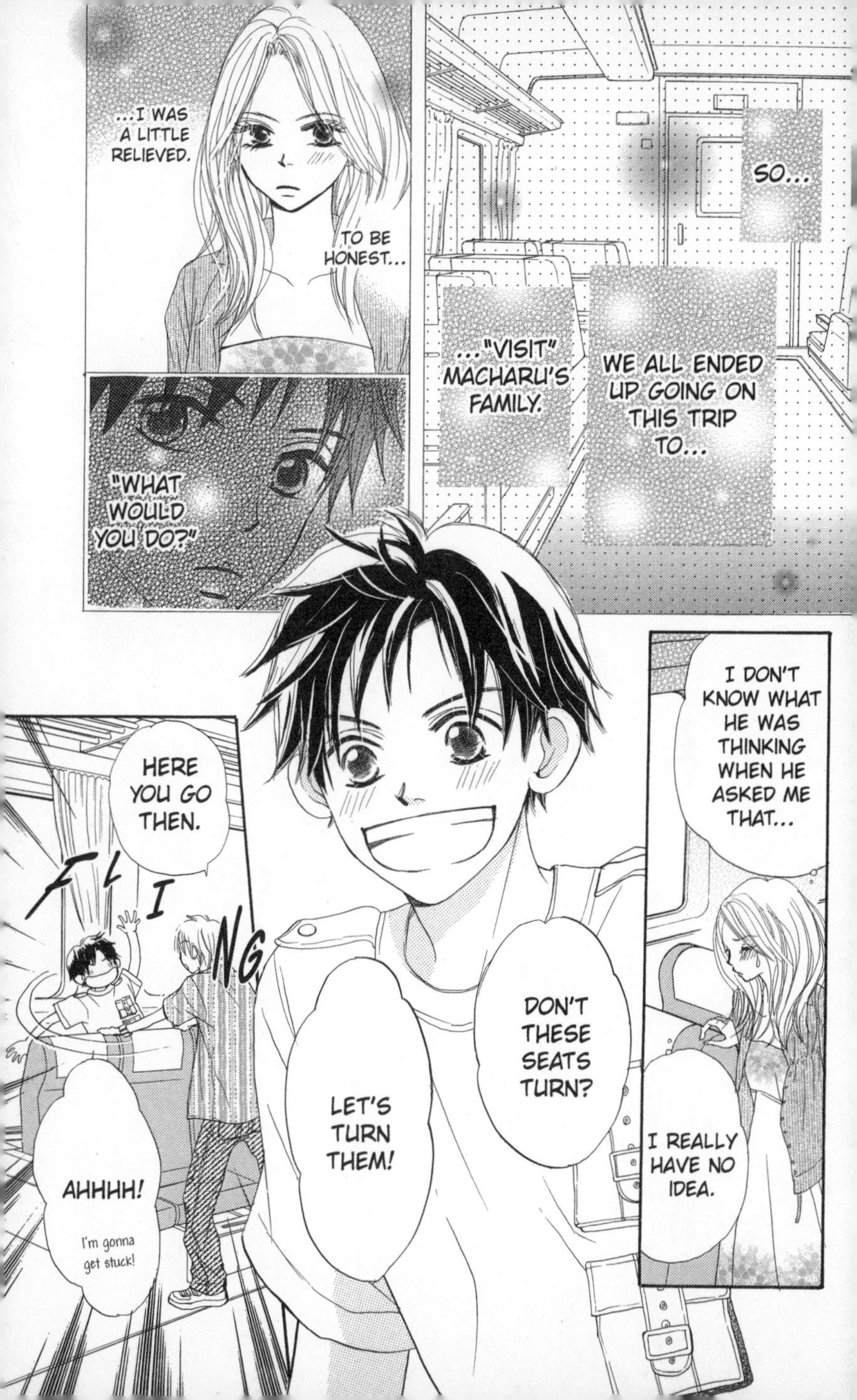
SO...
WE ALL ENDED UP GOING ON THIS TRIP TO...
..."VISIT" MACHARU'S FAMILY.
TO BE HONEST...
...I WAS A LITTLE RELIEVED.
"WHAT WOULD YOU DO?"
I DON'T KNOW WHAT HE WAS THINKING WHEN HE ASKED ME THAT...
I REALLY HAVE NO IDEA.
DON'T THESE SEATS TURN?
LET'S TURN THEM!
HERE YOU GO THEN.
FLING
AHHHH!
I'm gonna get stuck!

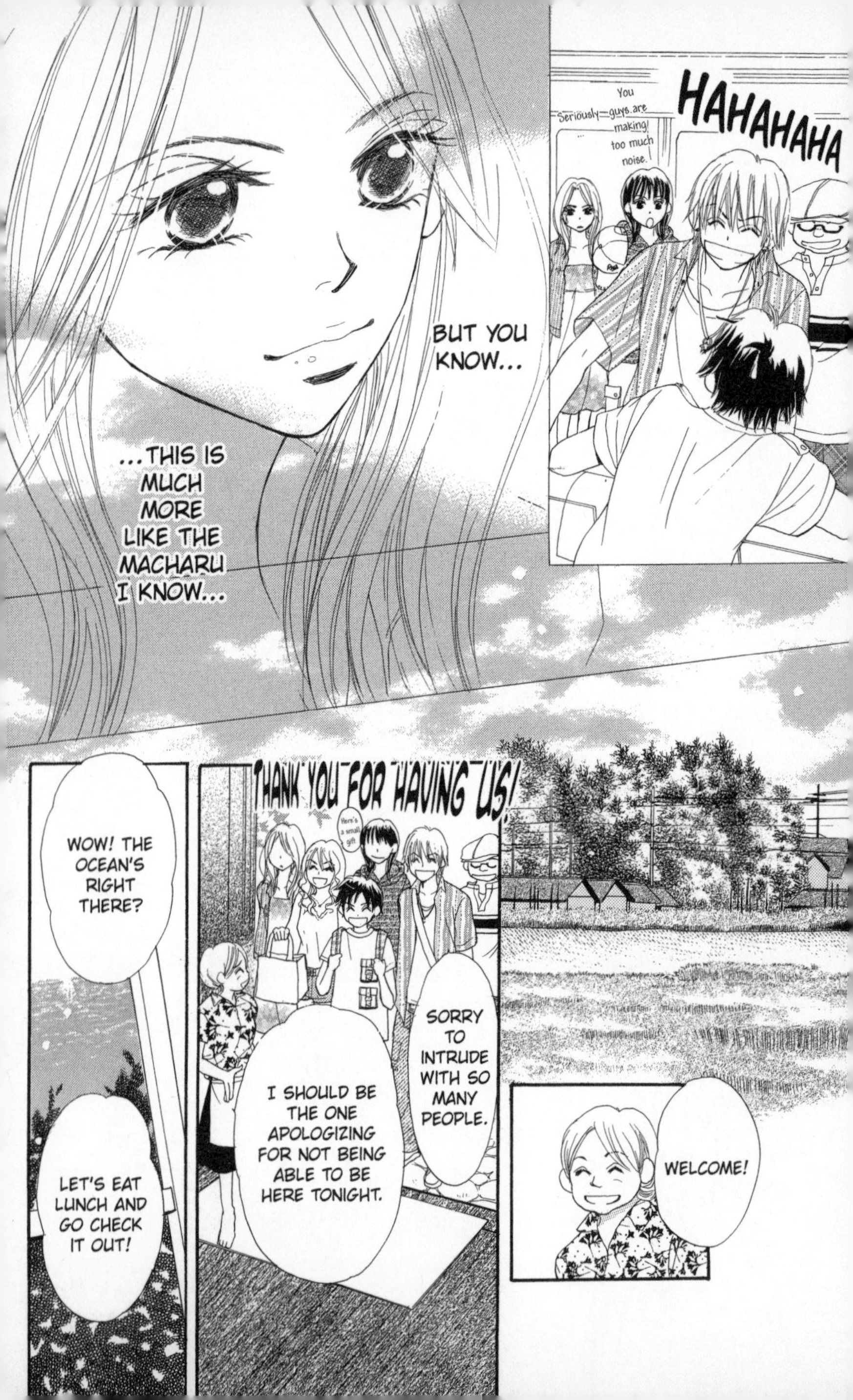
HAHAHAHA
You guys are making too much noise!
Seriously...
BUT YOU KNOW...
...THIS IS MUCH MORE LIKE THE MACHARU I KNOW...
WELCOME!
THANK YOU FOR HAVING US!
Here's a small gift
SORRY TO INTRUDE WITH SO MANY PEOPLE.
I SHOULD BE THE ONE APOLOGIZING FOR NOT BEING ABLE TO BE HERE TONIGHT.
WOW! THE OCEAN'S RIGHT THERE?
LET'S EAT LUNCH AND GO CHECK IT OUT!

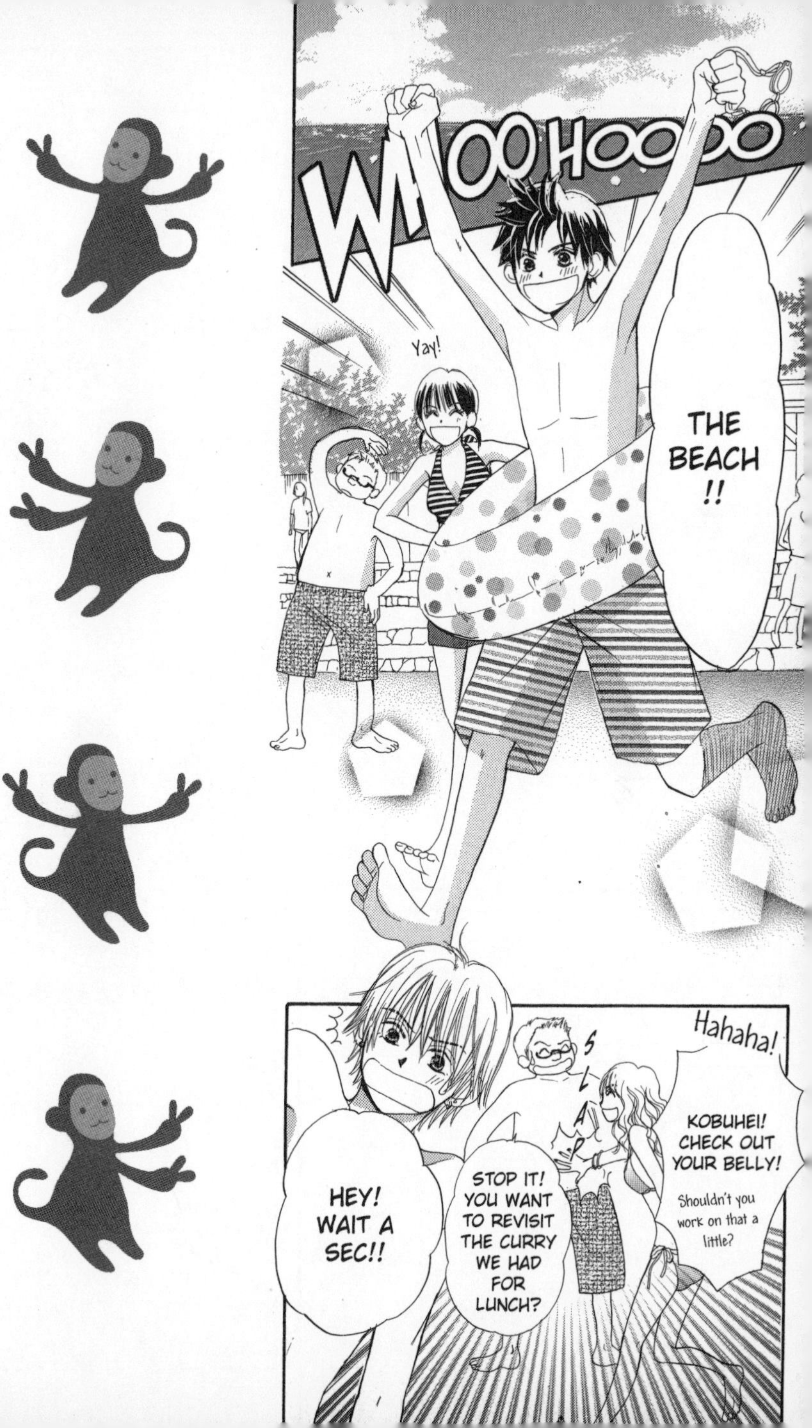
WA OO HOOOO
THE BEACH!!
Yay!
Hahaha!
KOBUHEI! CHECK OUT YOUR BELLY!
Shouldn't you work on that a little?
SLAP
STOP IT! YOU WANT TO REVISIT THE CURRY WE HAD FOR LUNCH?
HEY! WAIT A SEC!!

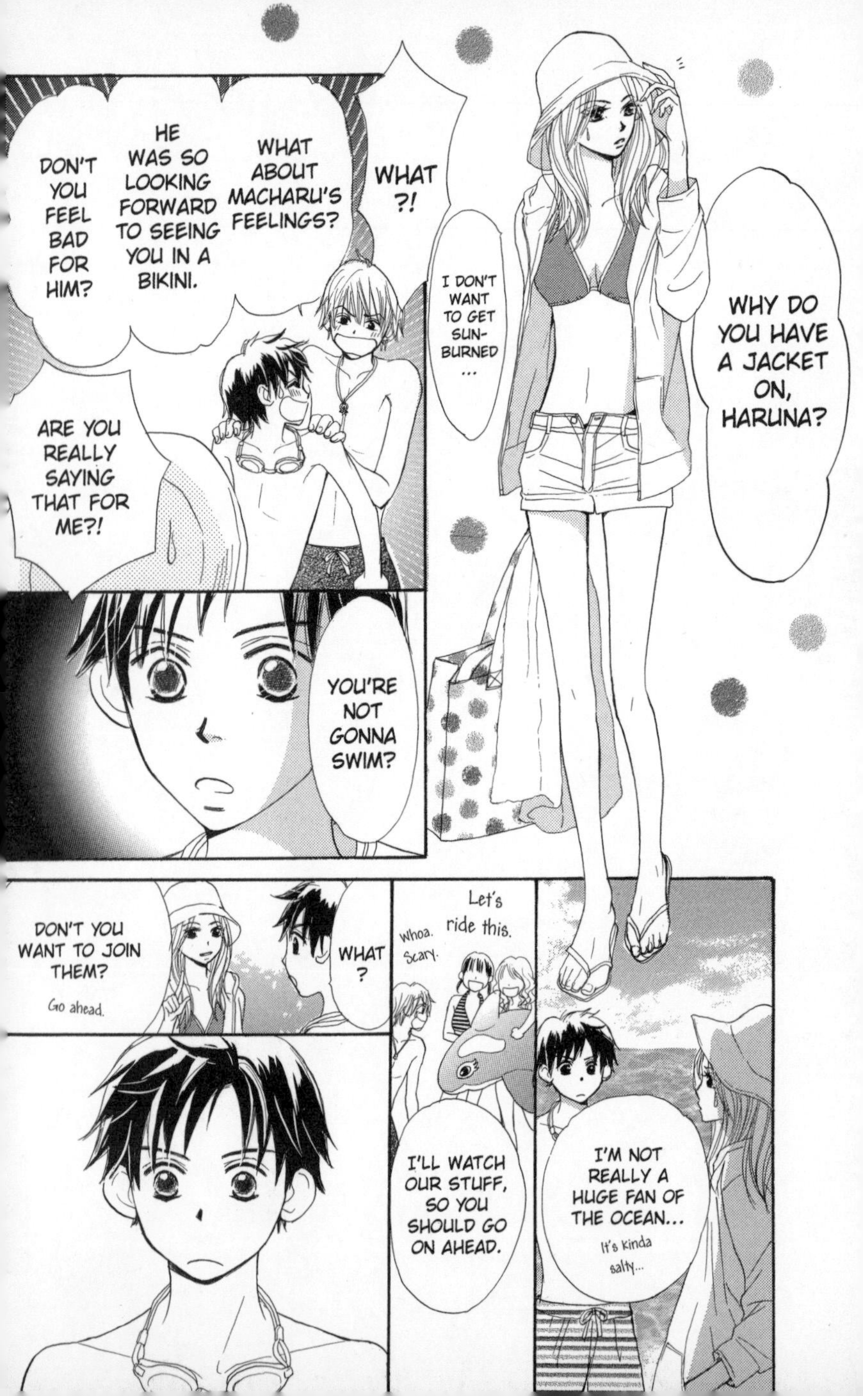
WHY DO YOU HAVE A JACKET ON, HARUNA?
I DON'T WANT TO GET SUN-BURNED ...
WHAT ?!
WHAT ABOUT MACHARU'S FEELINGS?
HE WAS SO LOOKING FORWARD TO SEEING YOU IN A BIKINI.
DON'T YOU FEEL BAD FOR HIM?
ARE YOU REALLY SAYING THAT FOR ME?!
YOU'RE NOT GONNA SWIM?
I'M NOT REALLY A HUGE FAN OF THE OCEAN...
It's kinda salty...
Let's ride this.
Whoa. Scary.
I'LL WATCH OUR STUFF, SO YOU SHOULD GO ON AHEAD.
WHAT ?
DON'T YOU WANT TO JOIN THEM?
Go ahead.

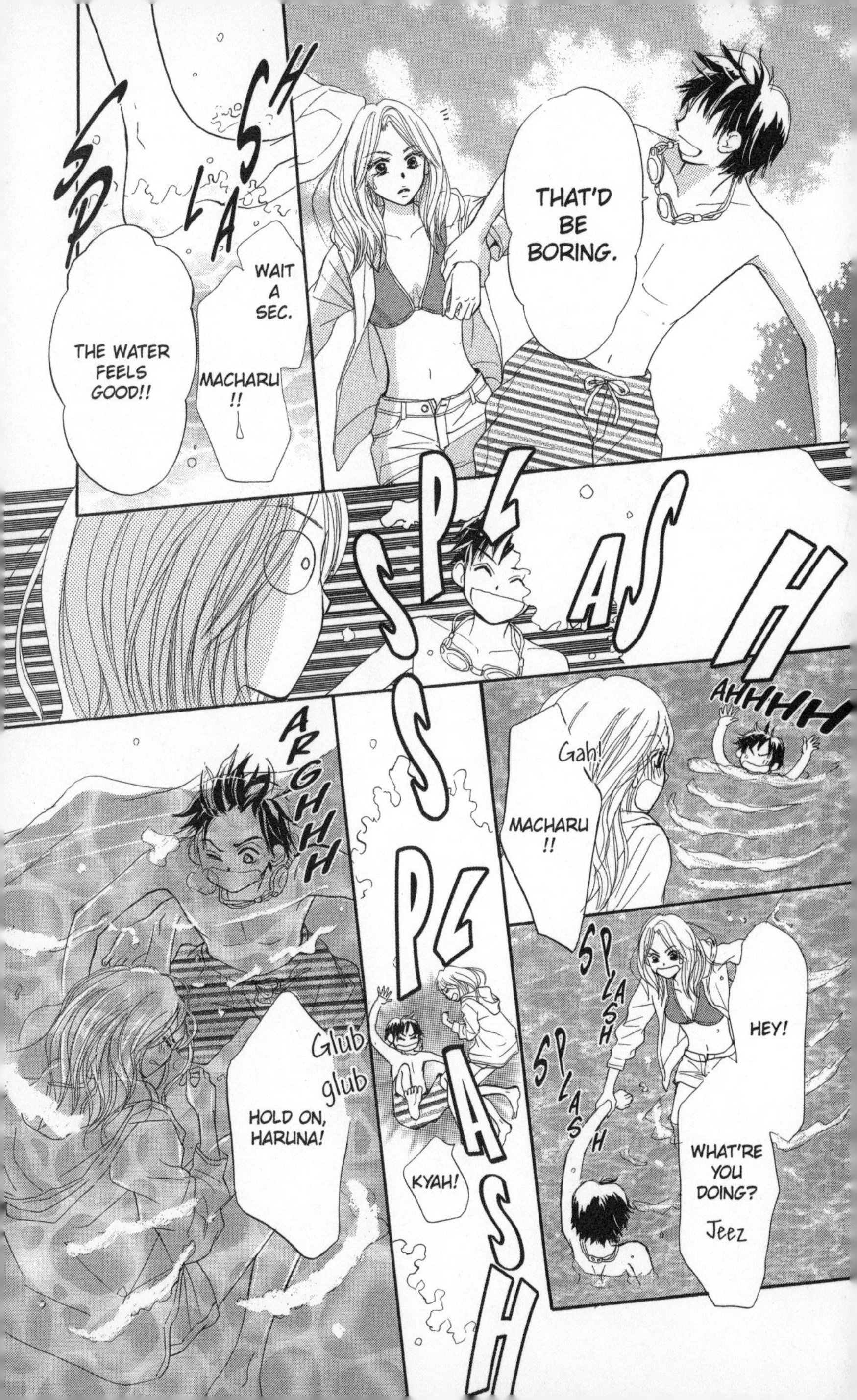
THAT'D BE BORING.
SPLASH
WAIT A SEC.
MACHARU!!
THE WATER FEELS GOOD!!
SPLASH
AHHHHH
Gah!
MACHARU!!
SPLASH
SPLASH
HEY!
WHAT'RE YOU DOING?
Jeez
SPLASH
KYAH!
ARGHHHH
Glub glub
HOLD ON, HARUNA!

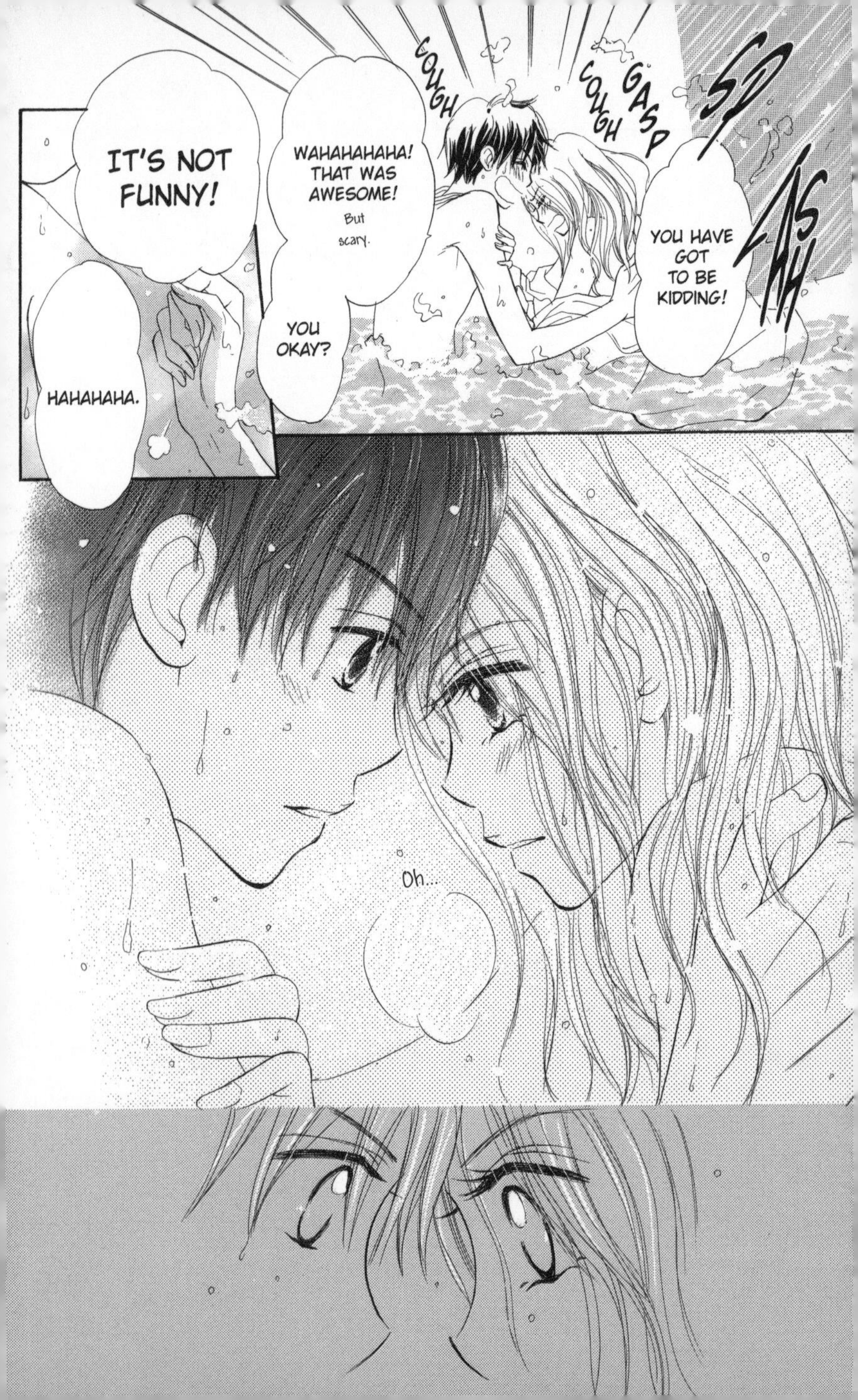
SPLASH
YOU HAVE GOT TO BE KIDDING!
GASP
COUGH
COUGH
WAHAHAHAHA! THAT WAS AWESOME!
But scary.
YOU OKAY?
IT'S NOT FUNNY!
HAHAHAHA.
Oh...

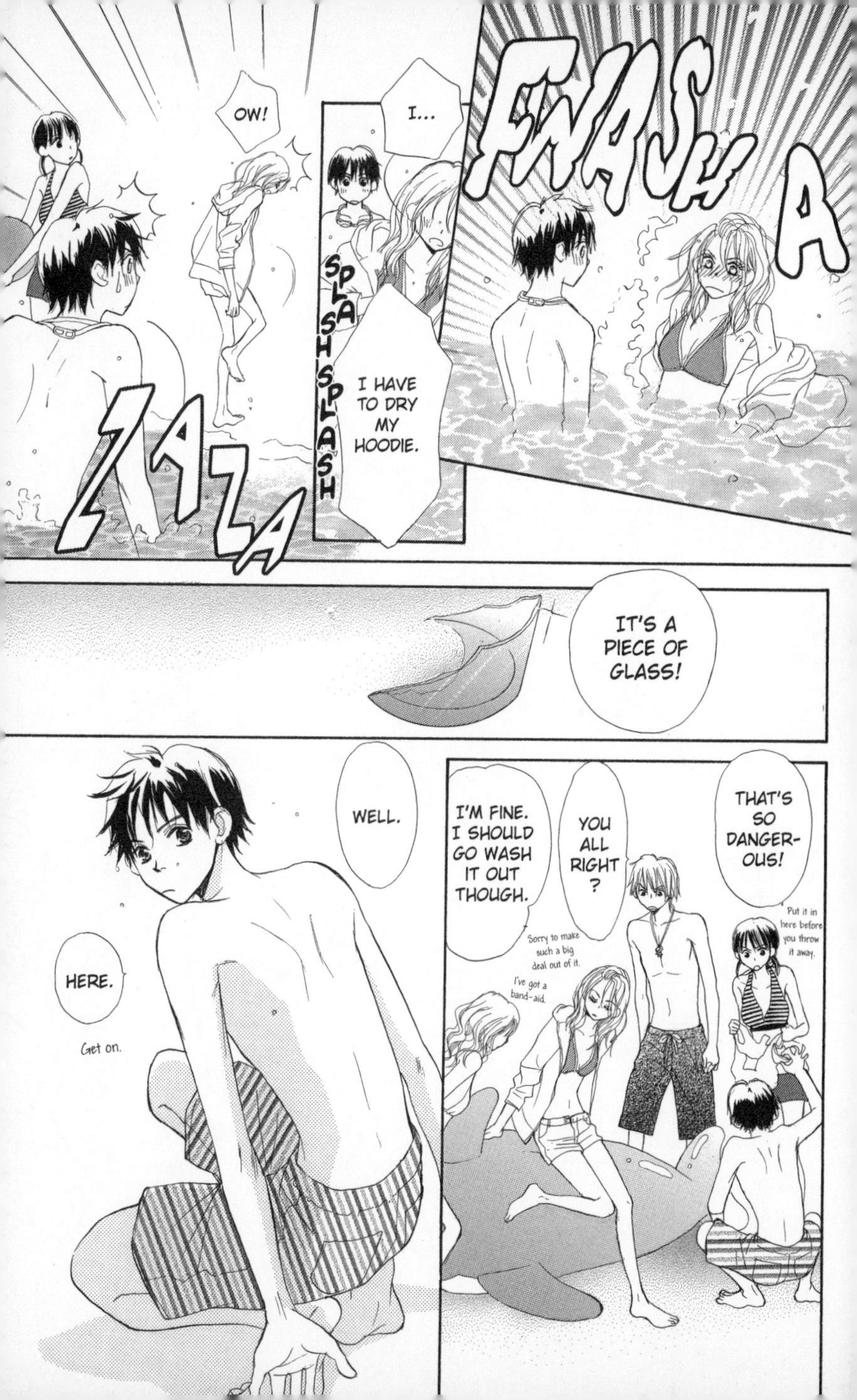
FWASHA
I...
SPLASH SPLASH
I HAVE TO DRY MY HOODIE.
OW!
ZAZA
IT'S A PIECE OF GLASS!
THAT'S SO DANGER-OUS!
Put it in here before you throw it away.
YOU ALL RIGHT?
I'M FINE. I SHOULD GO WASH IT OUT THOUGH.
Sorry to make such a big deal out of it.
I've got a band-aid.
WELL.
HERE.
Get on.

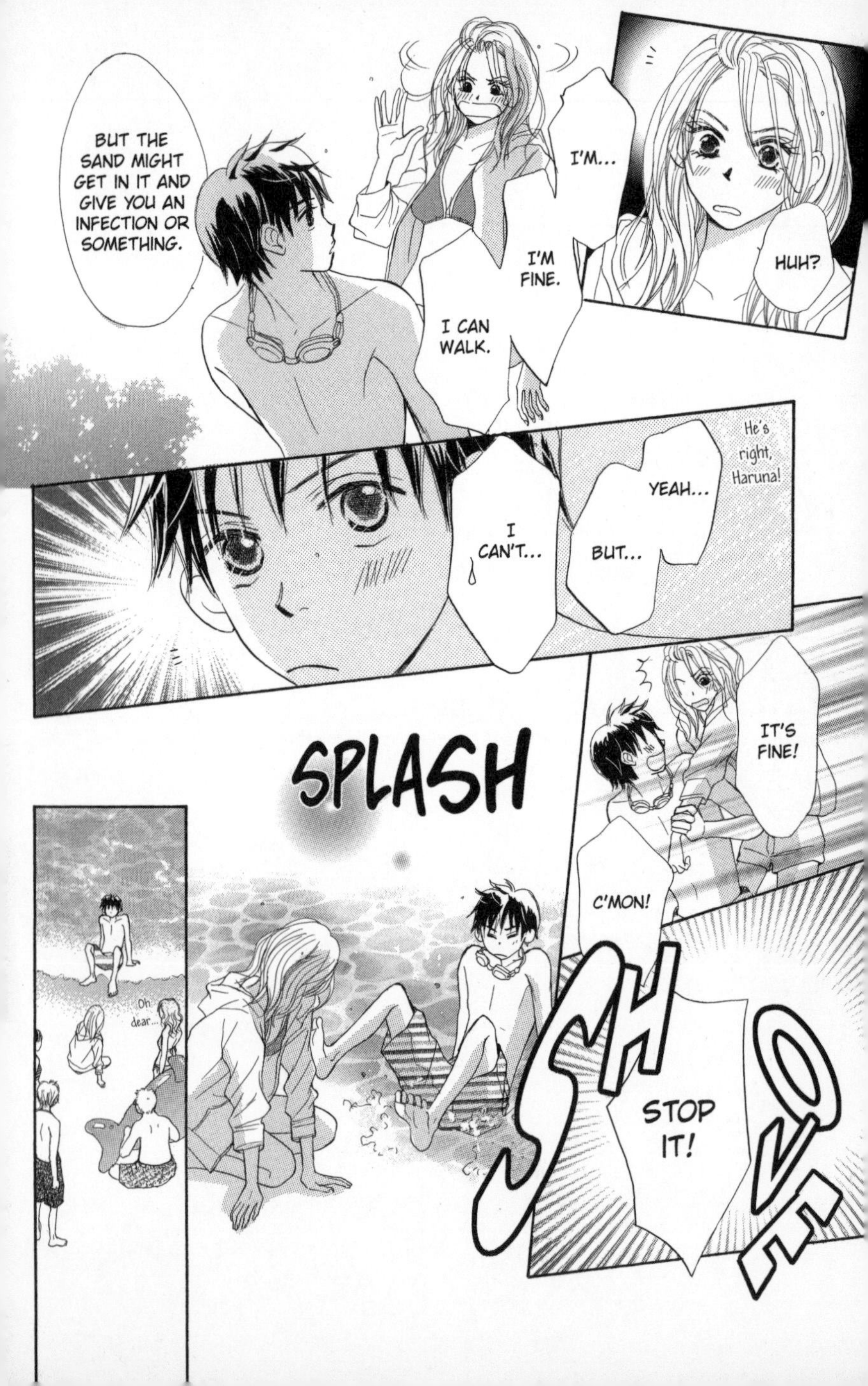
HUH?
I'M...
I'M FINE.
I CAN WALK.
BUT THE SAND MIGHT GET IN IT AND GIVE YOU AN INFECTION OR SOMETHING.
He's right, Haruna!
YEAH...
BUT...
I CAN'T...
IT'S FINE!
C'MON!
SPLASH
STOP IT!
Oh dear...

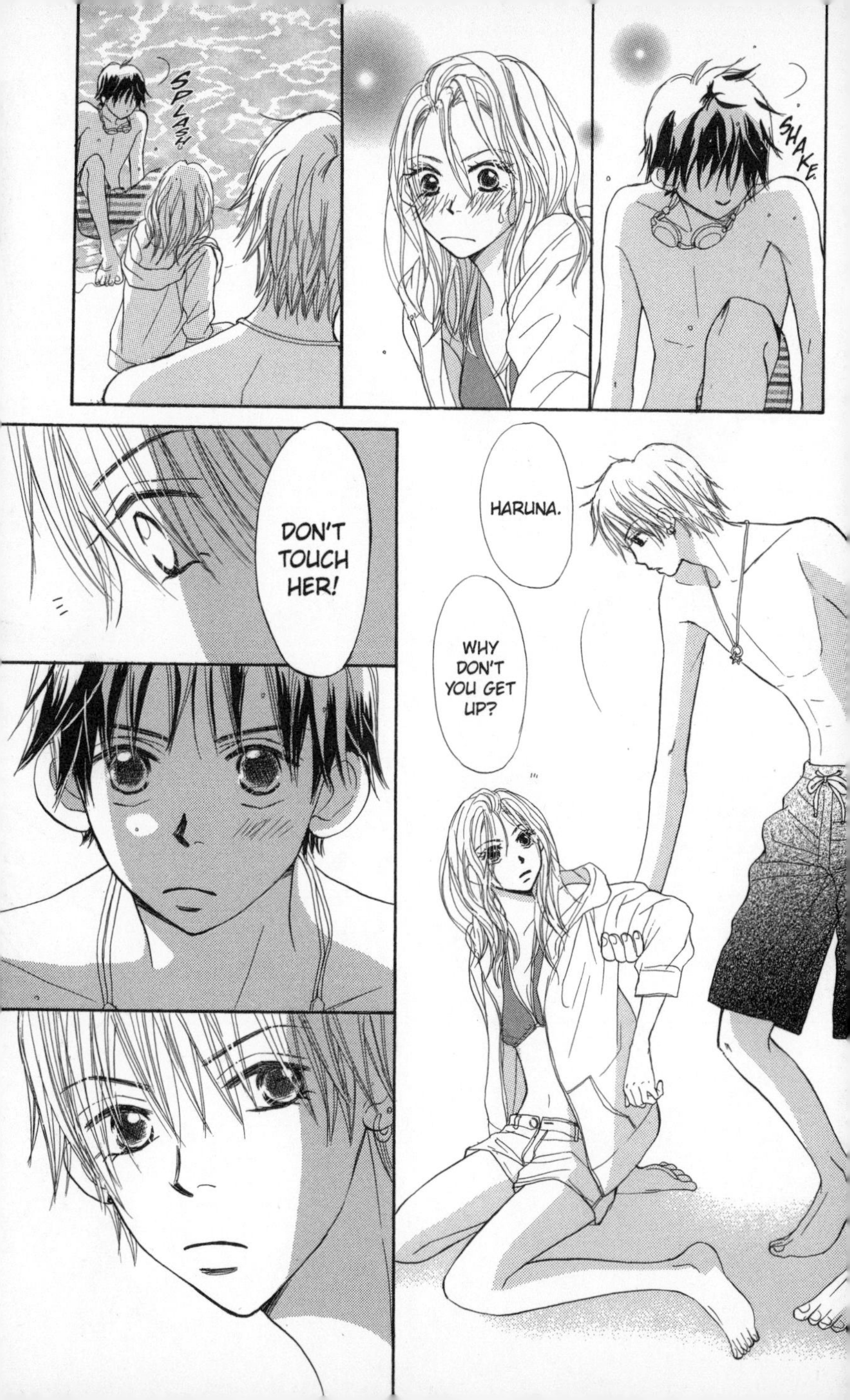
SHAKE.
SPLASH
HARUNA.
WHY DON'T YOU GET UP?
DON'T TOUCH HER!

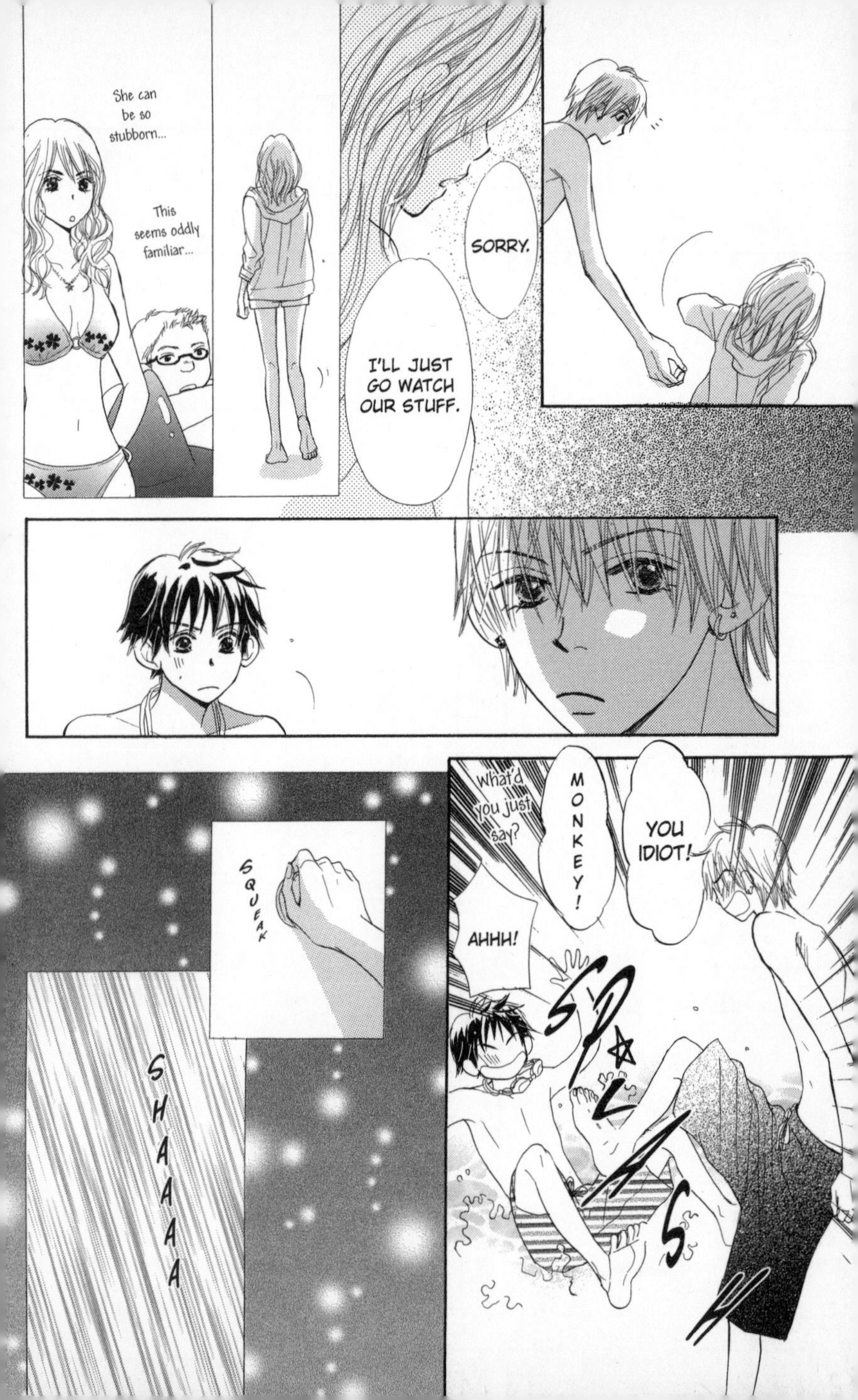
SORRY.
I'LL JUST GO WATCH OUR STUFF.
She can be so stubborn...
This seems oddly familiar...
YOU IDIOT!
MONKEY!
What'd you just say?
AHHH!
SPLASH
SQUEAK
SHAAAAA

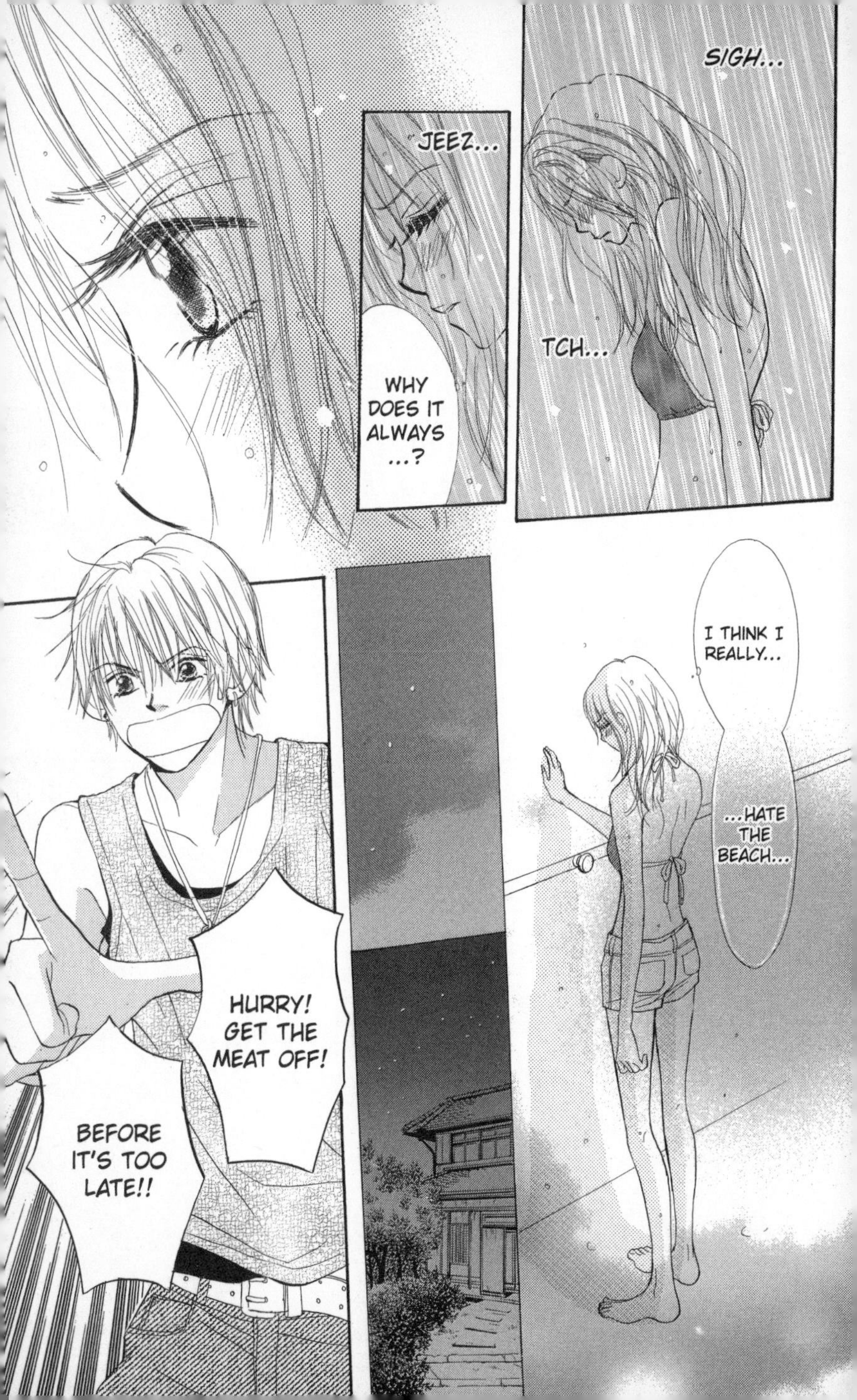
SIGH...
TCH...
JEEZ...
WHY DOES IT ALWAYS ...?
I THINK I REALLY...
...HATE THE BEACH...
HURRY! GET THE MEAT OFF!
BEFORE IT'S TOO LATE!!

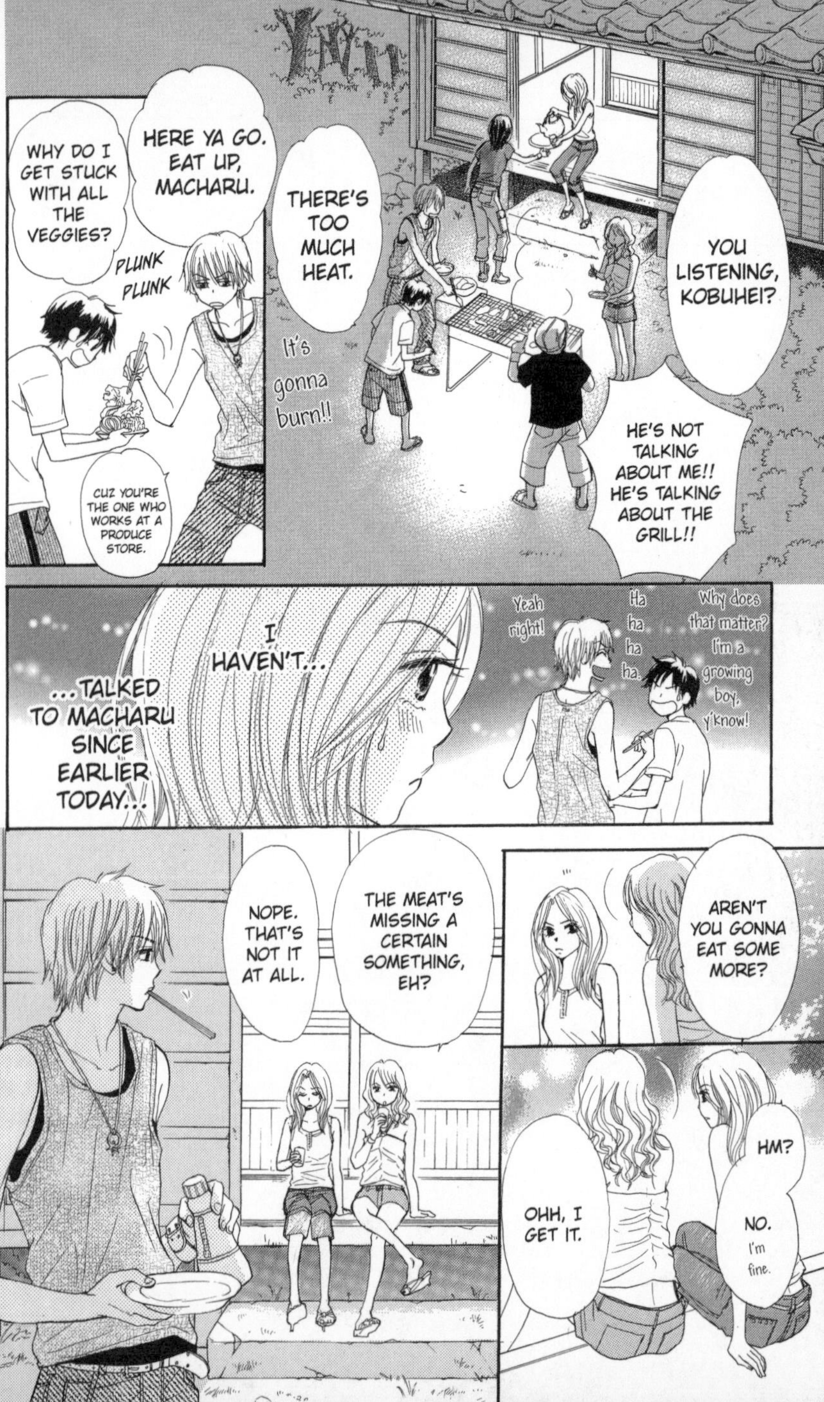
YOU LISTENING, KOBUHEI?
HE'S NOT TALKING ABOUT ME!! HE'S TALKING ABOUT THE GRILL!!
THERE'S TOO MUCH HEAT.
It's gonna burn!!
HERE YA GO. EAT UP, MACHARU.
WHY DO I GET STUCK WITH ALL THE VEGGIES?
PLUNK PLUNK
CUZ YOU'RE THE ONE WHO WORKS AT A PRODUCE STORE.
Why does that matter? I'm a growing boy, y'know!
Ha ha ha ha.
Yeah right!
I HAVEN'T...
...TALKED TO MACHARU SINCE EARLIER TODAY...
AREN'T YOU GONNA EAT SOME MORE?
HM?
NO. I'm fine.
OHH, I GET IT.
THE MEAT'S MISSING A CERTAIN SOMETHING, EH?
NOPE. THAT'S NOT IT AT ALL.

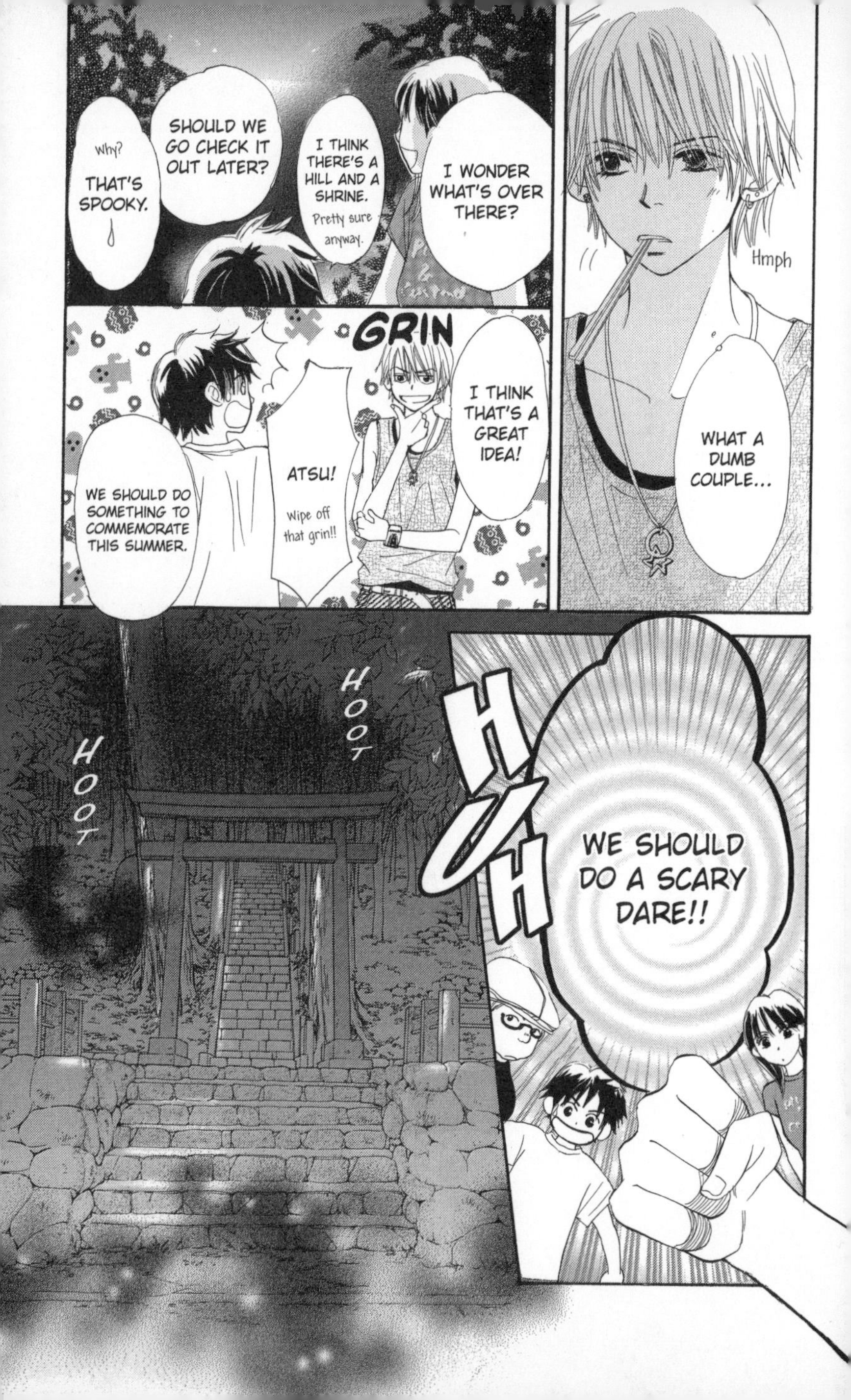
Hmph
WHAT A DUMB COUPLE...
I WONDER WHAT'S OVER THERE?
I THINK THERE'S A HILL AND A SHRINE.
Pretty sure anyway.
SHOULD WE GO CHECK IT OUT LATER?
Why?
THAT'S SPOOKY.
GRIN
I THINK THAT'S A GREAT IDEA!
ATSU!
Wipe off that grin!!
WE SHOULD DO SOMETHING TO COMMEMORATE THIS SUMMER.
HUH
WE SHOULD DO A SCARY DARE!!
HOOT
HOOT

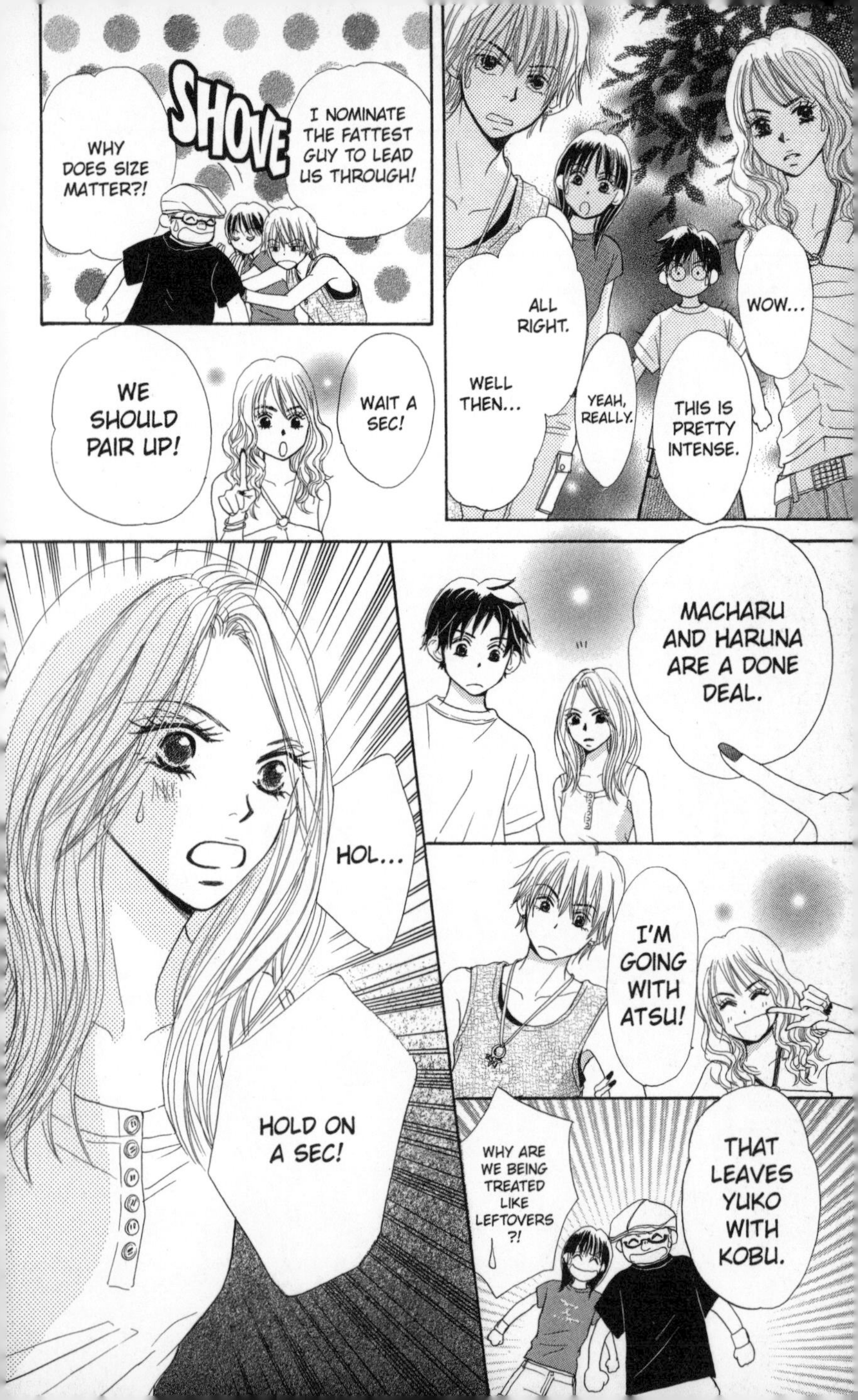
WOW...
THIS IS PRETTY INTENSE.
YEAH, REALLY.
ALL RIGHT.
WELL THEN...
I NOMINATE THE FATTEST GUY TO LEAD US THROUGH!
SHOVE
WHY DOES SIZE MATTER?!
WAIT A SEC!
WE SHOULD PAIR UP!
MACHARU AND HARUNA ARE A DONE DEAL.
I'M GOING WITH ATSU!
THAT LEAVES YUKO WITH KOBU.
WHY ARE WE BEING TREATED LIKE LEFTOVERS?!
HOL...
HOLD ON A SEC!

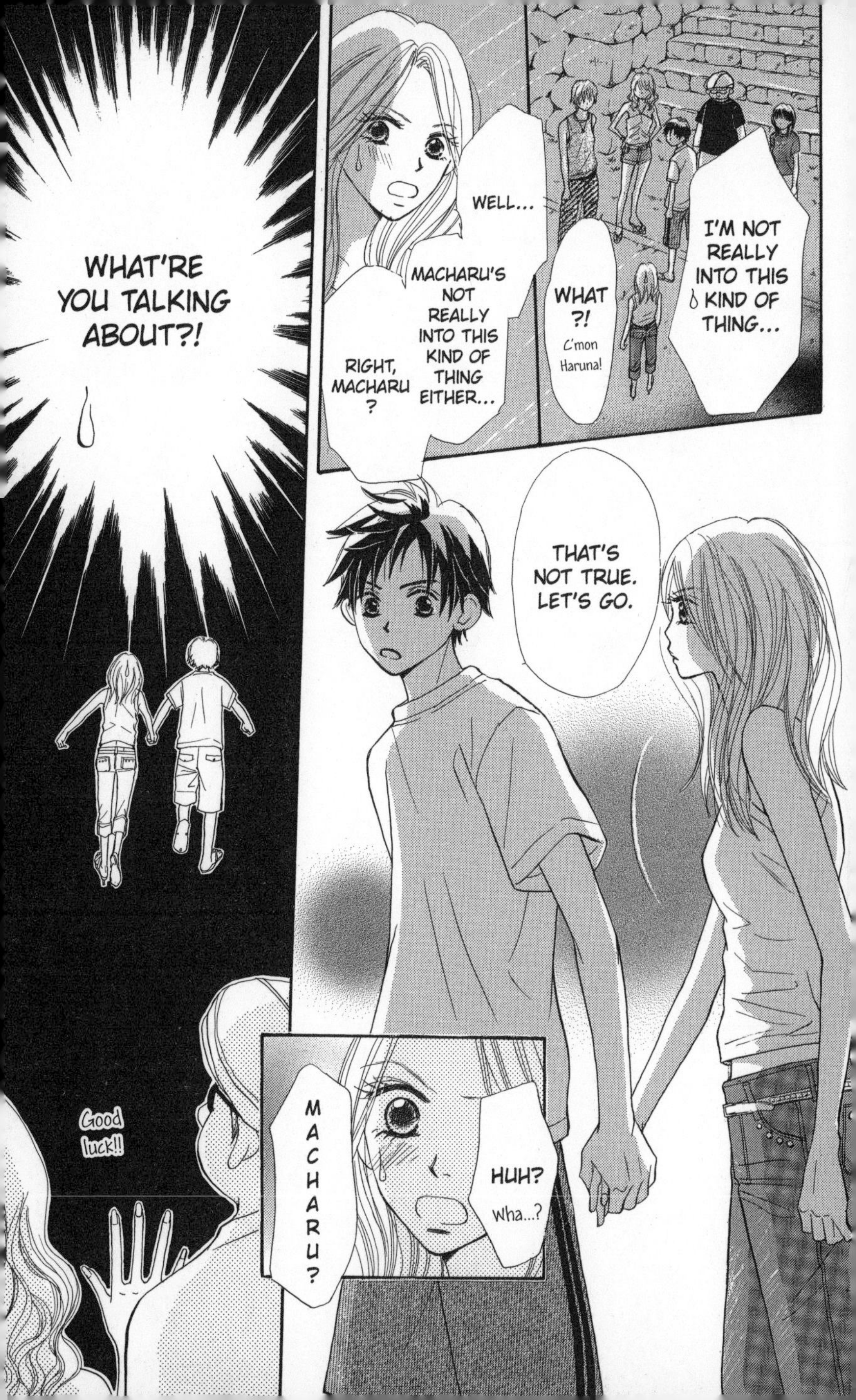
I'M NOT REALLY INTO THIS KIND OF THING...
WHAT?!
C'mon Haruna!
WELL...
MACHARU'S NOT REALLY INTO THIS KIND OF THING EITHER...
RIGHT, MACHARU?
THAT'S NOT TRUE. LET'S GO.
MACHARU?
HUH?
Wha...?
WHAT'RE YOU TALKING ABOUT?!
Good luck!!

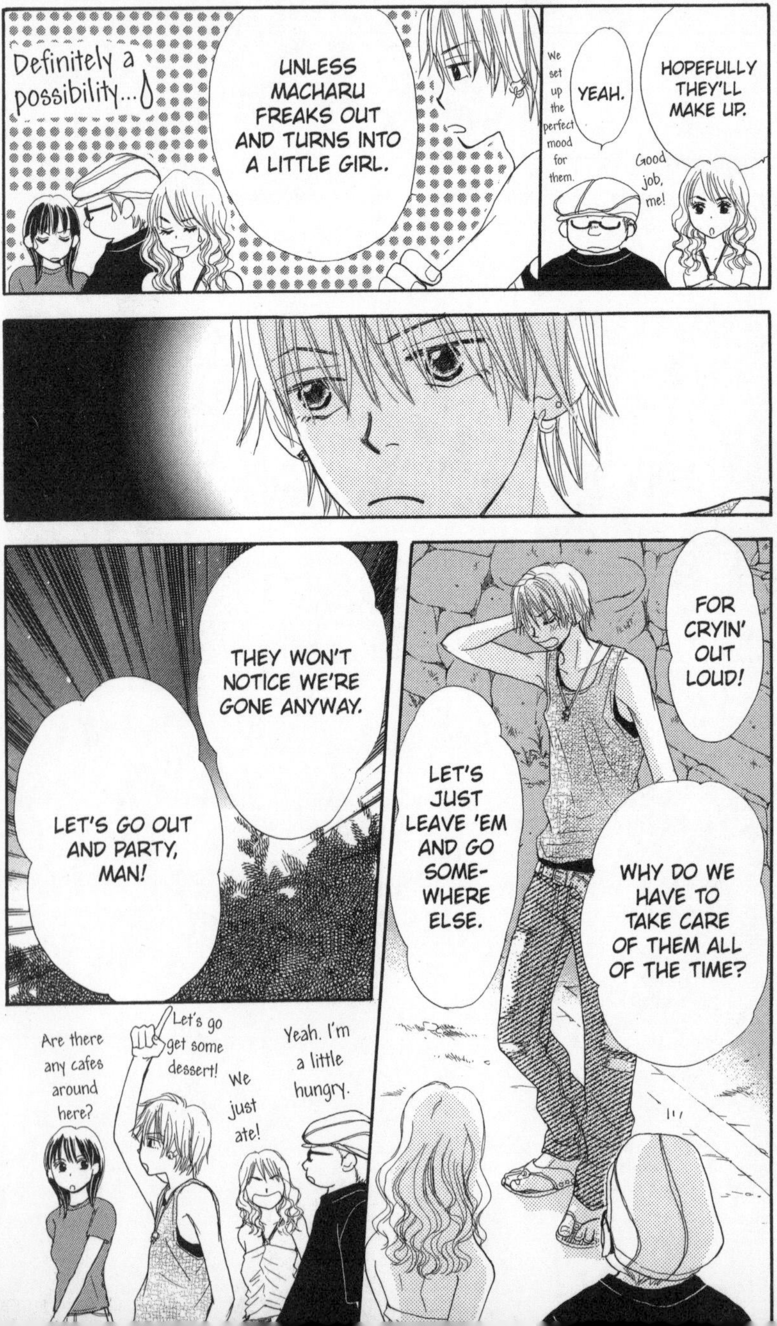
HOPEFULLY THEY'LL MAKE UP.
YEAH.
We set up the perfect mood for them.
Good job, me!
UNLESS MACHARU FREAKS OUT AND TURNS INTO A LITTLE GIRL.
Definitely a possibility...
FOR CRYIN' OUT LOUD!
WHY DO WE HAVE TO TAKE CARE OF THEM ALL OF THE TIME?
LET'S JUST LEAVE 'EM AND GO SOME-WHERE ELSE.
THEY WON'T NOTICE WE'RE GONE ANYWAY.
LET'S GO OUT AND PARTY, MAN!
Yeah. I'm a little hungry.
We just ate!
Let's go get some dessert!
Are there any cafes around here?

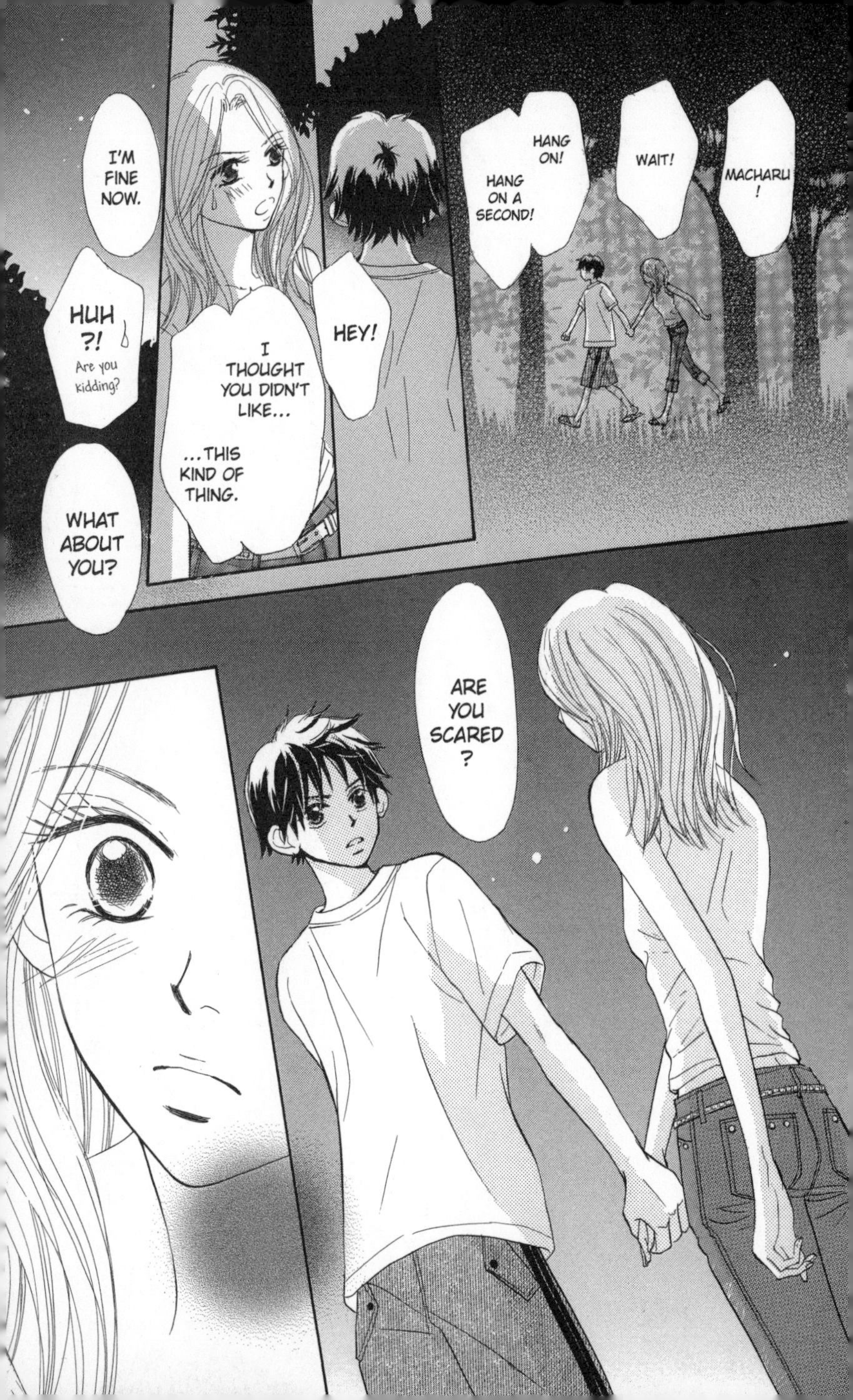
MACHARU!
WAIT!
HANG ON!
HANG ON A SECOND!
HEY!
I THOUGHT YOU DIDN'T LIKE...
...THIS KIND OF THING.
I'M FINE NOW.
HUH?!
Are you kidding?
WHAT ABOUT YOU?
ARE YOU SCARED?

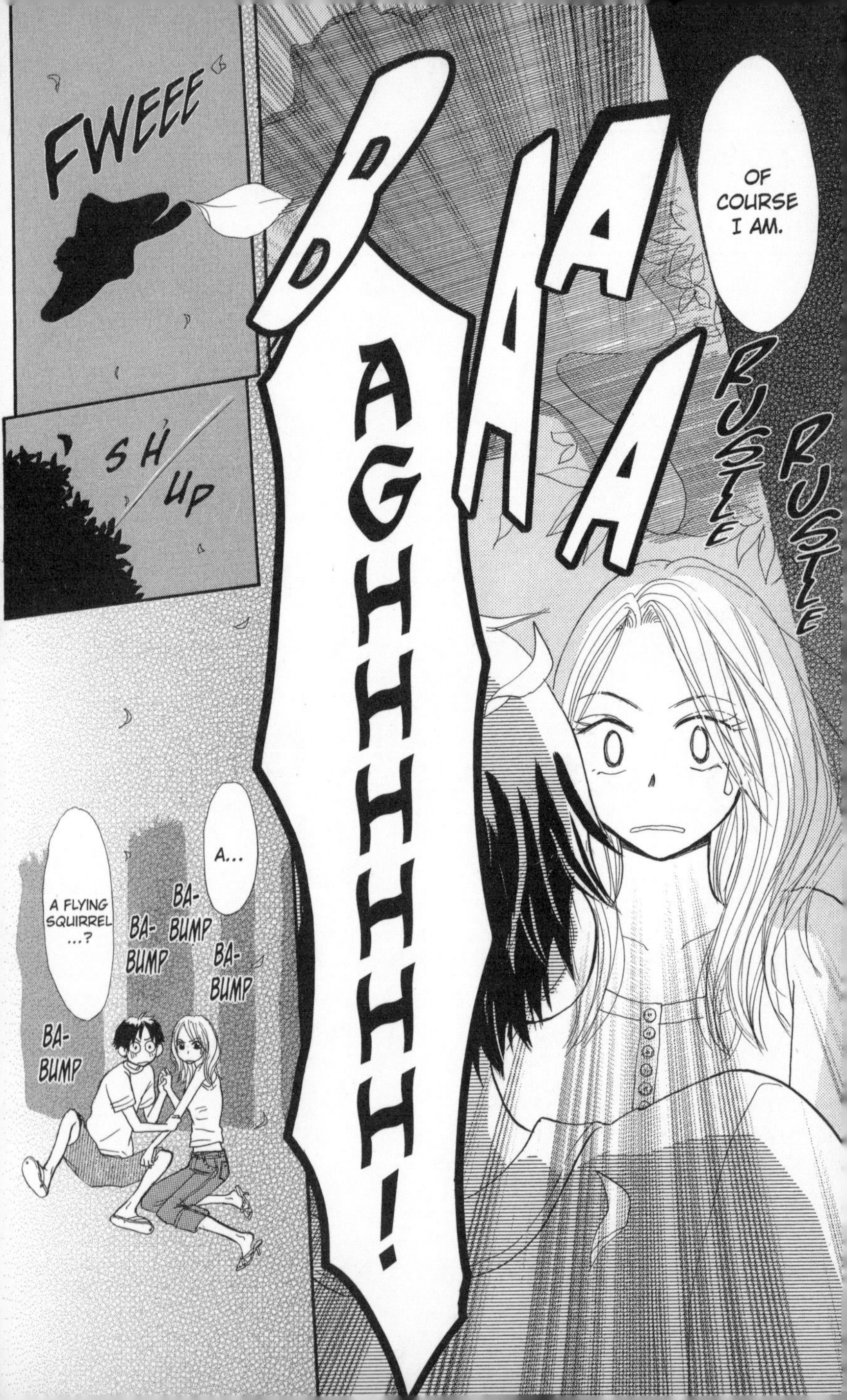
OF COURSE I AM.
BAAAAGHHHHHHH!
RUSTLE RUSTLE
FWEEE
SHUP
A...
A FLYING SQUIRREL ...?
BA-BUMP BA-BUMP
BA-BUMP BA-BUMP

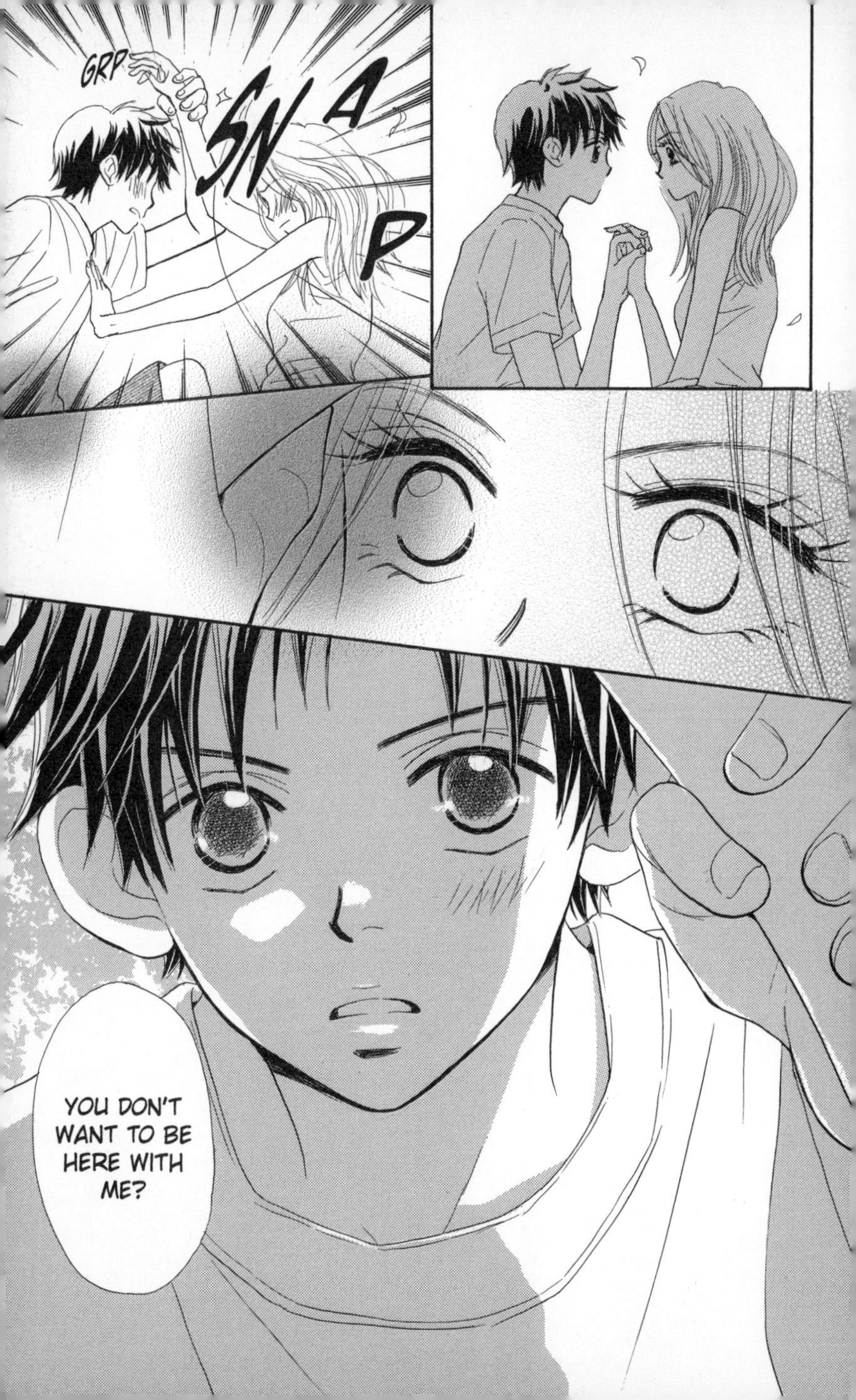
GRP
SNAP
YOU DON'T WANT TO BE HERE WITH ME?

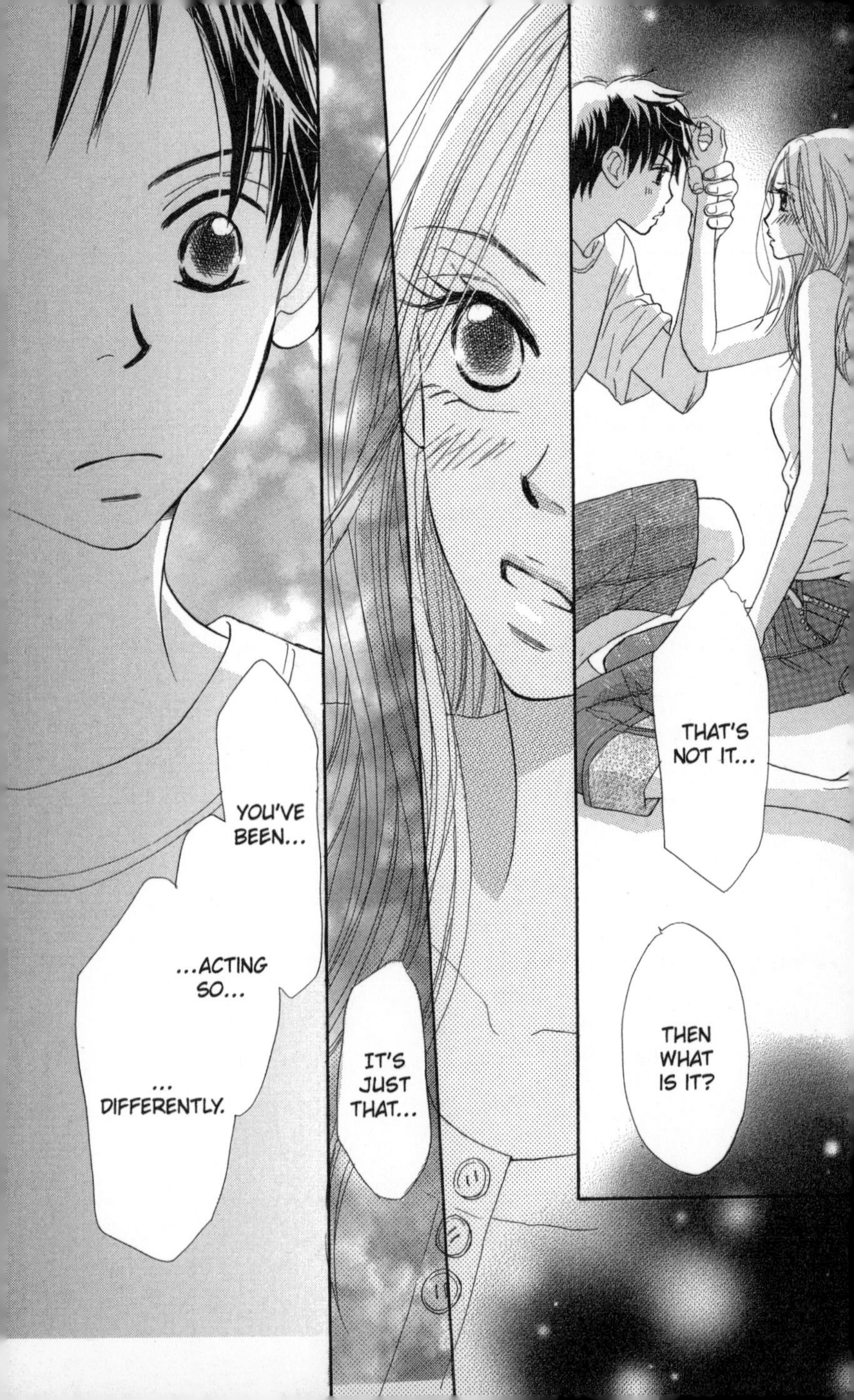
THAT'S NOT IT...
THEN WHAT IS IT?
IT'S JUST THAT...
YOU'VE BEEN...
...ACTING SO...
...DIFFERENTLY.

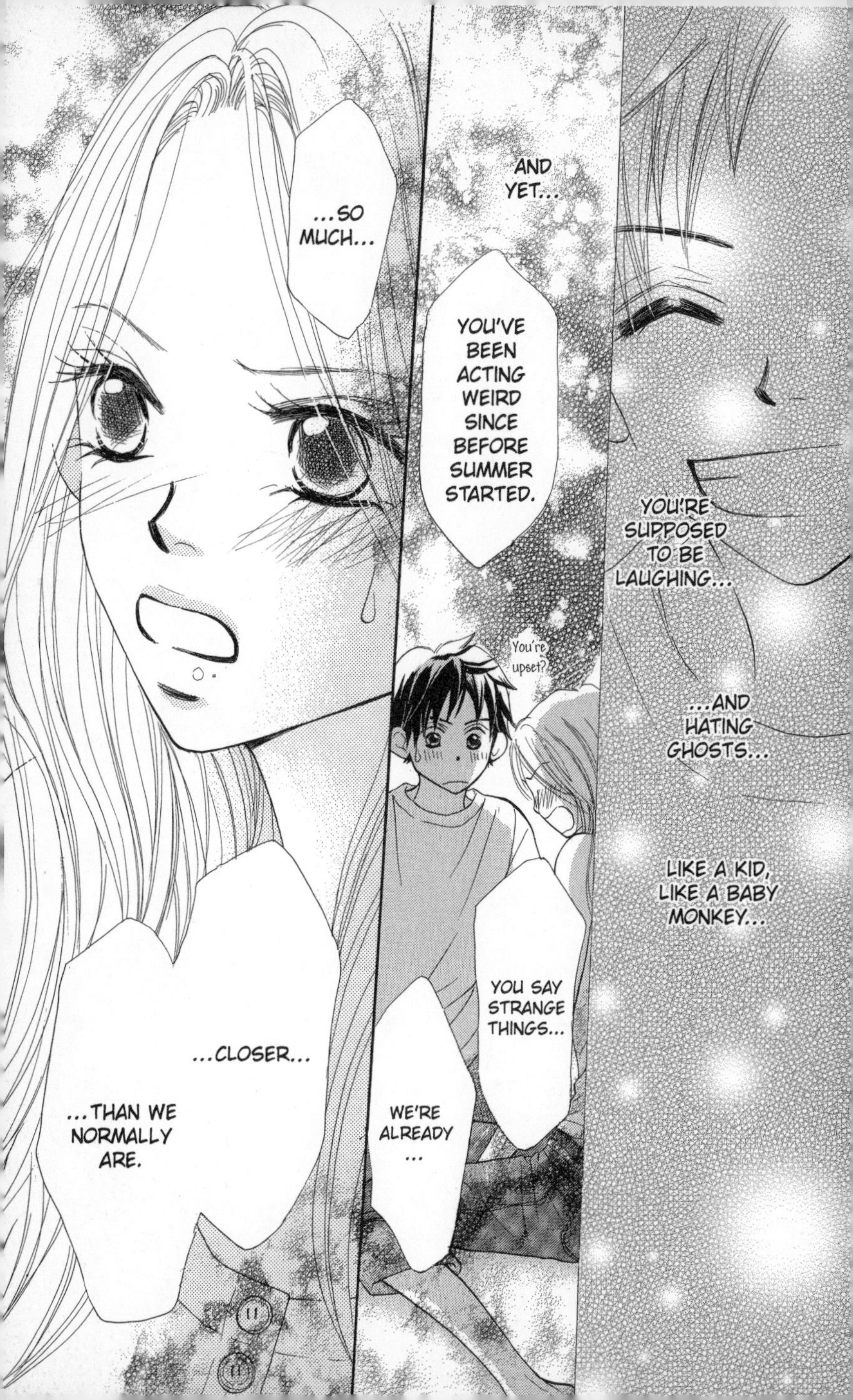
YOU'RE SUPPOSED TO BE LAUGHING...
...AND HATING GHOSTS...
LIKE A KID, LIKE A BABY MONKEY...
AND YET...
YOU'VE BEEN ACTING WEIRD SINCE BEFORE SUMMER STARTED.
You're upset?
YOU SAY STRANGE THINGS...
WE'RE ALREADY ...
...SO MUCH...
...CLOSER...
...THAN WE NORMALLY ARE.

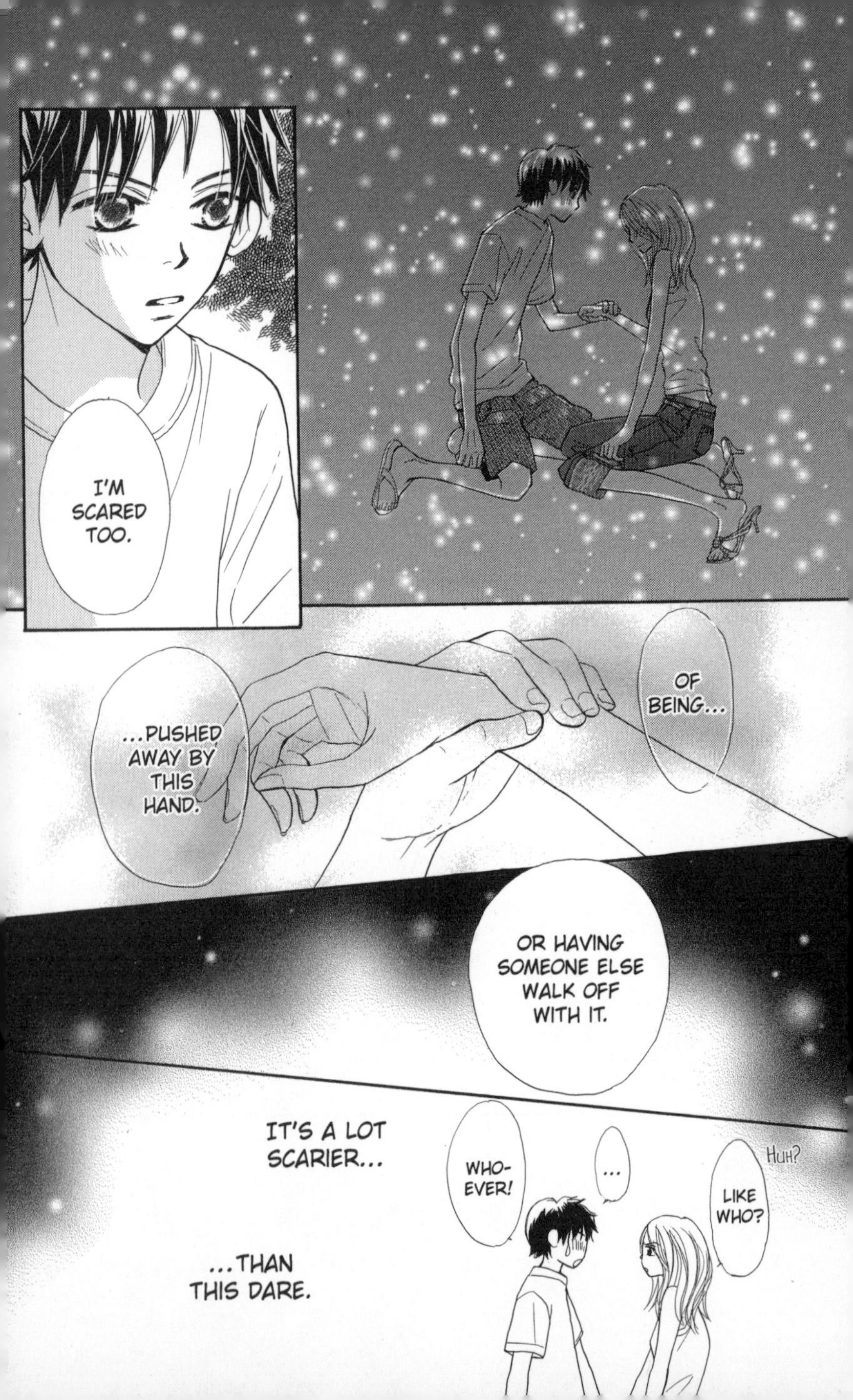
I'M SCARED TOO.
OF BEING...
...PUSHED AWAY BY THIS HAND.
OR HAVING SOMEONE ELSE WALK OFF WITH IT.
HUH?
LIKE WHO?
...
WHO-EVER!
IT'S A LOT SCARIER...
...THAN THIS DARE.

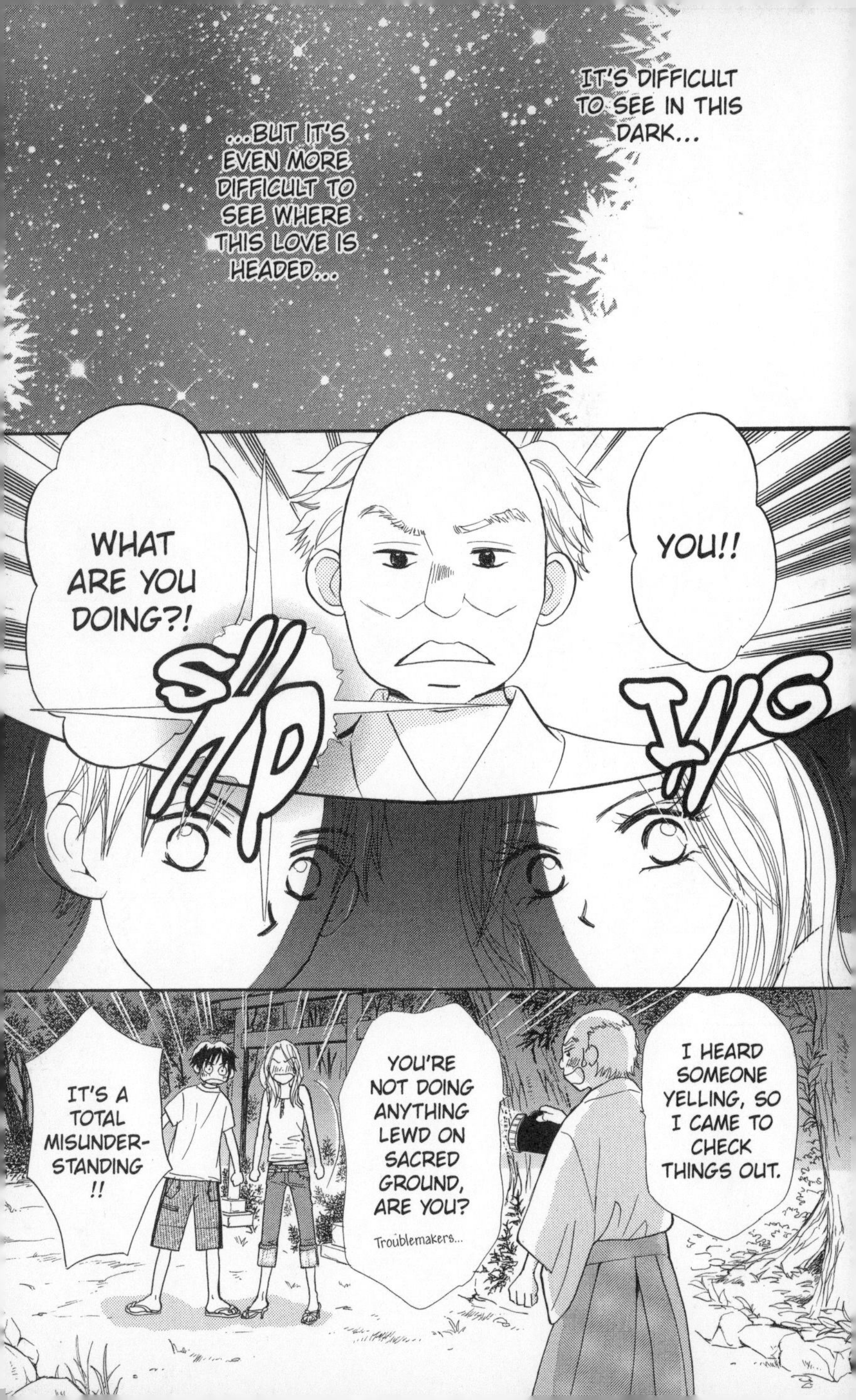
IT'S DIFFICULT TO SEE IN THIS DARK...
...BUT IT'S EVEN MORE DIFFICULT TO SEE WHERE THIS LOVE IS HEADED...
YOU!!
WHAT ARE YOU DOING?!
I HEARD SOMEONE YELLING, SO I CAME TO CHECK THINGS OUT.
YOU'RE NOT DOING ANYTHING LEWD ON SACRED GROUND, ARE YOU?
Troublemakers...
IT'S A TOTAL MISUNDERSTANDING!!

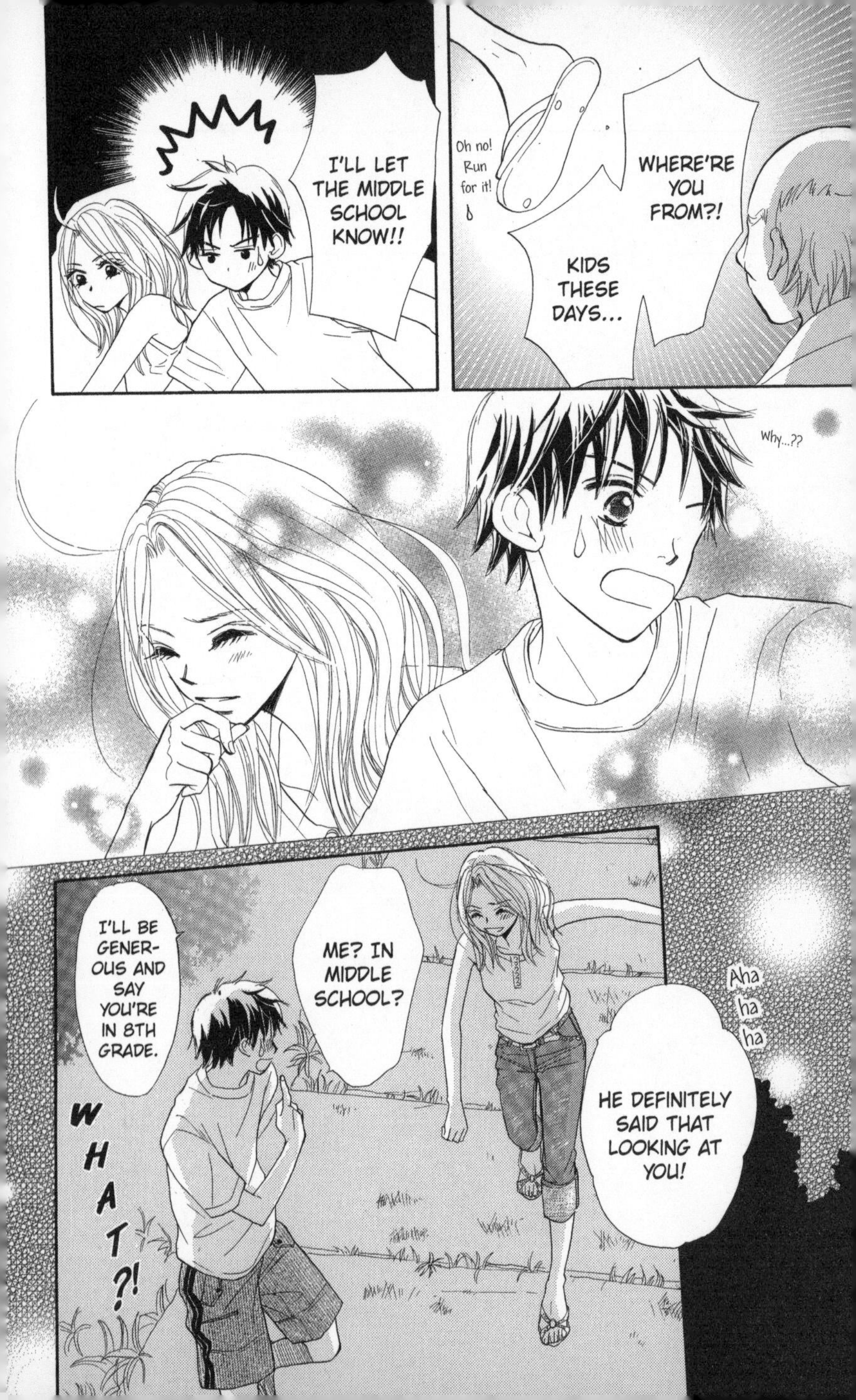
WHERE'RE YOU FROM?!
KIDS THESE DAYS...
Oh no! Run for it!
I'LL LET THE MIDDLE SCHOOL KNOW!!
Why...??
Aha ha ha
HE DEFINITELY SAID THAT LOOKING AT YOU!
ME? IN MIDDLE SCHOOL?
I'LL BE GENER-OUS AND SAY YOU'RE IN 8TH GRADE.
WHAT?!

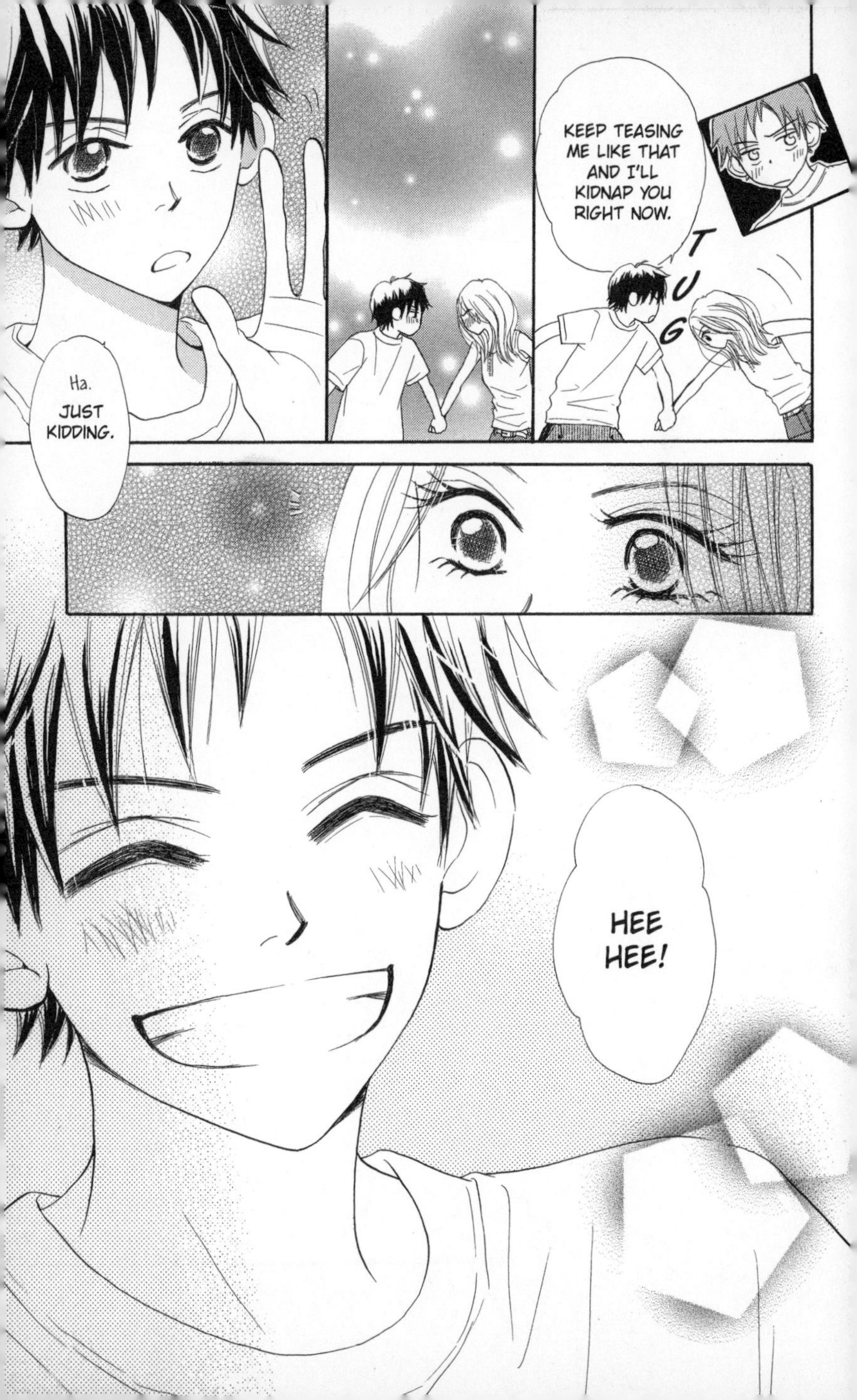
KEEP TEASING ME LIKE THAT AND I'LL KIDNAP YOU RIGHT NOW.
TUG
Ha. JUST KIDDING.
HEE HEE!

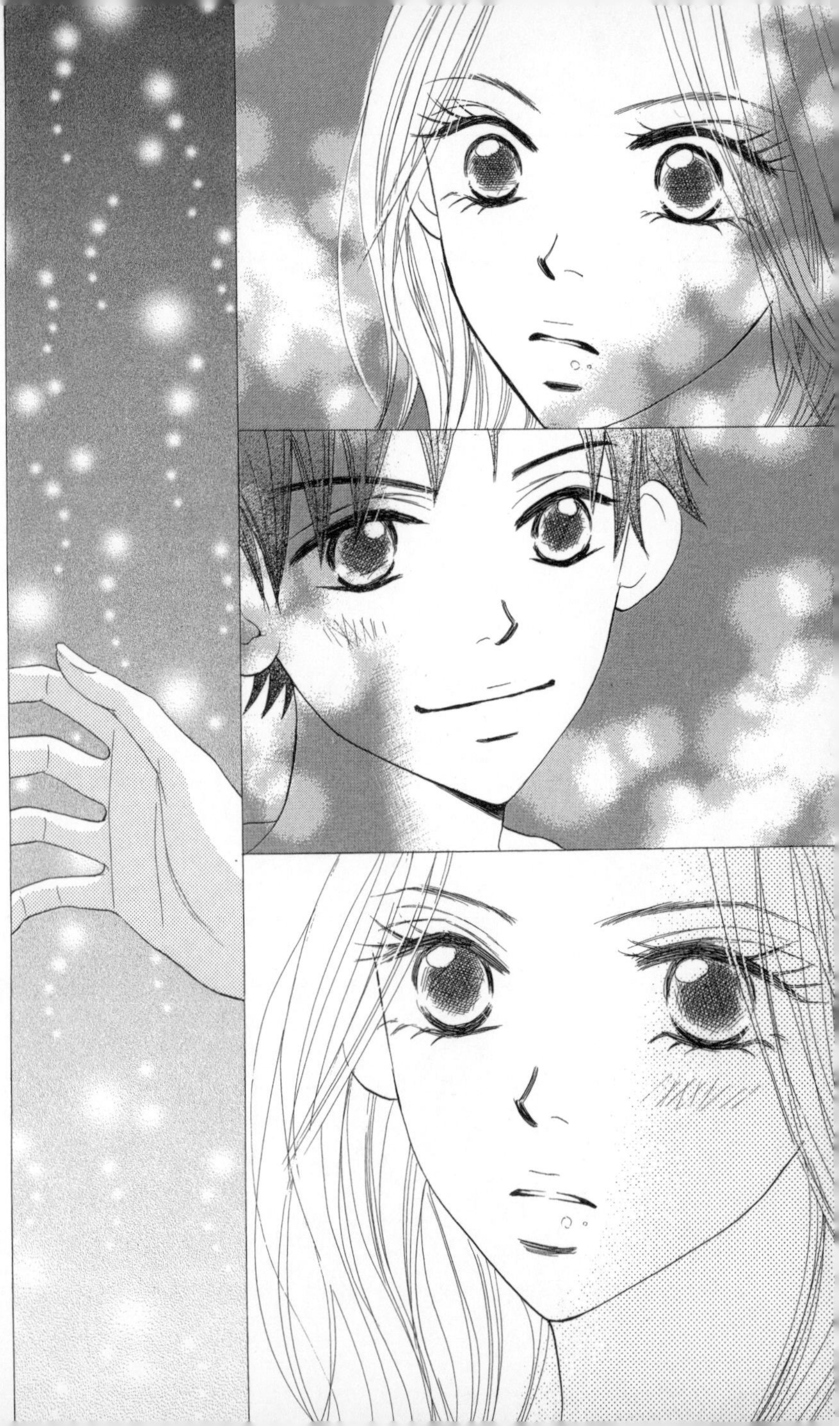

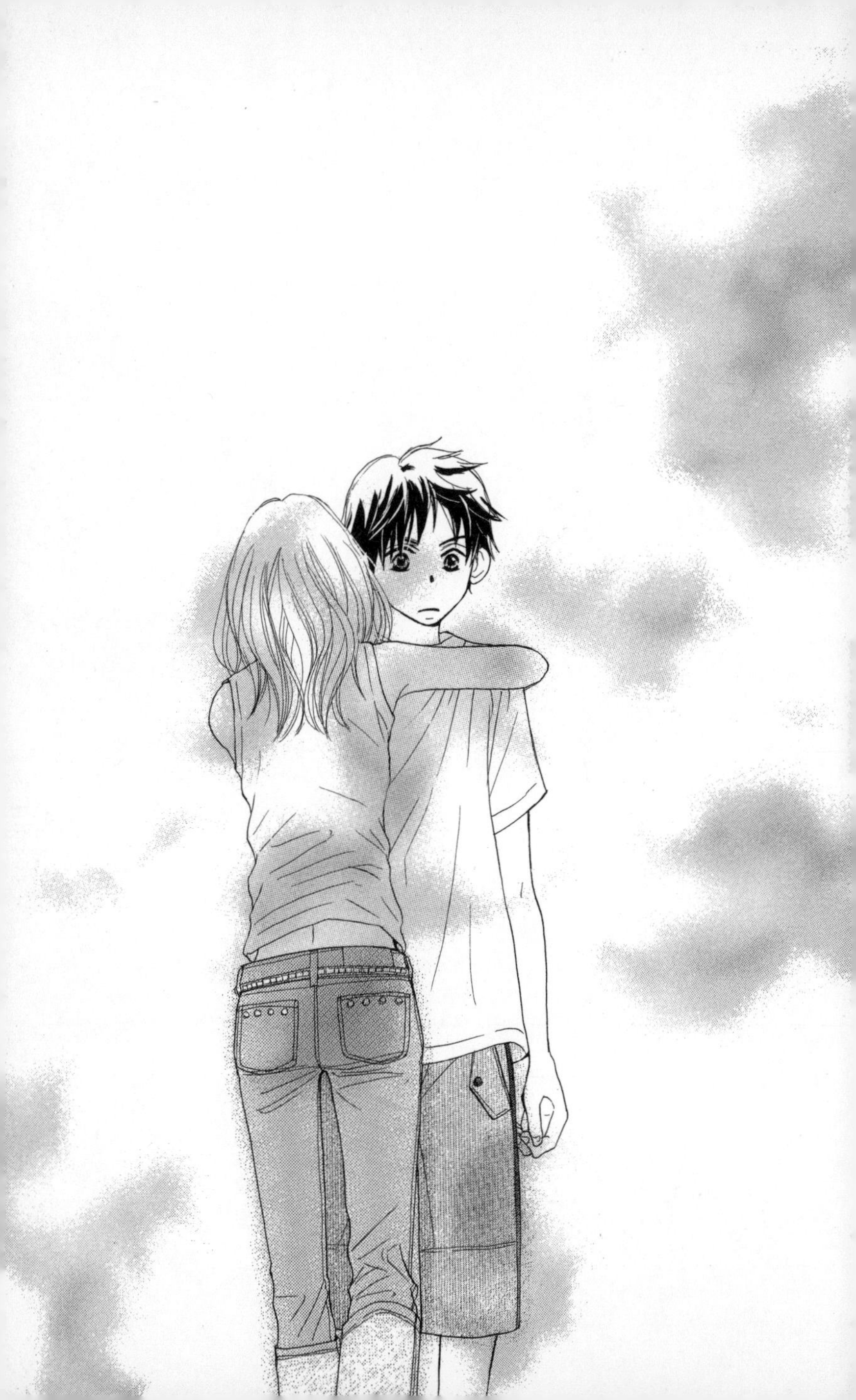

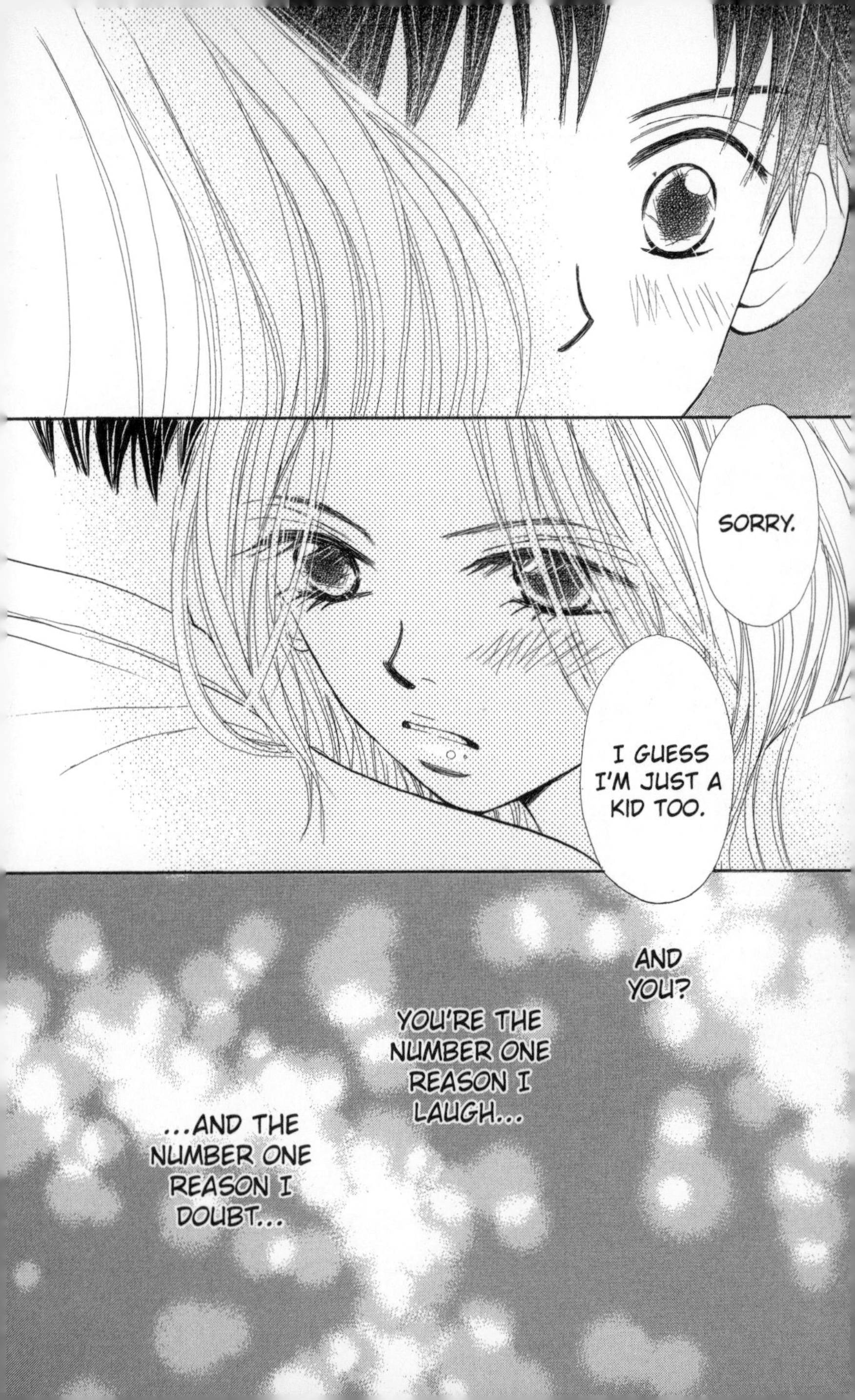
SORRY.
I GUESS I'M JUST A KID TOO.
AND YOU?
YOU'RE THE NUMBER ONE REASON I LAUGH...
...AND THE NUMBER ONE REASON I DOUBT...

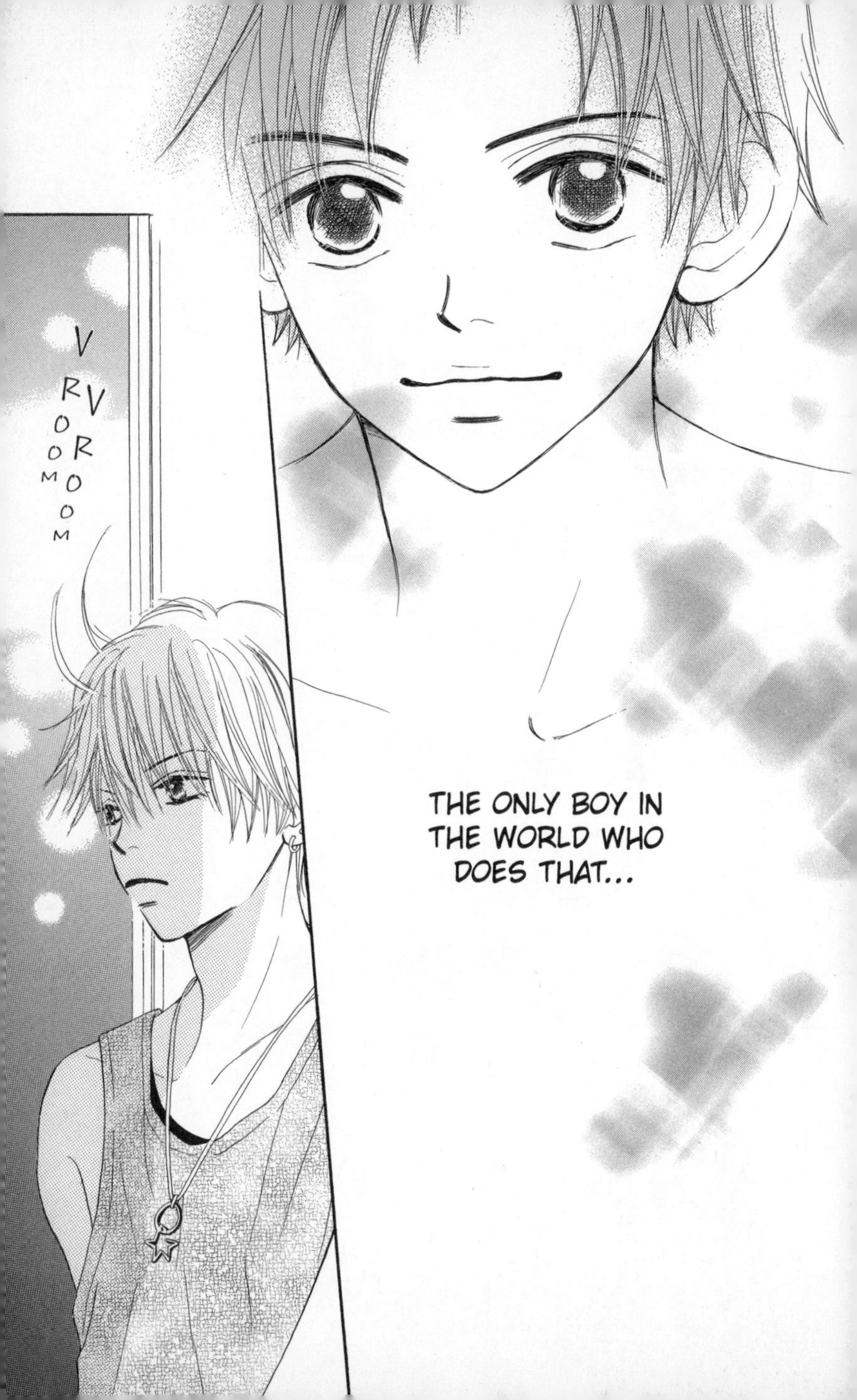
THE ONLY BOY IN THE WORLD WHO DOES THAT...
VROOM VROOM

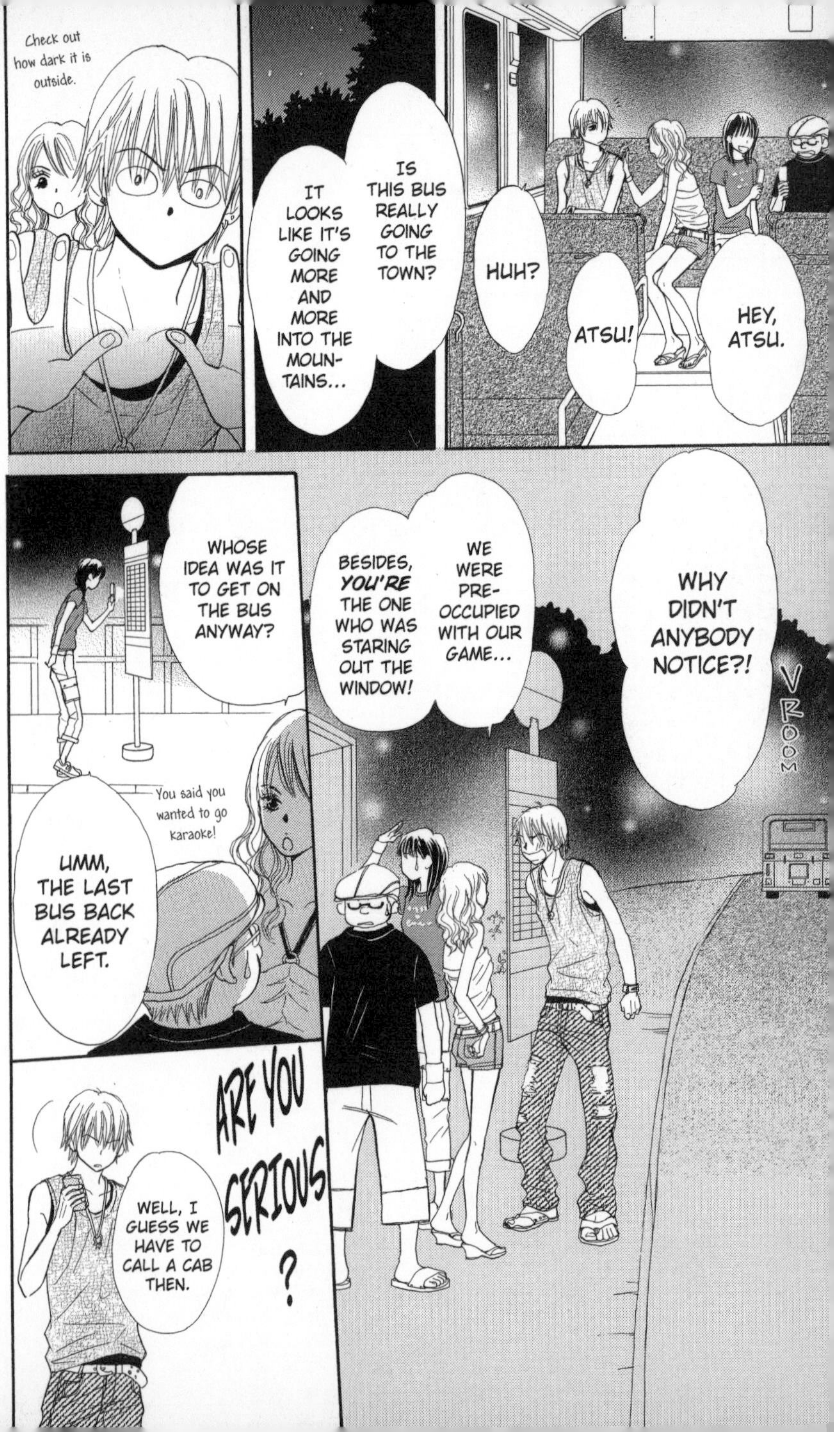
HEY, ATSU.
ATSU!
HUH?
IS THIS BUS REALLY GOING TO THE TOWN?
IT LOOKS LIKE IT'S GOING MORE AND MORE INTO THE MOUNTAINS...
Check out how dark it is outside.
WHY DIDN'T ANYBODY NOTICE?!
VROOM
WE WERE PREOCCUPIED WITH OUR GAME...
BESIDES, *YOU'RE* THE ONE WHO WAS STARING OUT THE WINDOW!
WHOSE IDEA WAS IT TO GET ON THE BUS ANYWAY?
You said you wanted to go karaoke!
UMM, THE LAST BUS BACK ALREADY LEFT.
ARE YOU SERIOUS?
WELL, I GUESS WE HAVE TO CALL A CAB THEN.

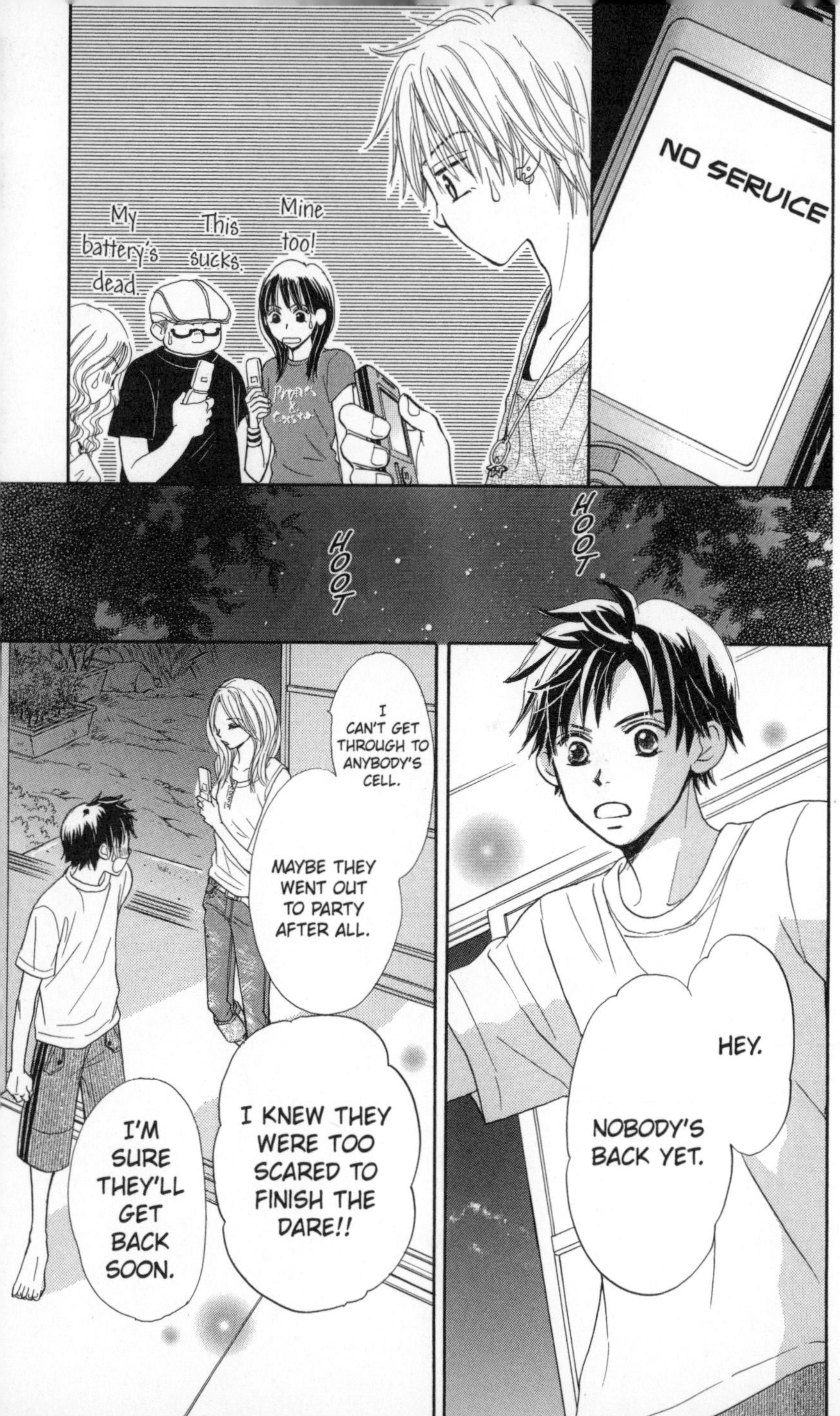
NO SERVICE
Mine too!
This sucks.
My battery's dead.
HOOT
HOOT
HEY.
NOBODY'S BACK YET.
I CAN'T GET THROUGH TO ANYBODY'S CELL.
MAYBE THEY WENT OUT TO PARTY AFTER ALL.
I KNEW THEY WERE TOO SCARED TO FINISH THE DARE!!
I'M SURE THEY'LL GET BACK SOON.

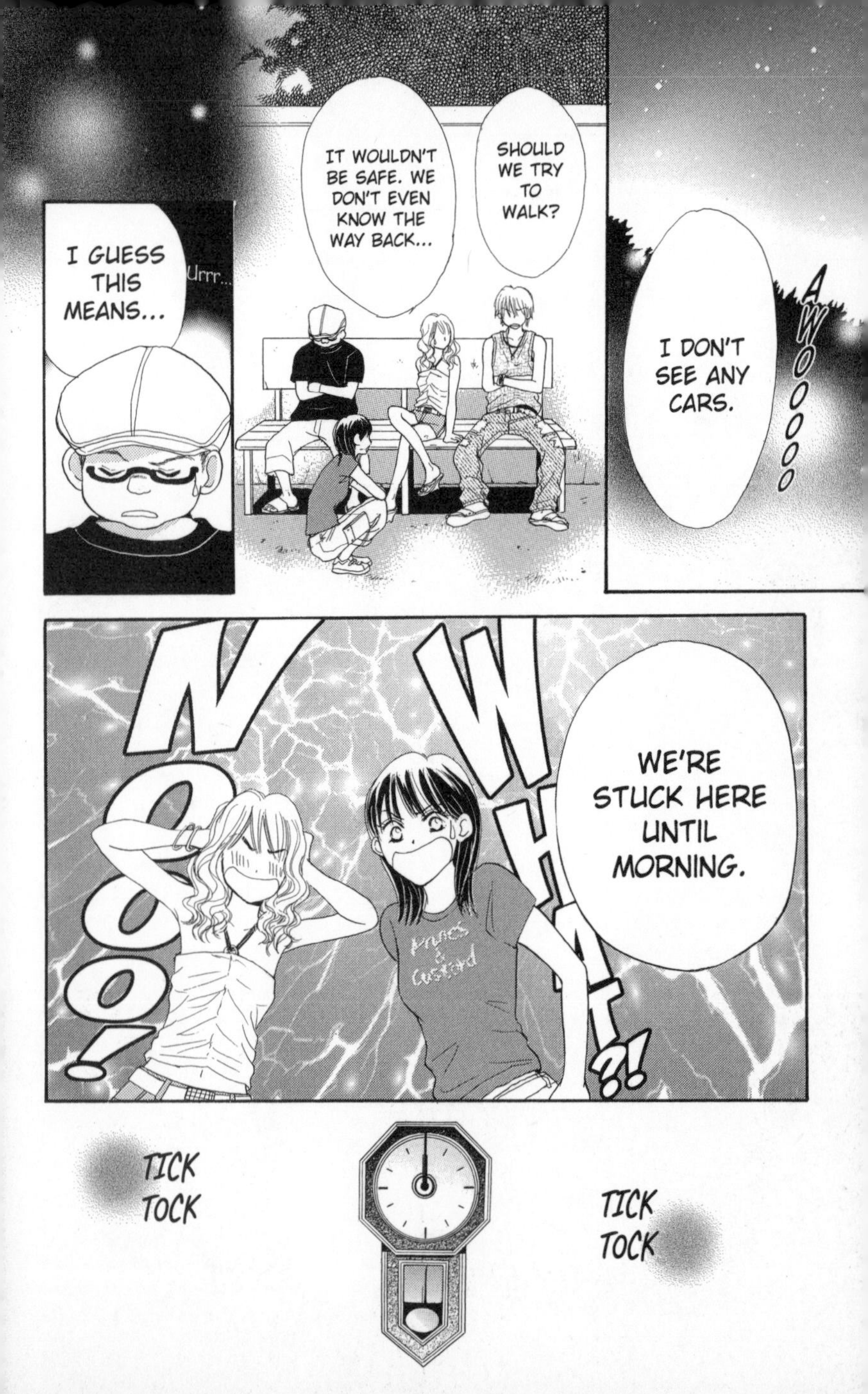
AWOOOOOOO
I DON'T SEE ANY CARS.
SHOULD WE TRY TO WALK?
IT WOULDN'T BE SAFE. WE DON'T EVEN KNOW THE WAY BACK...
Urrr...
I GUESS THIS MEANS...
WE'RE STUCK HERE UNTIL MORNING.
WHAT?!
NOOO!
TICK TOCK
TICK TOCK

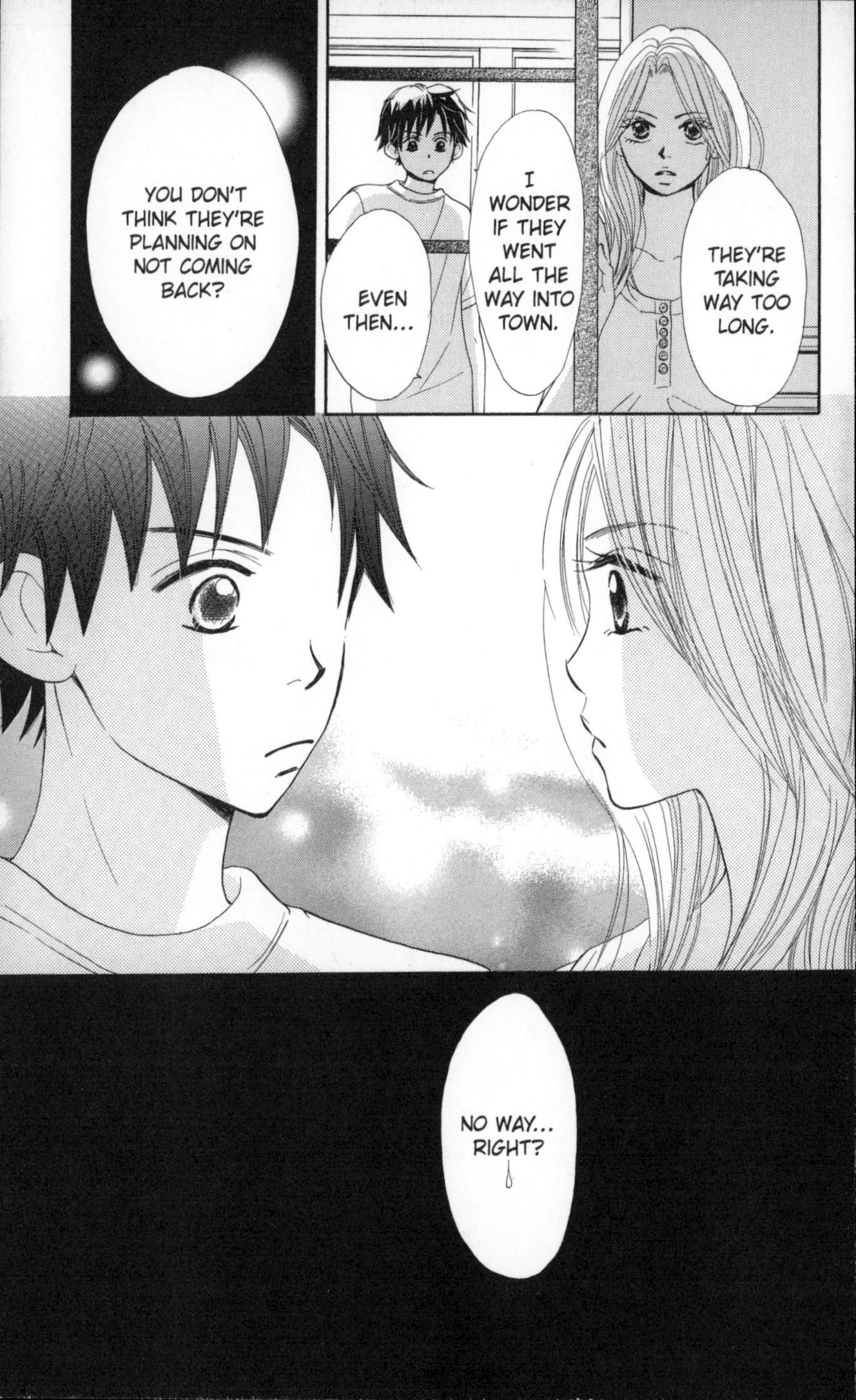
THEY'RE TAKING WAY TOO LONG.
I WONDER IF THEY WENT ALL THE WAY INTO TOWN.
EVEN THEN...
YOU DON'T THINK THEY'RE PLANNING ON NOT COMING BACK?
NO WAY... RIGHT?

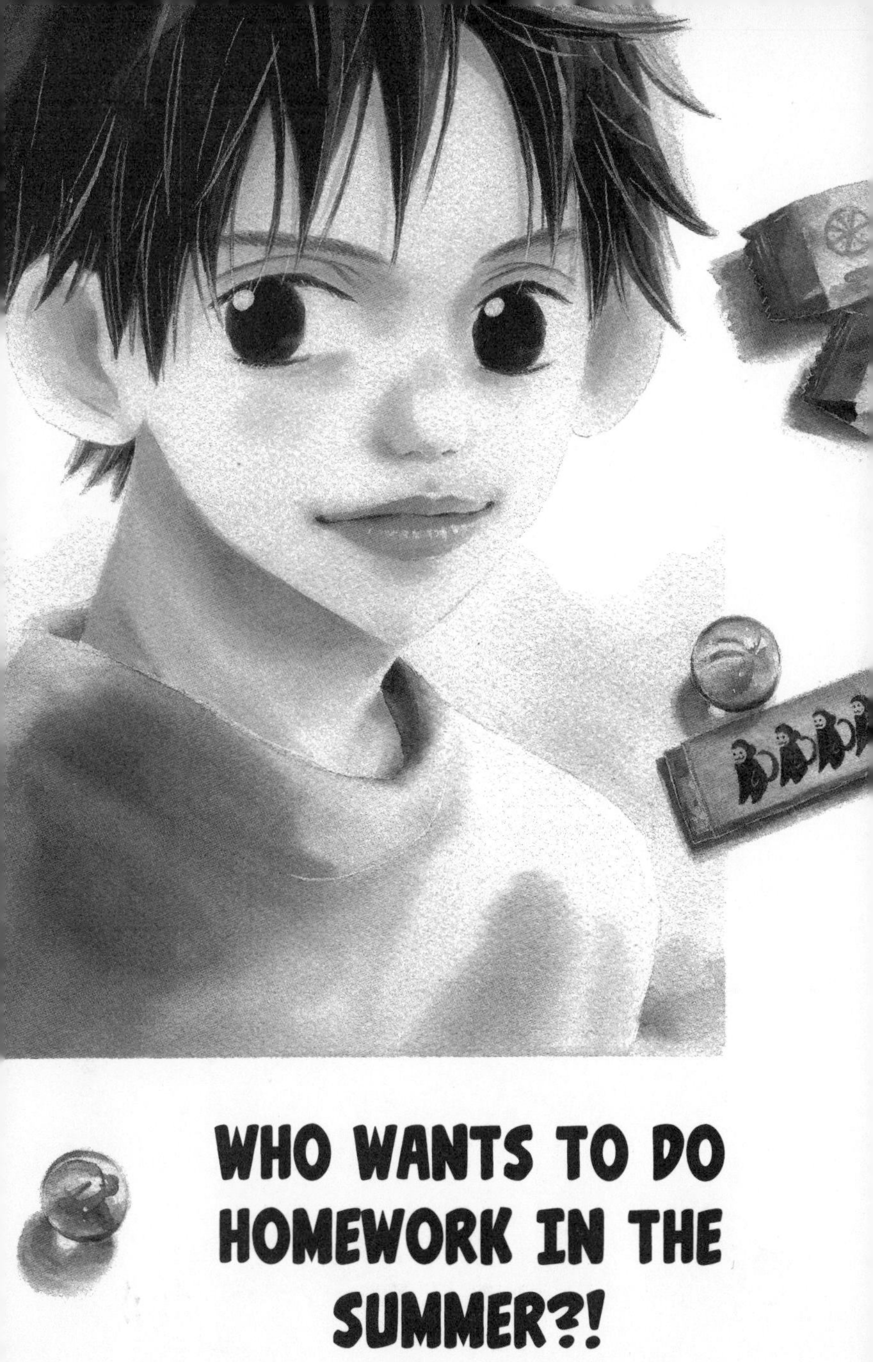

WHO WANTS TO DO HOMEWORK IN THE SUMMER?!

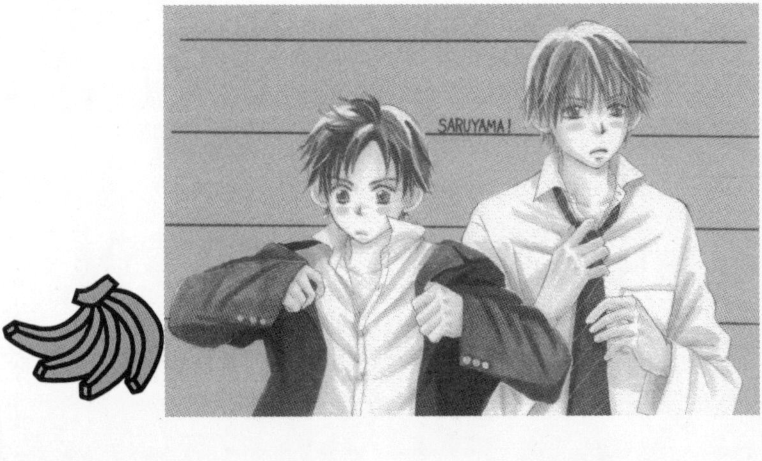
SARUYAMA!

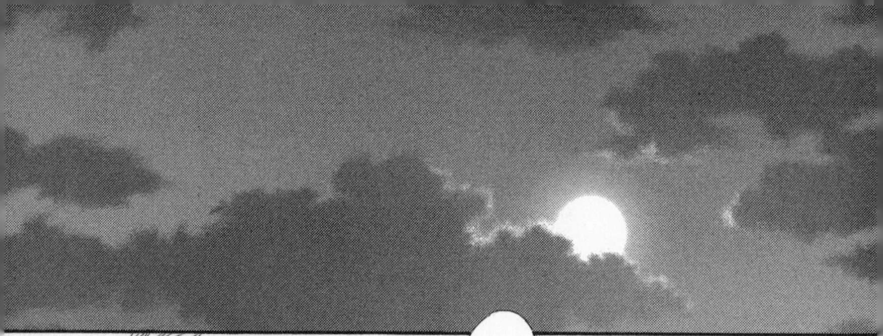

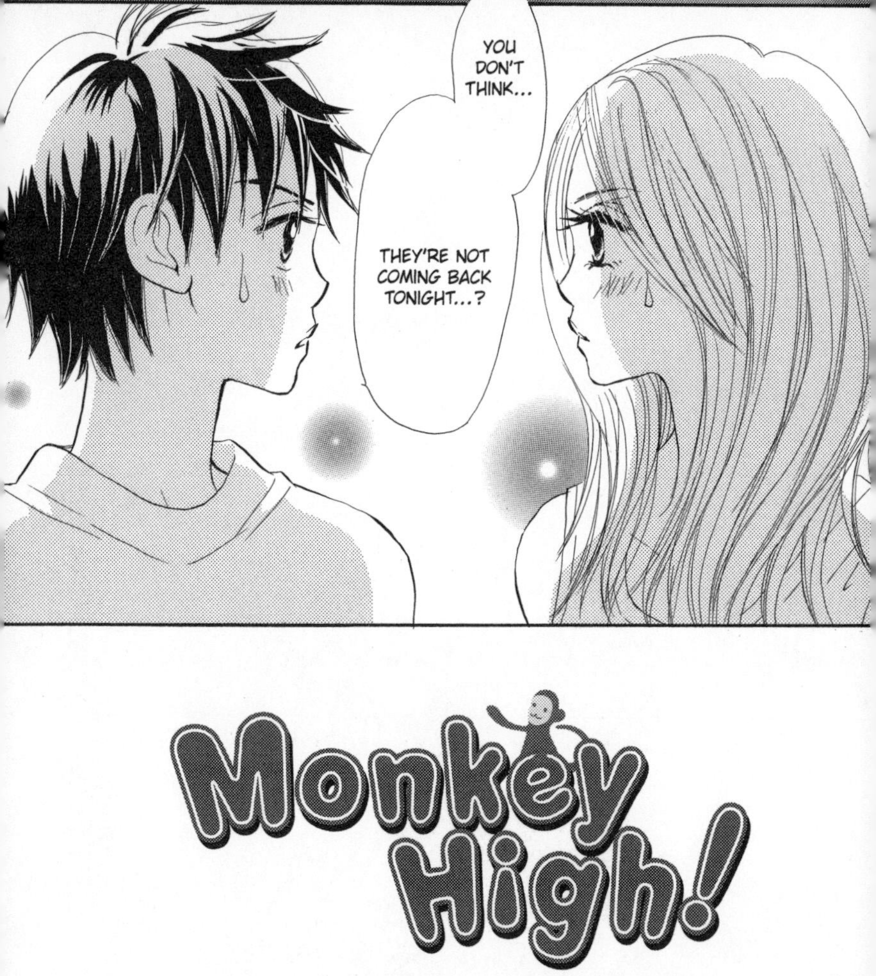
YOU DON'T THINK...
THEY'RE NOT COMING BACK TONIGHT...?

Monkey High!

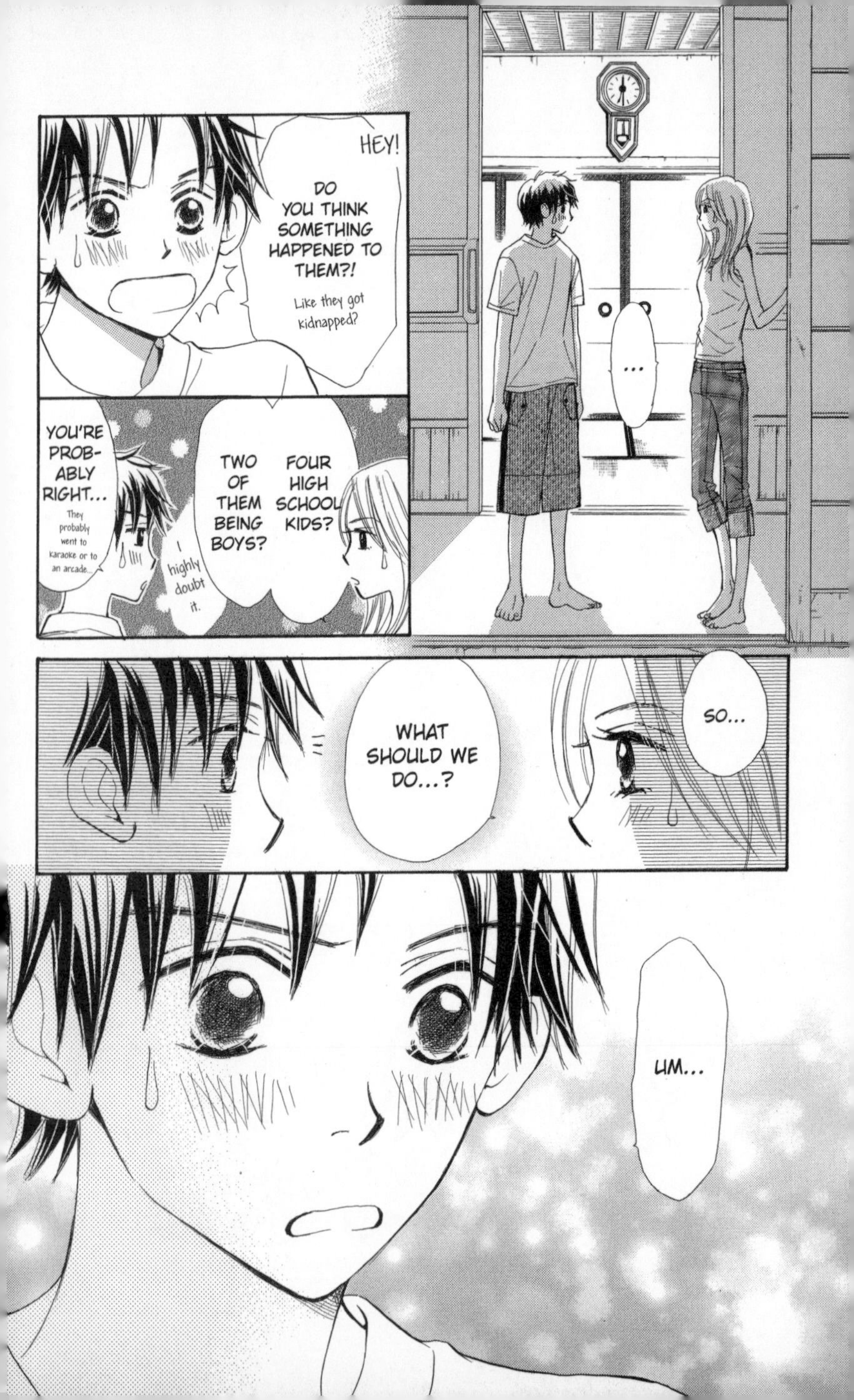
...
HEY!
DO YOU THINK SOMETHING HAPPENED TO THEM?!
Like they got kidnapped?
FOUR HIGH SCHOOL KIDS?
TWO OF THEM BEING BOYS?
I highly doubt it.
YOU'RE PROB-ABLY RIGHT...
They probably went to karaoke or to an arcade...
SO...
WHAT SHOULD WE DO...?
UM...

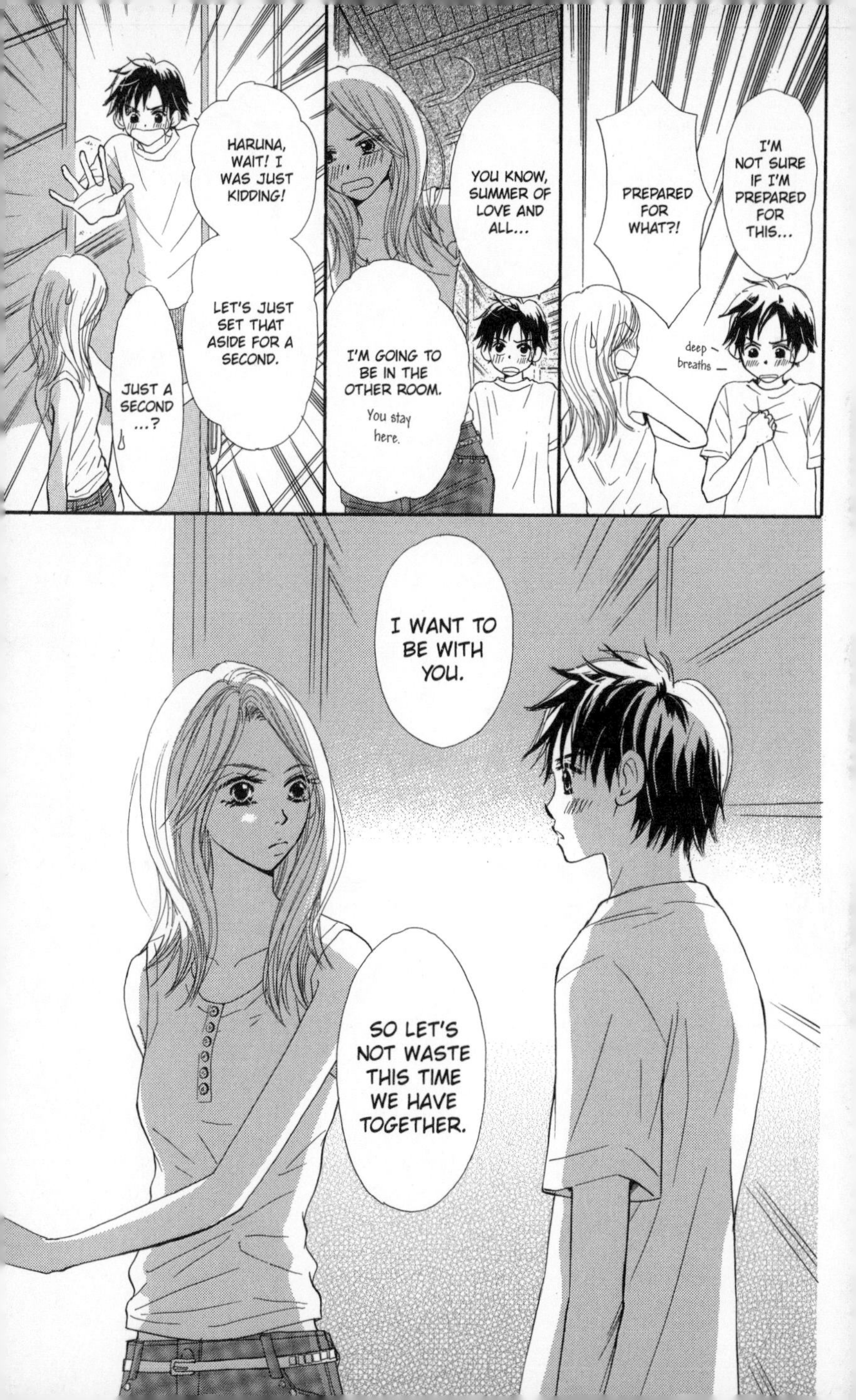
I'M NOT SURE IF I'M PREPARED FOR THIS...
PREPARED FOR WHAT?!
deep breaths
YOU KNOW, SUMMER OF LOVE AND ALL...
I'M GOING TO BE IN THE OTHER ROOM.
You stay here.
HARUNA, WAIT! I WAS JUST KIDDING!
LET'S JUST SET THAT ASIDE FOR A SECOND.
JUST A SECOND ...?
I WANT TO BE WITH YOU.
SO LET'S NOT WASTE THIS TIME WE HAVE TOGETHER.

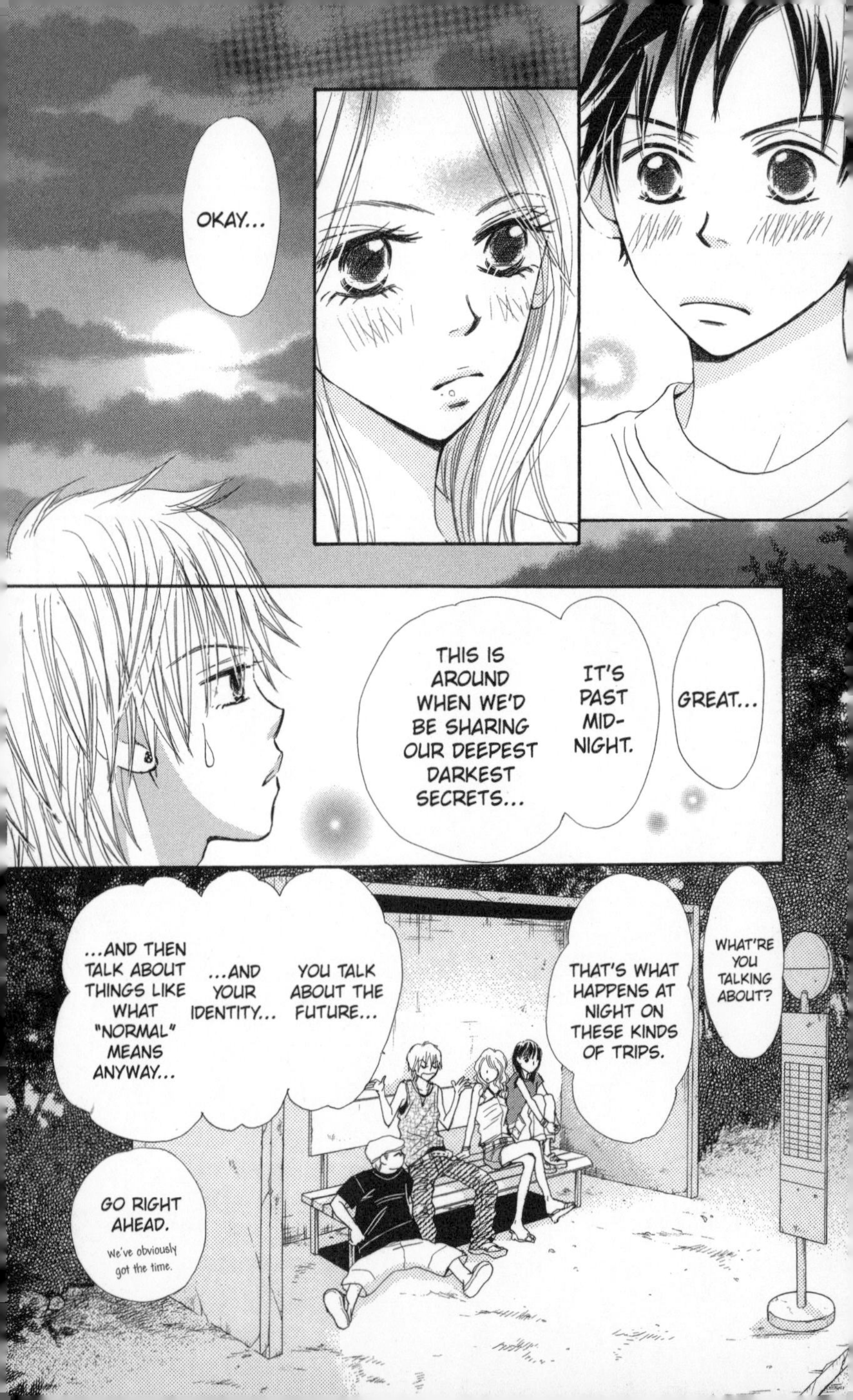
OKAY...
GREAT...
IT'S PAST MID-NIGHT.
THIS IS AROUND WHEN WE'D BE SHARING OUR DEEPEST DARKEST SECRETS...
WHAT'RE YOU TALKING ABOUT?
THAT'S WHAT HAPPENS AT NIGHT ON THESE KINDS OF TRIPS.
YOU TALK ABOUT THE FUTURE...
...AND YOUR IDENTITY...
...AND THEN TALK ABOUT THINGS LIKE WHAT "NORMAL" MEANS ANYWAY...
GO RIGHT AHEAD.
We've obviously got the time.

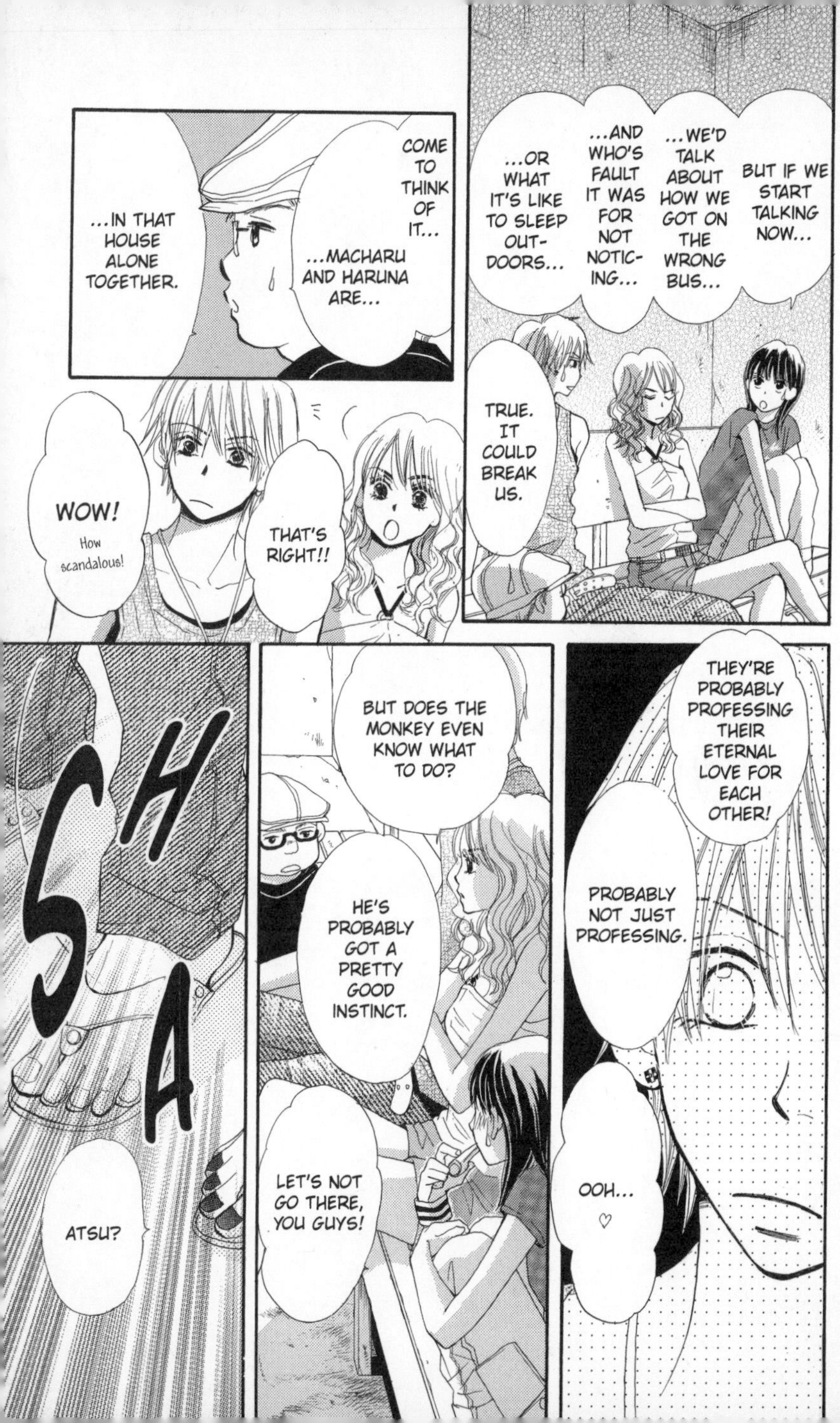
BUT IF WE START TALKING NOW...
...WE'D TALK ABOUT HOW WE GOT ON THE WRONG BUS...
...AND WHO'S FAULT IT WAS FOR NOT NOTICING...
...OR WHAT IT'S LIKE TO SLEEP OUTDOORS...
TRUE. IT COULD BREAK US.
COME TO THINK OF IT...
...MACHARU AND HARUNA ARE...
...IN THAT HOUSE ALONE TOGETHER.
THAT'S RIGHT!!
WOW! How scandalous!
THEY'RE PROBABLY PROFESSING THEIR ETERNAL LOVE FOR EACH OTHER!
PROBABLY NOT JUST PROFESSING.
OOH... ♡
BUT DOES THE MONKEY EVEN KNOW WHAT TO DO?
HE'S PROBABLY GOT A PRETTY GOOD INSTINCT.
LET'S NOT GO THERE, YOU GUYS!
SHA
ATSU?

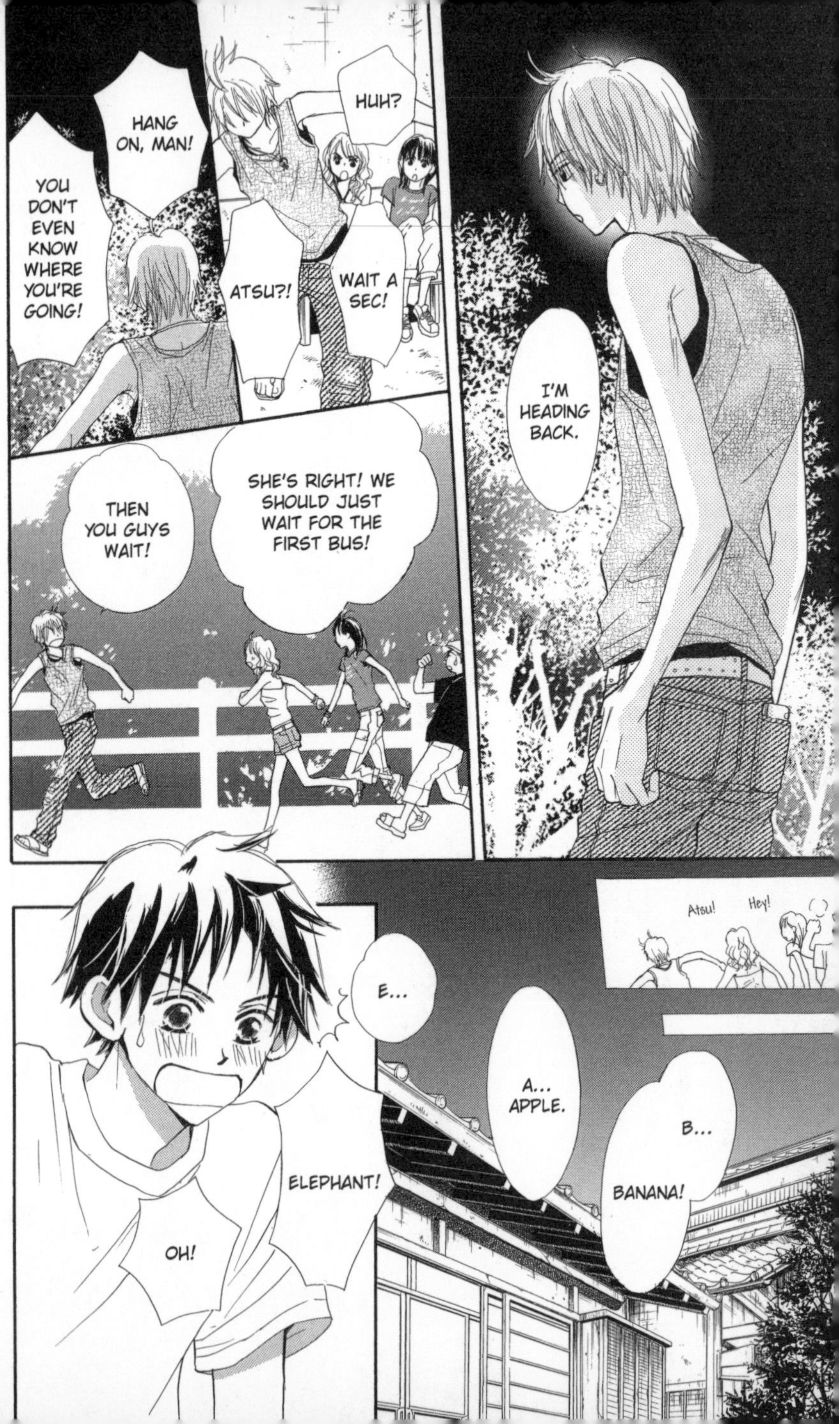
I'M HEADING BACK.
HUH?
WAIT A SEC!
ATSU?!
HANG ON, MAN!
YOU DON'T EVEN KNOW WHERE YOU'RE GOING!
SHE'S RIGHT! WE SHOULD JUST WAIT FOR THE FIRST BUS!
THEN YOU GUYS WAIT!
Hey!
Atsu!
B...
BANANA!
A... APPLE.
E...
ELEPHANT!
OH!

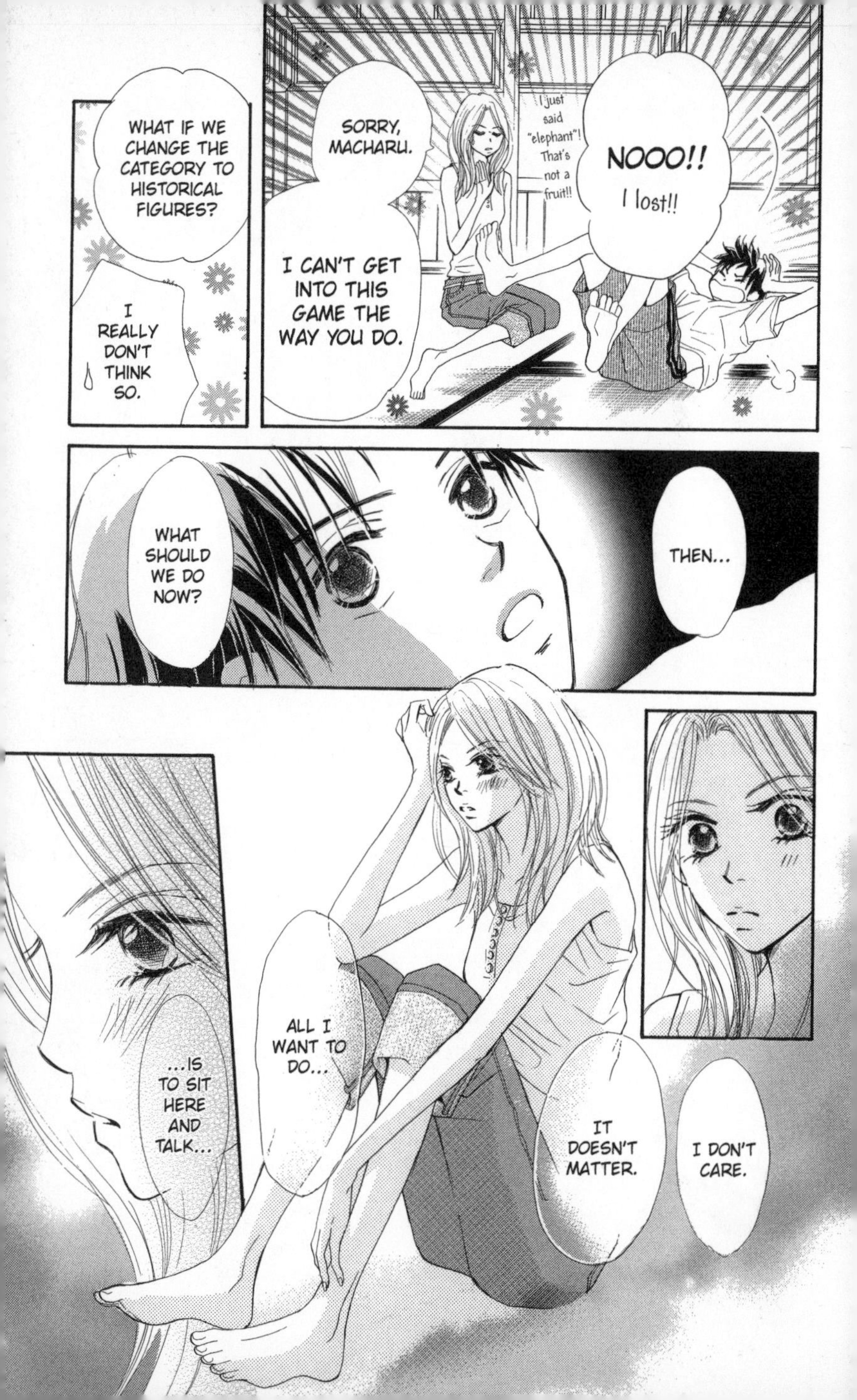
NOOO!! I lost!!
I just said "elephant"! That's not a fruit!!
SORRY, MACHARU.
I CAN'T GET INTO THIS GAME THE WAY YOU DO.
WHAT IF WE CHANGE THE CATEGORY TO HISTORICAL FIGURES?
I REALLY DON'T THINK SO.
THEN...
WHAT SHOULD WE DO NOW?
I DON'T CARE.
IT DOESN'T MATTER.
ALL I WANT TO DO...
...IS TO SIT HERE AND TALK...

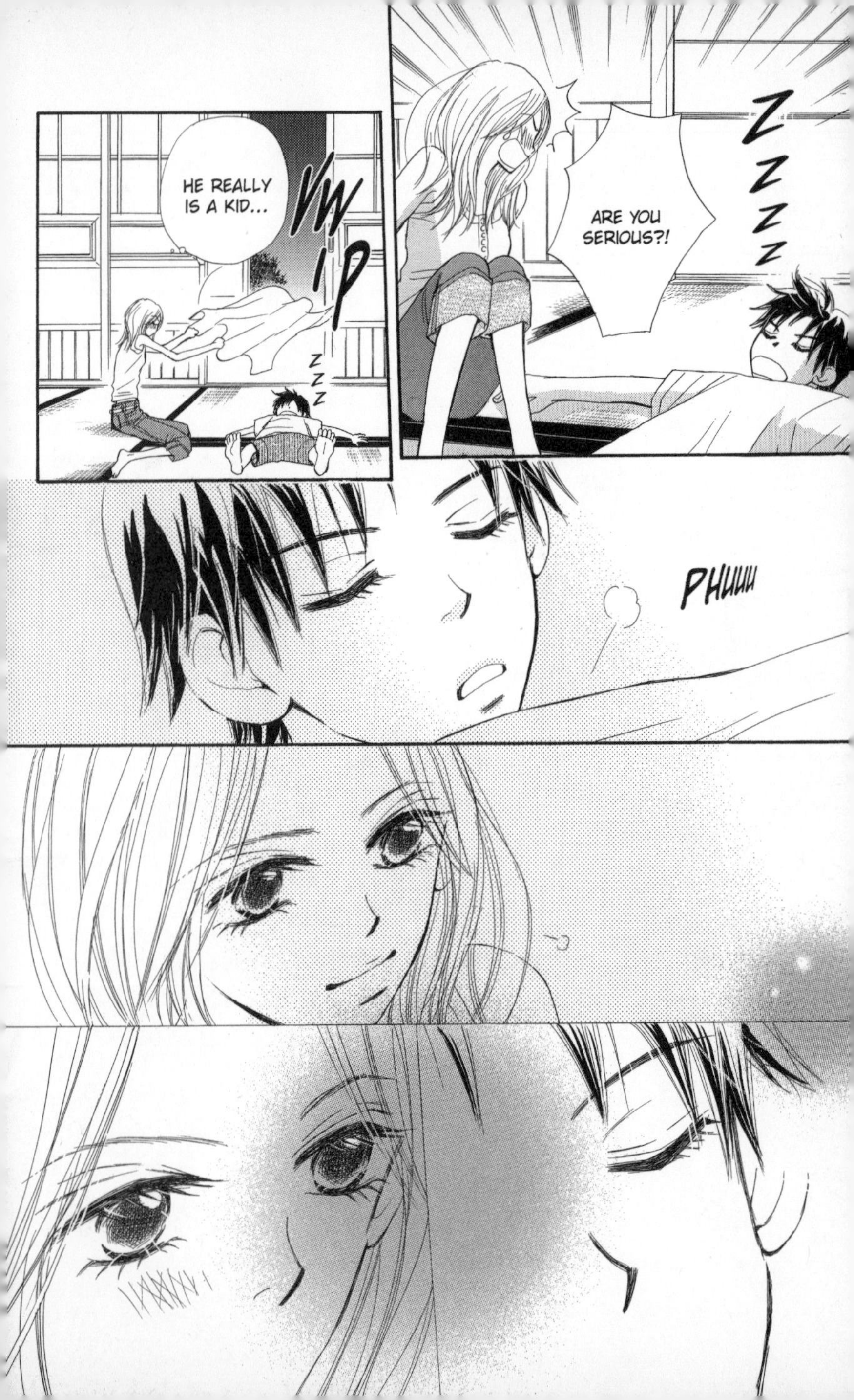
ZZZZ
ARE YOU SERIOUS?!
HE REALLY IS A KID...
WIP
ZZZ
PHUUU

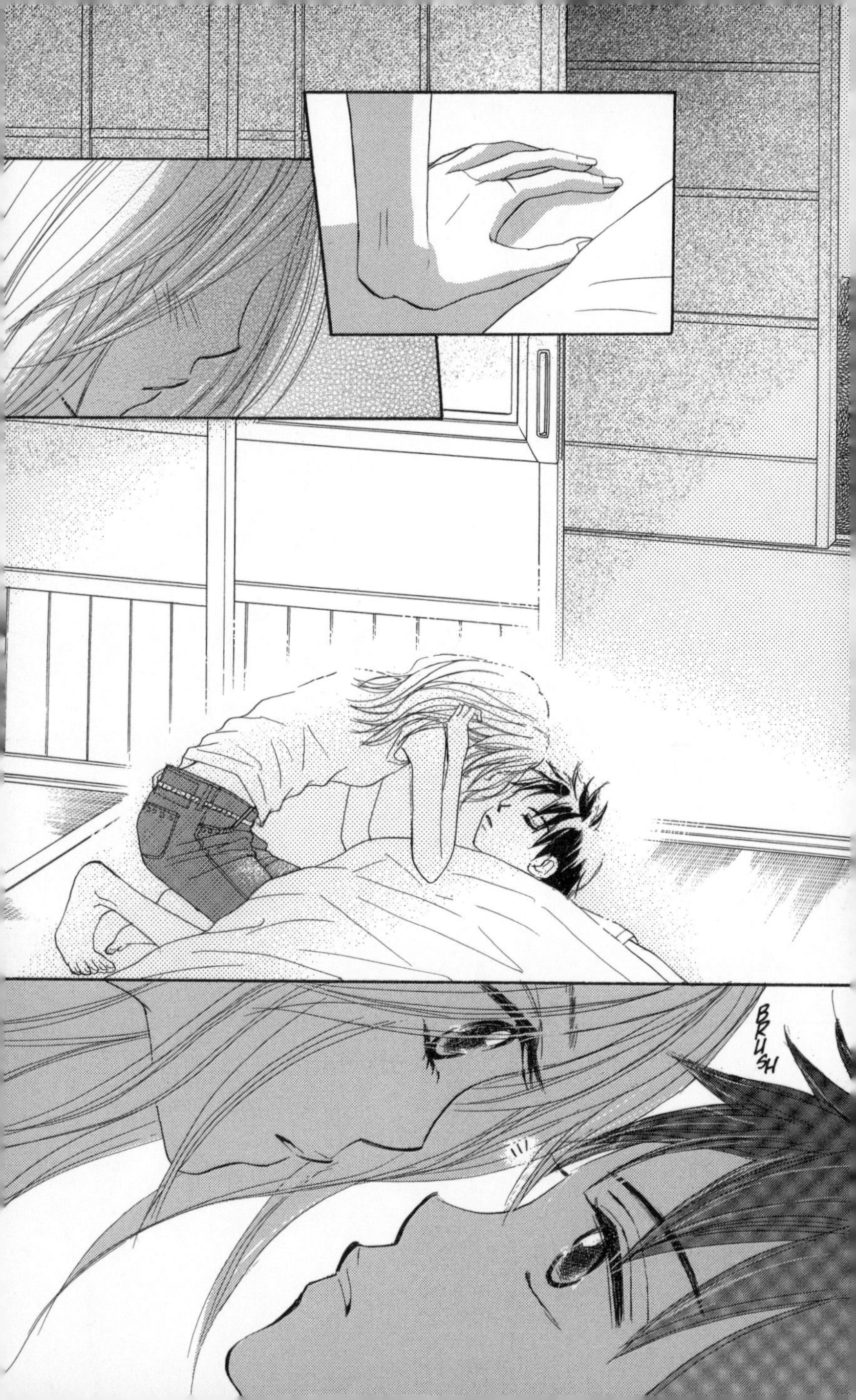
BRUSH

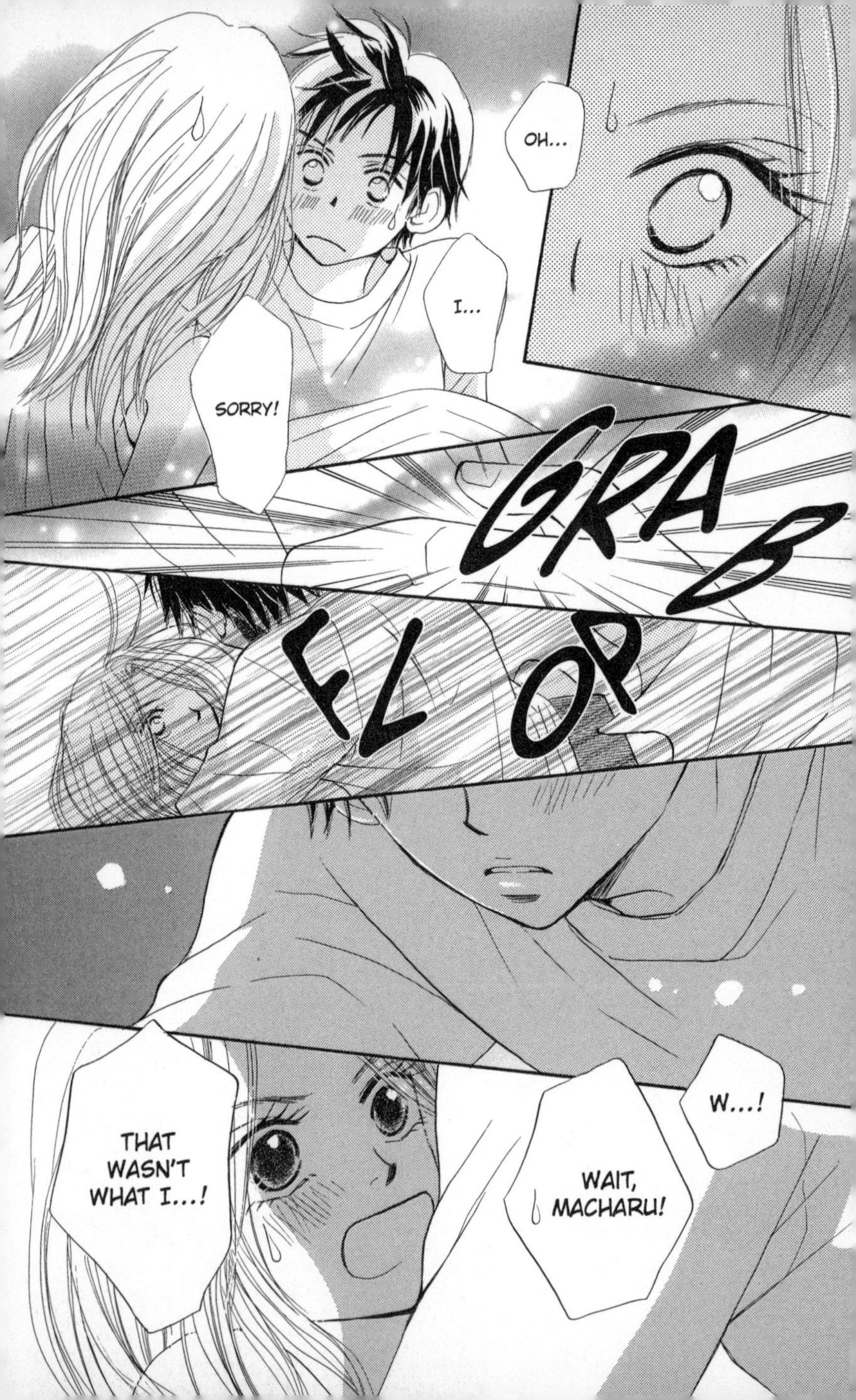
OH...
I...
SORRY!
GRAB
FLOP
W...!
WAIT, MACHARU!
THAT WASN'T WHAT I...!

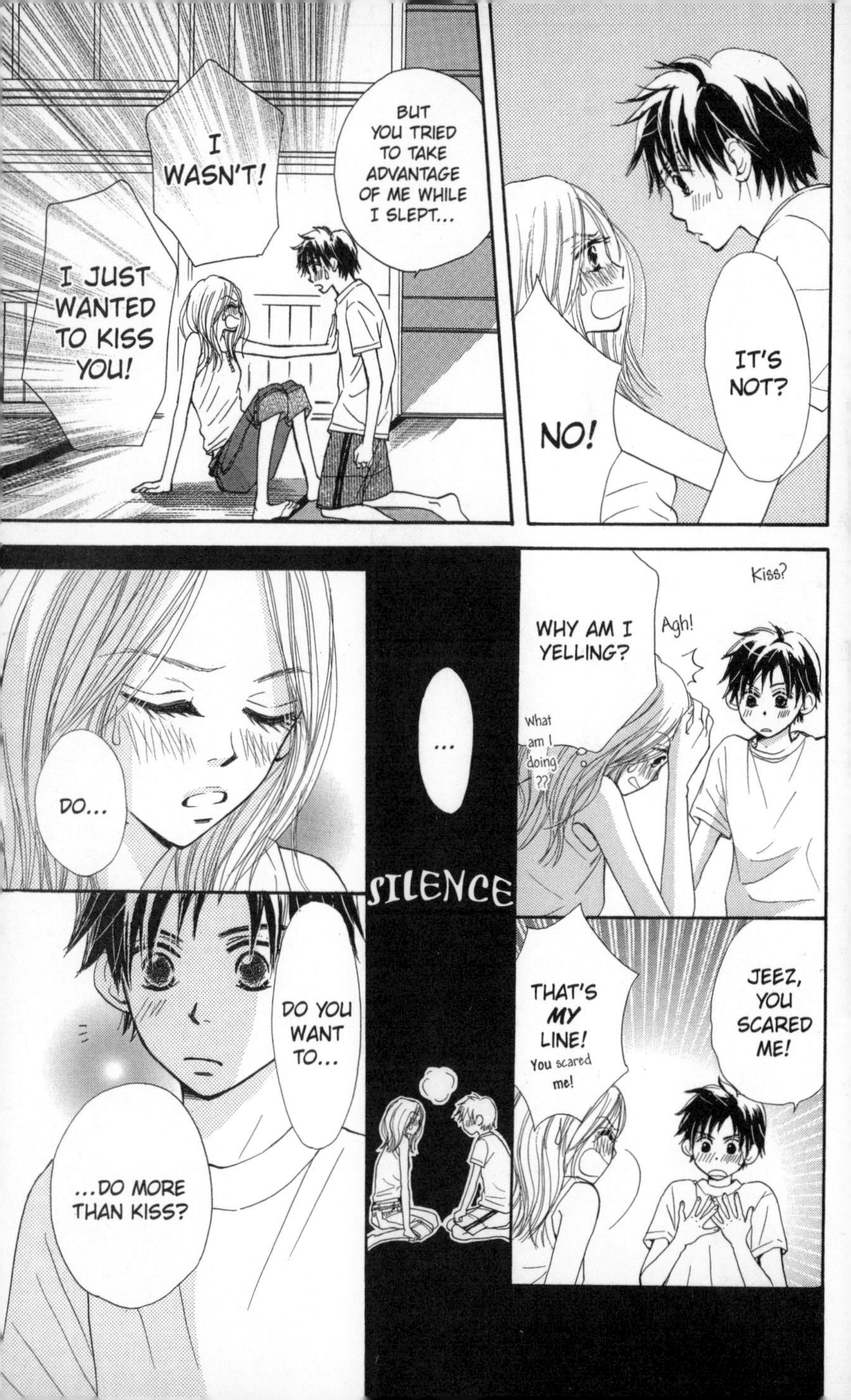
IT'S NOT?
NO!
BUT YOU TRIED TO TAKE ADVANTAGE OF ME WHILE I SLEPT...
I WASN'T!
I JUST WANTED TO KISS YOU!
Kiss?
Agh!
WHY AM I YELLING?
What am I doing??
JEEZ, YOU SCARED ME!
THAT'S MY LINE! You scared me!
...
SILENCE
DO...
DO YOU WANT TO...
...DO MORE THAN KISS?

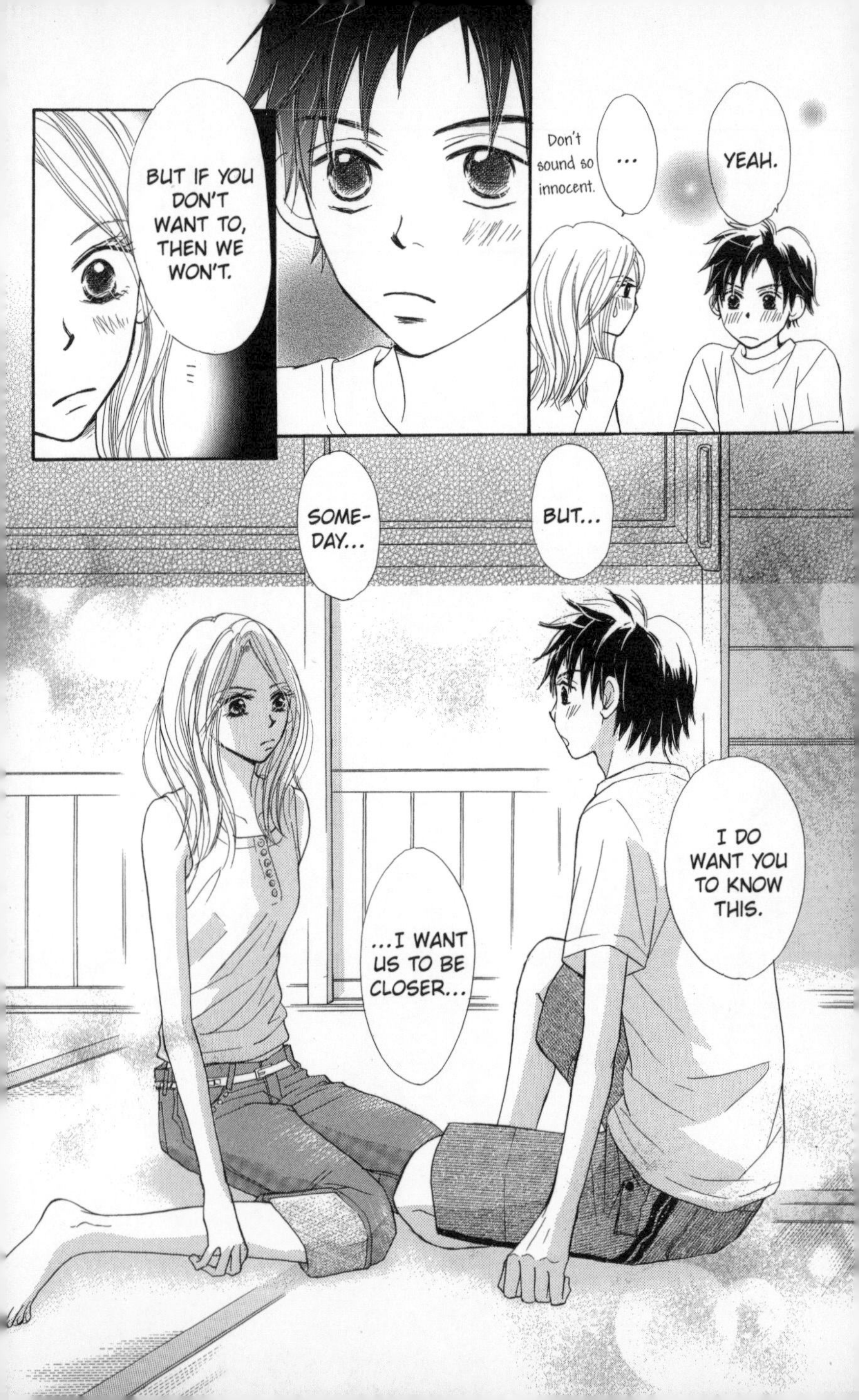
YEAH.
...
Don't sound so innocent.
BUT IF YOU DON'T WANT TO, THEN WE WON'T.
BUT...
SOME-DAY...
...I WANT US TO BE CLOSER...
I DO WANT YOU TO KNOW THIS.

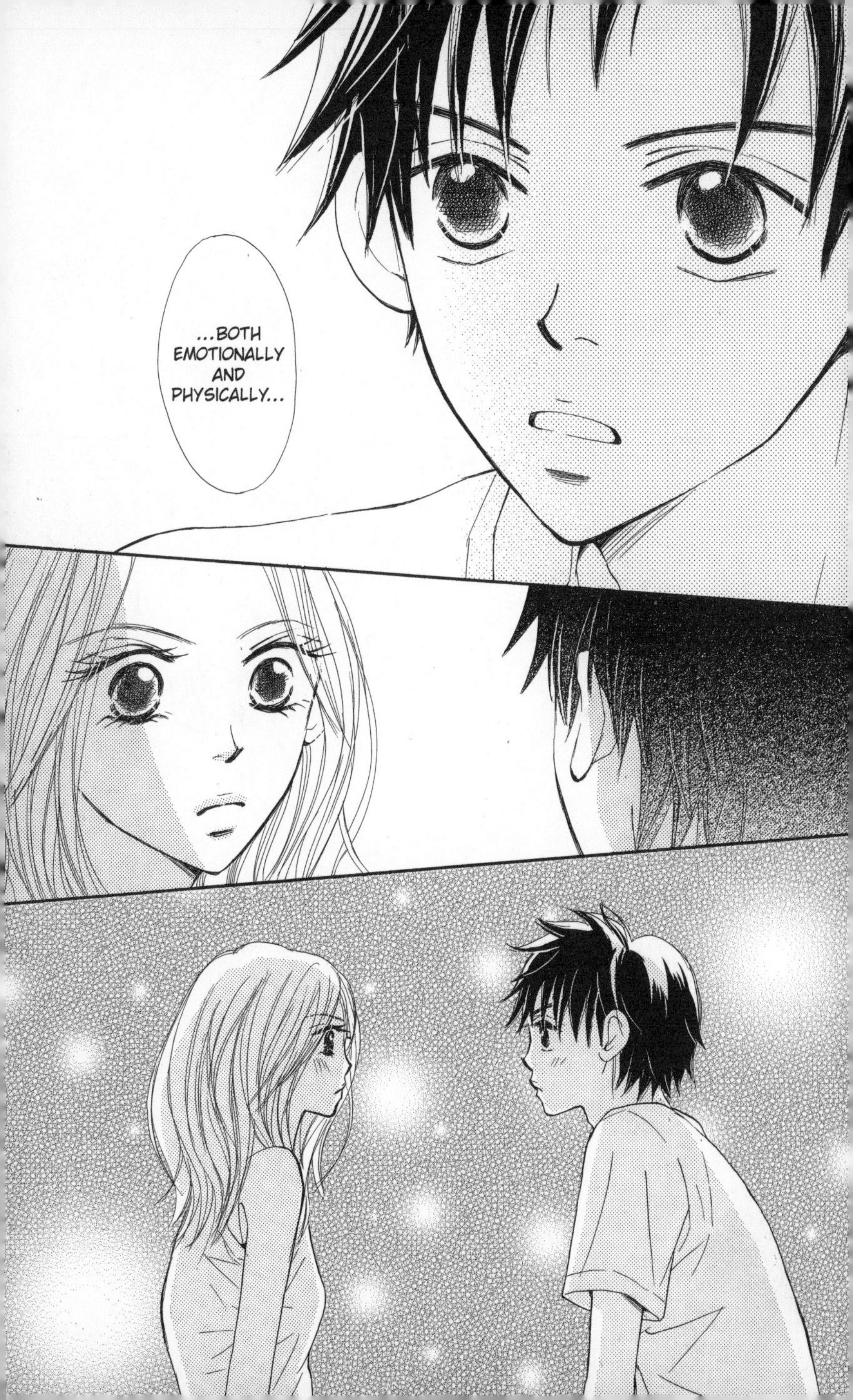
...BOTH EMOTIONALLY AND PHYSICALLY...

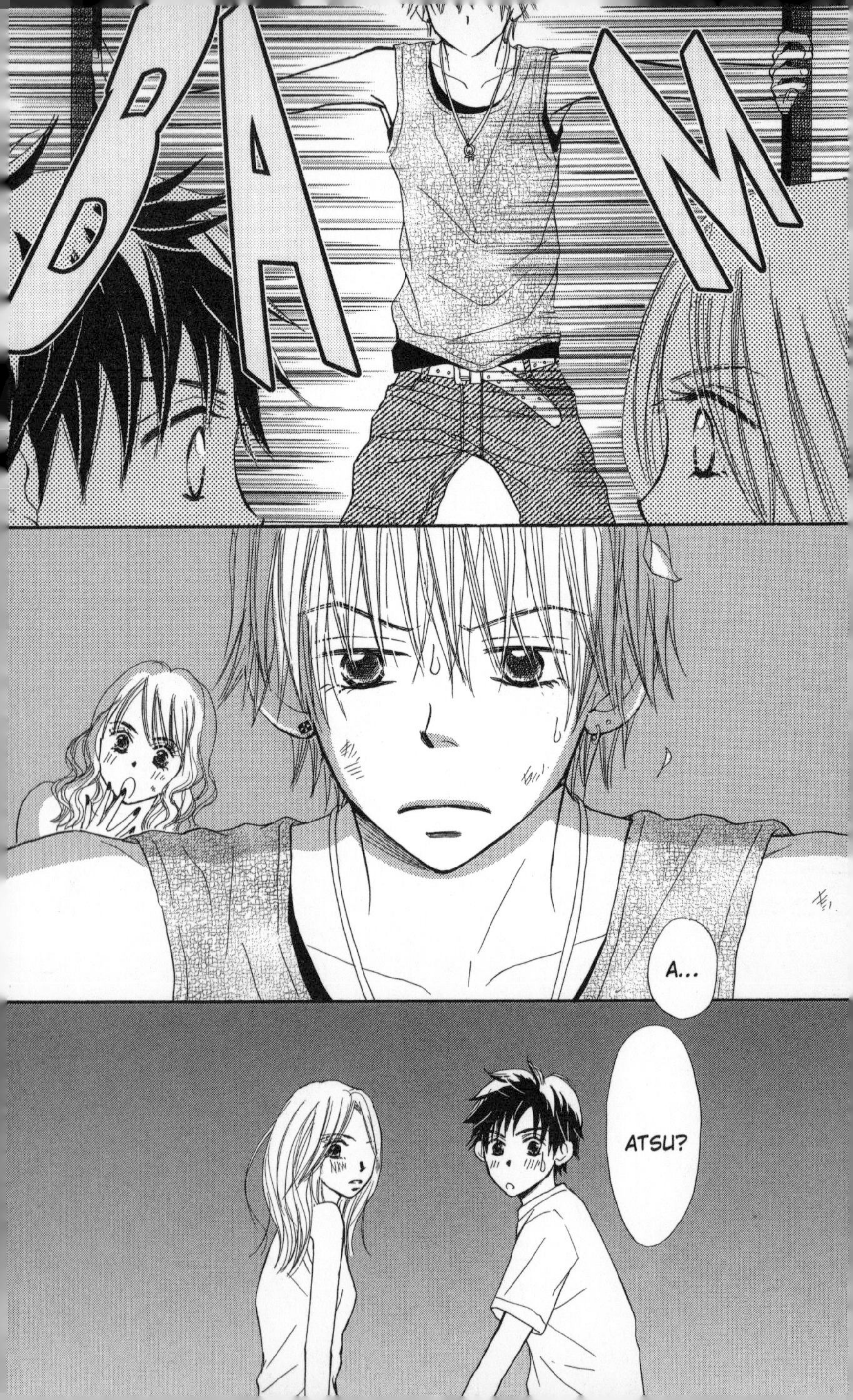
BAM
A...
ATSU?

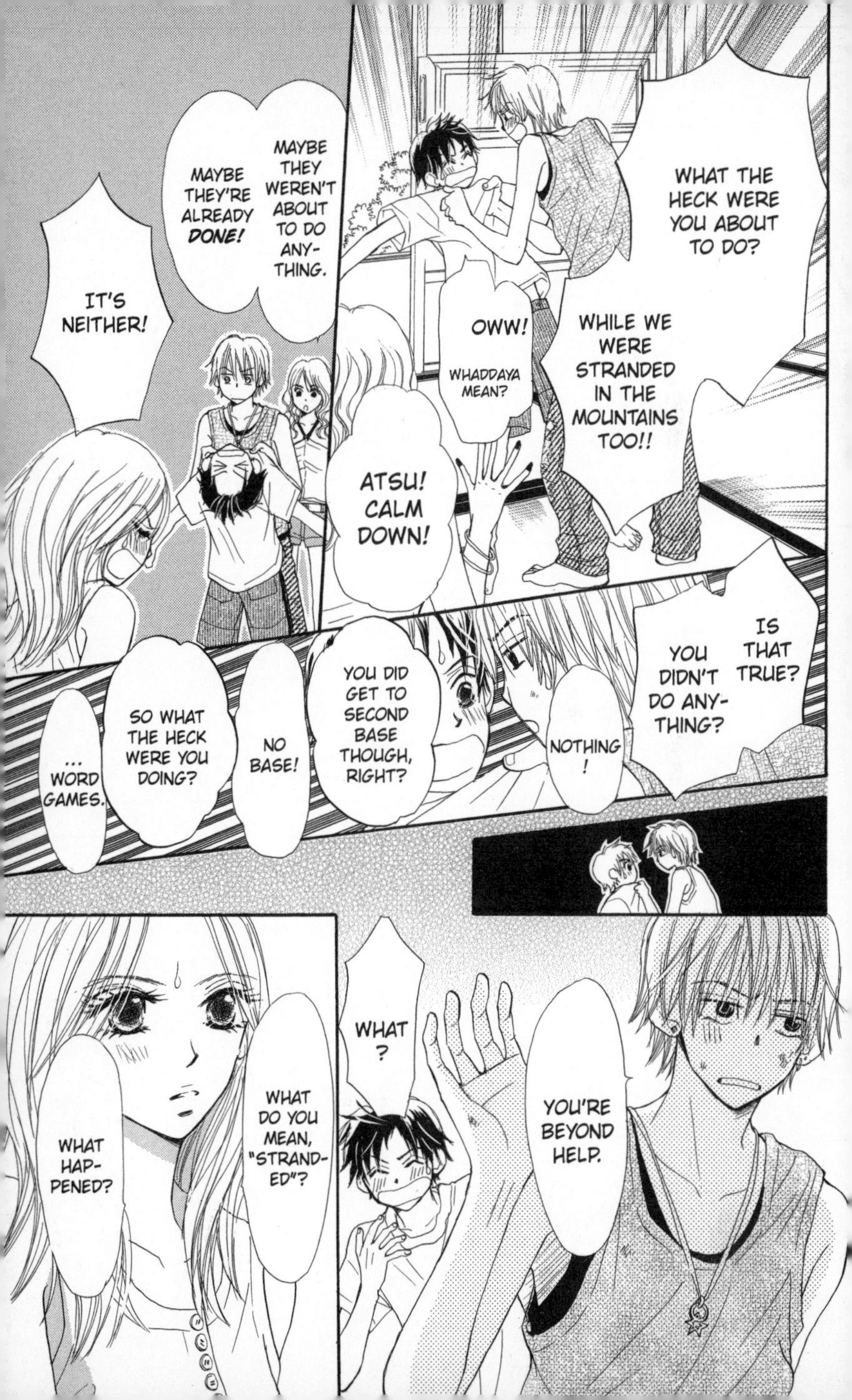
WHAT THE HECK WERE YOU ABOUT TO DO?
WHILE WE WERE STRANDED IN THE MOUNTAINS TOO!!
OWW!
WHADDAYA MEAN?
ATSU! CALM DOWN!
MAYBE THEY WEREN'T ABOUT TO DO ANY-THING.
MAYBE THEY'RE ALREADY DONE!
IT'S NEITHER!
IS THAT TRUE?
YOU DIDN'T DO ANY-THING?
NOTHING!
YOU DID GET TO SECOND BASE THOUGH, RIGHT?
NO BASE!
SO WHAT THE HECK WERE YOU DOING?
... WORD GAMES.
YOU'RE BEYOND HELP.
WHAT?
WHAT DO YOU MEAN, "STRAND-ED"?
WHAT HAP-PENED?

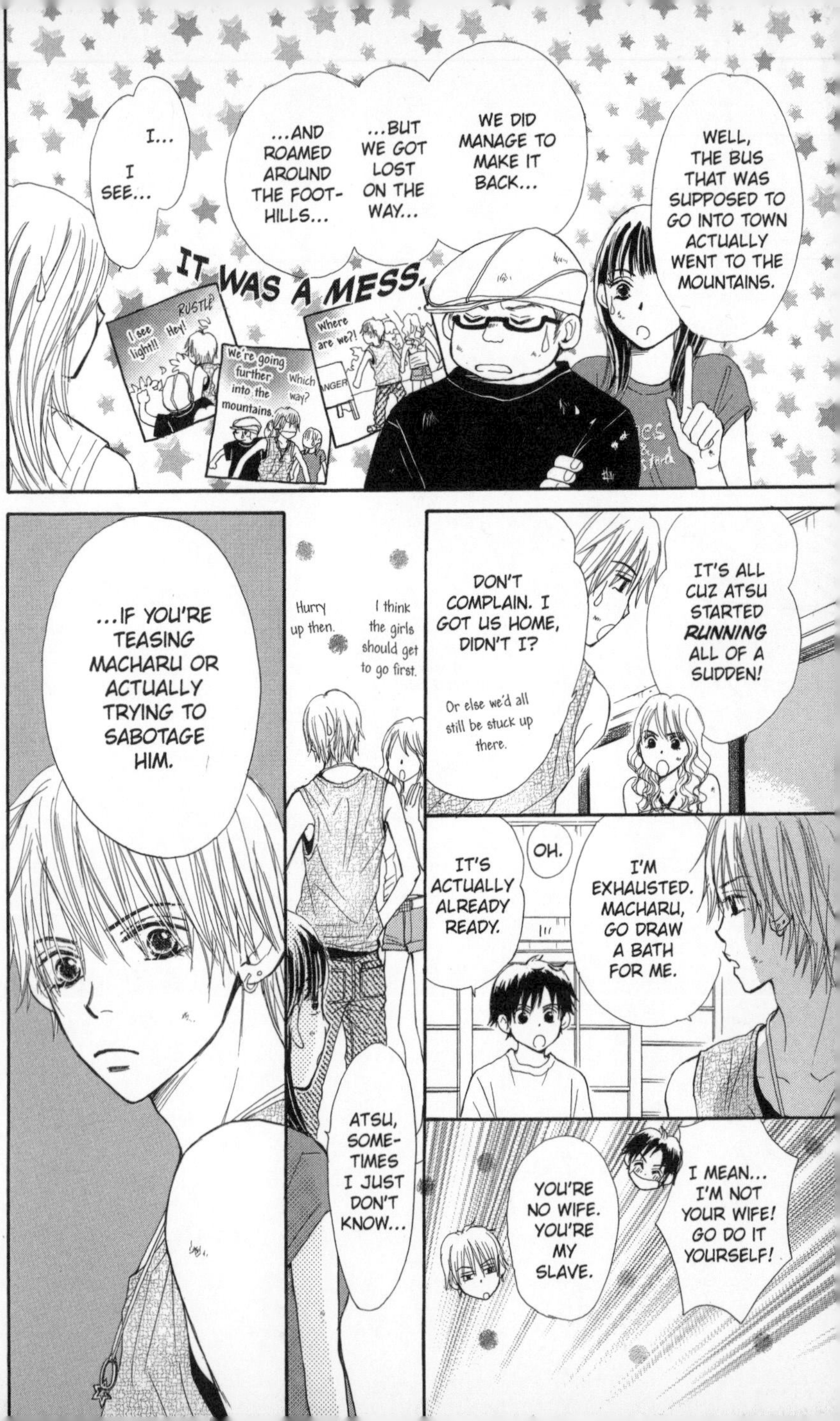
WELL, THE BUS THAT WAS SUPPOSED TO GO INTO TOWN ACTUALLY WENT TO THE MOUNTAINS.
WE DID MANAGE TO MAKE IT BACK...
...BUT WE GOT LOST ON THE WAY...
...AND ROAMED AROUND THE FOOT-HILLS...
I... I SEE...
IT WAS A MESS.
Where are we?!
We're going further into the mountains.
Which way?
I see light!!
Hey!
RUSTLE
IT'S ALL CUZ ATSU STARTED RUNNING ALL OF A SUDDEN!
DON'T COMPLAIN. I GOT US HOME, DIDN'T I?
Or else we'd all still be stuck up there.
I'M EXHAUSTED. MACHARU, GO DRAW A BATH FOR ME.
OH.
IT'S ACTUALLY ALREADY READY.
I MEAN... I'M NOT YOUR WIFE! GO DO IT YOURSELF!
YOU'RE NO WIFE. YOU'RE MY SLAVE.
I think the girls should get to go first.
Hurry up then.
ATSU, SOME-TIMES I JUST DON'T KNOW...
...IF YOU'RE TEASING MACHARU OR ACTUALLY TRYING TO SABOTAGE HIM.

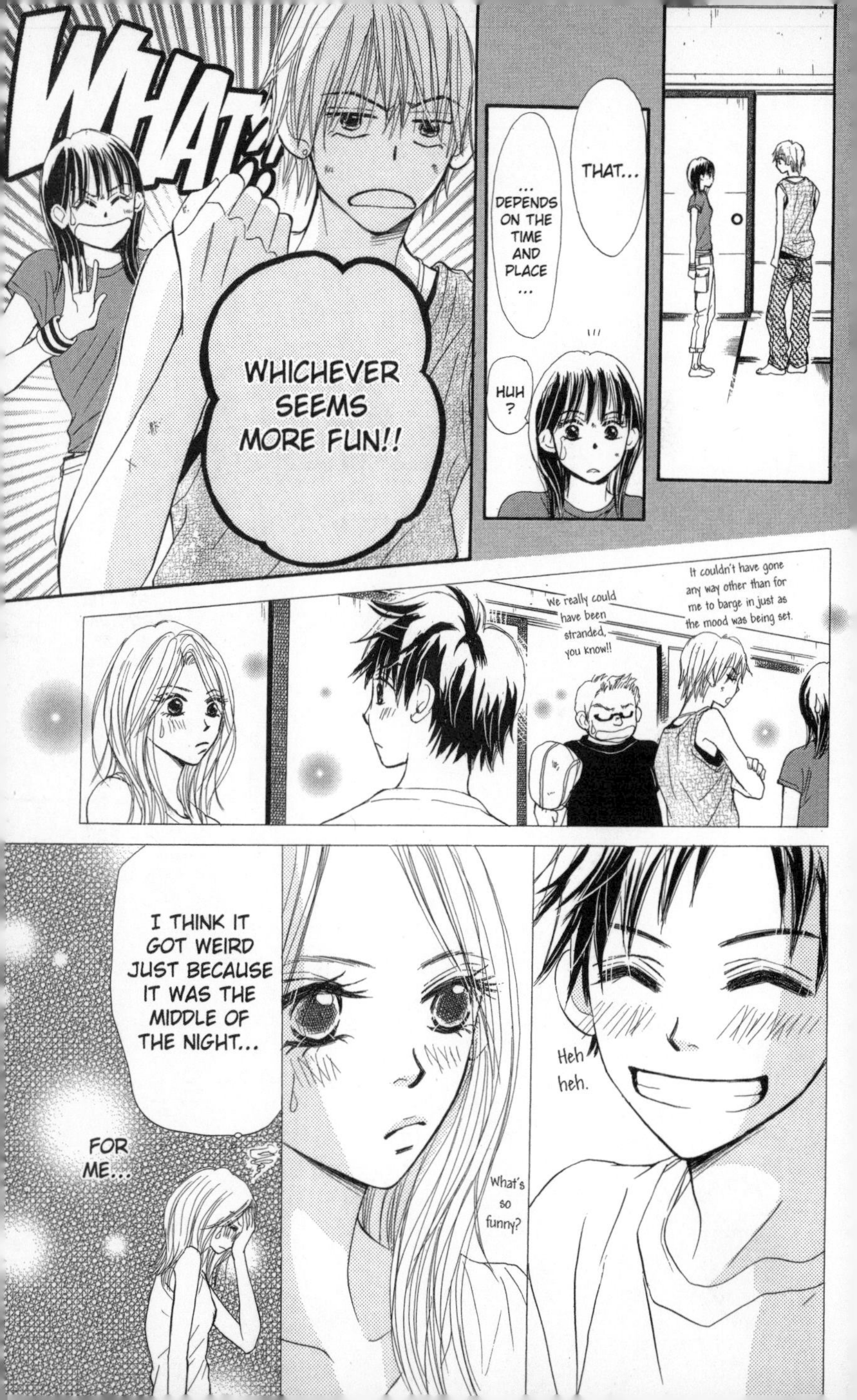
THAT...
...DEPENDS ON THE TIME AND PLACE...
HUH?
WHAT
WHICHEVER SEEMS MORE FUN!!
It couldn't have gone any way other than for me to barge in just as the mood was being set.
We really could have been stranded, you know!!
Heh heh.
What's so funny?
I THINK IT GOT WEIRD JUST BECAUSE IT WAS THE MIDDLE OF THE NIGHT...
FOR ME...

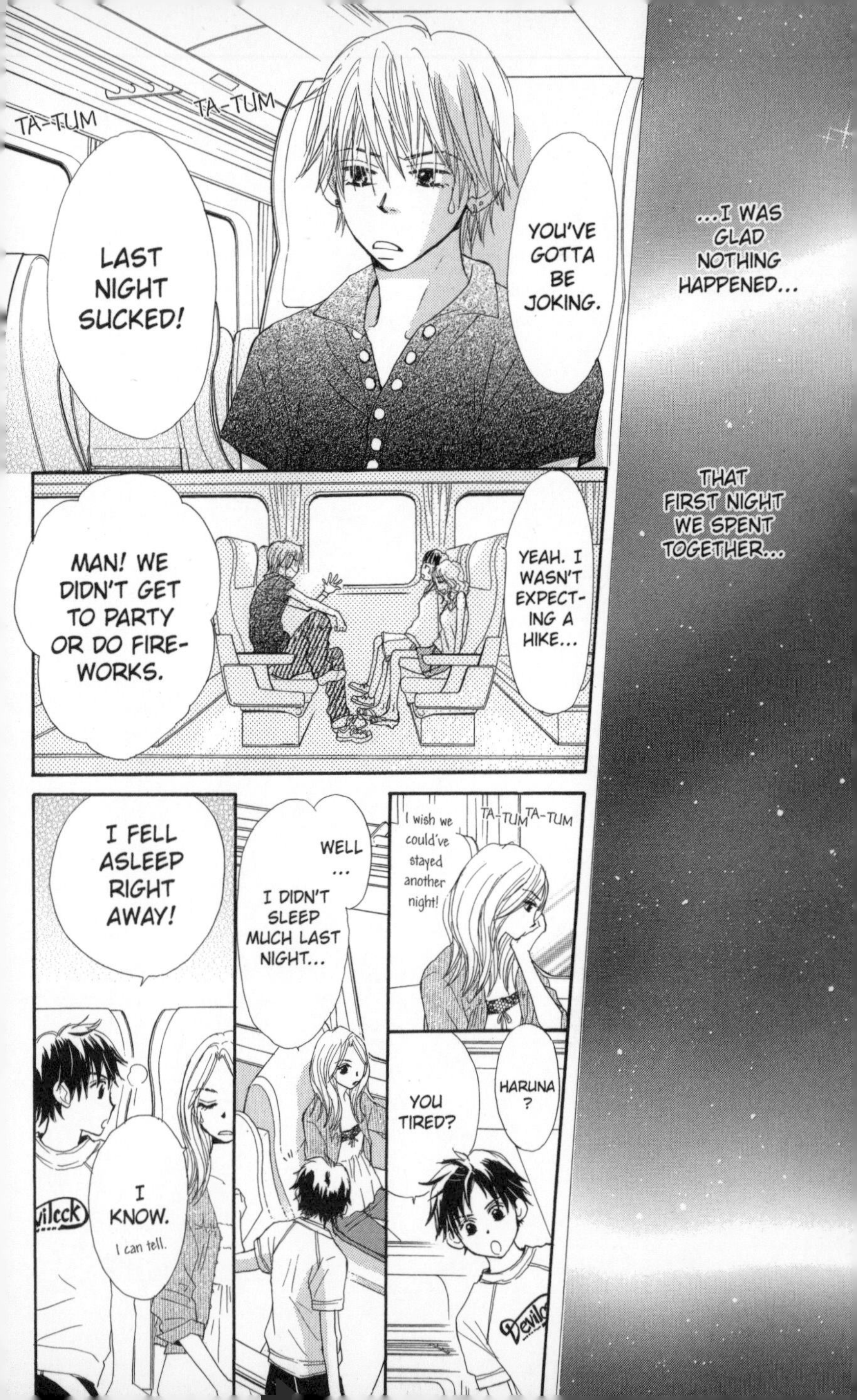
...I WAS GLAD NOTHING HAPPENED...
THAT FIRST NIGHT WE SPENT TOGETHER...
TA-TUM
TA-TUM
YOU'VE GOTTA BE JOKING.
LAST NIGHT SUCKED!
YEAH. I WASN'T EXPECT-ING A HIKE...
MAN! WE DIDN'T GET TO PARTY OR DO FIRE-WORKS.
TA-TUM TA-TUM
I wish we could've stayed another night!
HARUNA?
YOU TIRED?
WELL...
I DIDN'T SLEEP MUCH LAST NIGHT...
I FELL ASLEEP RIGHT AWAY!
I KNOW.
I can tell.

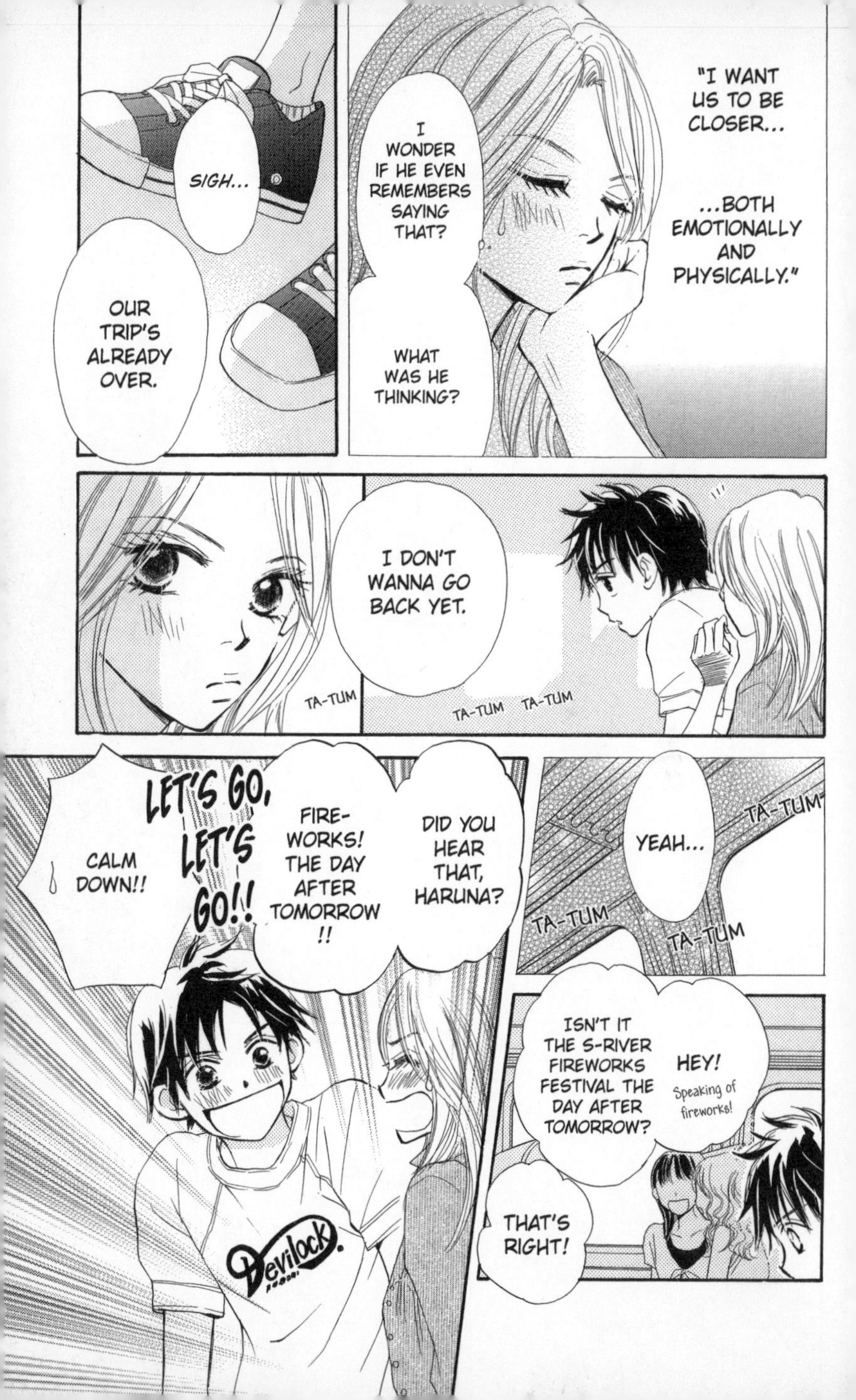
"I WANT US TO BE CLOSER...
...BOTH EMOTIONALLY AND PHYSICALLY."
I WONDER IF HE EVEN REMEMBERS SAYING THAT?
WHAT WAS HE THINKING?
SIGH...
OUR TRIP'S ALREADY OVER.
I DON'T WANNA GO BACK YET.
TA-TUM TA-TUM
TA-TUM
TA-TUM
YEAH...
TA-TUM
TA-TUM
HEY!
Speaking of fireworks!
ISN'T IT THE S-RIVER FIREWORKS FESTIVAL THE DAY AFTER TOMORROW?
THAT'S RIGHT!
DID YOU HEAR THAT, HARUNA?
FIRE-WORKS! THE DAY AFTER TOMORROW!!
LET'S GO, LET'S GO!!
CALM DOWN!!
Devilock

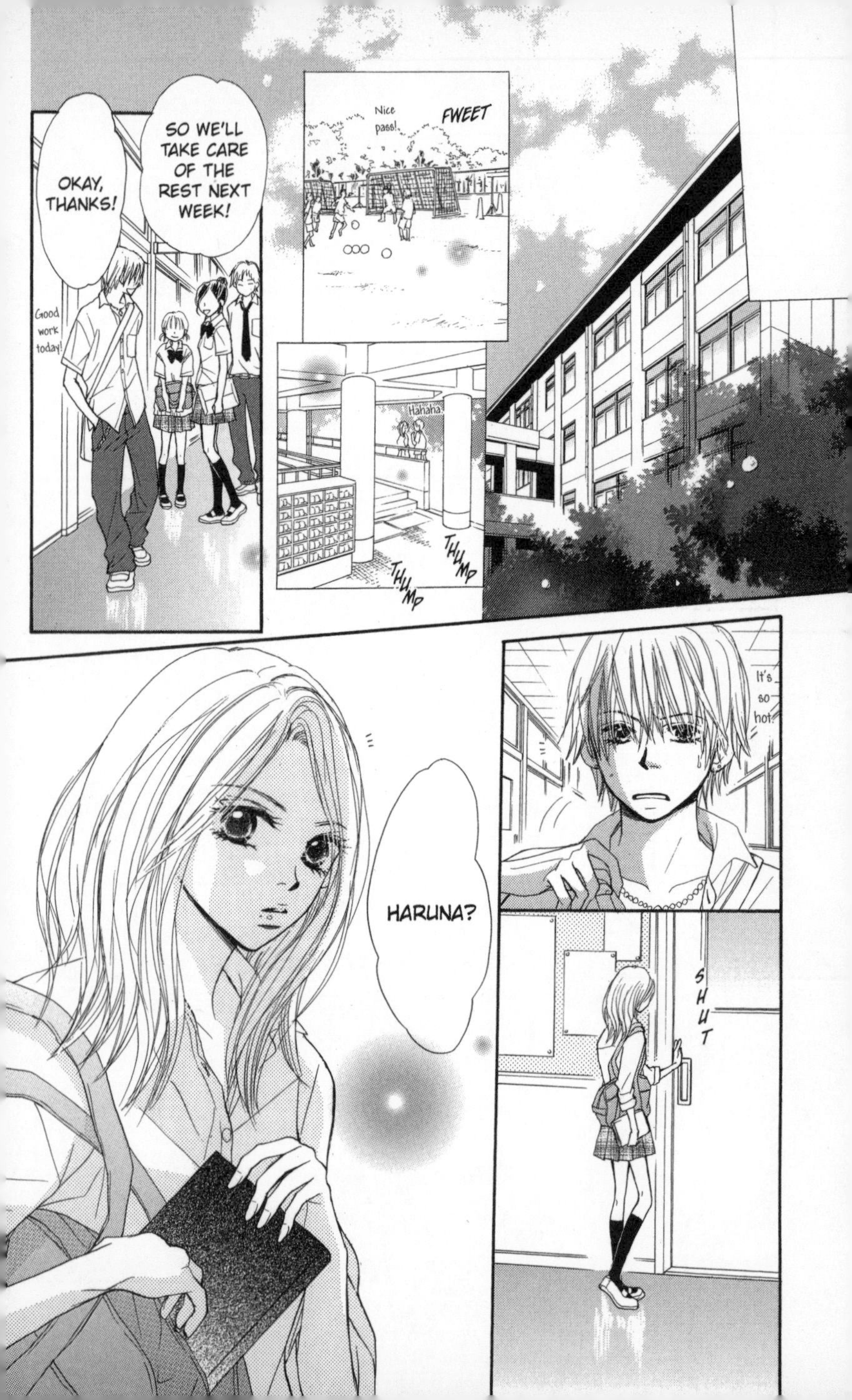
Nice pass!
FWEET
Hahaha
THUMP
THUMP
SO WE'LL TAKE CARE OF THE REST NEXT WEEK!
OKAY, THANKS!
Good work today!
It's so hot
SHUT
HARUNA?

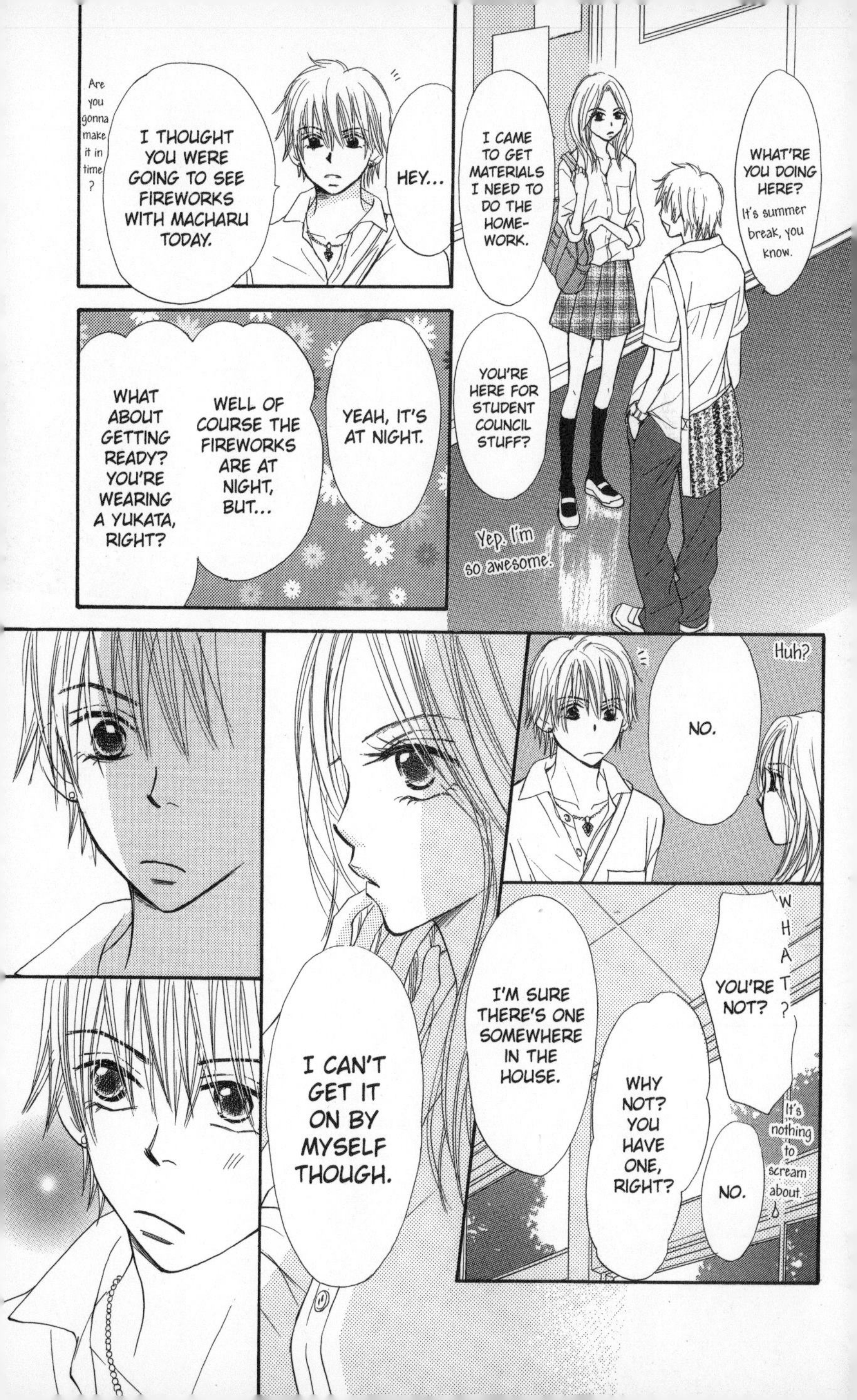
WHAT'RE YOU DOING HERE?
It's summer break, you know.
I CAME TO GET MATERIALS I NEED TO DO THE HOMEWORK.
YOU'RE HERE FOR STUDENT COUNCIL STUFF?
Yep. I'm so awesome.
HEY...
I THOUGHT YOU WERE GOING TO SEE FIREWORKS WITH MACHARU TODAY.
Are you gonna make it in time?
YEAH, IT'S AT NIGHT.
WELL OF COURSE THE FIREWORKS ARE AT NIGHT, BUT...
WHAT ABOUT GETTING READY? YOU'RE WEARING A YUKATA, RIGHT?
Huh?
NO.
WHAT?
YOU'RE NOT?
It's nothing to scream about.
WHY NOT? YOU HAVE ONE, RIGHT?
NO.
I'M SURE THERE'S ONE SOMEWHERE IN THE HOUSE.
I CAN'T GET IT ON BY MYSELF THOUGH.

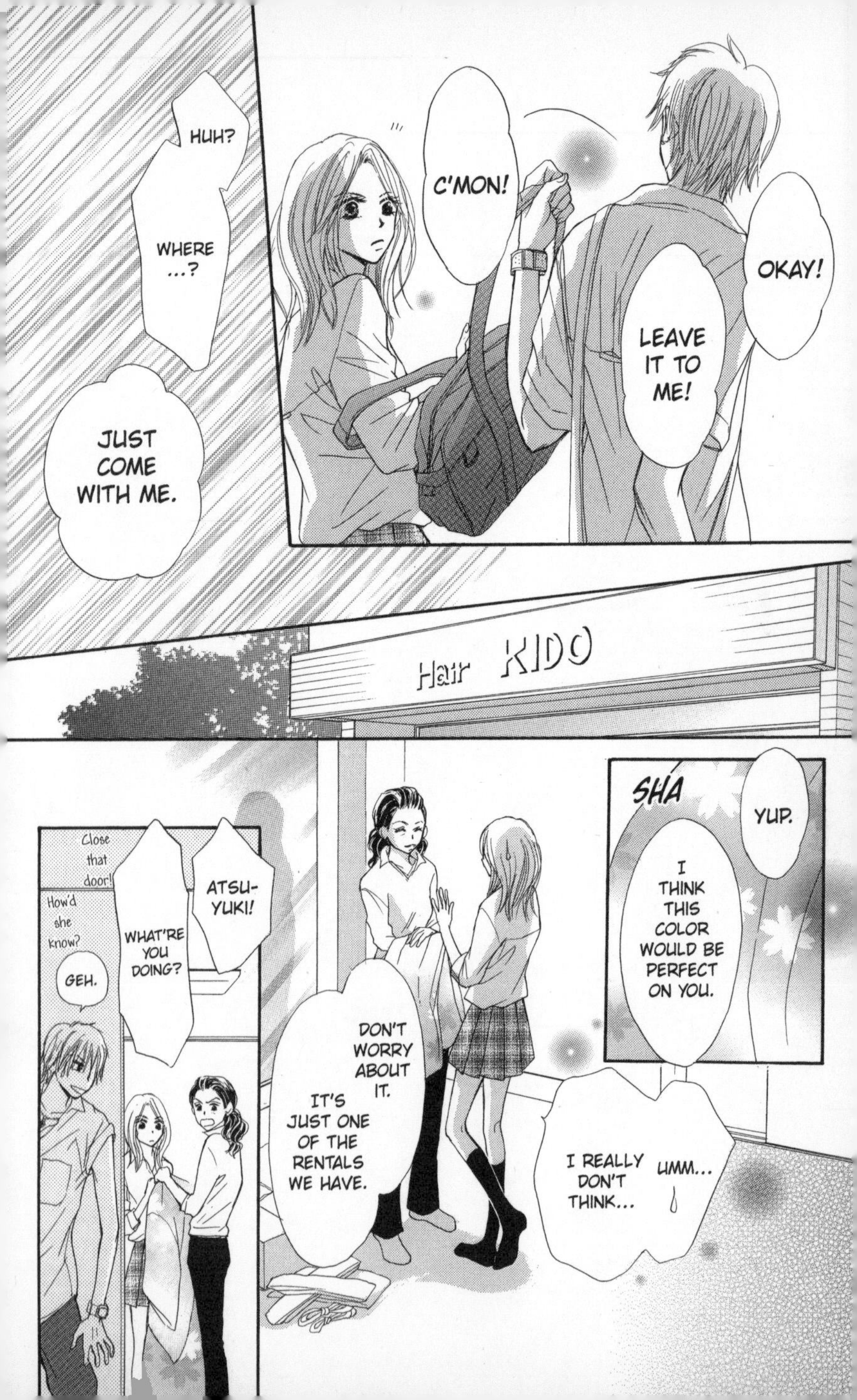
OKAY!
LEAVE IT TO ME!
C'MON!
HUH?
WHERE ...?
JUST COME WITH ME.
Hair KIDO
SHA
YUP.
I THINK THIS COLOR WOULD BE PERFECT ON YOU.
UMM...
I REALLY DON'T THINK...
DON'T WORRY ABOUT IT.
IT'S JUST ONE OF THE RENTALS WE HAVE.
ATSU-YUKI!
WHAT'RE YOU DOING?
Close that door!
How'd she know?
GEH.

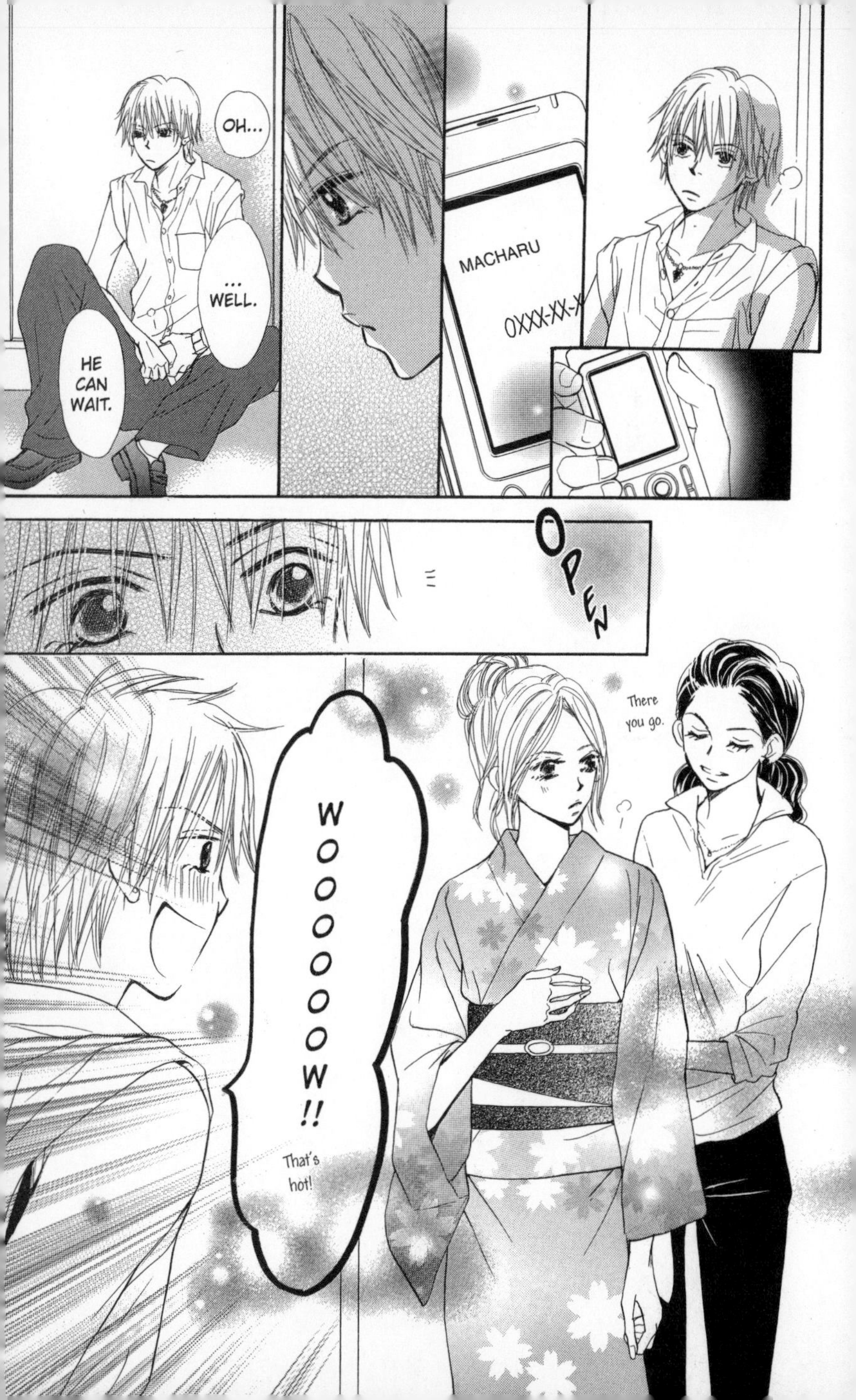
MACHARU
0XXX-XX-X
OH...
... WELL.
HE CAN WAIT.
OPEN
There you go.
WOOOOOOOW!!
That's hot!

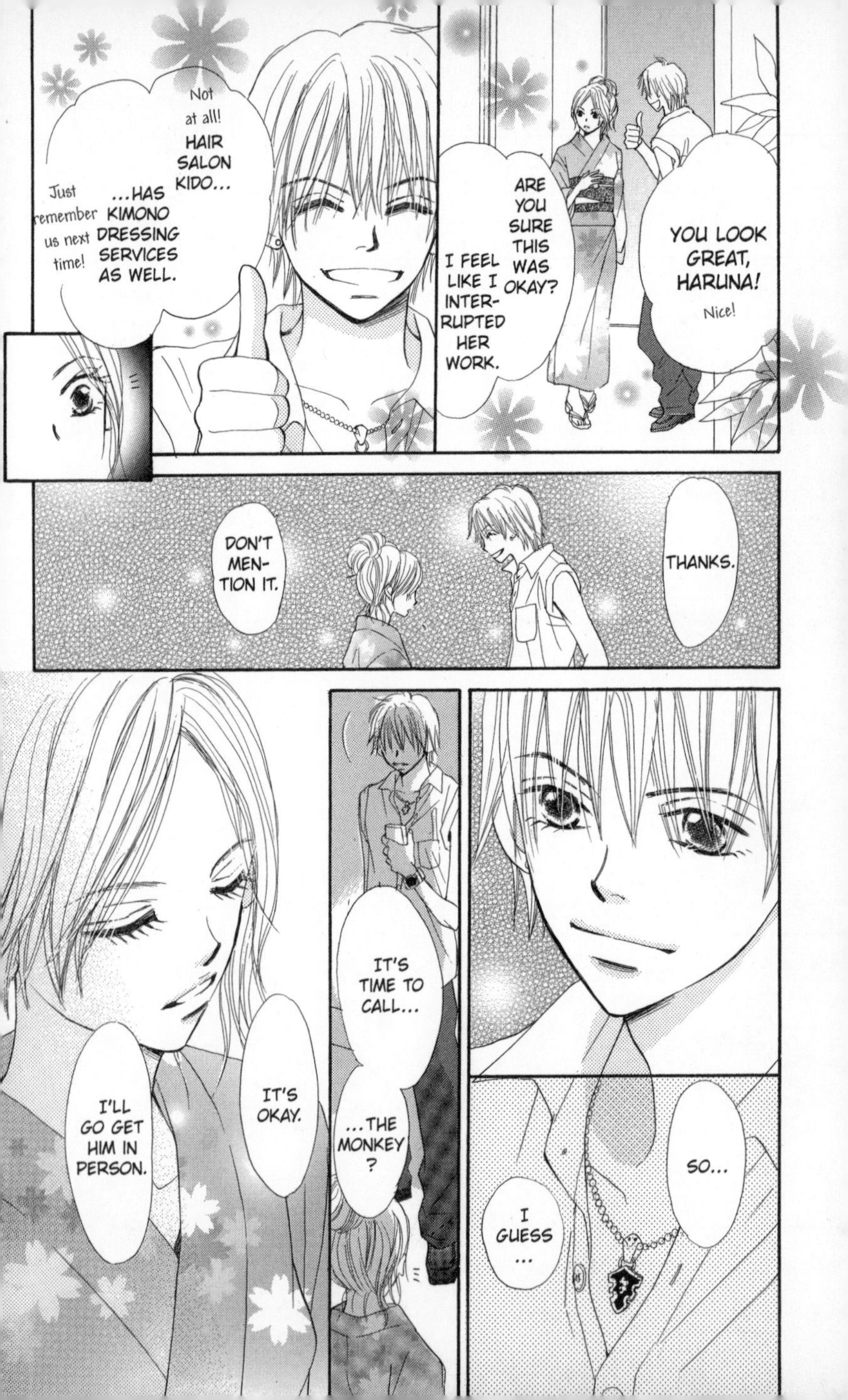
YOU LOOK GREAT, HARUNA!
Nice!
ARE YOU SURE THIS WAS OKAY?
I FEEL LIKE I INTERRUPTED HER WORK.
Not at all!
HAIR SALON KIDO...
...HAS KIMONO DRESSING SERVICES AS WELL.
Just remember us next time!
THANKS.
DON'T MENTION IT.
SO...
I GUESS...
IT'S TIME TO CALL...
...THE MONKEY?
IT'S OKAY.
I'LL GO GET HIM IN PERSON.

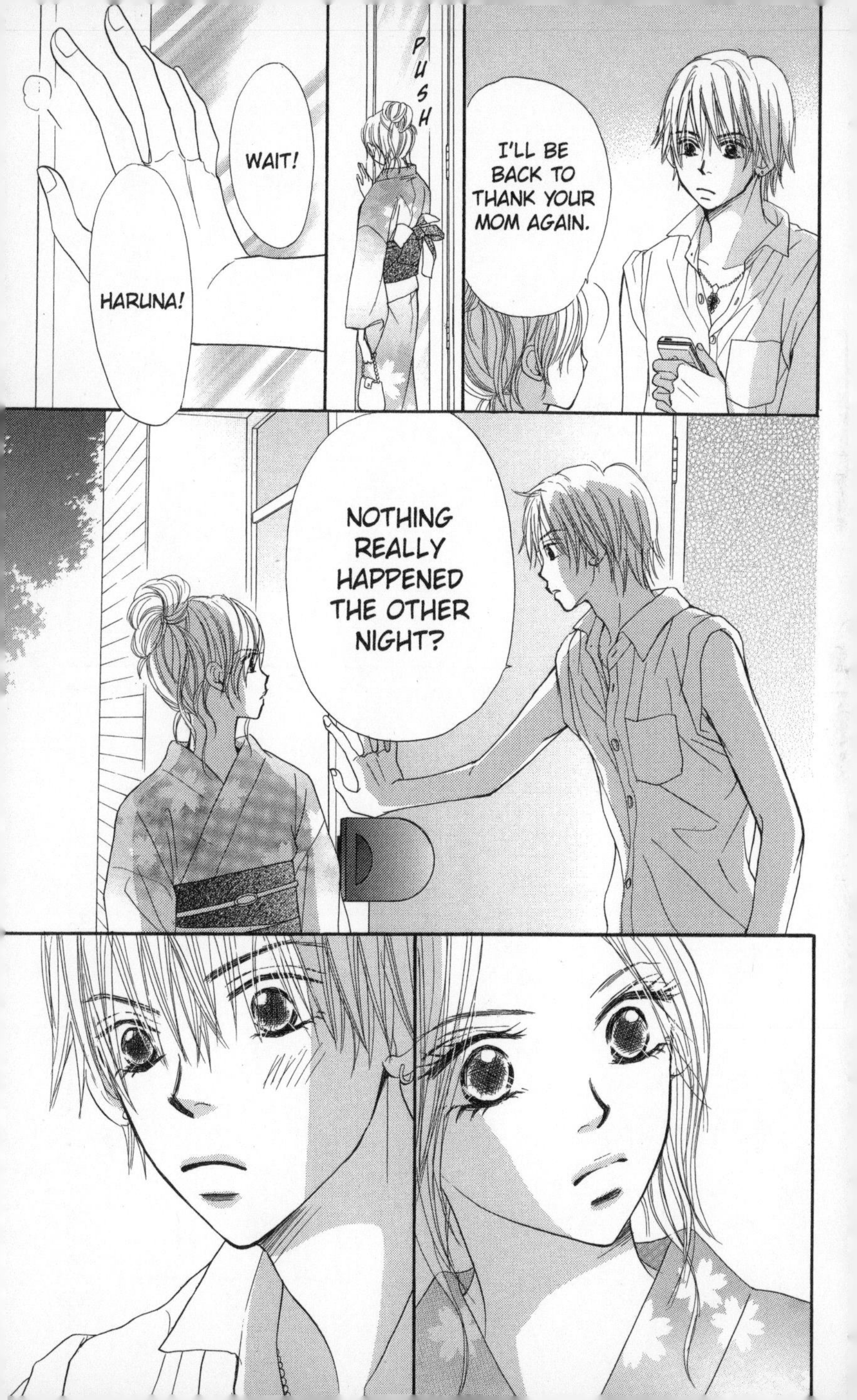
I'LL BE BACK TO THANK YOUR MOM AGAIN.
PUSH
WAIT!
HARUNA!
NOTHING REALLY HAPPENED THE OTHER NIGHT?

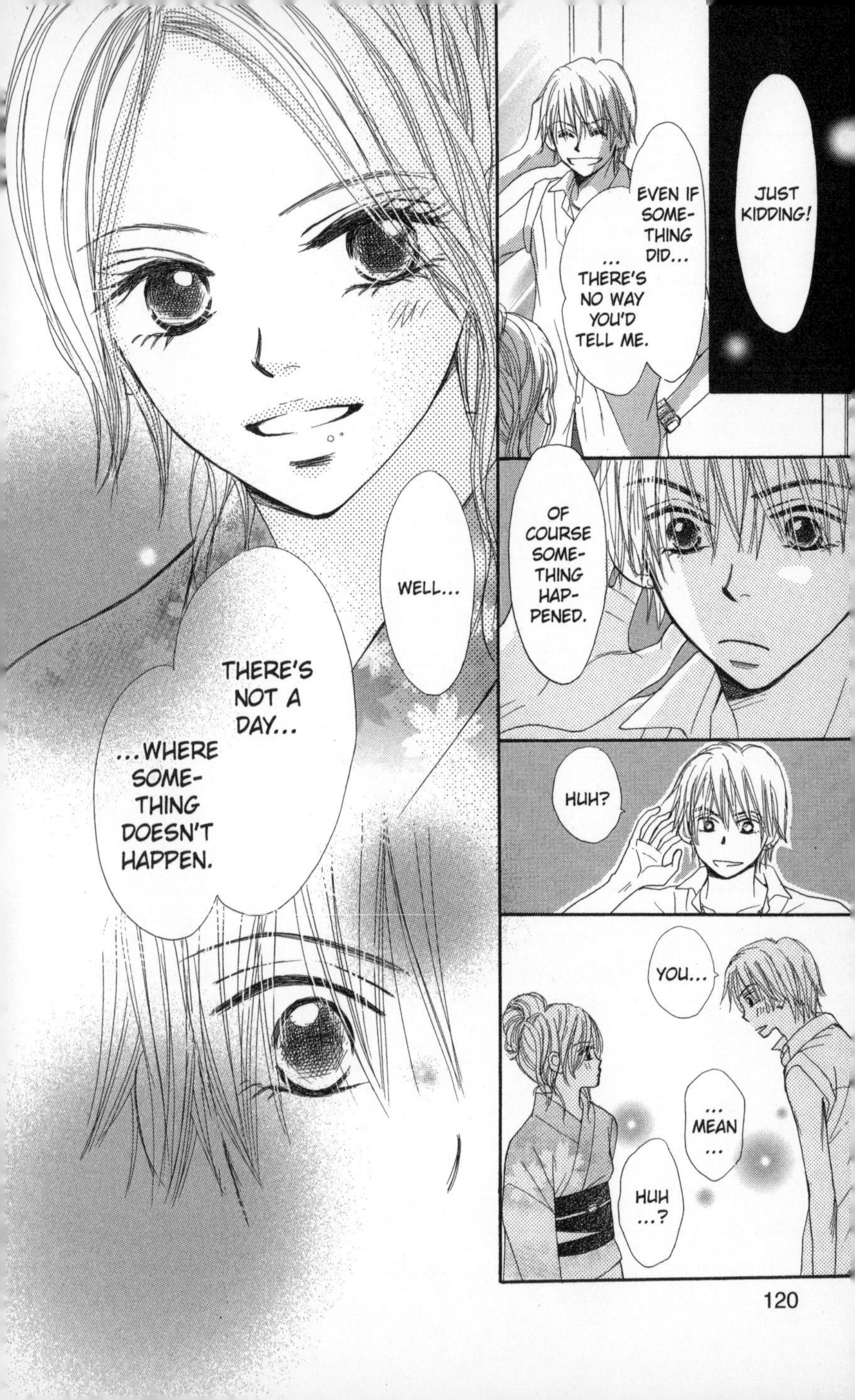
JUST KIDDING!
EVEN IF SOMETHING DID...
...THERE'S NO WAY YOU'D TELL ME.
OF COURSE SOMETHING HAPPENED.
HUH?
YOU...
...MEAN...
HUH...?
WELL...
THERE'S NOT A DAY...
...WHERE SOMETHING DOESN'T HAPPEN.

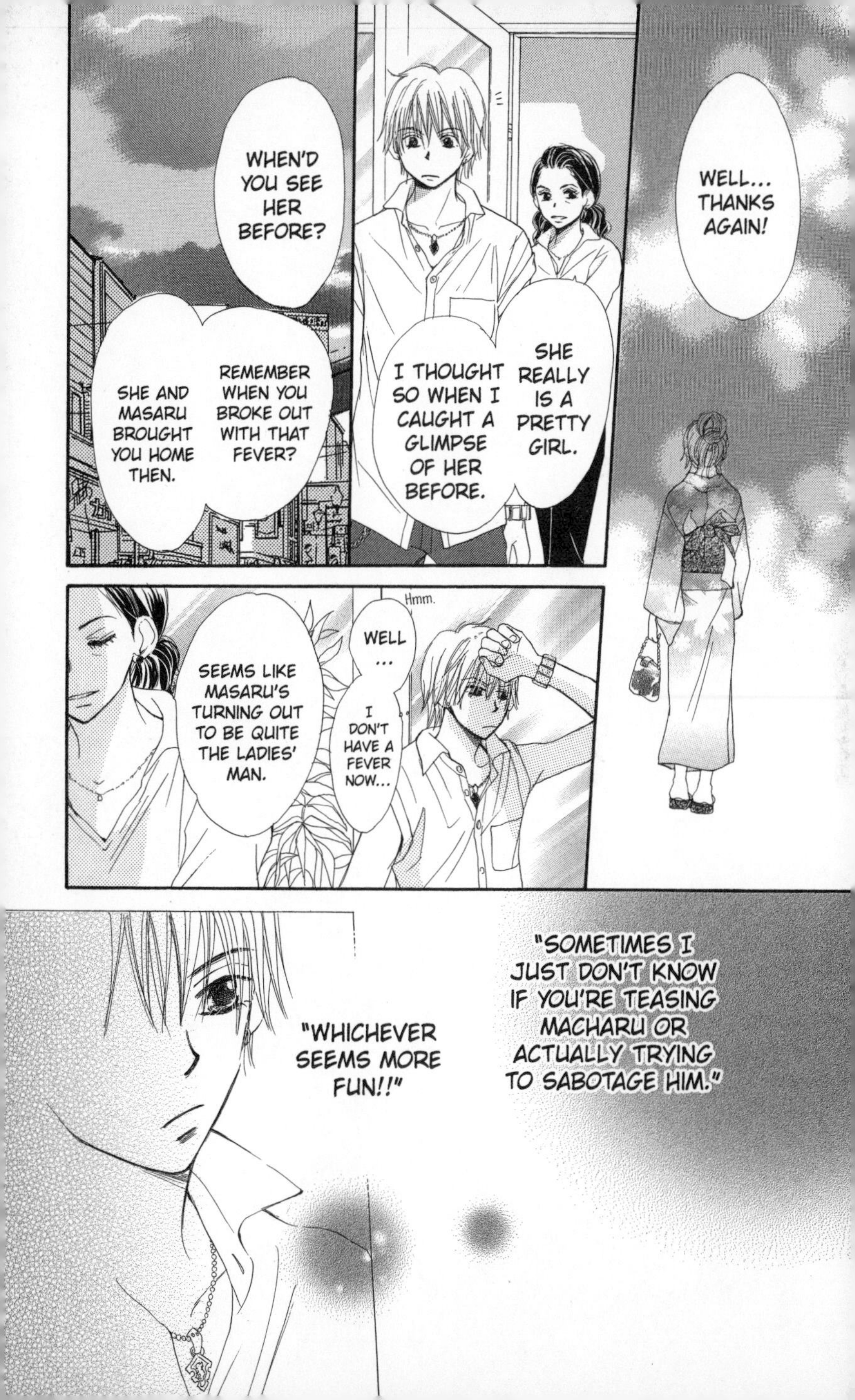
WELL... THANKS AGAIN!
SHE REALLY IS A PRETTY GIRL.
I THOUGHT SO WHEN I CAUGHT A GLIMPSE OF HER BEFORE.
WHEN'D YOU SEE HER BEFORE?
REMEMBER WHEN YOU BROKE OUT WITH THAT FEVER?
SHE AND MASARU BROUGHT YOU HOME THEN.
Hmm.
WELL ...
I DON'T HAVE A FEVER NOW...
SEEMS LIKE MASARU'S TURNING OUT TO BE QUITE THE LADIES' MAN.
"SOMETIMES I JUST DON'T KNOW IF YOU'RE TEASING MACHARU OR ACTUALLY TRYING TO SABOTAGE HIM."
"WHICHEVER SEEMS MORE FUN!!"

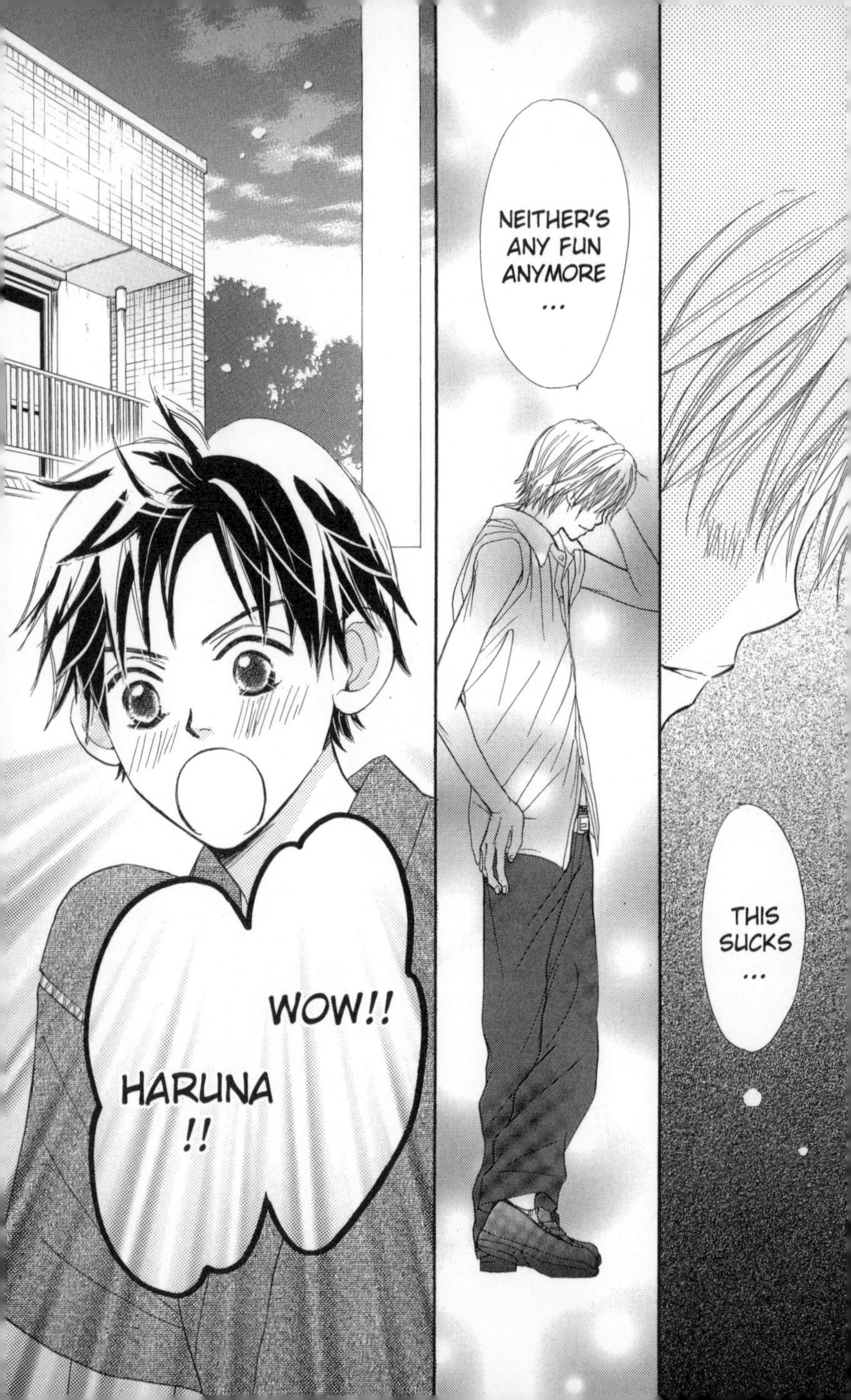
THIS SUCKS ...
NEITHER'S ANY FUN ANYMORE ...
WOW!!
HARUNA !!

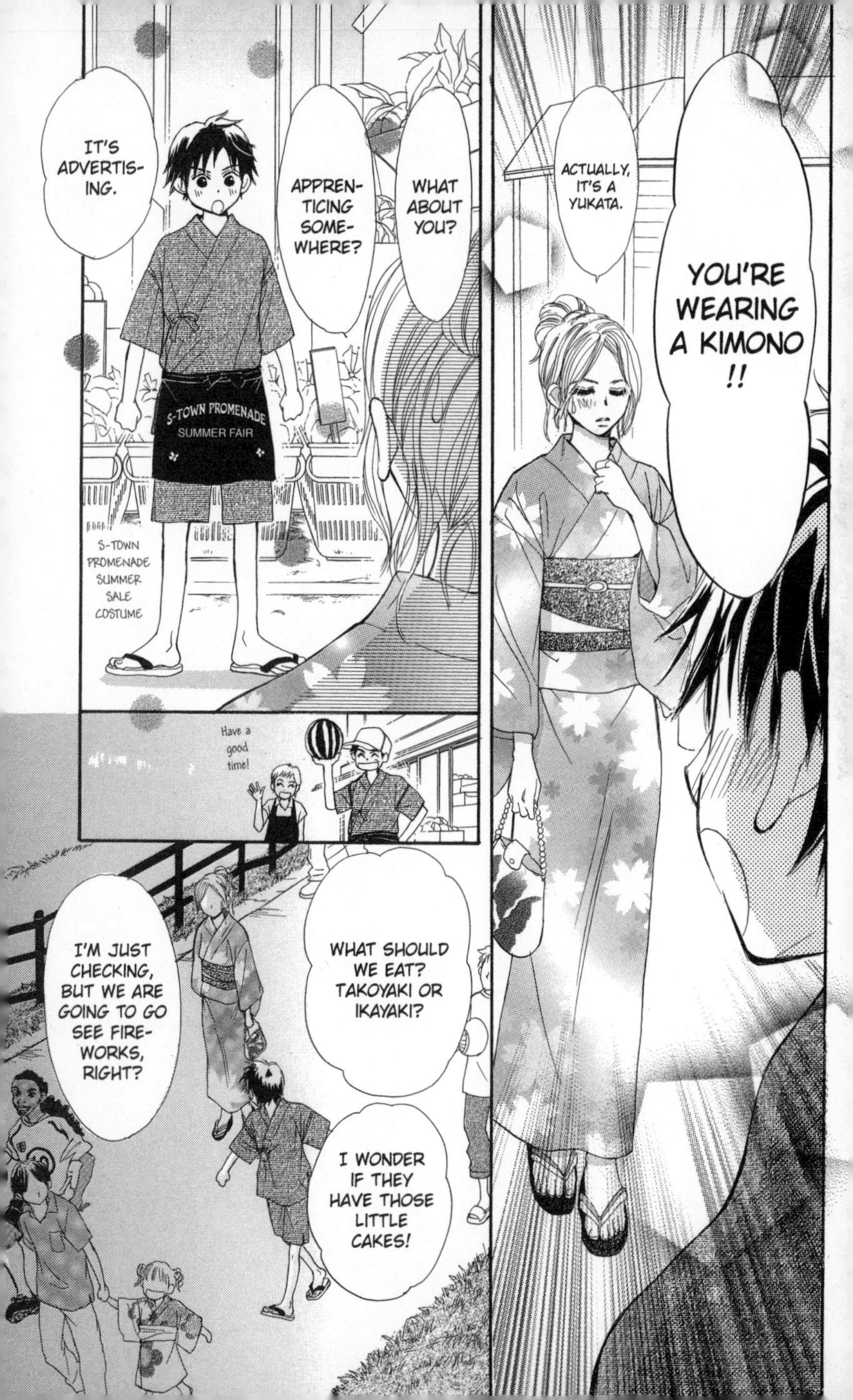
YOU'RE WEARING A KIMONO !!
ACTUALLY, IT'S A YUKATA.
WHAT ABOUT YOU?
APPRENTICING SOMEWHERE?
IT'S ADVERTISING.
S-TOWN PROMENADE SUMMER FAIR
S-TOWN PROMENADE SUMMER SALE COSTUME
Have a good time!
WHAT SHOULD WE EAT? TAKOYAKI OR IKAYAKI?
I WONDER IF THEY HAVE THOSE LITTLE CAKES!
I'M JUST CHECKING, BUT WE ARE GOING TO GO SEE FIREWORKS, RIGHT?

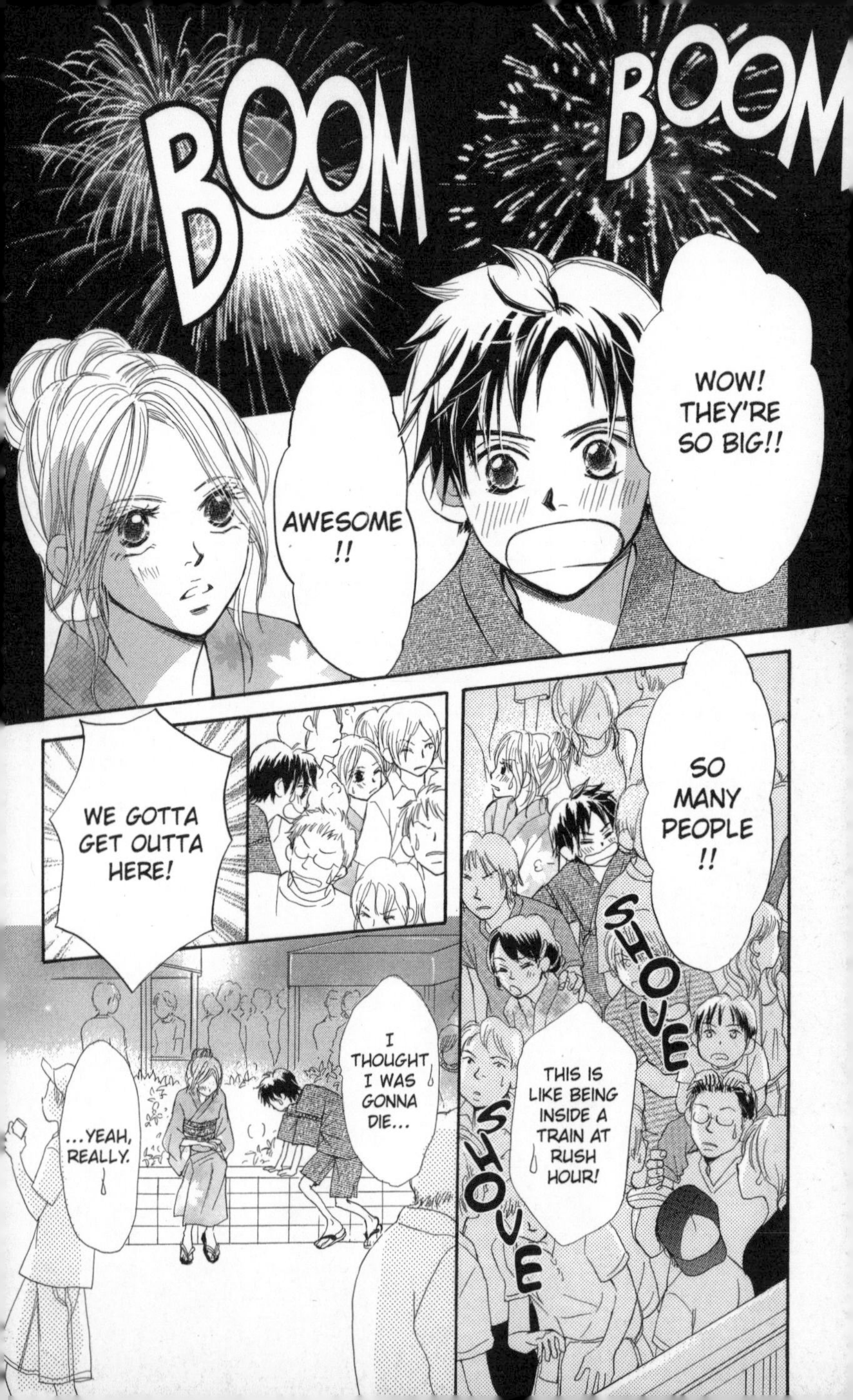
BOOM
BOOM
WOW! THEY'RE SO BIG!!
AWESOME!!
SO MANY PEOPLE!!
SHOVE
SHOVE
THIS IS LIKE BEING INSIDE A TRAIN AT RUSH HOUR!
WE GOTTA GET OUTTA HERE!
I THOUGHT I WAS GONNA DIE...
...YEAH, REALLY.

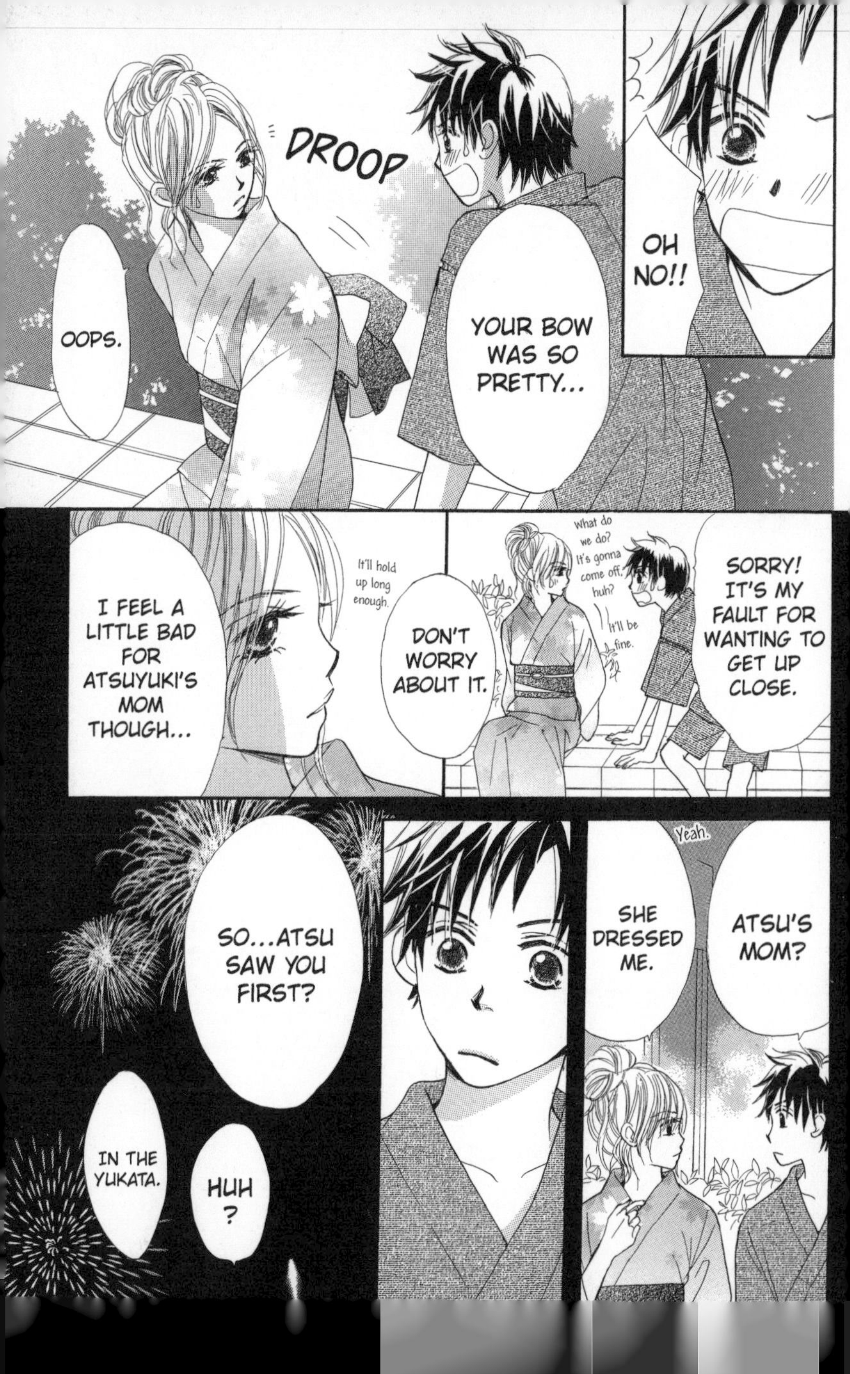
OH NO!!
YOUR BOW WAS SO PRETTY...
DROOP
OOPS.
SORRY! IT'S MY FAULT FOR WANTING TO GET UP CLOSE.
What do we do? It's gonna come off, huh?
It'll be fine.
It'll hold up long enough.
DON'T WORRY ABOUT IT.
I FEEL A LITTLE BAD FOR ATSUYUKI'S MOM THOUGH...
ATSU'S MOM?
Yeah.
SHE DRESSED ME.
SO...ATSU SAW YOU FIRST?
HUH?
IN THE YUKATA.

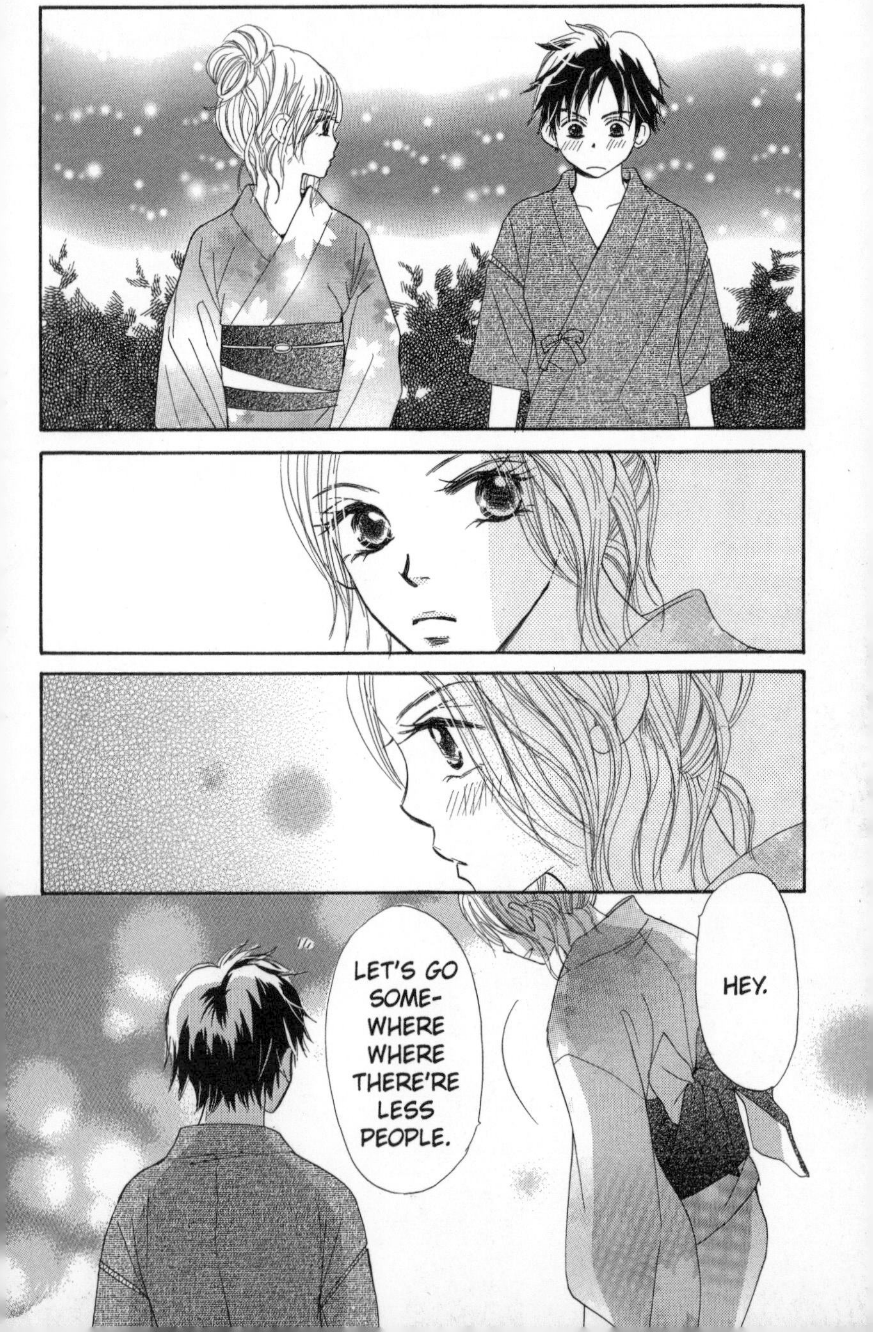
HEY.
LET'S GO SOMEWHERE WHERE THERE'RE LESS PEOPLE.

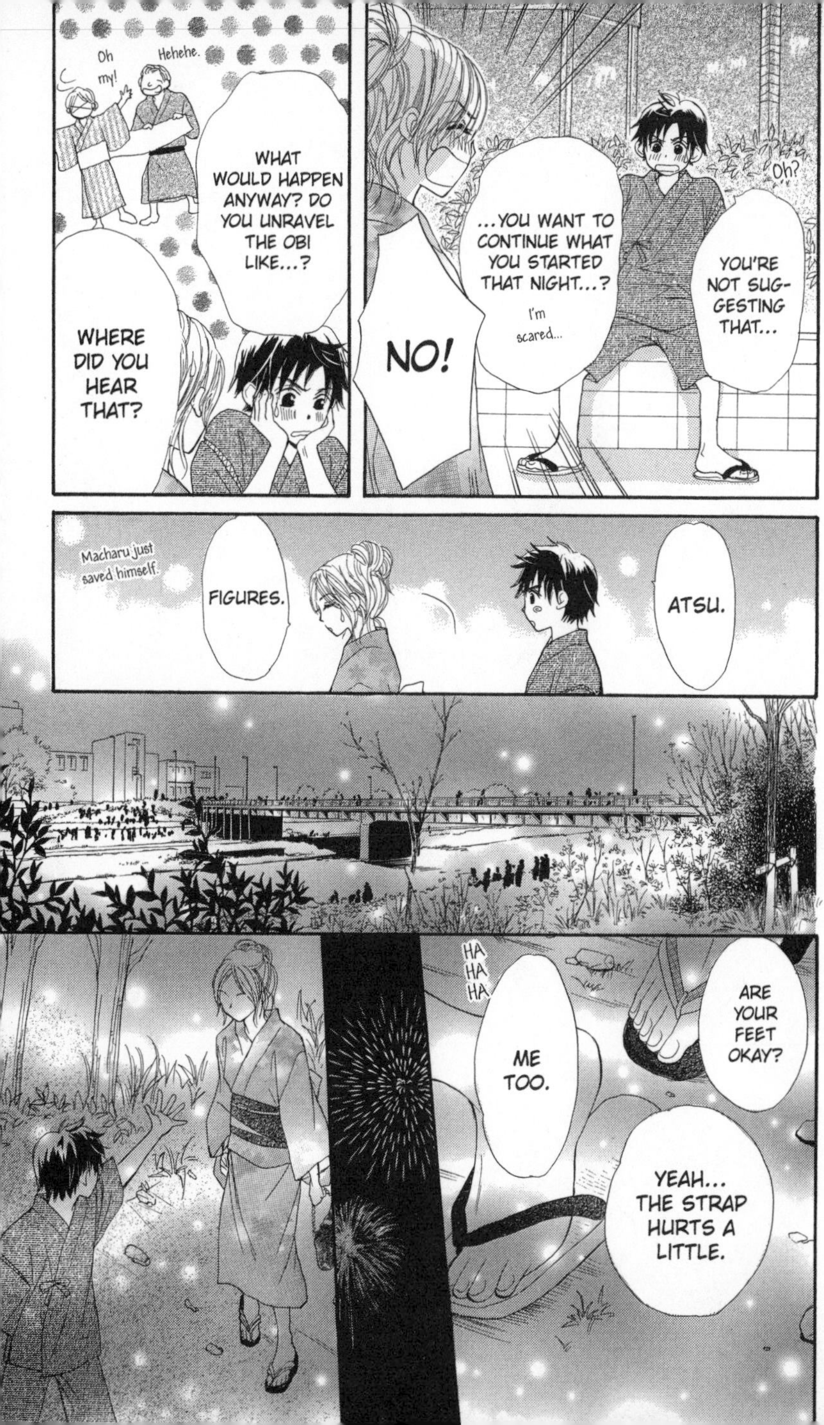
Oh?
YOU'RE NOT SUG-GESTING THAT...
...YOU WANT TO CONTINUE WHAT YOU STARTED THAT NIGHT...?
I'm scared...
NO!
Hehehe.
Oh my!
WHAT WOULD HAPPEN ANYWAY? DO YOU UNRAVEL THE OBI LIKE...?
WHERE DID YOU HEAR THAT?
ATSU.
FIGURES.
Macharu just saved himself.
ARE YOUR FEET OKAY?
YEAH... THE STRAP HURTS A LITTLE.
ME TOO.
HA HA HA

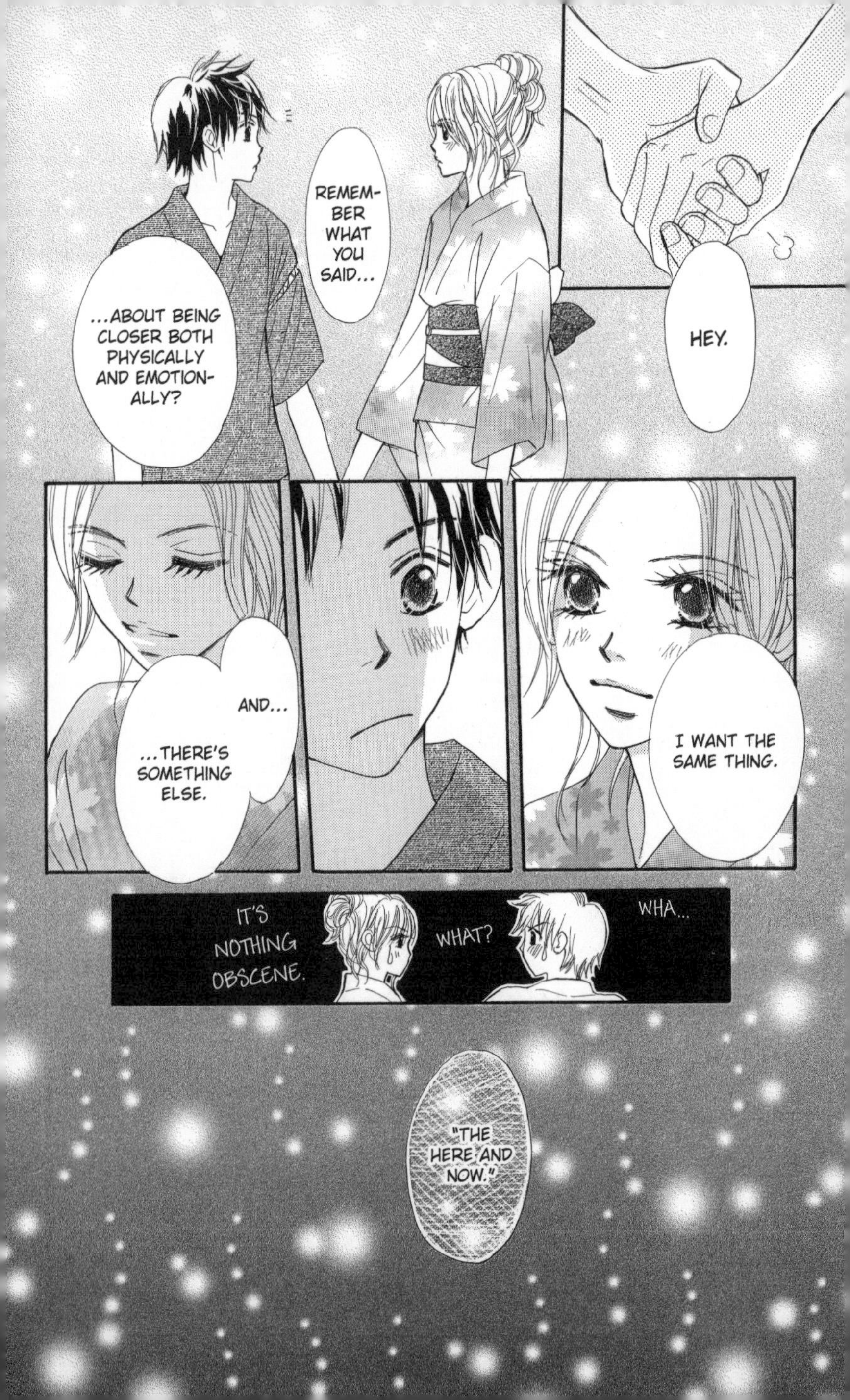
HEY.
REMEM-BER WHAT YOU SAID...
...ABOUT BEING CLOSER BOTH PHYSICALLY AND EMOTION-ALLY?
I WANT THE SAME THING.
AND...
...THERE'S SOMETHING ELSE.
WHA...
WHAT?
IT'S NOTHING OBSCENE.
"THE HERE AND NOW."

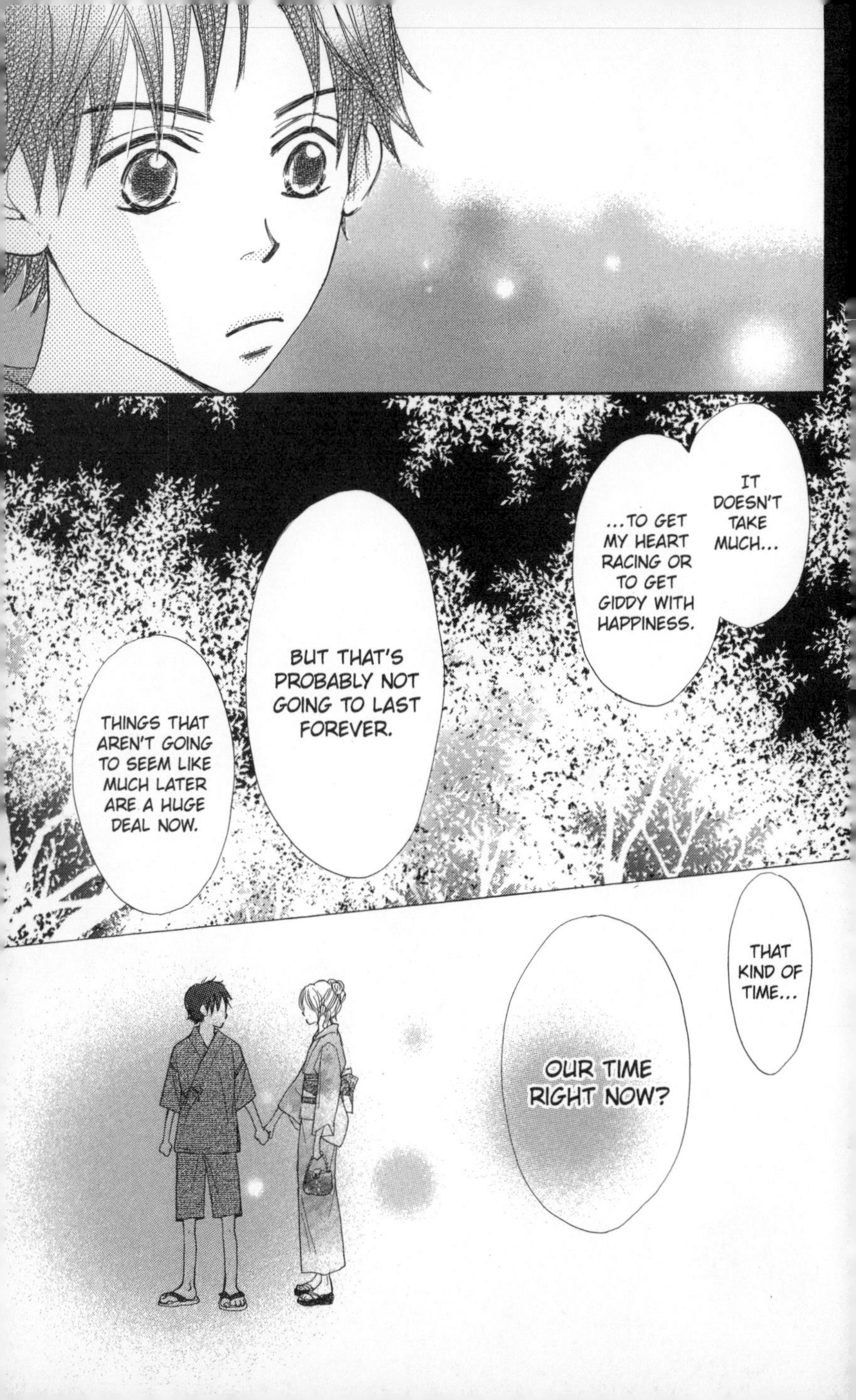
IT DOESN'T TAKE MUCH...
...TO GET MY HEART RACING OR TO GET GIDDY WITH HAPPINESS.
BUT THAT'S PROBABLY NOT GOING TO LAST FOREVER.
THINGS THAT AREN'T GOING TO SEEM LIKE MUCH LATER ARE A HUGE DEAL NOW.
THAT KIND OF TIME...
OUR TIME RIGHT NOW?

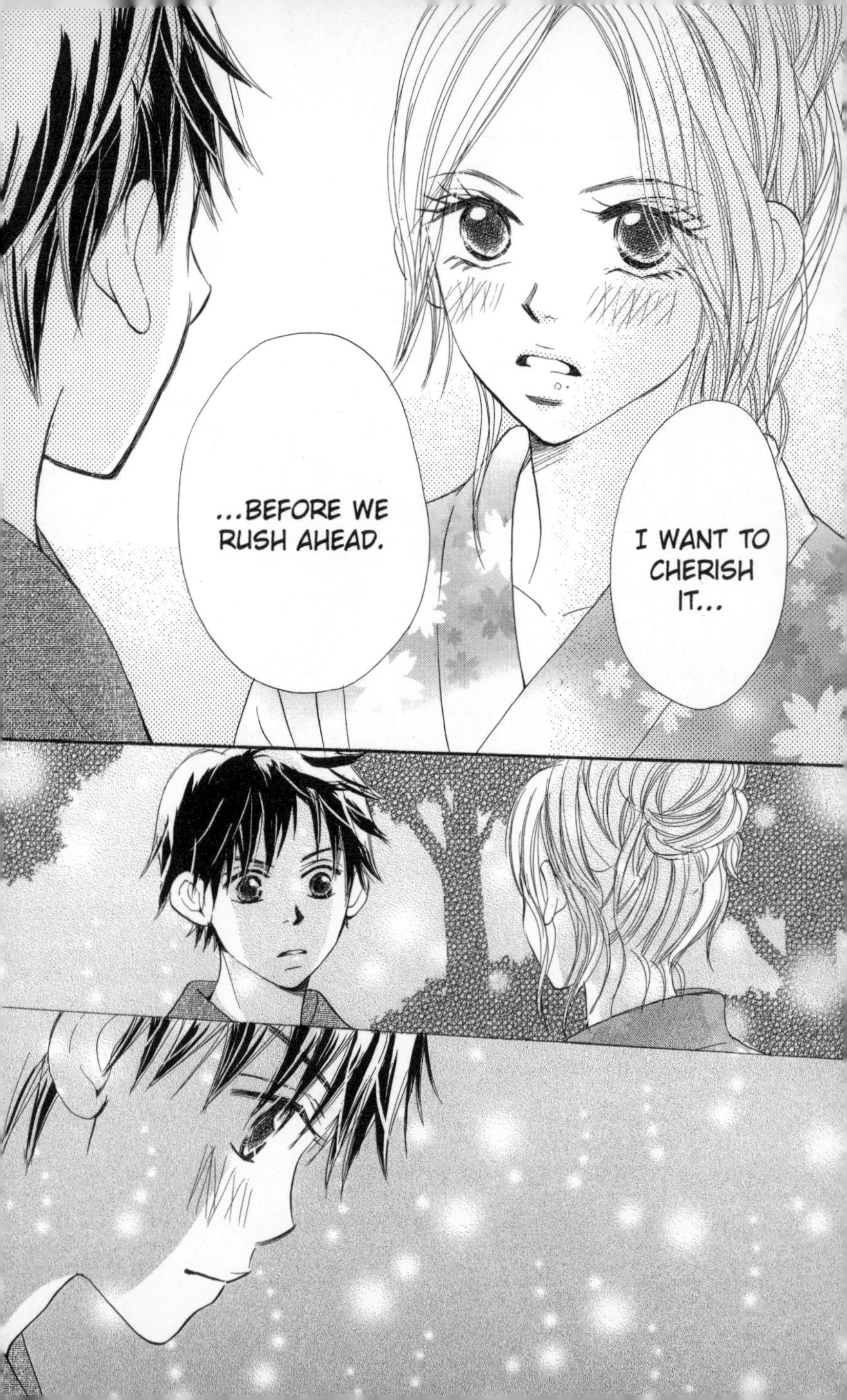
I WANT TO CHERISH IT...
...BEFORE WE RUSH AHEAD.

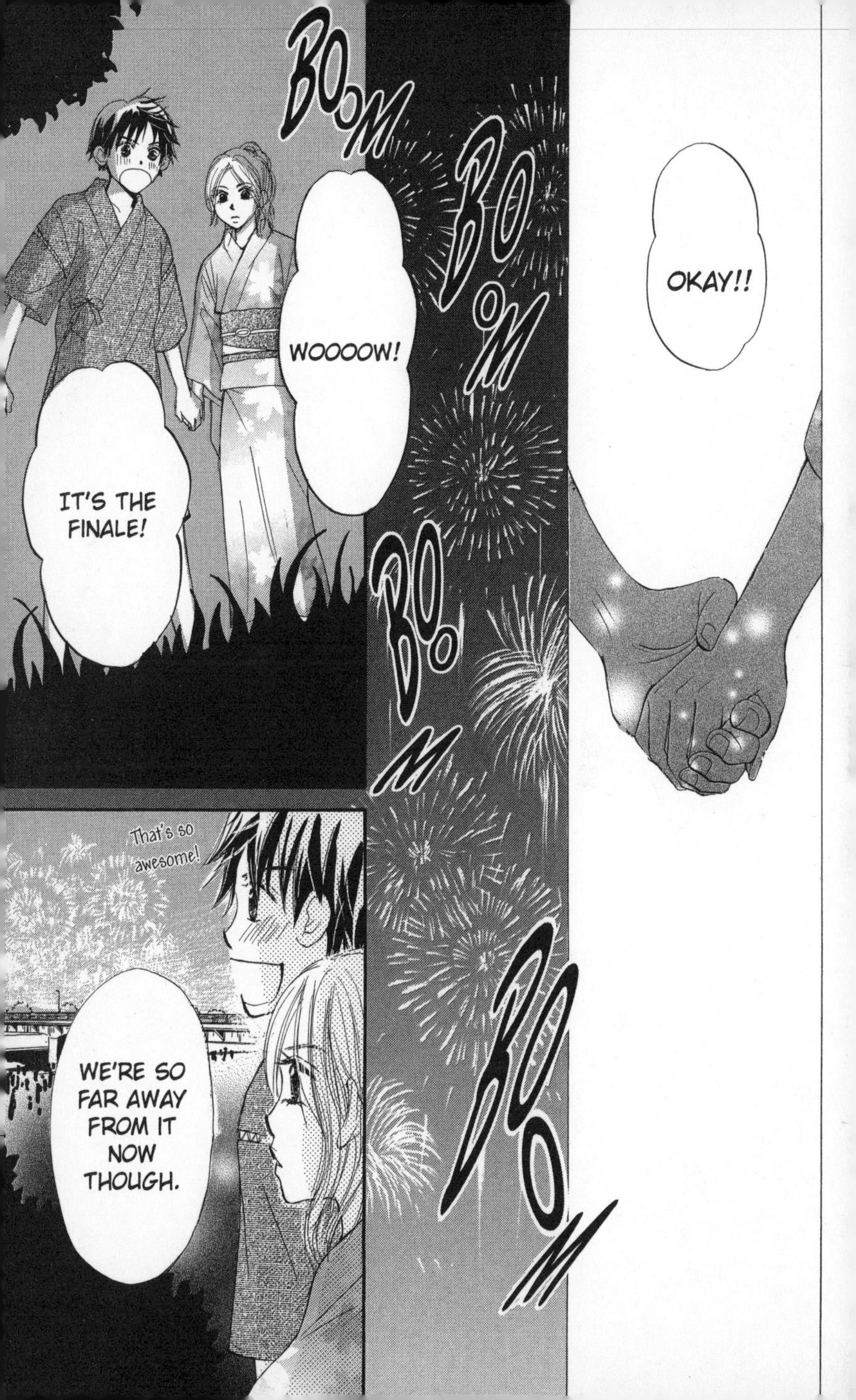
OKAY!!
BOOM
BOOM
BOOM
BOOOM
WOOOOW!
IT'S THE FINALE!
That's so awesome!
WE'RE SO FAR AWAY FROM IT NOW THOUGH.

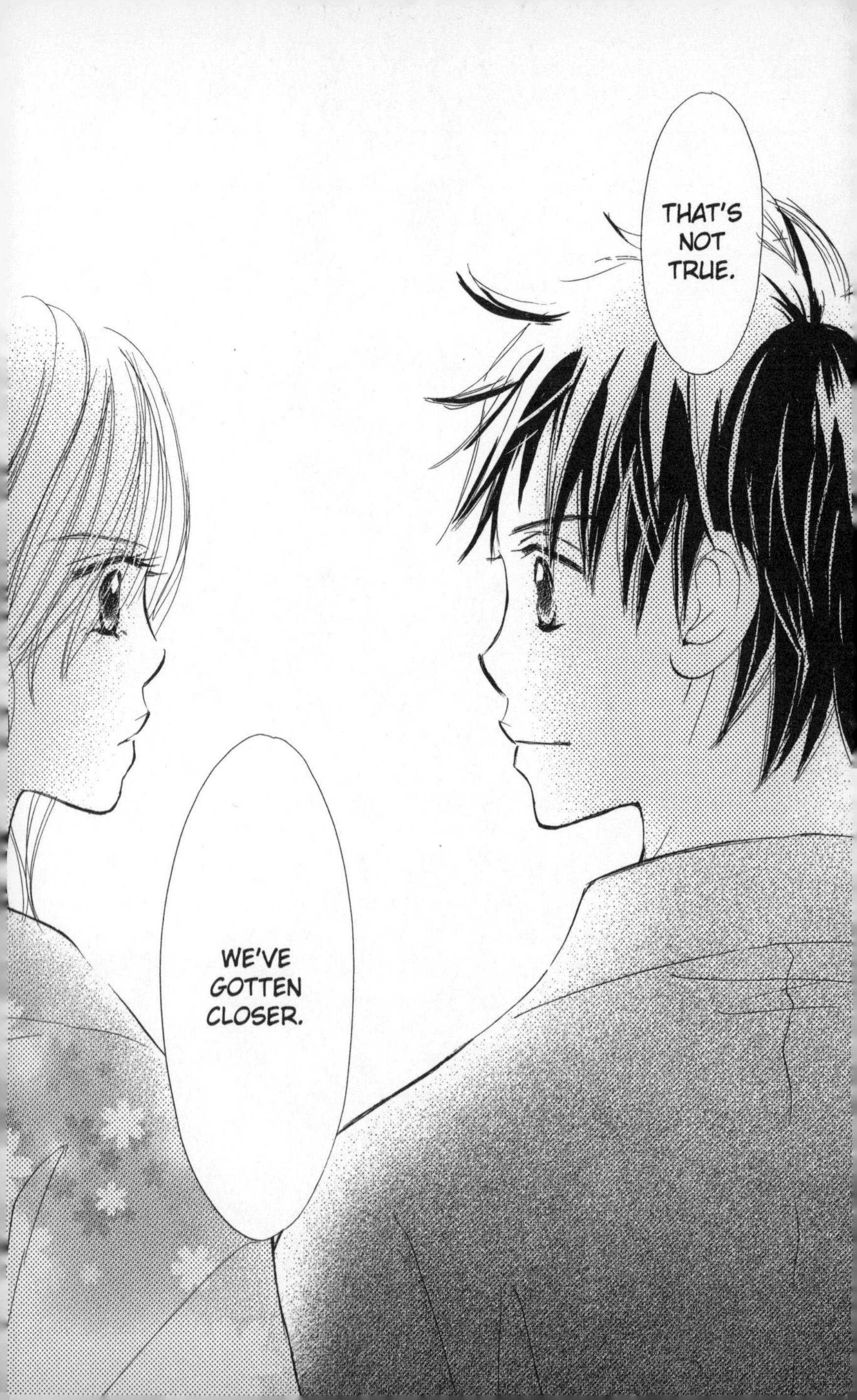
THAT'S NOT TRUE.
WE'VE GOTTEN CLOSER.

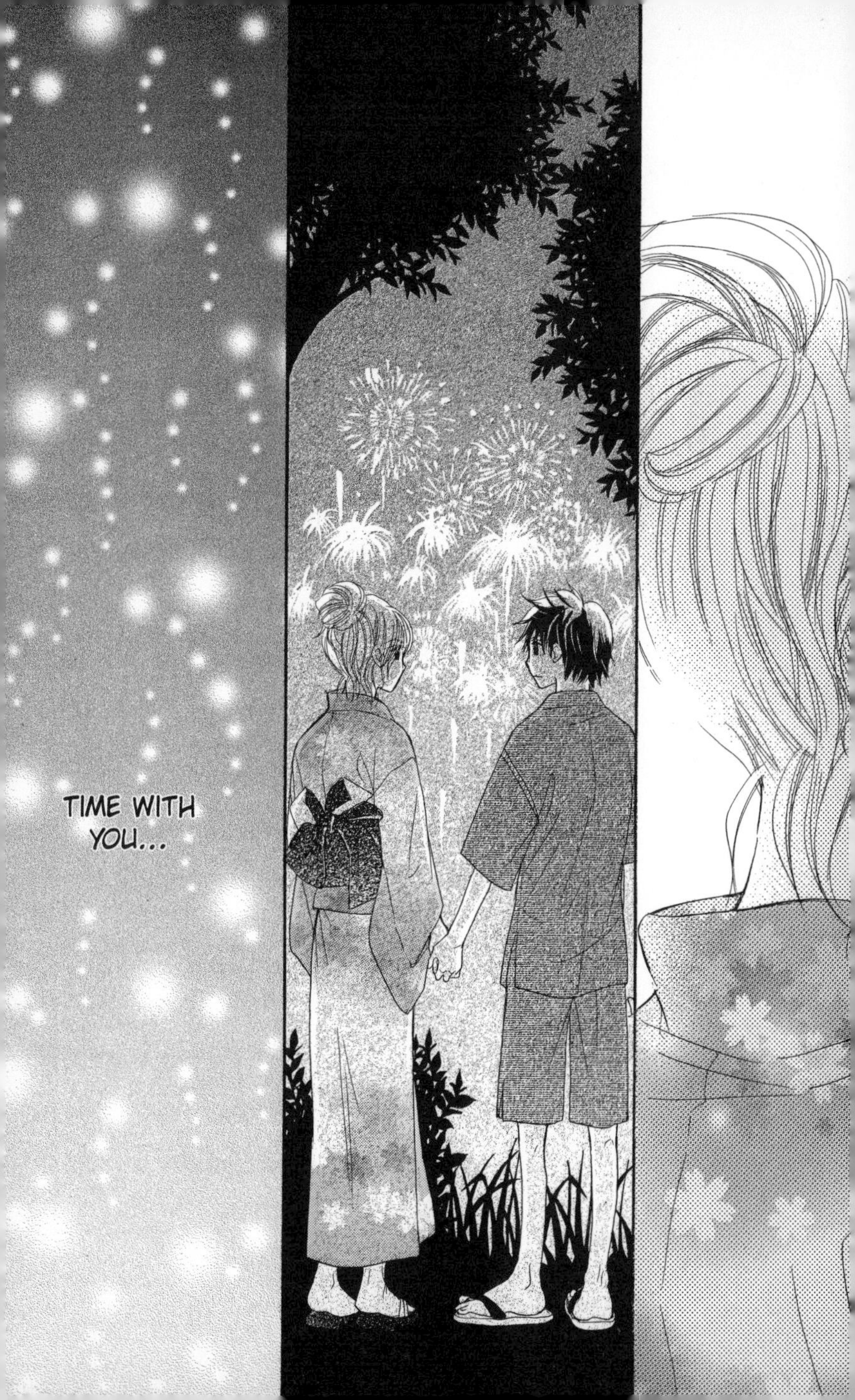
TIME WITH YOU...

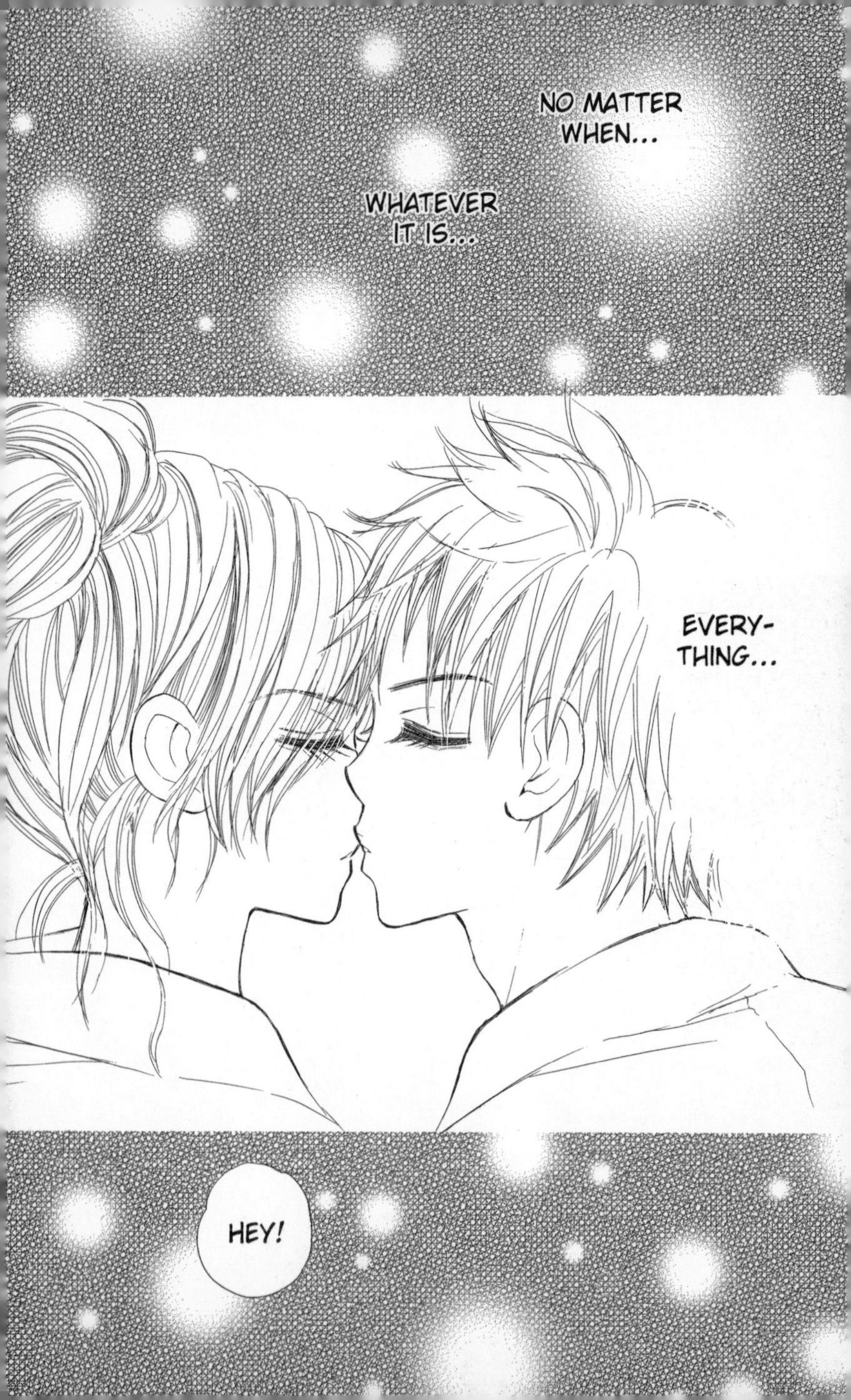
NO MATTER WHEN...
WHATEVER IT IS...
EVERY-THING...
HEY!

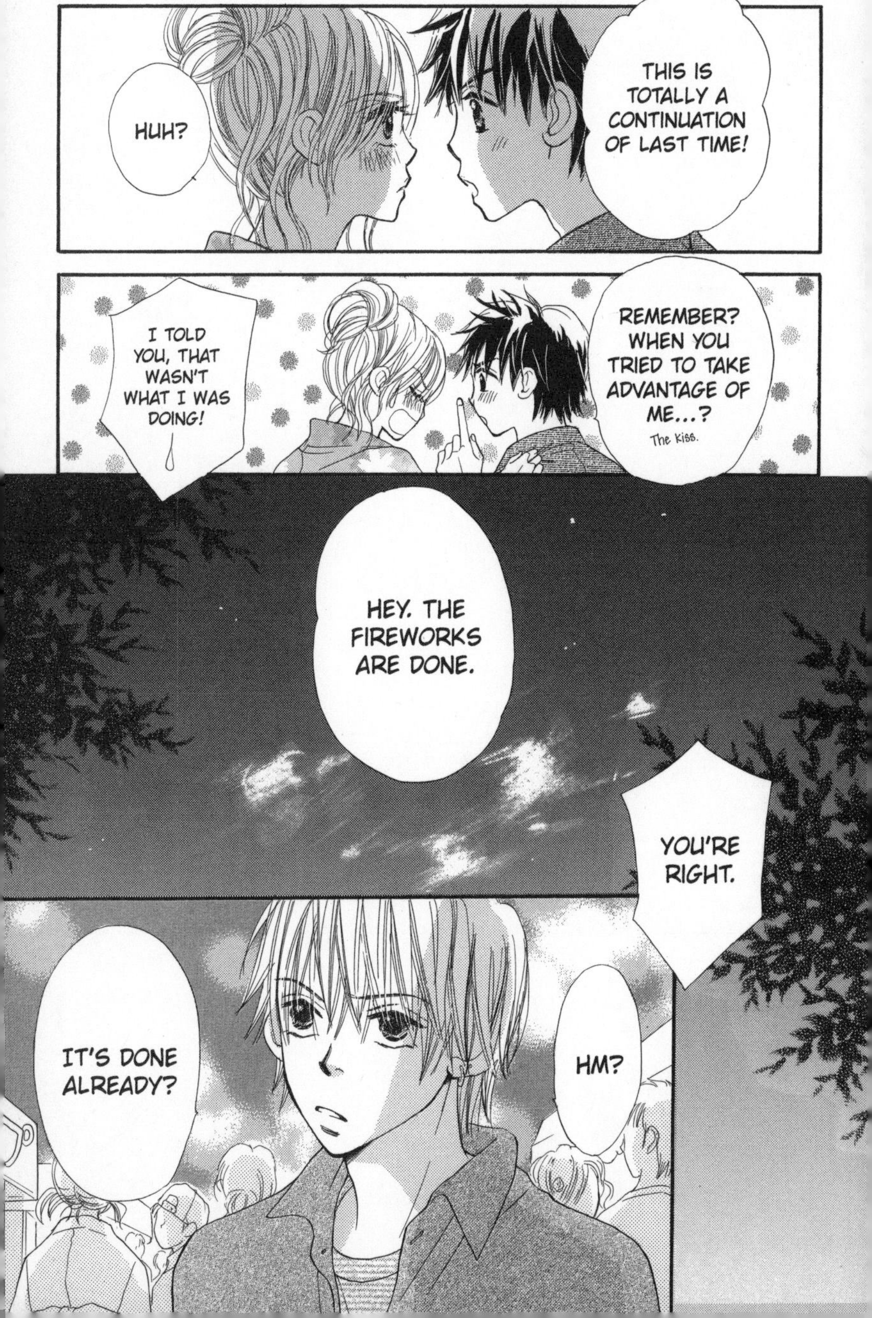
THIS IS TOTALLY A CONTINUATION OF LAST TIME!
HUH?
REMEMBER? WHEN YOU TRIED TO TAKE ADVANTAGE OF ME...?
The kiss.
I TOLD YOU, THAT WASN'T WHAT I WAS DOING!
HEY. THE FIREWORKS ARE DONE.
YOU'RE RIGHT.
HM?
IT'S DONE ALREADY?

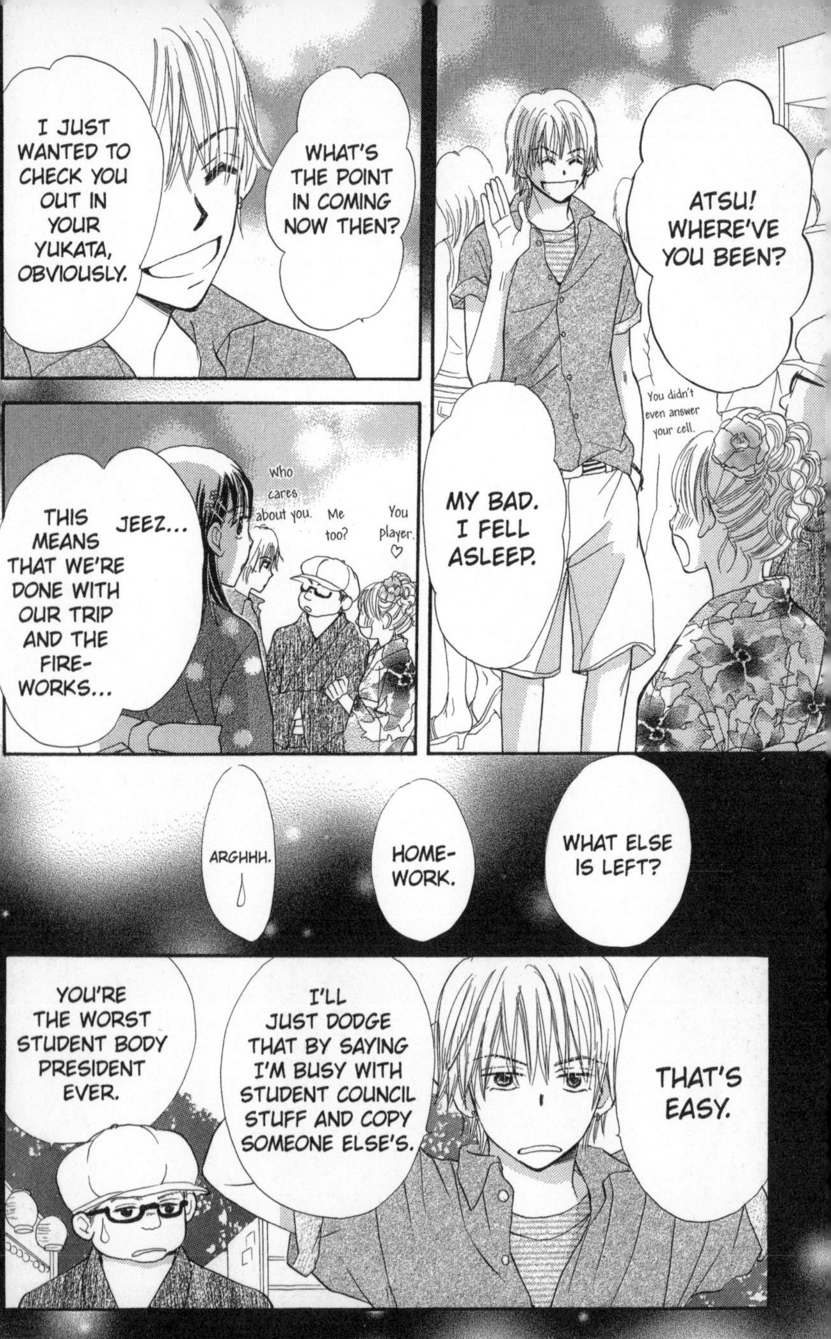
ATSU! WHERE'VE YOU BEEN?
You didn't even answer your cell.
MY BAD. I FELL ASLEEP.
WHAT'S THE POINT IN COMING NOW THEN?
I JUST WANTED TO CHECK YOU OUT IN YOUR YUKATA, OBVIOUSLY.
You player. ♡
Me too?
Who cares about you.
JEEZ...
THIS MEANS THAT WE'RE DONE WITH OUR TRIP AND THE FIRE-WORKS...
WHAT ELSE IS LEFT?
HOME-WORK.
ARGHHH.
THAT'S EASY.
I'LL JUST DODGE THAT BY SAYING I'M BUSY WITH STUDENT COUNCIL STUFF AND COPY SOMEONE ELSE'S.
YOU'RE THE WORST STUDENT BODY PRESIDENT EVER.

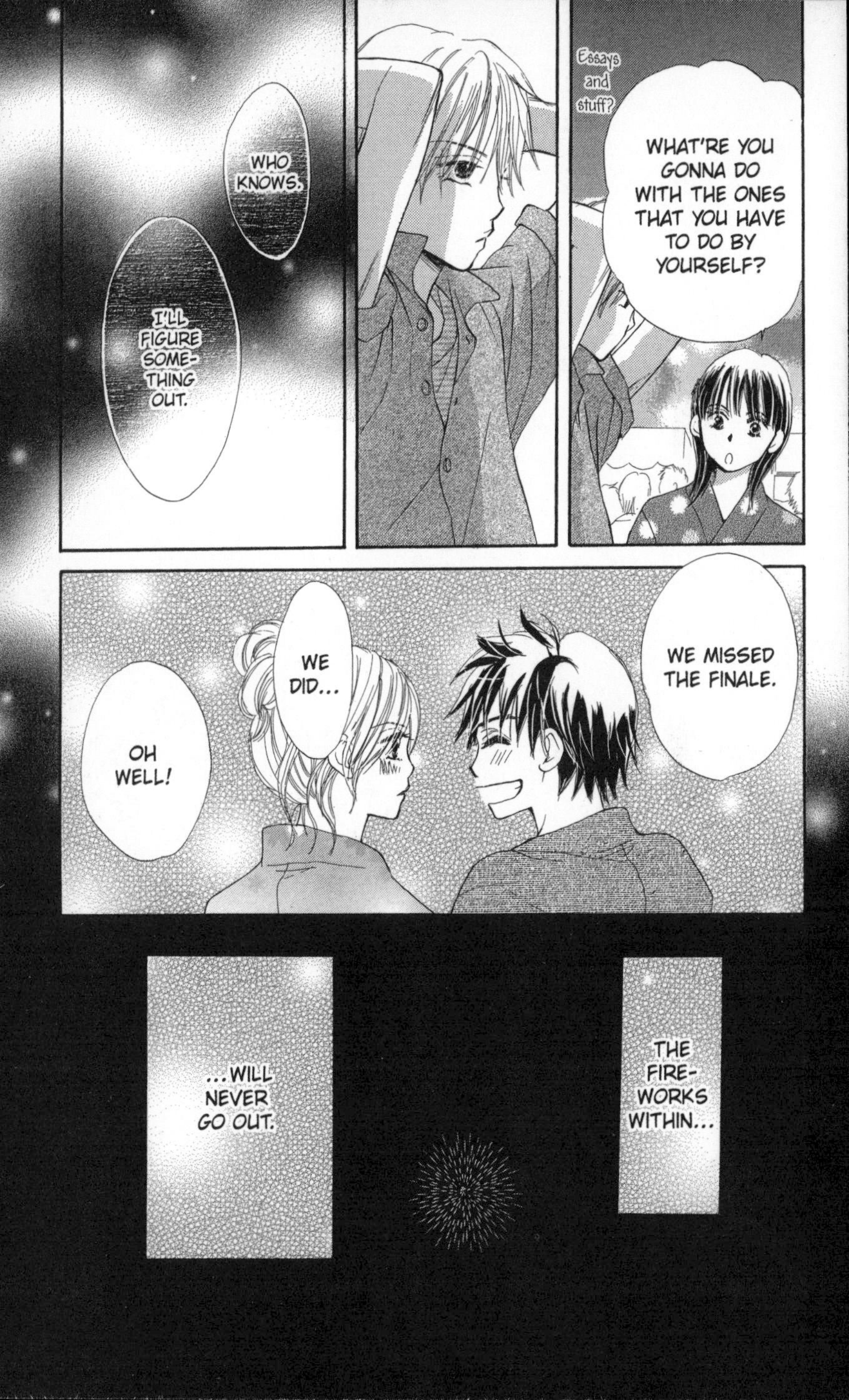
WHAT'RE YOU GONNA DO WITH THE ONES THAT YOU HAVE TO DO BY YOURSELF?
Essays and stuff?
WHO KNOWS.
I'LL FIGURE SOME-THING OUT.
WE MISSED THE FINALE.
WE DID...
OH WELL!
THE FIRE-WORKS WITHIN...
...WILL NEVER GO OUT.

FINISH YOUR HOMEWORK BEFORE THE NEW SEMESTER! (HOPEFULLY)

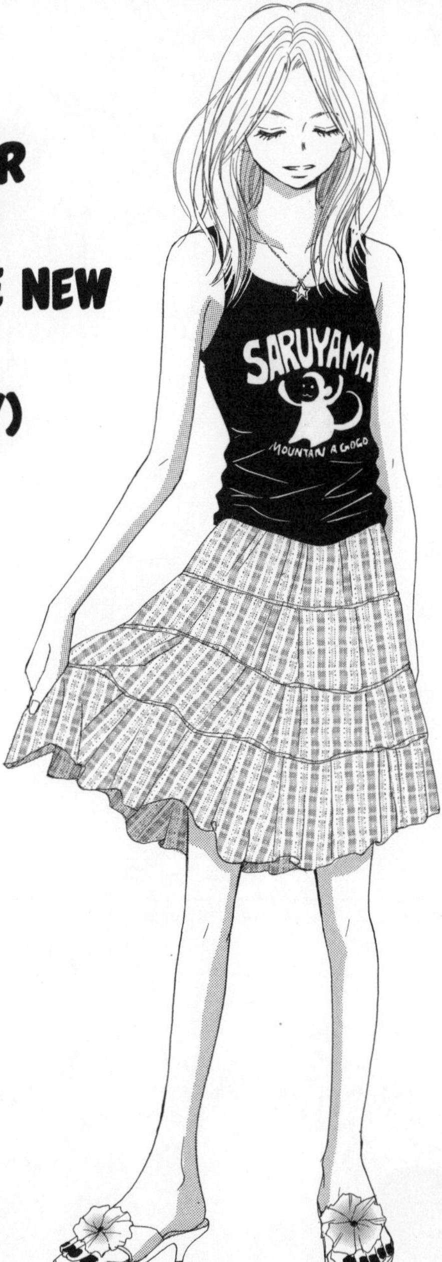
SARUYAMA
MOUNTAN A GOGO

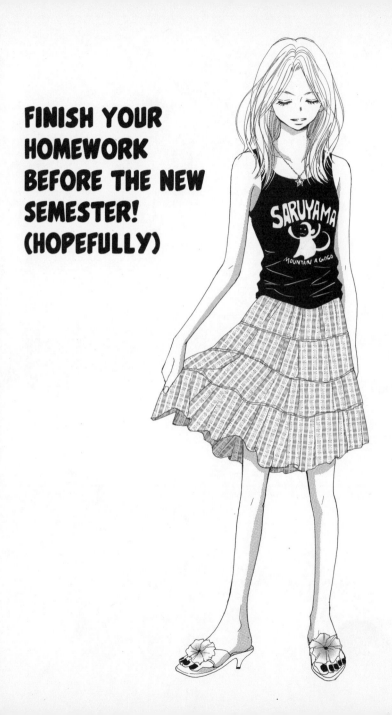

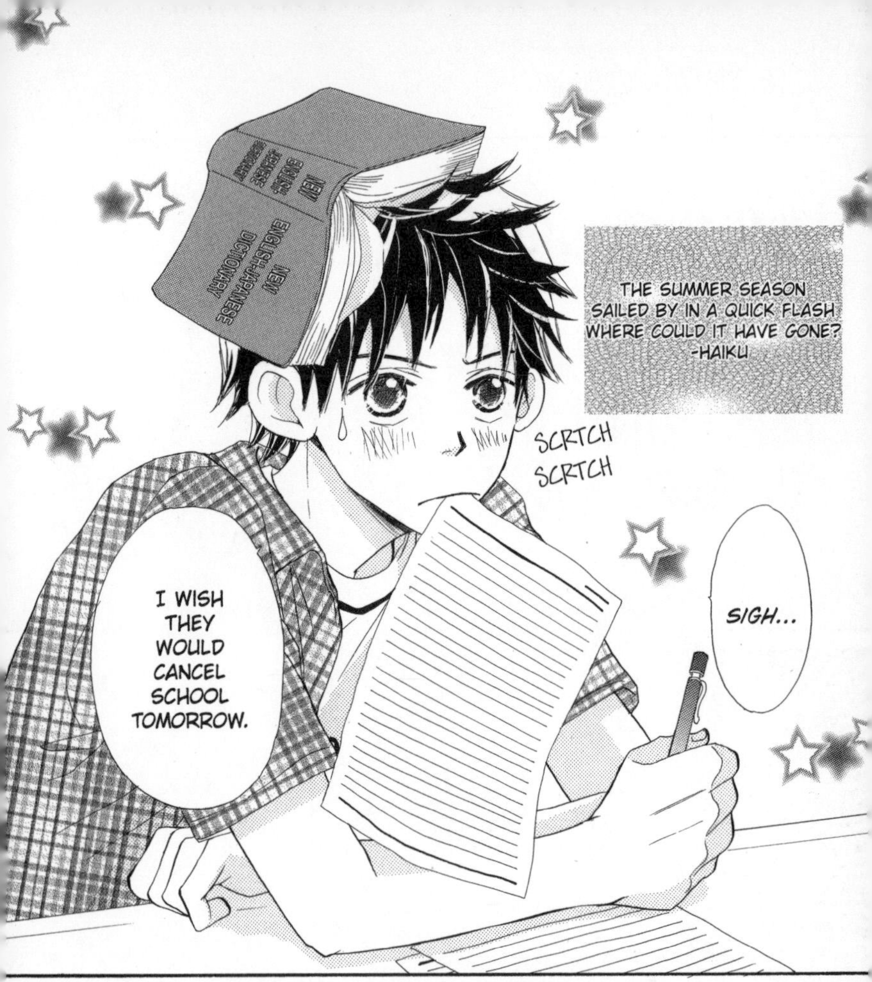
THE SUMMER SEASON SAILED BY IN A QUICK FLASH WHERE COULD IT HAVE GONE? -HAIKU
NEW ENGLISH-JAPANESE DICTIONARY
SCRTCH SCRTCH
SIGH...
I WISH THEY WOULD CANCEL SCHOOL TOMORROW.

Monkey High!

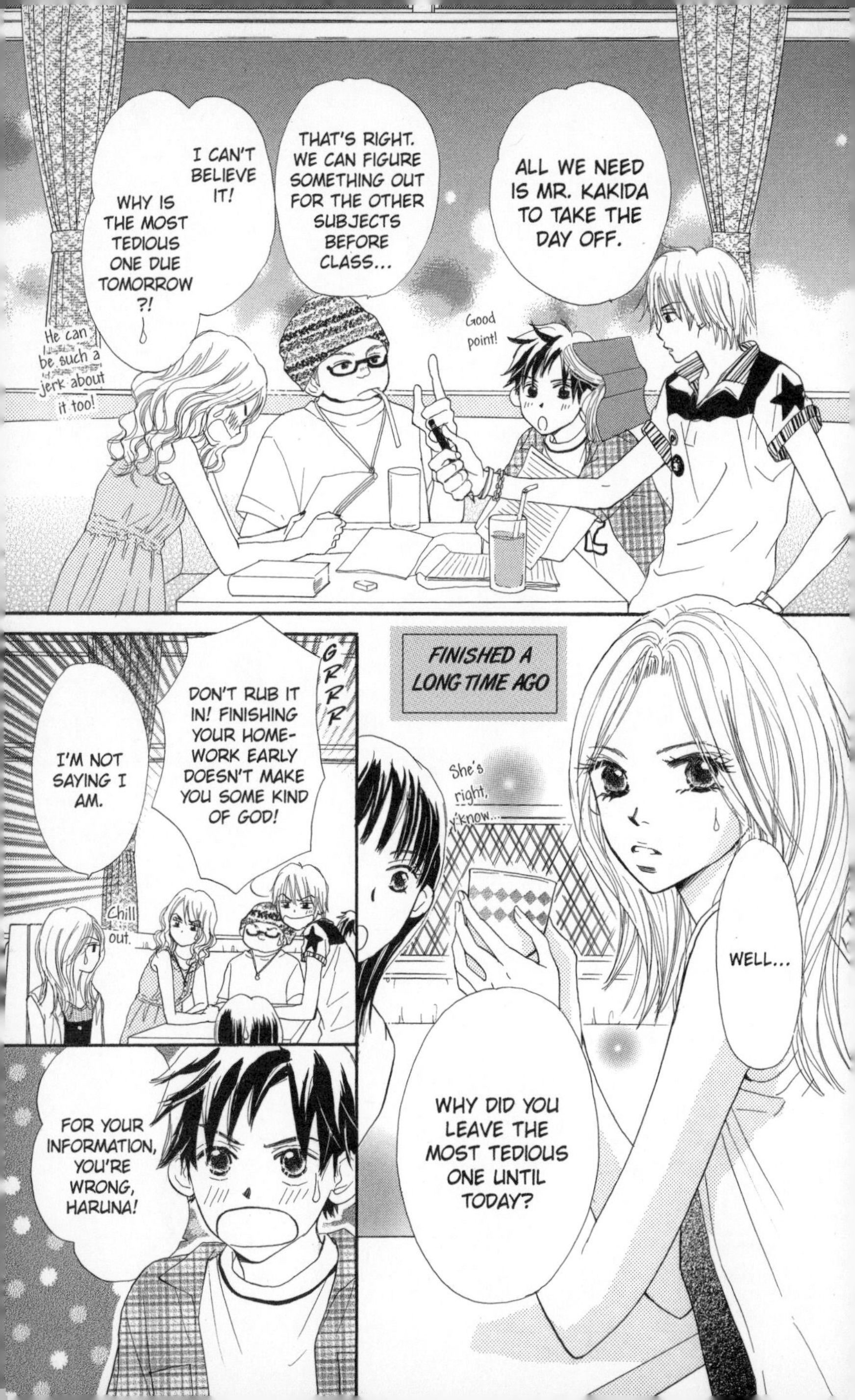
ALL WE NEED IS MR. KAKIDA TO TAKE THE DAY OFF.
Good point!
THAT'S RIGHT. WE CAN FIGURE SOMETHING OUT FOR THE OTHER SUBJECTS BEFORE CLASS...
I CAN'T BELIEVE IT!
WHY IS THE MOST TEDIOUS ONE DUE TOMORROW?!
He can be such a jerk about it too!
FINISHED A LONG TIME AGO
She's right, y'know...
WELL...
WHY DID YOU LEAVE THE MOST TEDIOUS ONE UNTIL TODAY?
GRRR
DON'T RUB IT IN! FINISHING YOUR HOME-WORK EARLY DOESN'T MAKE YOU SOME KIND OF GOD!
I'M NOT SAYING I AM.
Chill out.
FOR YOUR INFORMATION, YOU'RE WRONG, HARUNA!

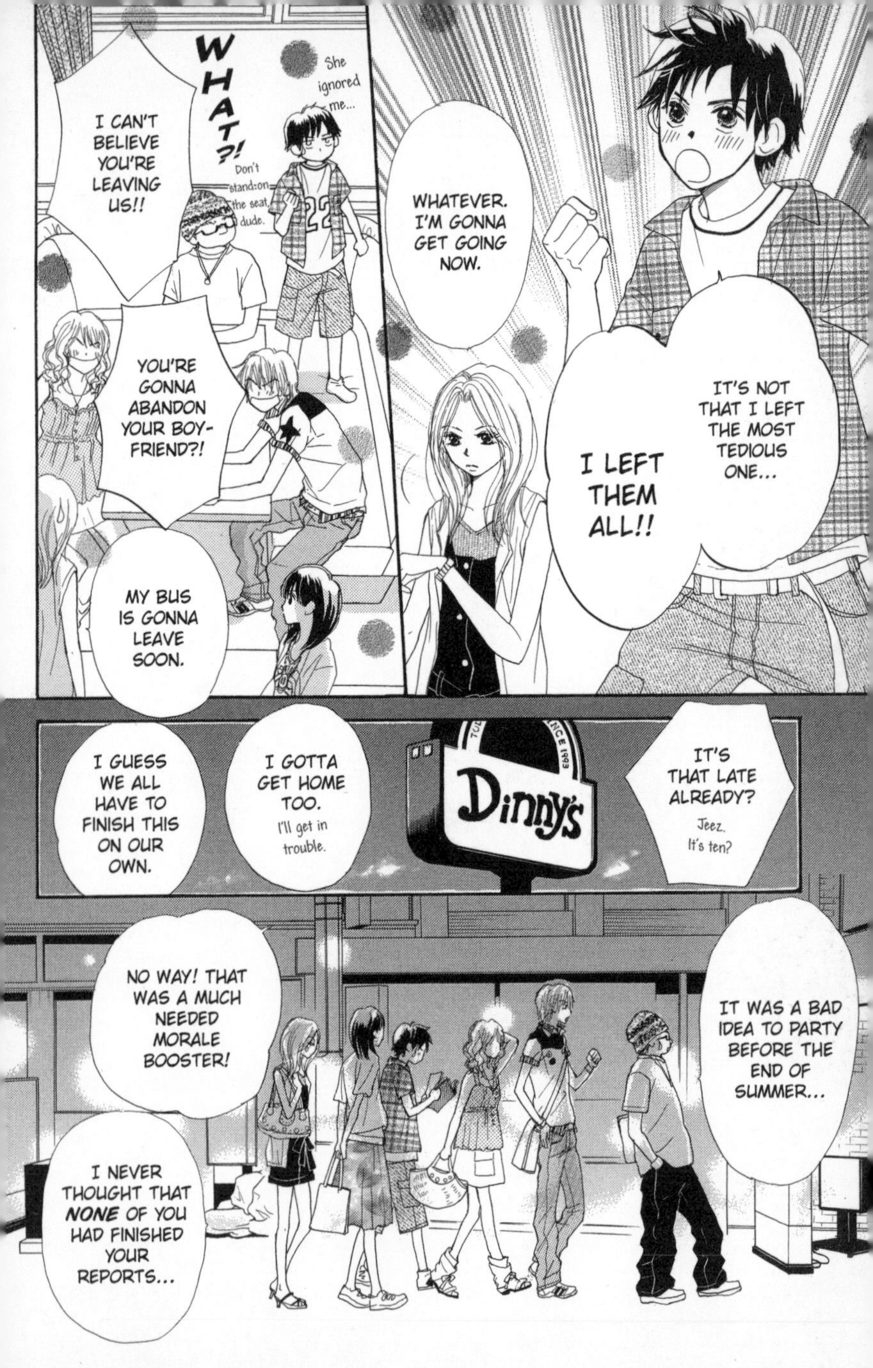
IT'S NOT THAT I LEFT THE MOST TEDIOUS ONE...
I LEFT THEM ALL!!
WHATEVER. I'M GONNA GET GOING NOW.
She ignored me...
WHAT?!
I CAN'T BELIEVE YOU'RE LEAVING US!!
Don't stand on the seat, dude.
YOU'RE GONNA ABANDON YOUR BOY-FRIEND?!
MY BUS IS GONNA LEAVE SOON.
IT'S THAT LATE ALREADY?
Jeez. It's ten?
Dinny's
I GOTTA GET HOME TOO.
I'll get in trouble.
I GUESS WE ALL HAVE TO FINISH THIS ON OUR OWN.
IT WAS A BAD IDEA TO PARTY BEFORE THE END OF SUMMER...
NO WAY! THAT WAS A MUCH NEEDED MORALE BOOSTER!
I NEVER THOUGHT THAT *NONE* OF YOU HAD FINISHED YOUR REPORTS...

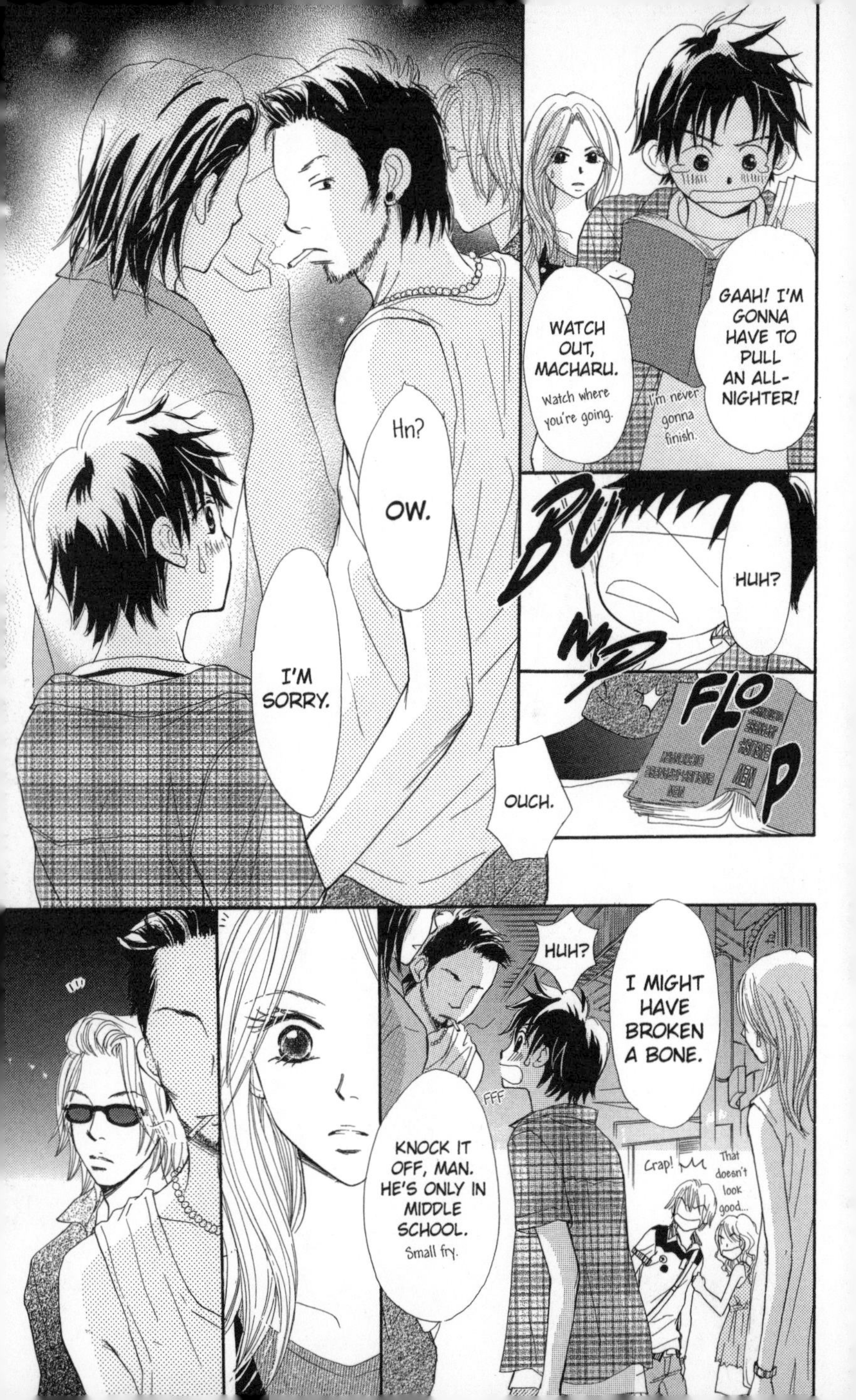
GAAH! I'M GONNA HAVE TO PULL AN ALL-NIGHTER!
I'm never gonna finish.
WATCH OUT, MACHARU.
Watch where you're going.
BUMP
HUH?
FLOP
OUCH.
Hn?
OW.
I'M SORRY.
HUH?
I MIGHT HAVE BROKEN A BONE.
Crap!
That doesn't look good...
FFF
KNOCK IT OFF, MAN. HE'S ONLY IN MIDDLE SCHOOL.
Small fry.

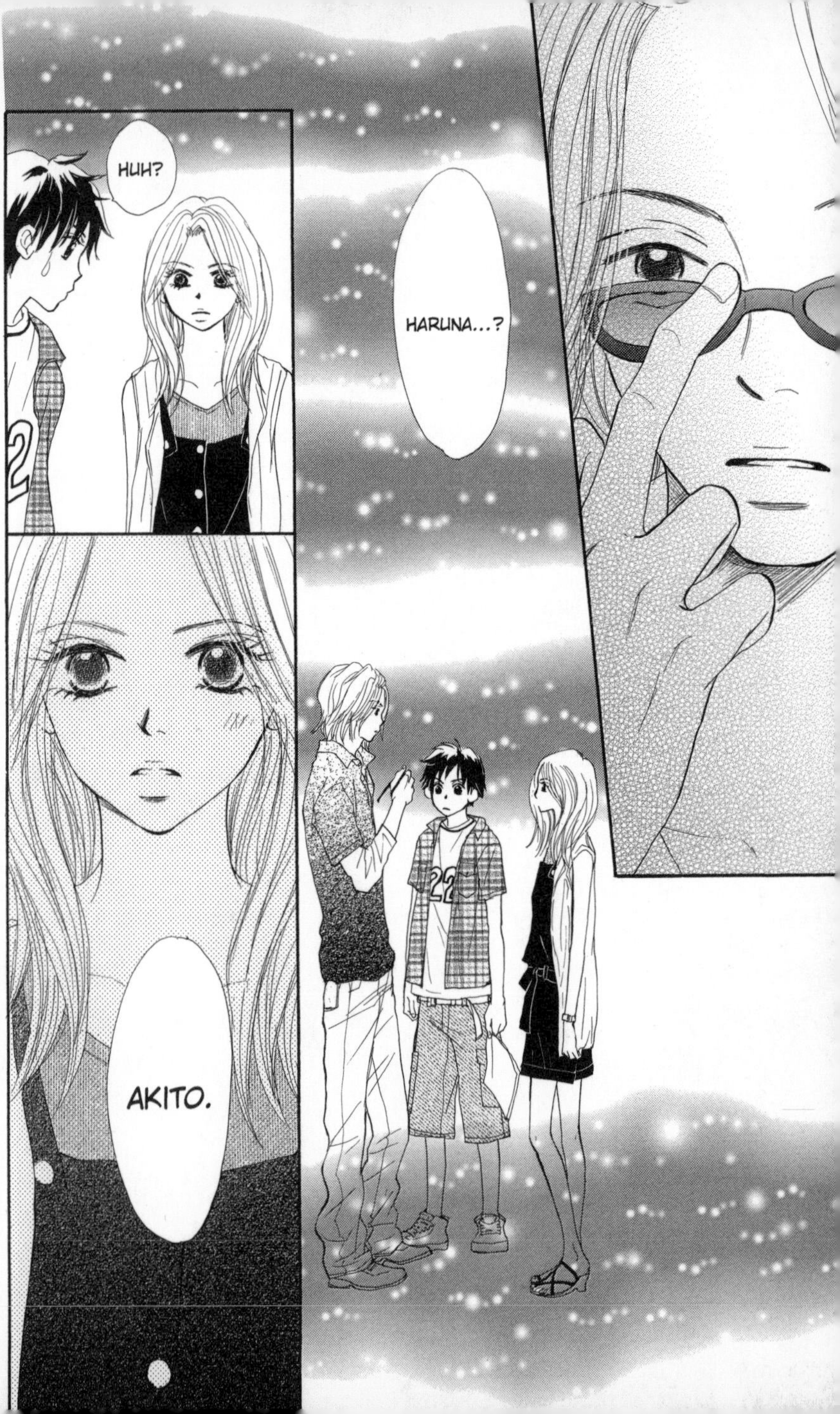
HARUNA...?
HUH?
AKITO.

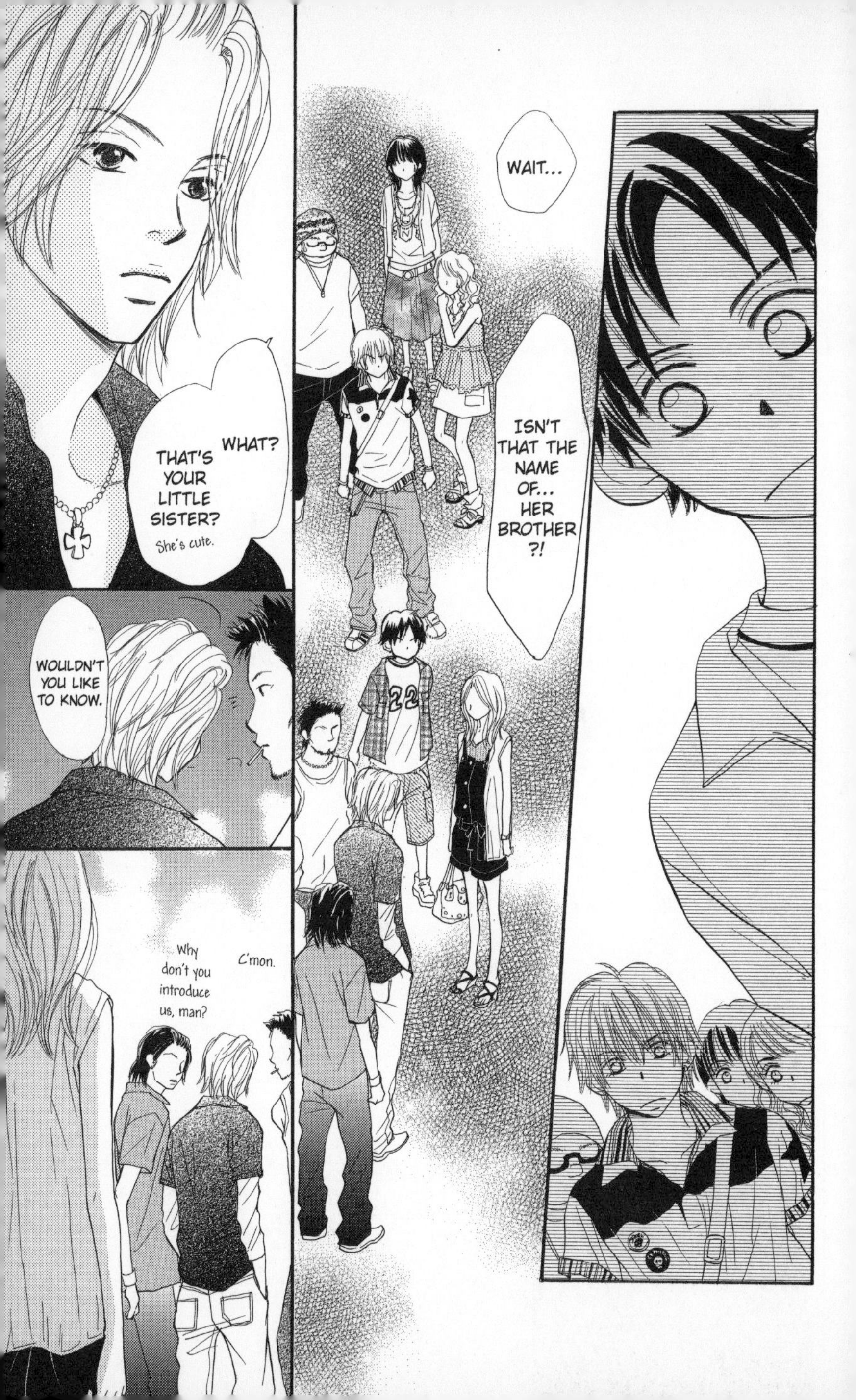
WAIT...
ISN'T THAT THE NAME OF... HER BROTHER?!
WHAT?
THAT'S YOUR LITTLE SISTER?
She's cute.
WOULDN'T YOU LIKE TO KNOW.
C'mon.
Why don't you introduce us, man?

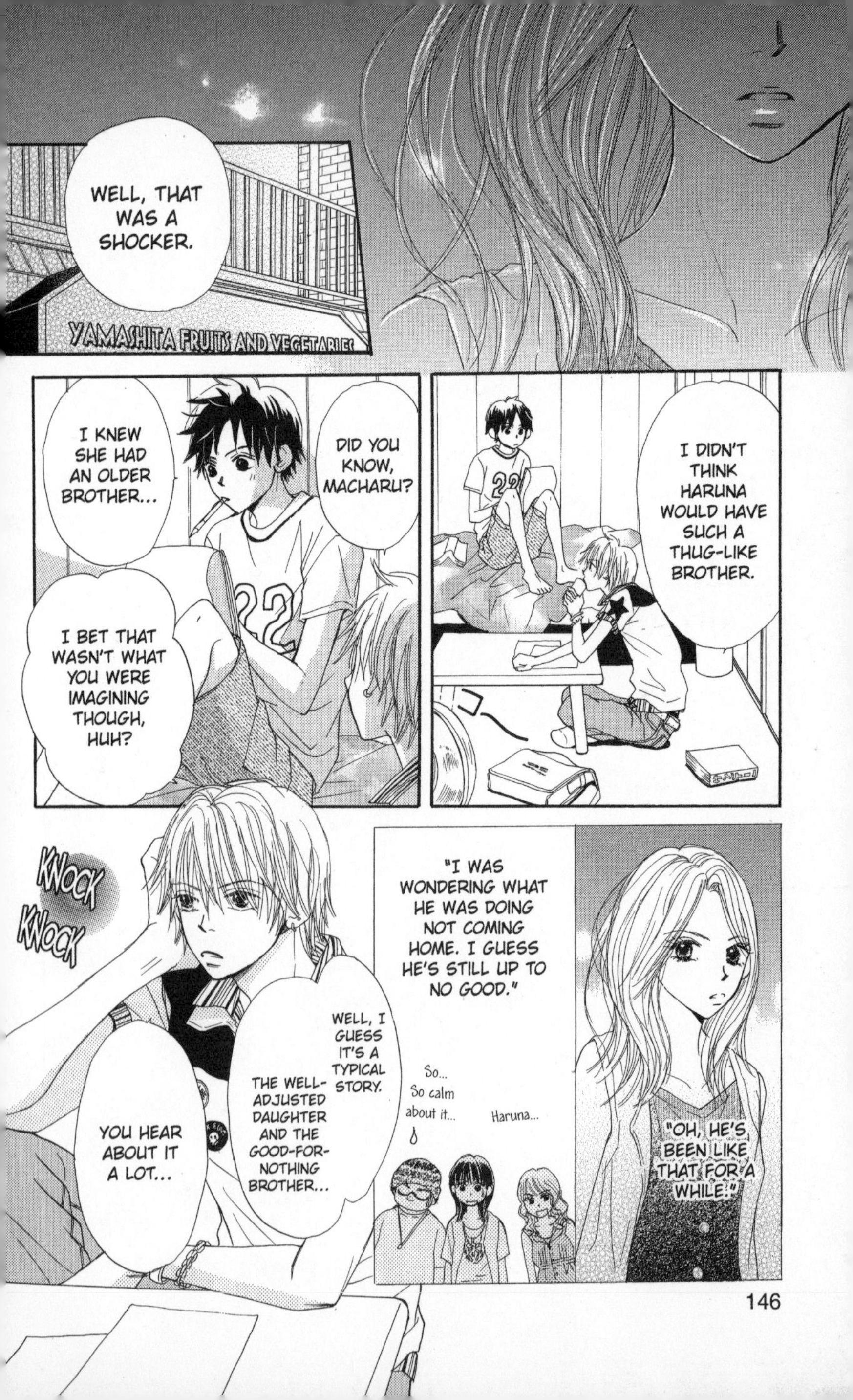
WELL, THAT WAS A SHOCKER.
YAMASHITA FRUITS AND VEGETABLES
I DIDN'T THINK HARUNA WOULD HAVE SUCH A THUG-LIKE BROTHER.
DID YOU KNOW, MACHARU?
I KNEW SHE HAD AN OLDER BROTHER...
I BET THAT WASN'T WHAT YOU WERE IMAGINING THOUGH, HUH?
"I WAS WONDERING WHAT HE WAS DOING NOT COMING HOME. I GUESS HE'S STILL UP TO NO GOOD."
"OH, HE'S BEEN LIKE THAT FOR A WHILE."
Haruna...
So... So calm about it...
KNOCK KNOCK
WELL, I GUESS IT'S A TYPICAL STORY.
THE WELL-ADJUSTED DAUGHTER AND THE GOOD-FOR-NOTHING BROTHER...
YOU HEAR ABOUT IT A LOT...

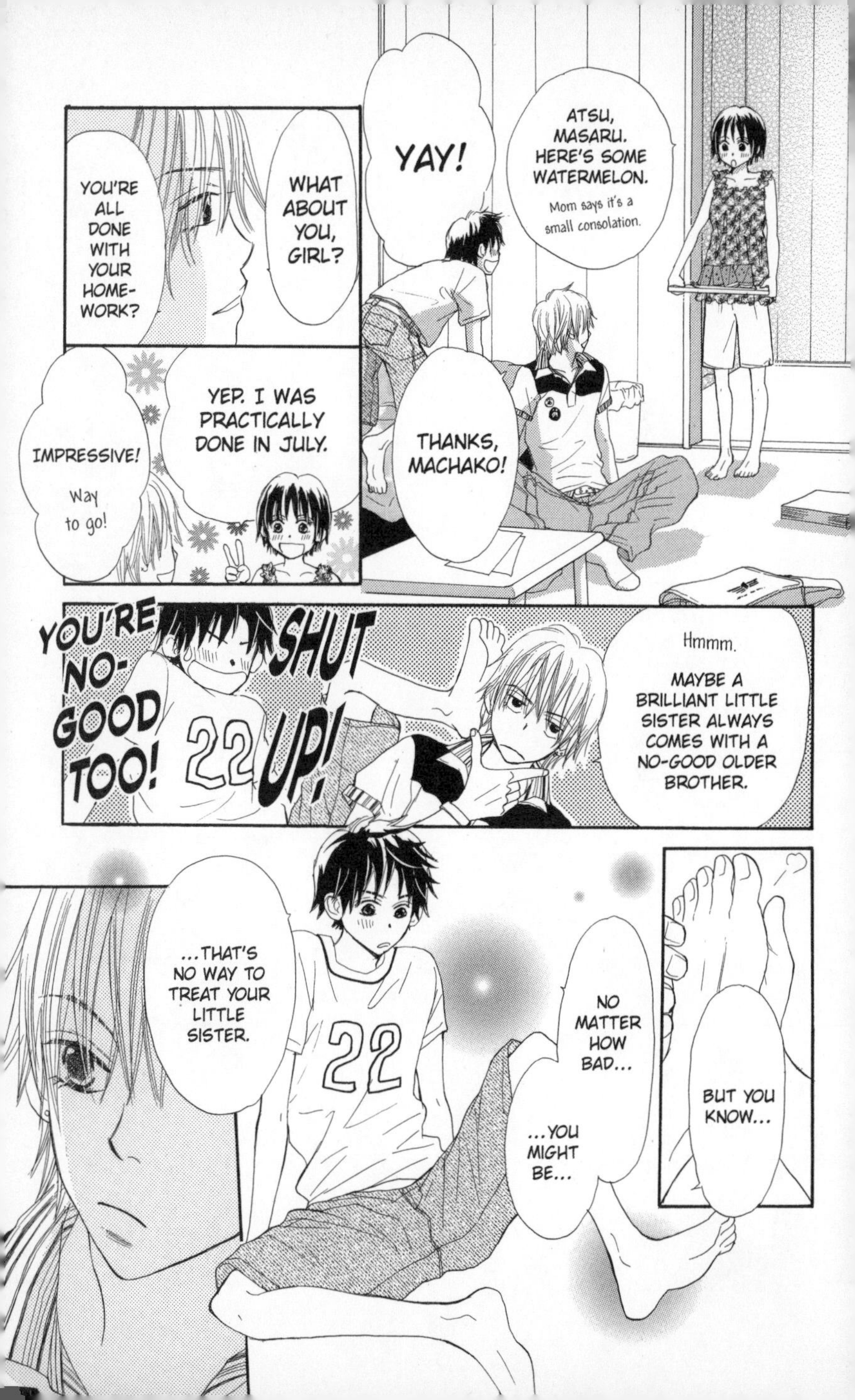
ATSU, MASARU. HERE'S SOME WATERMELON.
Mom says it's a small consolation.
YAY!
THANKS, MACHAKO!
WHAT ABOUT YOU, GIRL?
YOU'RE ALL DONE WITH YOUR HOME-WORK?
YEP. I WAS PRACTICALLY DONE IN JULY.
IMPRESSIVE!
Way to go!
Hmmm.
MAYBE A BRILLIANT LITTLE SISTER ALWAYS COMES WITH A NO-GOOD OLDER BROTHER.
SHUT UP!
YOU'RE NO-GOOD TOO!
22
BUT YOU KNOW...
NO MATTER HOW BAD...
...YOU MIGHT BE...
...THAT'S NO WAY TO TREAT YOUR LITTLE SISTER.
22

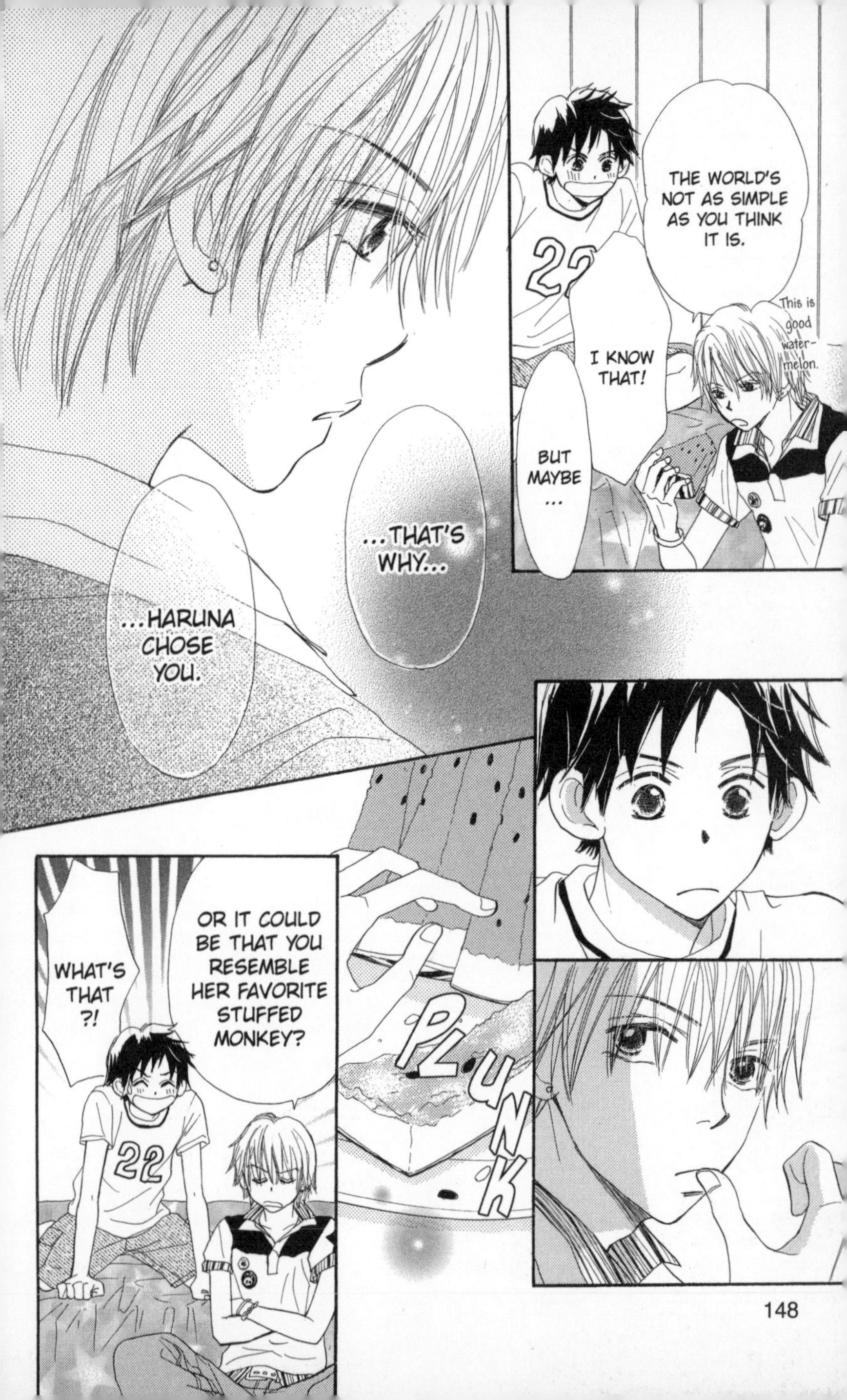
THE WORLD'S NOT AS SIMPLE AS YOU THINK IT IS.
This is good water-melon.
I KNOW THAT!
BUT MAYBE ...
...THAT'S WHY...
...HARUNA CHOSE YOU.
PLUNK
OR IT COULD BE THAT YOU RESEMBLE HER FAVORITE STUFFED MONKEY?
WHAT'S THAT ?!

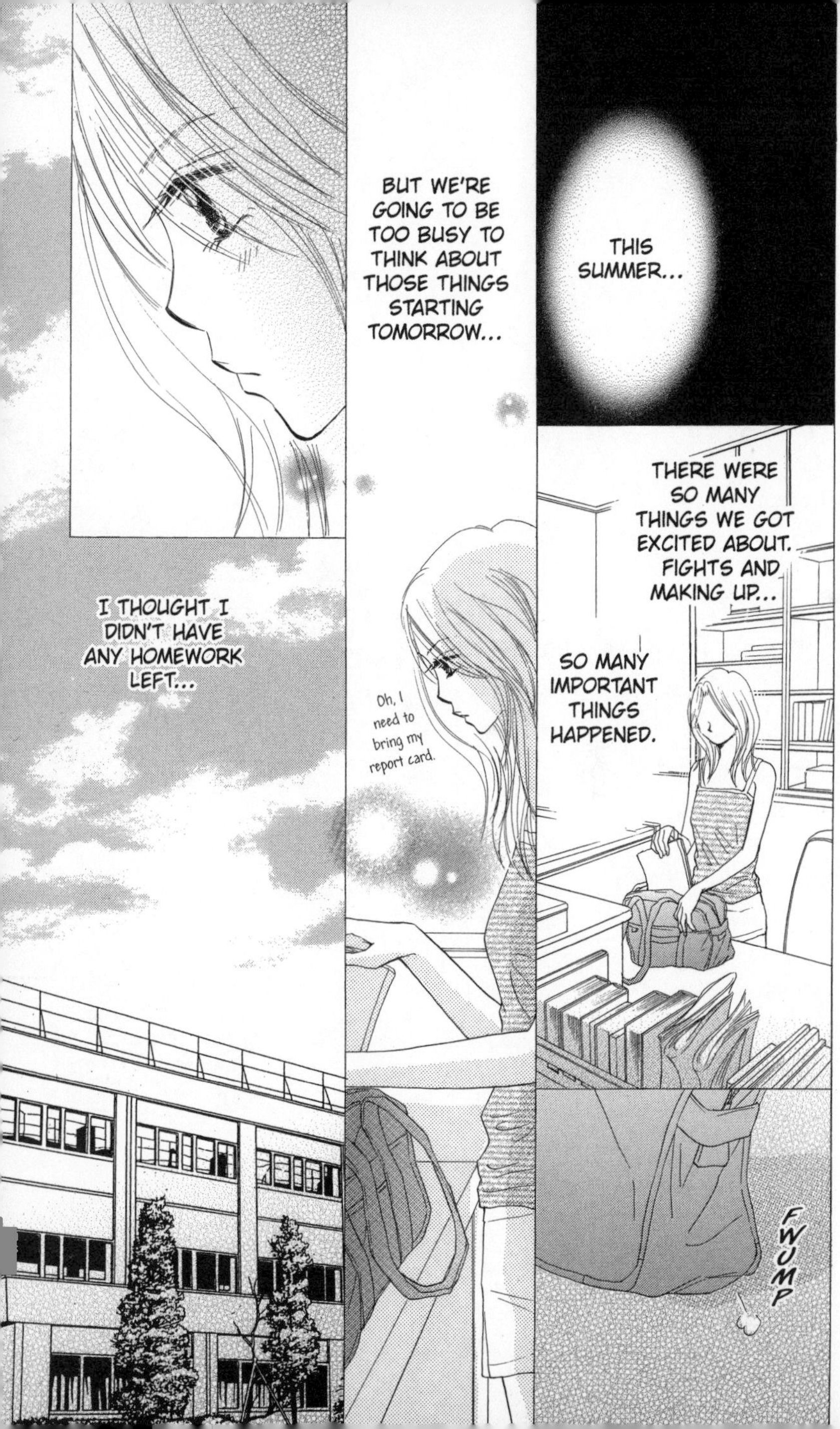
THIS SUMMER...
THERE WERE SO MANY THINGS WE GOT EXCITED ABOUT. FIGHTS AND MAKING UP...
SO MANY IMPORTANT THINGS HAPPENED.
FWUMP
BUT WE'RE GOING TO BE TOO BUSY TO THINK ABOUT THOSE THINGS STARTING TOMORROW...
Oh, I need to bring my report card.
I THOUGHT I DIDN'T HAVE ANY HOMEWORK LEFT...

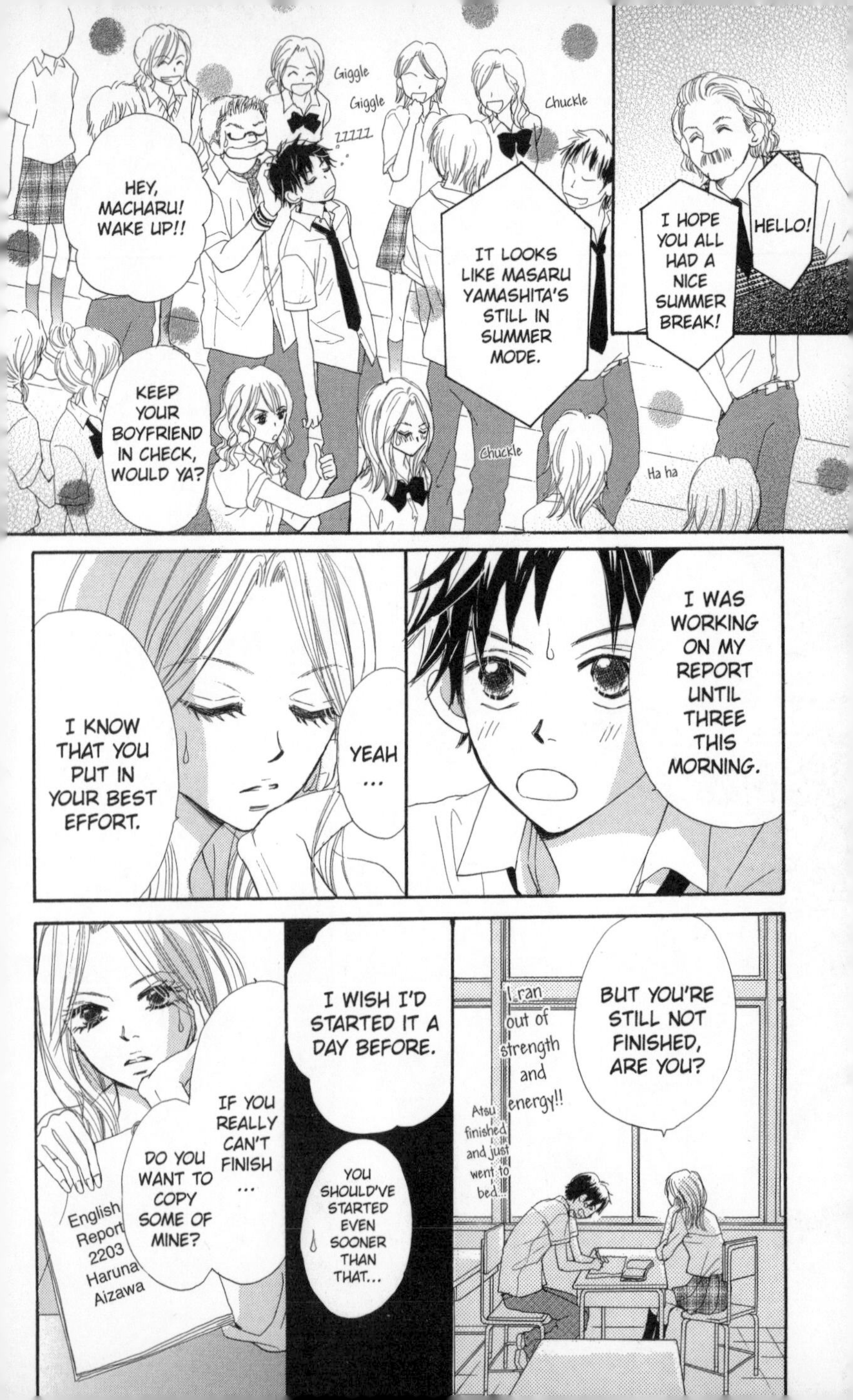
HELLO!
I HOPE YOU ALL HAD A NICE SUMMER BREAK!
IT LOOKS LIKE MASARU YAMASHITA'S STILL IN SUMMER MODE.
Chuckle
Giggle
Giggle
ZZZZZ
HEY, MACHARU! WAKE UP!!
Ha ha
Chuckle
KEEP YOUR BOYFRIEND IN CHECK, WOULD YA?
I WAS WORKING ON MY REPORT UNTIL THREE THIS MORNING.
YEAH ...
I KNOW THAT YOU PUT IN YOUR BEST EFFORT.
BUT YOU'RE STILL NOT FINISHED, ARE YOU?
I ran out of strength and energy!!
Atsu finished and just went to bed...
I WISH I'D STARTED IT A DAY BEFORE.
YOU SHOULD'VE STARTED EVEN SOONER THAN THAT...
IF YOU REALLY CAN'T FINISH ...
DO YOU WANT TO COPY SOME OF MINE?
English Report 2203 Haruna Aizawa

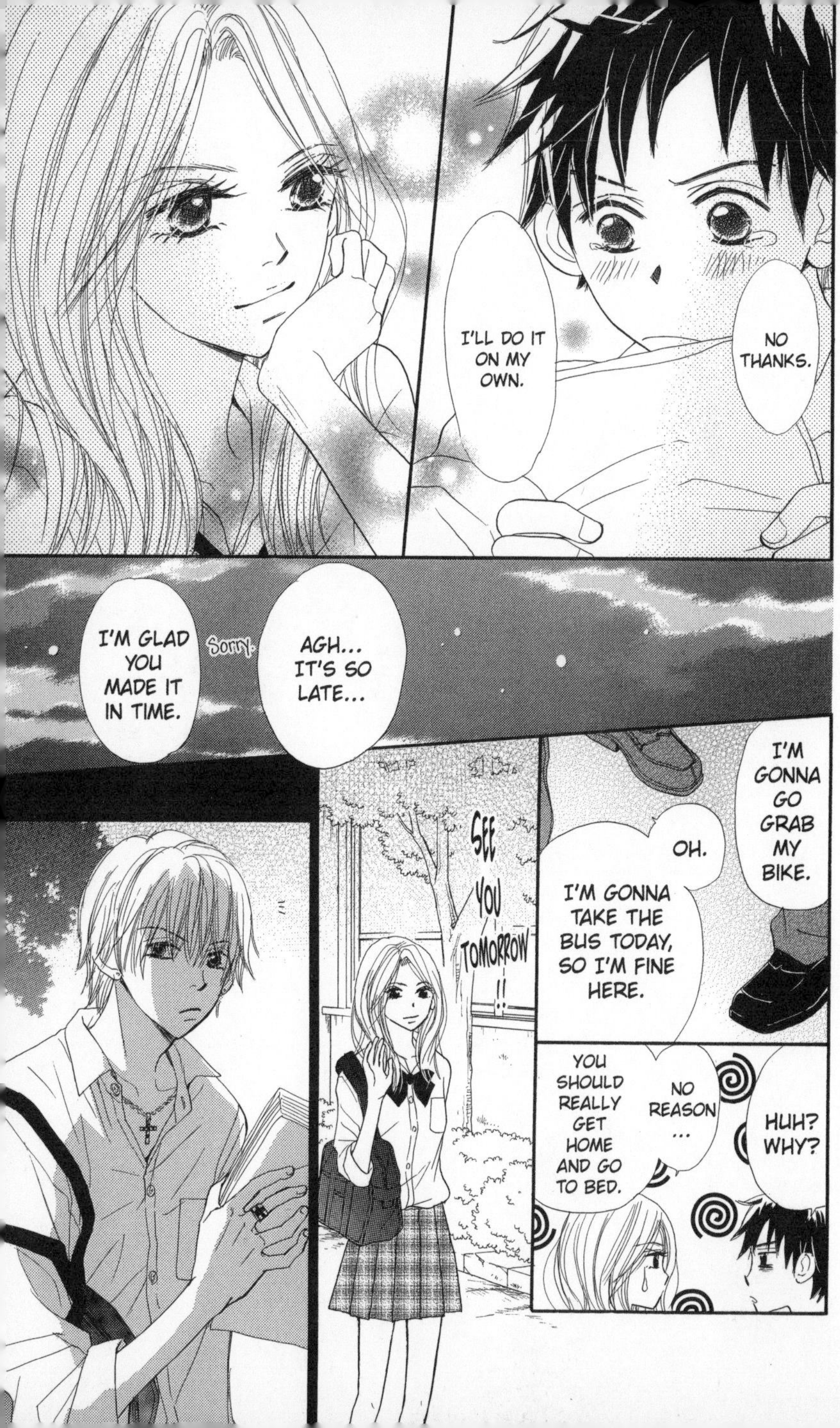
NO THANKS.
I'LL DO IT ON MY OWN.
AGH... IT'S SO LATE...
Sorry.
I'M GLAD YOU MADE IT IN TIME.
I'M GONNA GO GRAB MY BIKE.
OH.
I'M GONNA TAKE THE BUS TODAY, SO I'M FINE HERE.
HUH? WHY?
NO REASON...
YOU SHOULD REALLY GET HOME AND GO TO BED.
SEE YOU TOMORROW!!

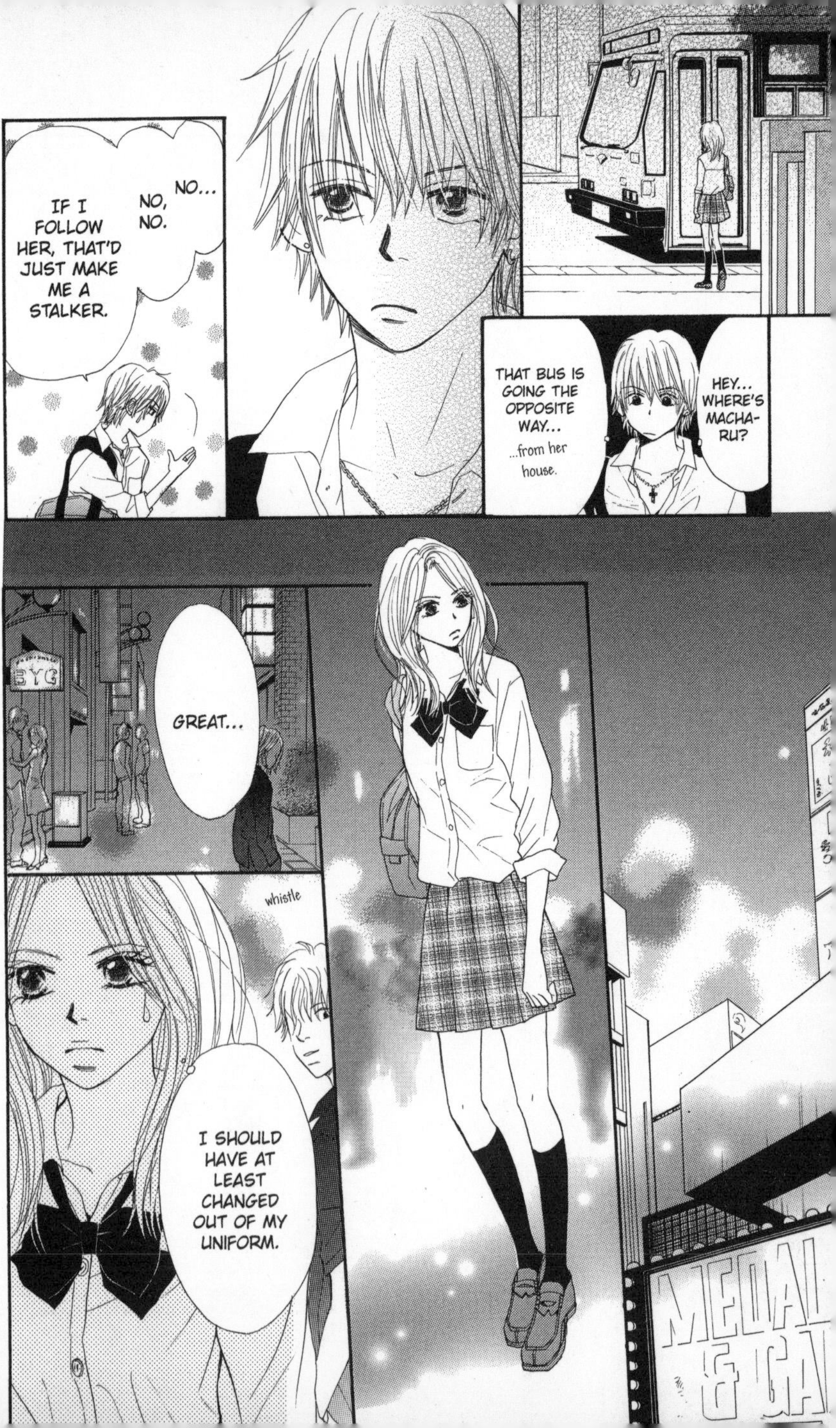
HEY... WHERE'S MACHA-RU?
THAT BUS IS GOING THE OPPOSITE WAY...
...from her house.
NO...
NO, NO.
IF I FOLLOW HER, THAT'D JUST MAKE ME A STALKER.
GREAT...
whistle
I SHOULD HAVE AT LEAST CHANGED OUT OF MY UNIFORM.

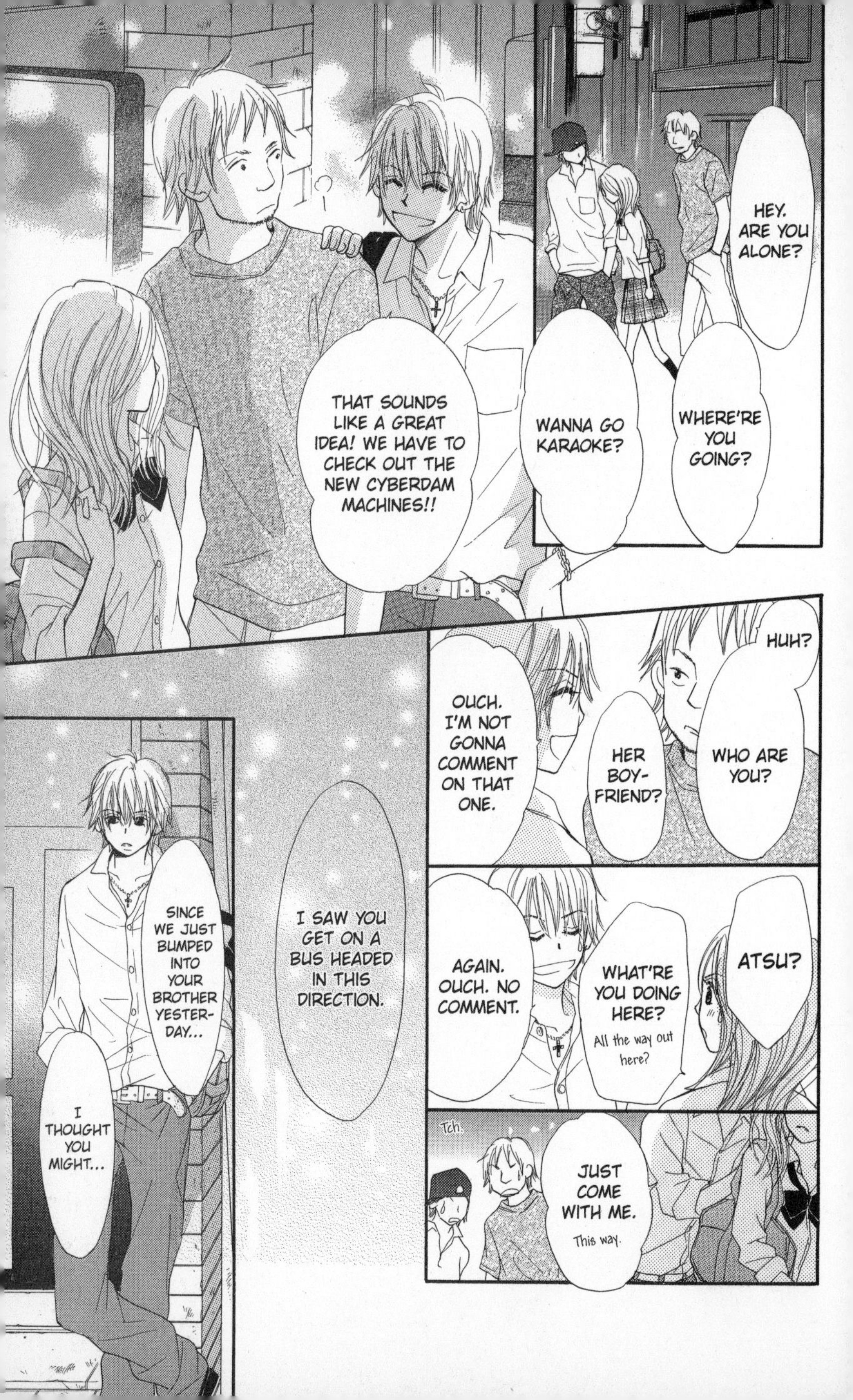
HEY. ARE YOU ALONE?
WHERE'RE YOU GOING?
WANNA GO KARAOKE?
THAT SOUNDS LIKE A GREAT IDEA! WE HAVE TO CHECK OUT THE NEW CYBERDAM MACHINES!!
HUH?
WHO ARE YOU?
HER BOY-FRIEND?
OUCH. I'M NOT GONNA COMMENT ON THAT ONE.
ATSU?
WHAT'RE YOU DOING HERE? All the way out here?
AGAIN. OUCH. NO COMMENT.
JUST COME WITH ME. This way.
Tch.
I SAW YOU GET ON A BUS HEADED IN THIS DIRECTION.
SINCE WE JUST BUMPED INTO YOUR BROTHER YESTER-DAY...
I THOUGHT YOU MIGHT...

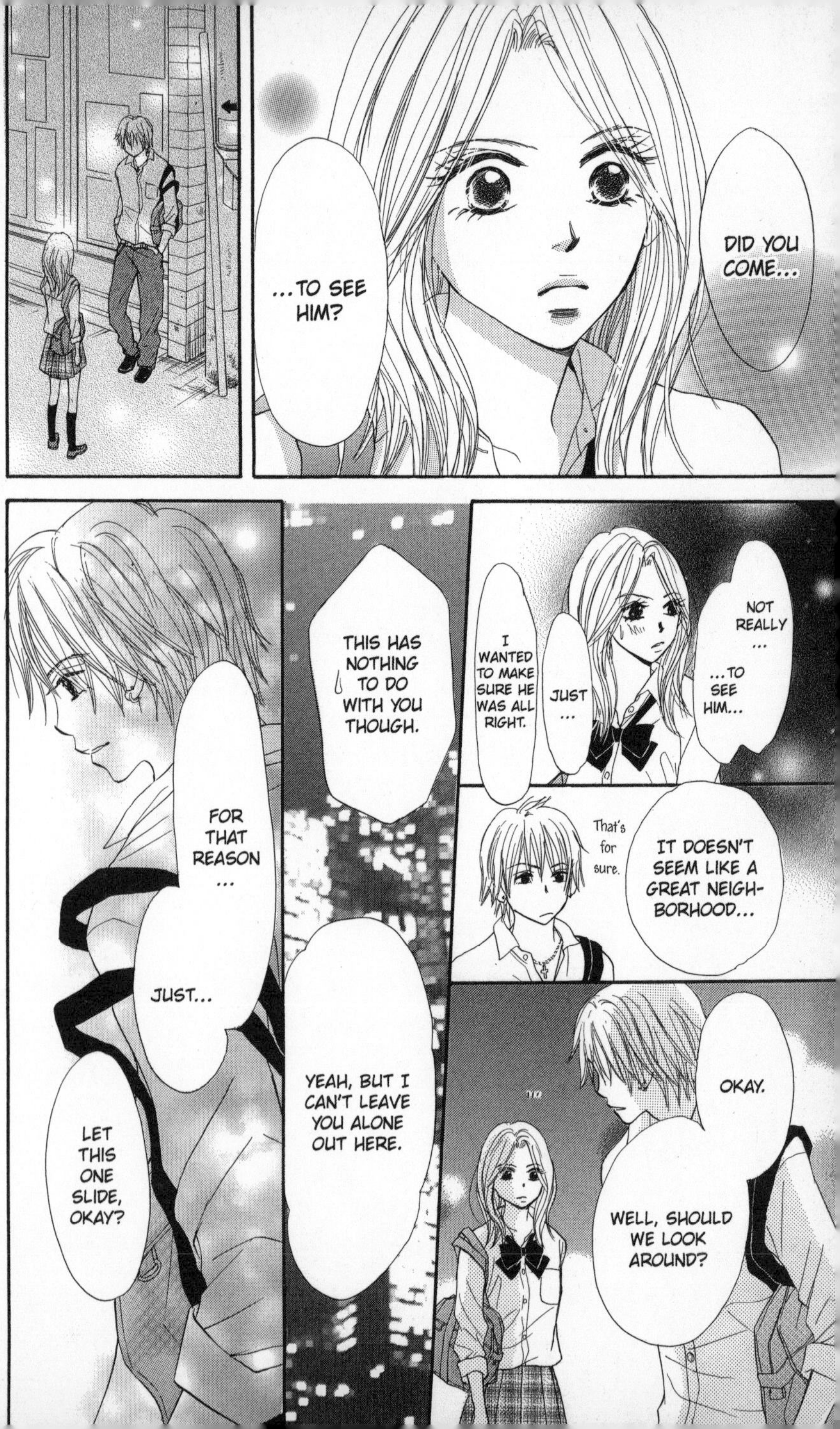
DID YOU COME...
...TO SEE HIM?
NOT REALLY ...
...TO SEE HIM...
JUST ...
I WANTED TO MAKE SURE HE WAS ALL RIGHT.
IT DOESN'T SEEM LIKE A GREAT NEIGH-BORHOOD...
That's for sure.
OKAY.
WELL, SHOULD WE LOOK AROUND?
THIS HAS NOTHING TO DO WITH YOU THOUGH.
YEAH, BUT I CAN'T LEAVE YOU ALONE OUT HERE.
FOR THAT REASON ...
JUST...
LET THIS ONE SLIDE, OKAY?

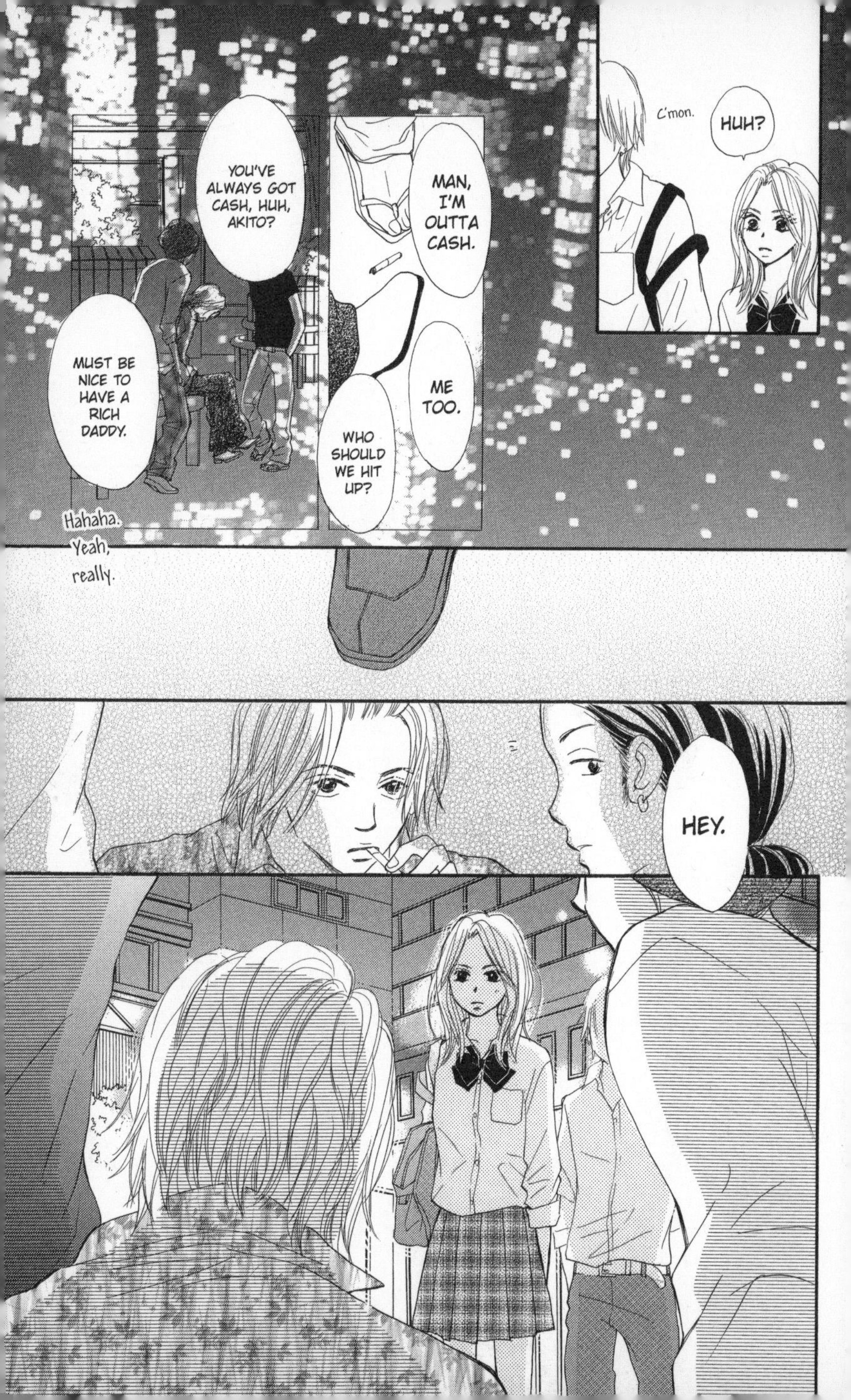
C'mon.
HUH?
MAN, I'M OUTTA CASH.
ME TOO.
WHO SHOULD WE HIT UP?
YOU'VE ALWAYS GOT CASH, HUH, AKITO?
MUST BE NICE TO HAVE A RICH DADDY.
Hahaha. Yeah, really.
HEY.

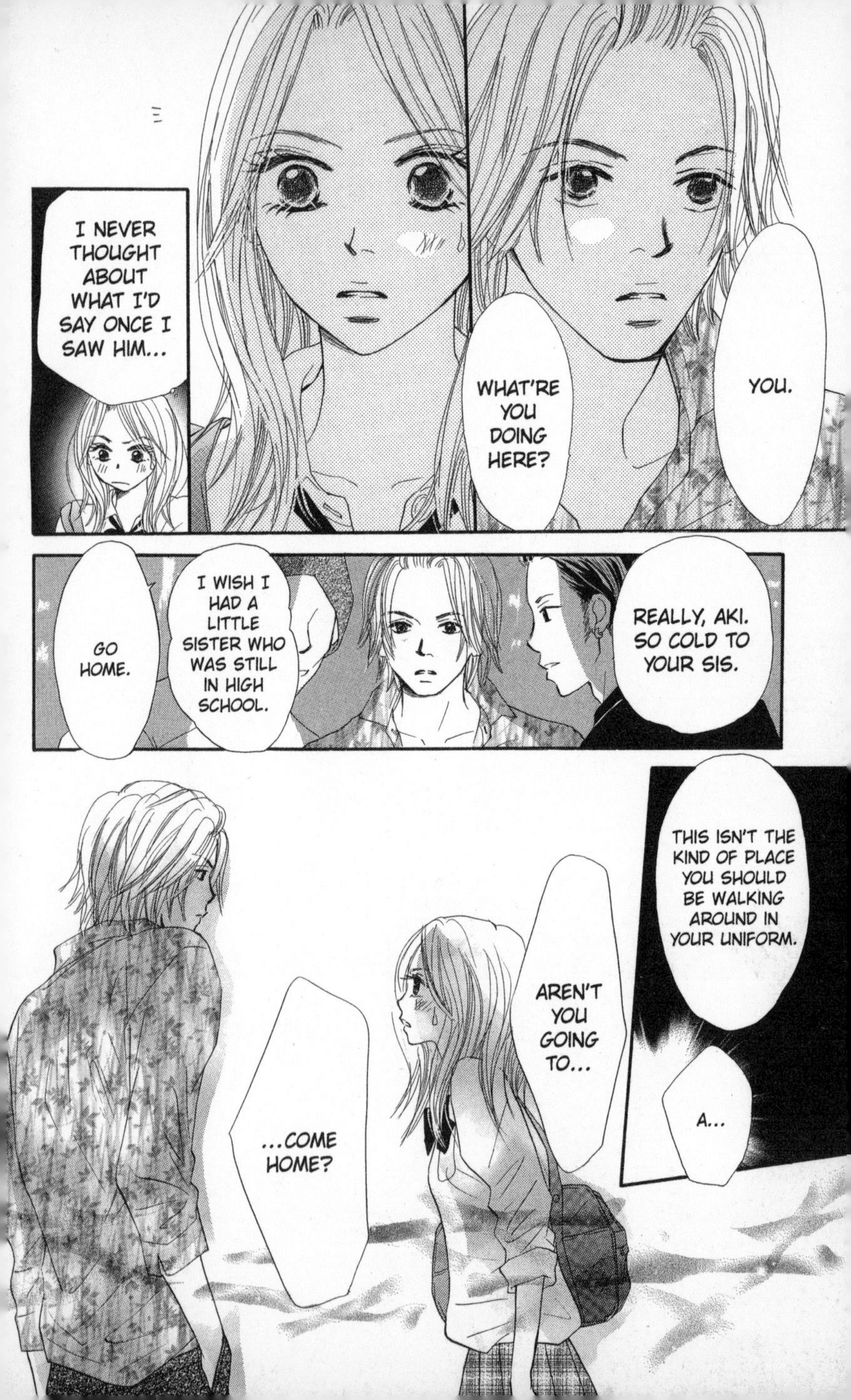
YOU.
WHAT'RE YOU DOING HERE?
I NEVER THOUGHT ABOUT WHAT I'D SAY ONCE I SAW HIM...
REALLY, AKI. SO COLD TO YOUR SIS.
I WISH I HAD A LITTLE SISTER WHO WAS STILL IN HIGH SCHOOL.
GO HOME.
THIS ISN'T THE KIND OF PLACE YOU SHOULD BE WALKING AROUND IN YOUR UNIFORM.
A...
AREN'T YOU GOING TO...
...COME HOME?

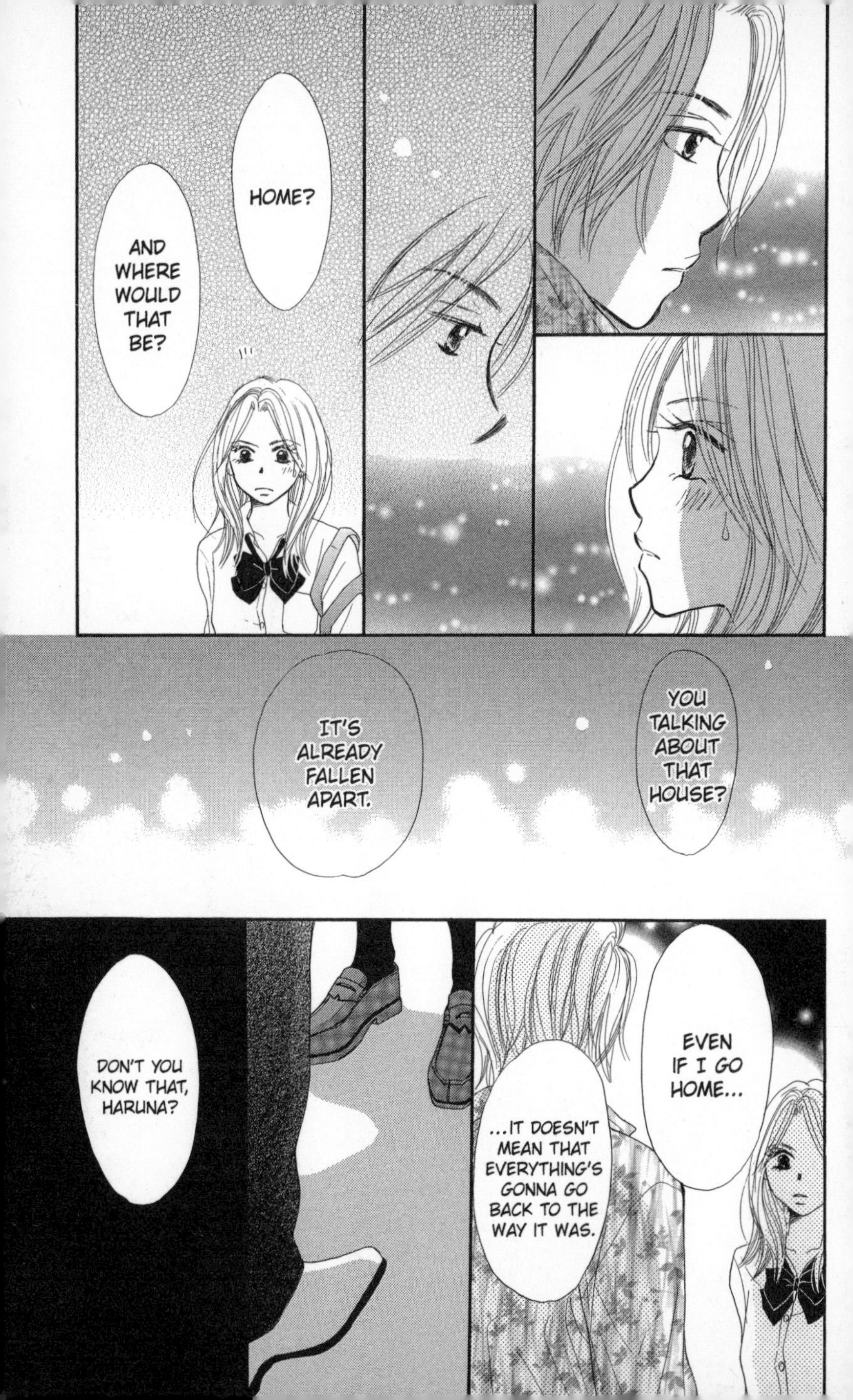
HOME?
AND WHERE WOULD THAT BE?
YOU TALKING ABOUT THAT HOUSE?
IT'S ALREADY FALLEN APART.
EVEN IF I GO HOME...
...IT DOESN'T MEAN THAT EVERYTHING'S GONNA GO BACK TO THE WAY IT WAS.
DON'T YOU KNOW THAT, HARUNA?

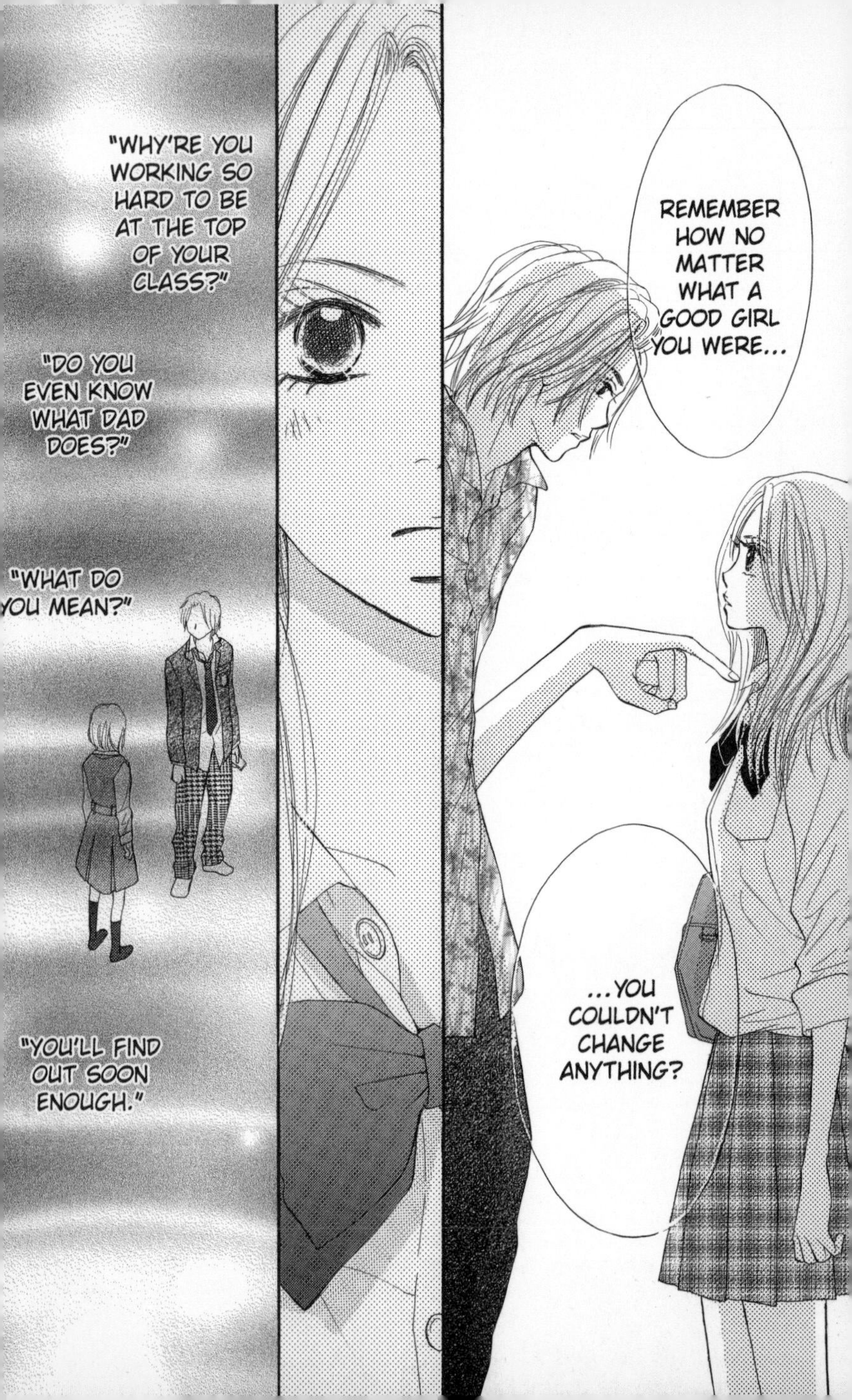
REMEMBER HOW NO MATTER WHAT A GOOD GIRL YOU WERE...
...YOU COULDN'T CHANGE ANYTHING?
"WHY'RE YOU WORKING SO HARD TO BE AT THE TOP OF YOUR CLASS?"
"DO YOU EVEN KNOW WHAT DAD DOES?"
"WHAT DO YOU MEAN?"
"YOU'LL FIND OUT SOON ENOUGH."

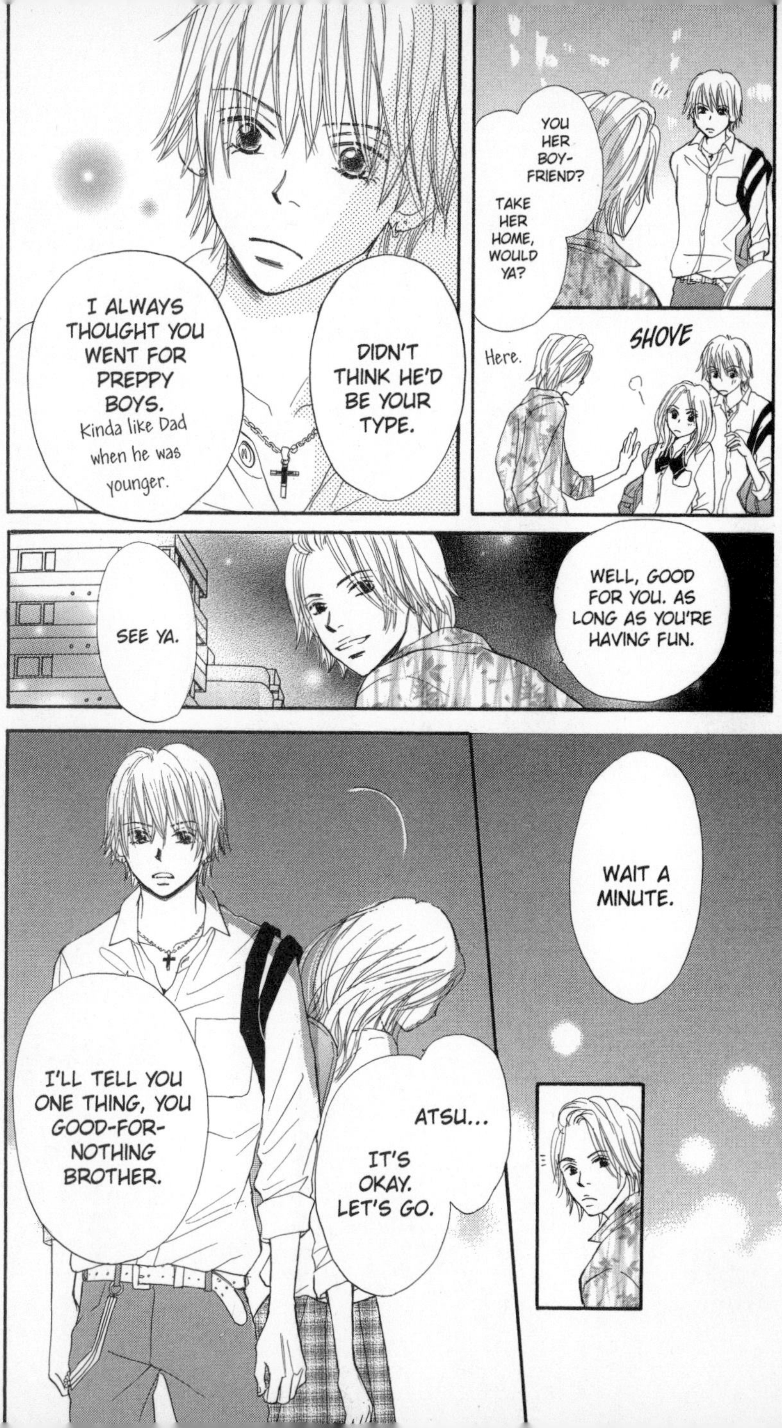
YOU HER BOY-FRIEND?
TAKE HER HOME, WOULD YA?
SHOVE
Here.
DIDN'T THINK HE'D BE YOUR TYPE.
I ALWAYS THOUGHT YOU WENT FOR PREPPY BOYS. Kinda like Dad when he was younger.
WELL, GOOD FOR YOU. AS LONG AS YOU'RE HAVING FUN.
SEE YA.
WAIT A MINUTE.
ATSU... IT'S OKAY. LET'S GO.
I'LL TELL YOU ONE THING, YOU GOOD-FOR-NOTHING BROTHER.

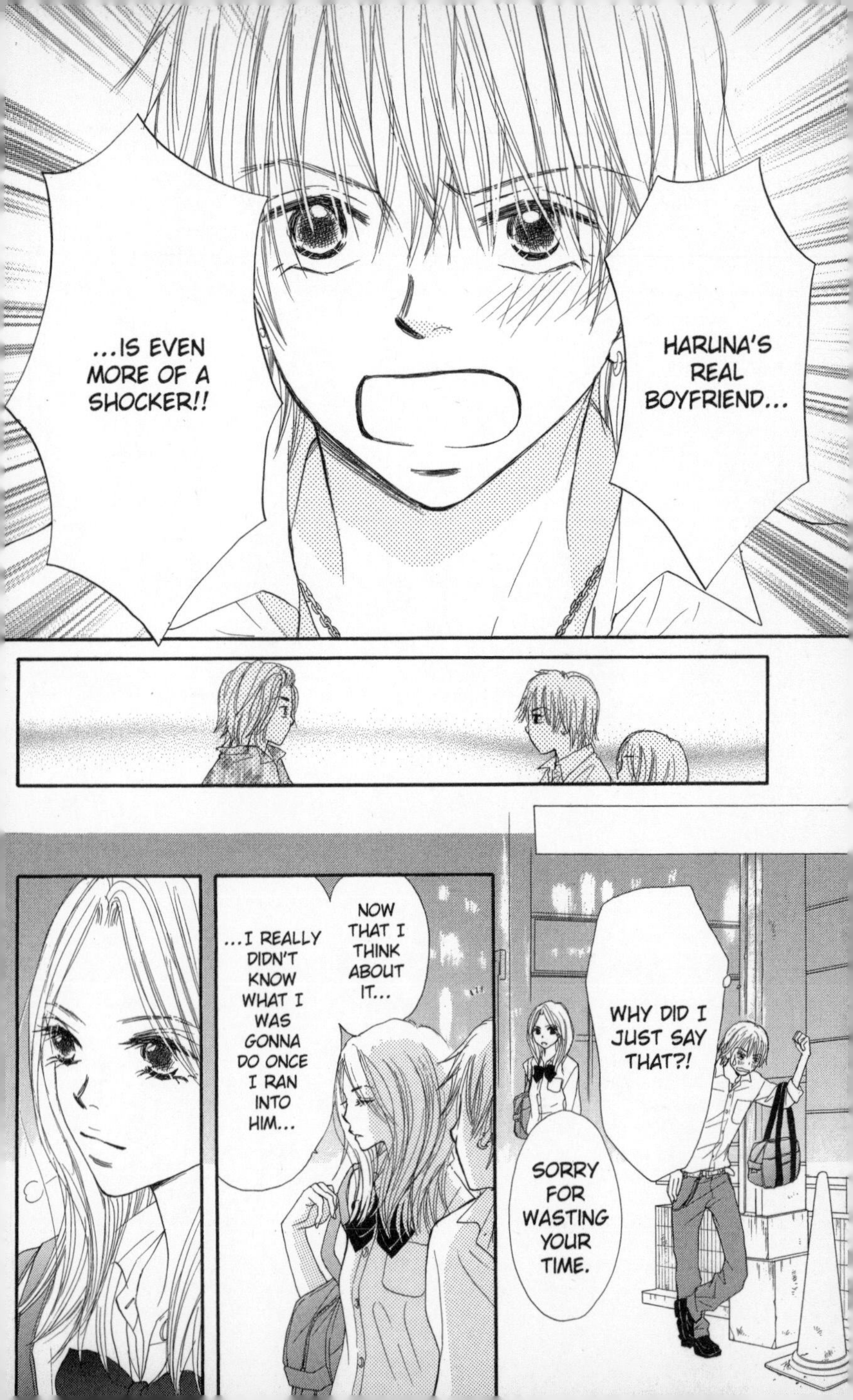
HARUNA'S REAL BOYFRIEND...
...IS EVEN MORE OF A SHOCKER!!
WHY DID I JUST SAY THAT?!
SORRY FOR WASTING YOUR TIME.
NOW THAT I THINK ABOUT IT...
...I REALLY DIDN'T KNOW WHAT I WAS GONNA DO ONCE I RAN INTO HIM...

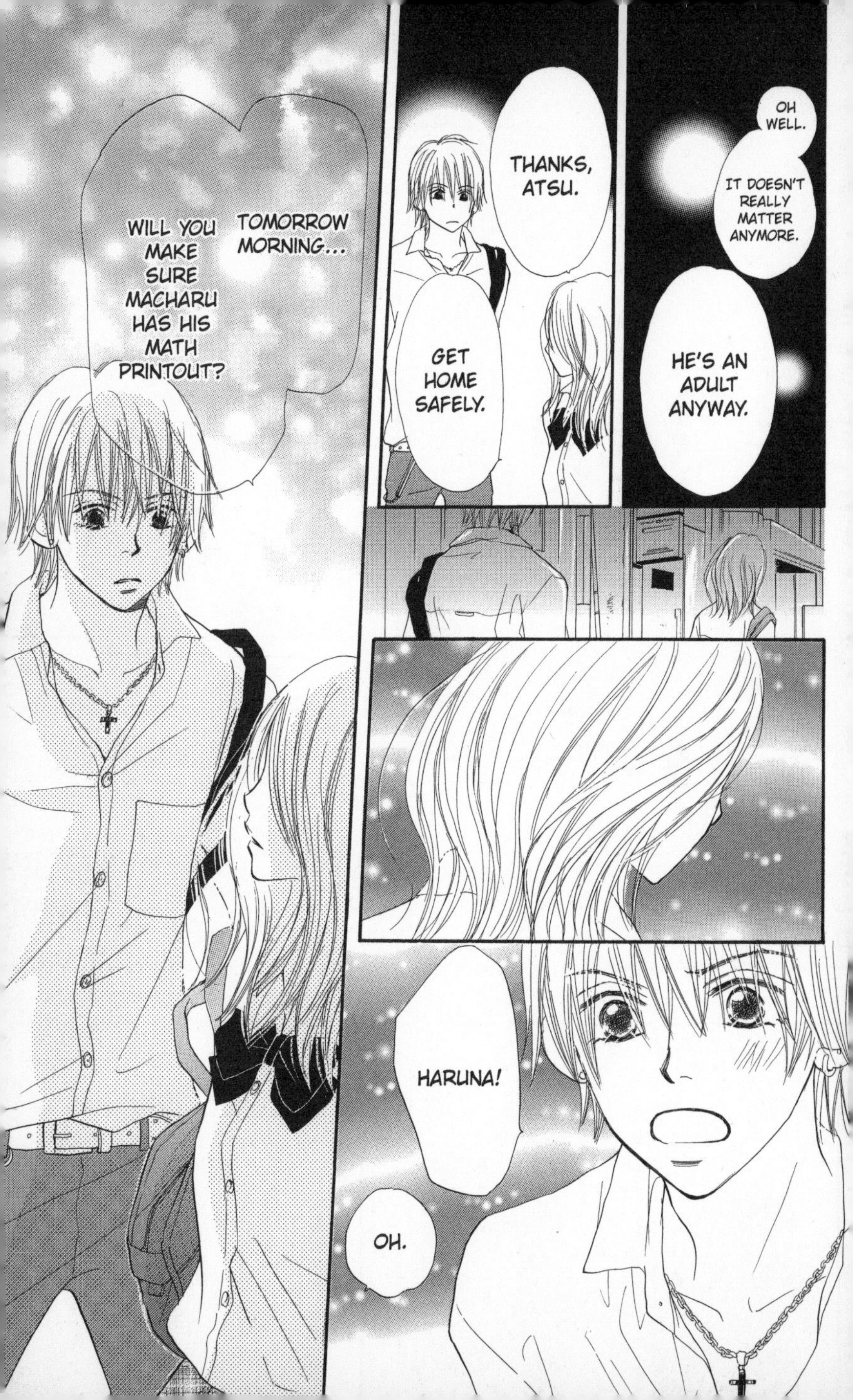
OH WELL.
IT DOESN'T REALLY MATTER ANYMORE.
HE'S AN ADULT ANYWAY.
THANKS, ATSU.
GET HOME SAFELY.
HARUNA!
OH.
TOMORROW MORNING...
WILL YOU MAKE SURE MACHARU HAS HIS MATH PRINTOUT?

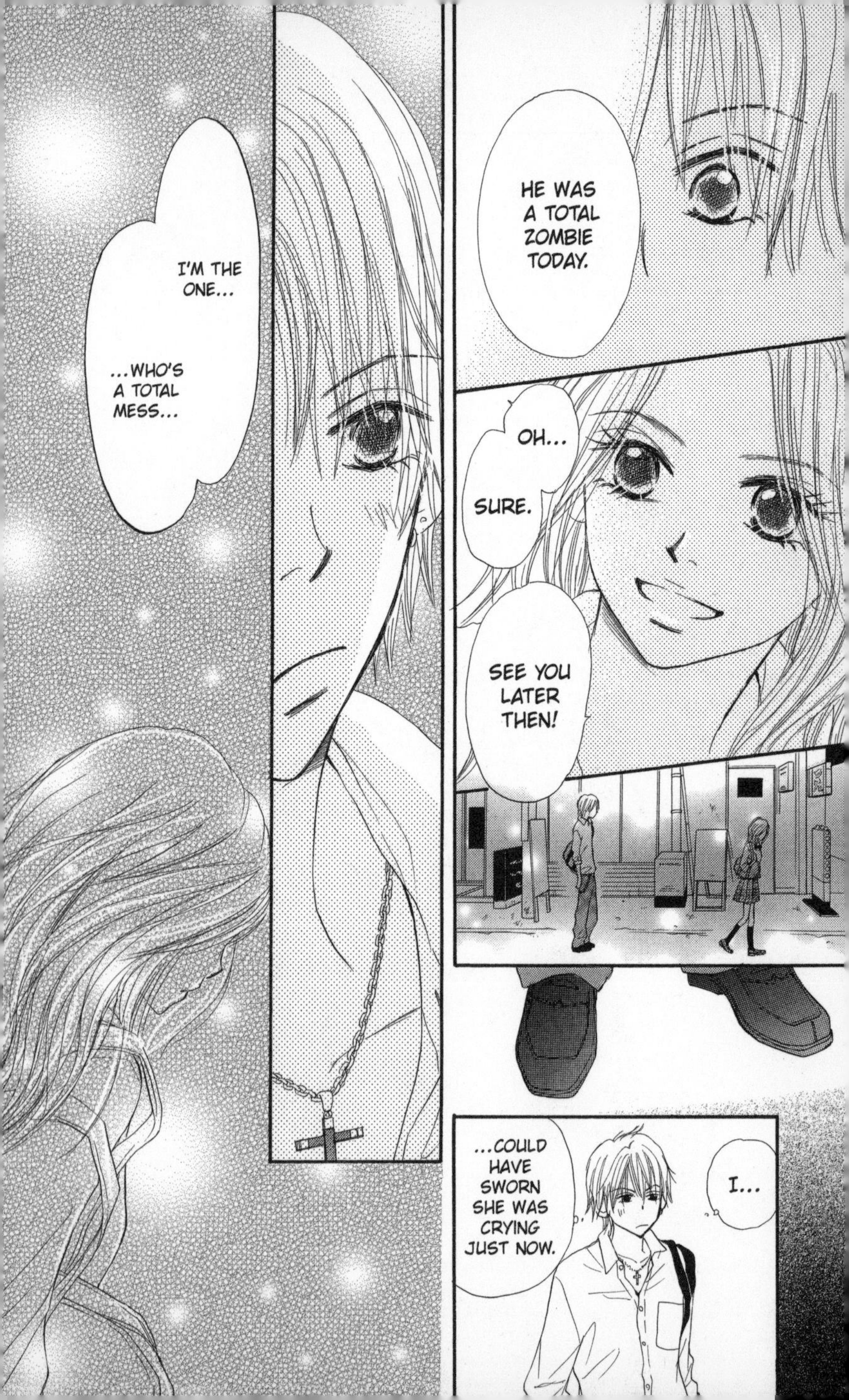
HE WAS A TOTAL ZOMBIE TODAY.
OH... SURE.
SEE YOU LATER THEN!
I...
...COULD HAVE SWORN SHE WAS CRYING JUST NOW.
I'M THE ONE...
...WHO'S A TOTAL MESS...

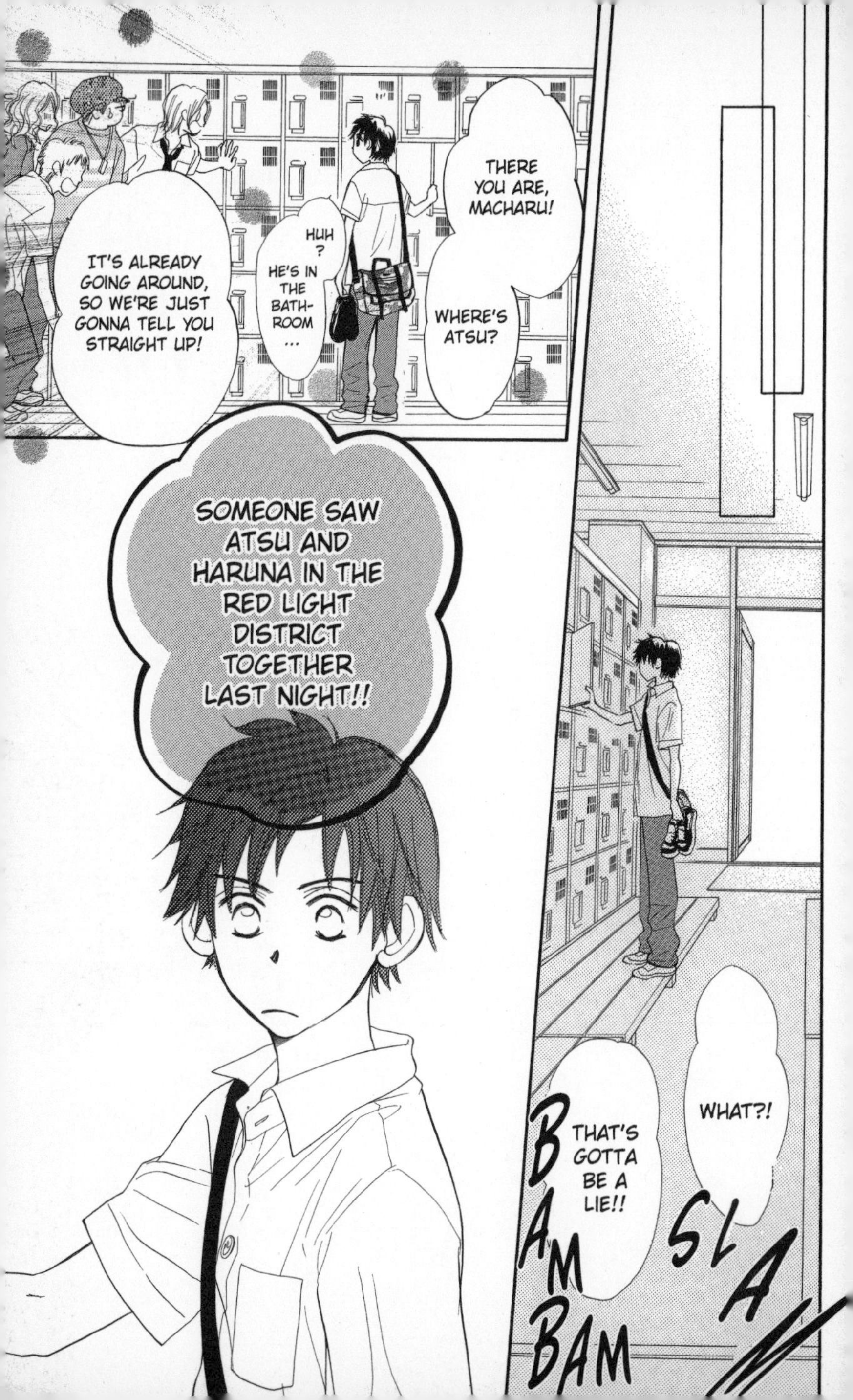
WHAT?!
THAT'S GOTTA BE A LIE!!
BAM BAM
SLAM
THERE YOU ARE, MACHARU!
WHERE'S ATSU?
HUH? HE'S IN THE BATHROOM...
IT'S ALREADY GOING AROUND, SO WE'RE JUST GONNA TELL YOU STRAIGHT UP!
SOMEONE SAW ATSU AND HARUNA IN THE RED LIGHT DISTRICT TOGETHER LAST NIGHT!!

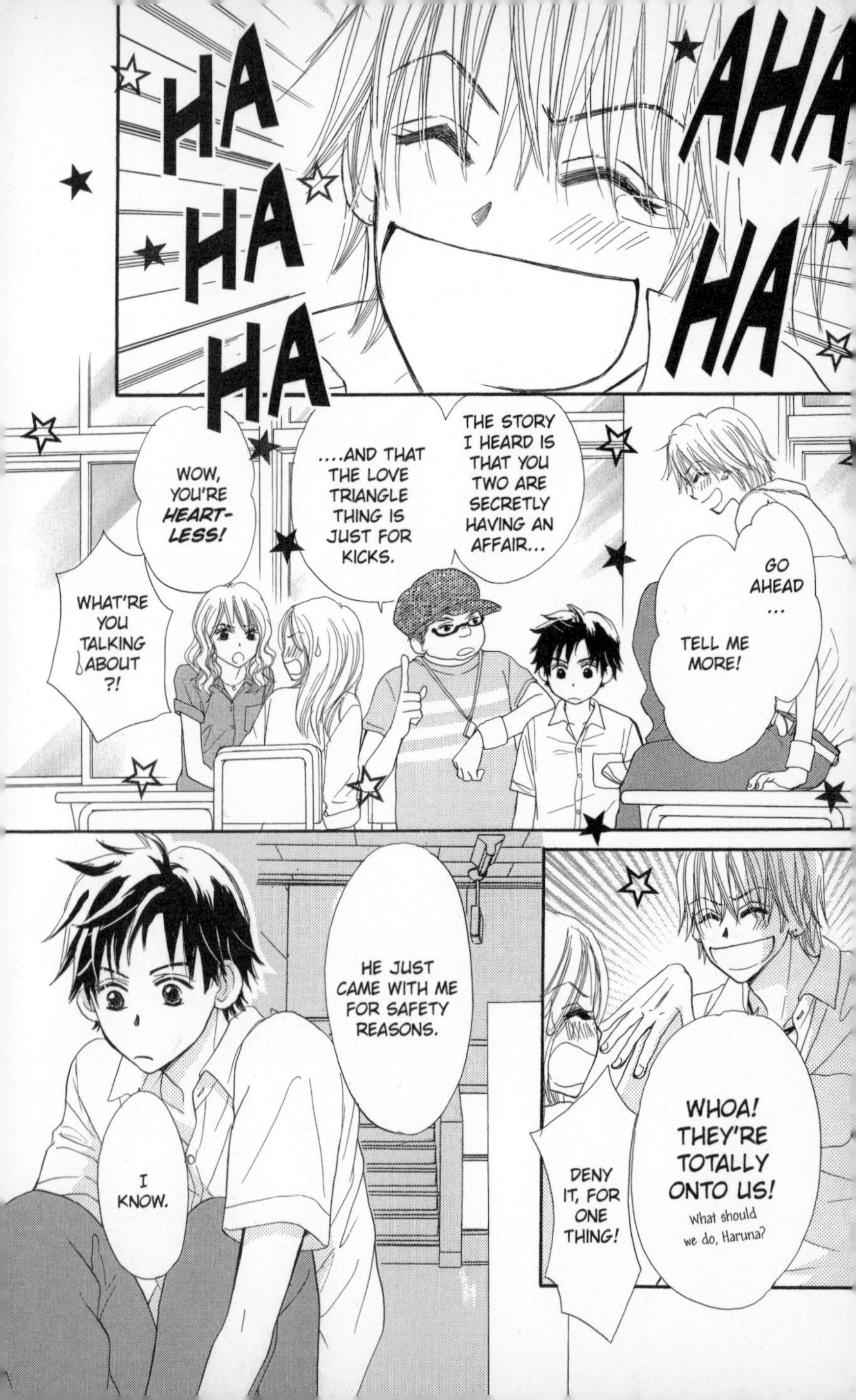

AHAHA HA
HA HA HA HA
GO AHEAD... TELL ME MORE!
THE STORY I HEARD IS THAT YOU TWO ARE SECRETLY HAVING AN AFFAIR...
....AND THAT THE LOVE TRIANGLE THING IS JUST FOR KICKS.
WOW, YOU'RE HEARTLESS!
WHAT'RE YOU TALKING ABOUT?!
WHOA! THEY'RE TOTALLY ONTO US!
What should we do, Haruna?
DENY IT, FOR ONE THING!
HE JUST CAME WITH ME FOR SAFETY REASONS.
I KNOW.

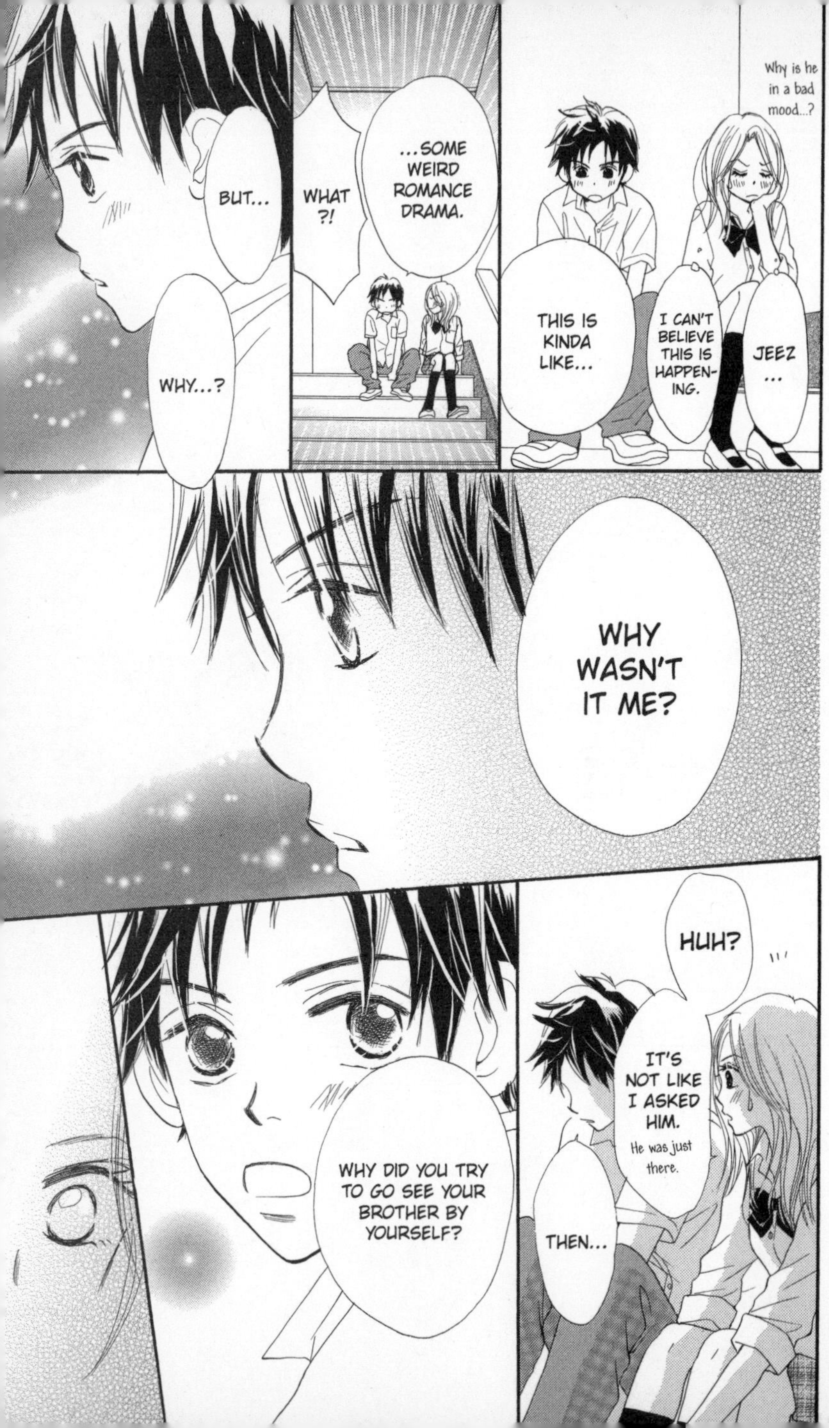
Why is he in a bad mood...?
JEEZ...
I CAN'T BELIEVE THIS IS HAPPENING.
THIS IS KINDA LIKE...
...SOME WEIRD ROMANCE DRAMA.
WHAT?!
BUT...
WHY...?
WHY WASN'T IT ME?
HUH?
IT'S NOT LIKE I ASKED HIM.
He was just there.
THEN...
WHY DID YOU TRY TO GO SEE YOUR BROTHER BY YOURSELF?

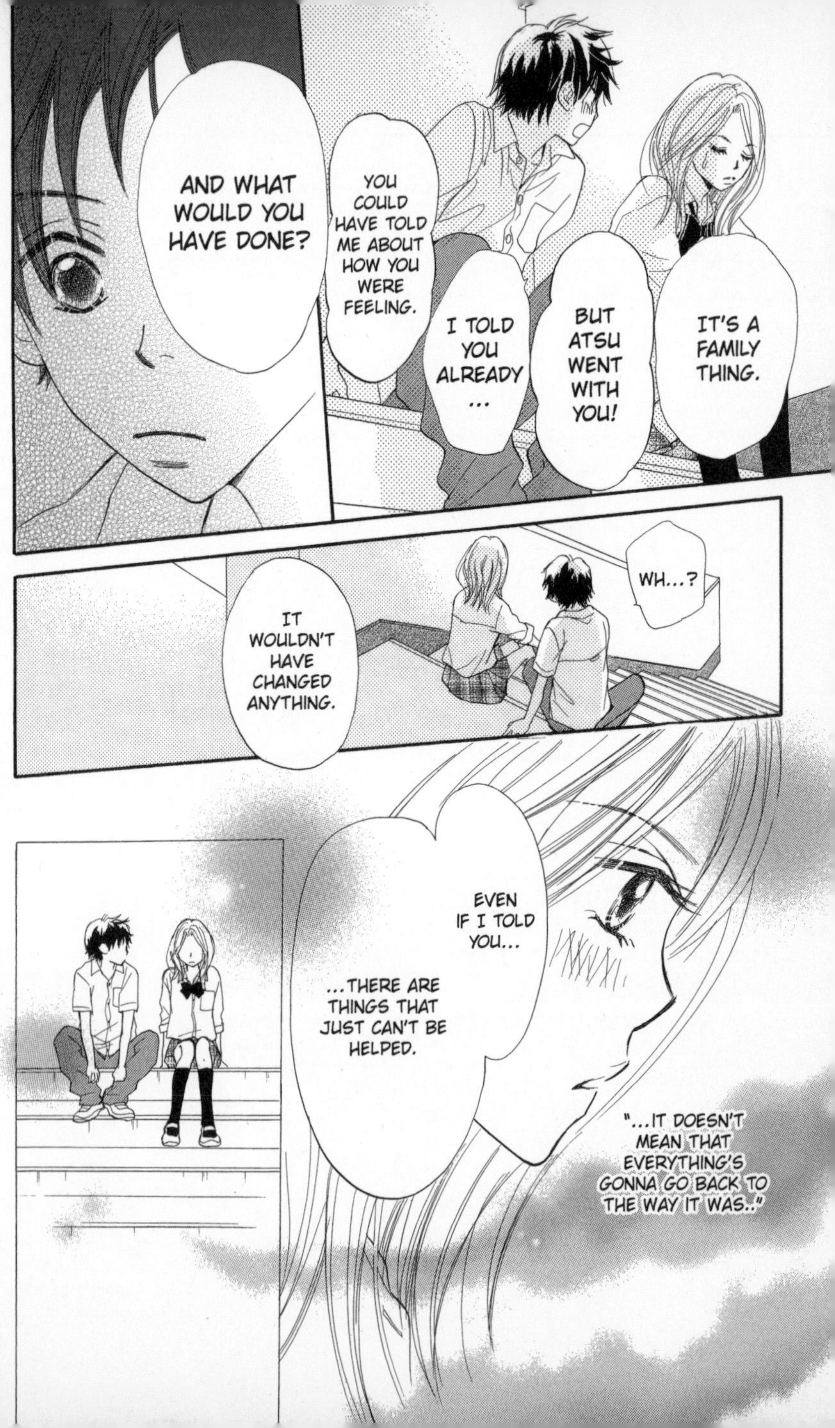
IT'S A FAMILY THING.
BUT ATSU WENT WITH YOU!
I TOLD YOU ALREADY...
YOU COULD HAVE TOLD ME ABOUT HOW YOU WERE FEELING.
AND WHAT WOULD YOU HAVE DONE?
WH...?
IT WOULDN'T HAVE CHANGED ANYTHING.
EVEN IF I TOLD YOU...
...THERE ARE THINGS THAT JUST CAN'T BE HELPED.
"...IT DOESN'T MEAN THAT EVERYTHING'S GONNA GO BACK TO THE WAY IT WAS.."

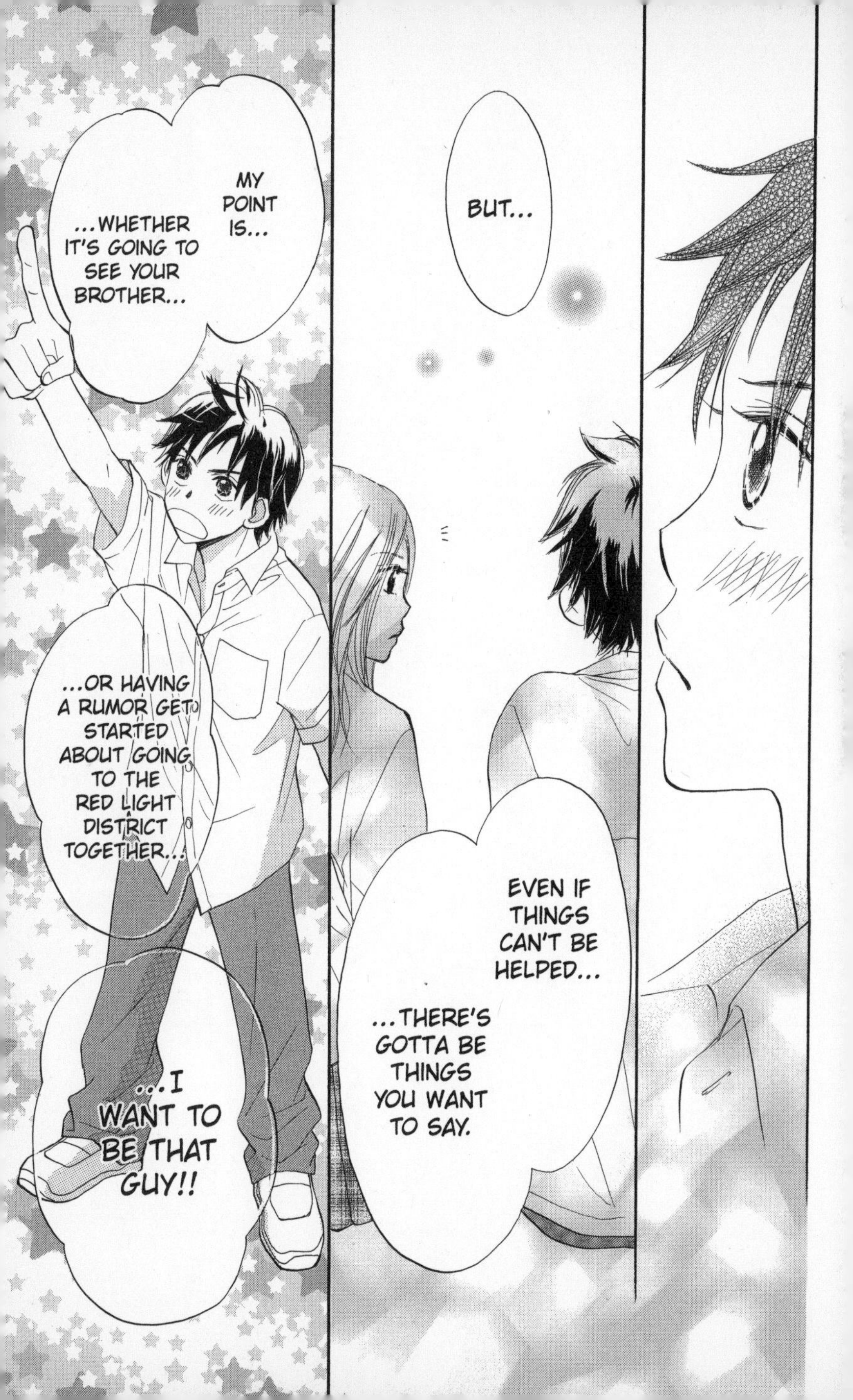
BUT...
EVEN IF THINGS CAN'T BE HELPED...
...THERE'S GOTTA BE THINGS YOU WANT TO SAY.
MY POINT IS...
...WHETHER IT'S GOING TO SEE YOUR BROTHER...
...OR HAVING A RUMOR GET STARTED ABOUT GOING TO THE RED LIGHT DISTRICT TOGETHER...
...I WANT TO BE THAT GUY!!

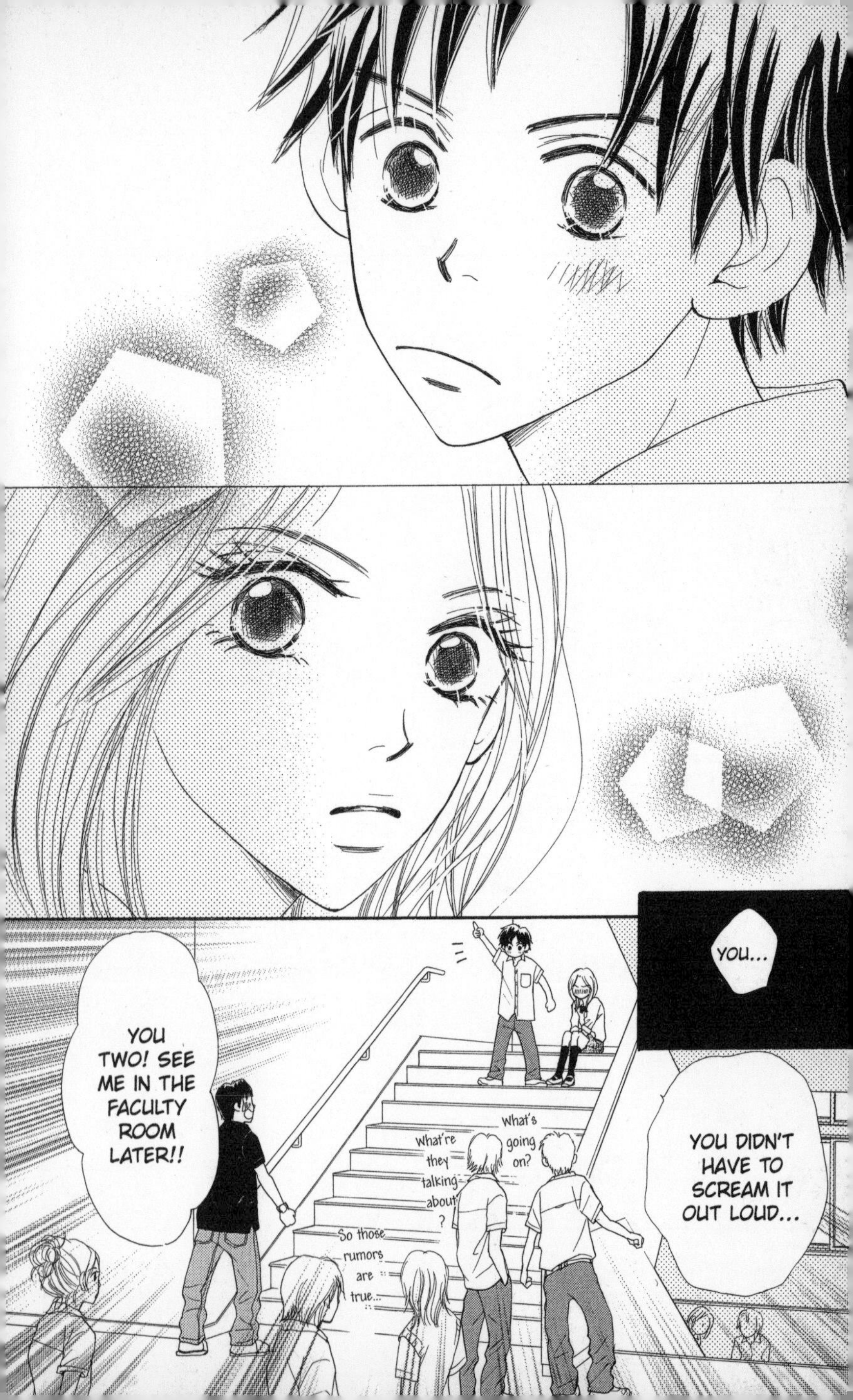
YOU...
YOU DIDN'T HAVE TO SCREAM IT OUT LOUD...
What's going on?
What're they talking about?
YOU TWO! SEE ME IN THE FACULTY ROOM LATER!!
So those rumors are true...

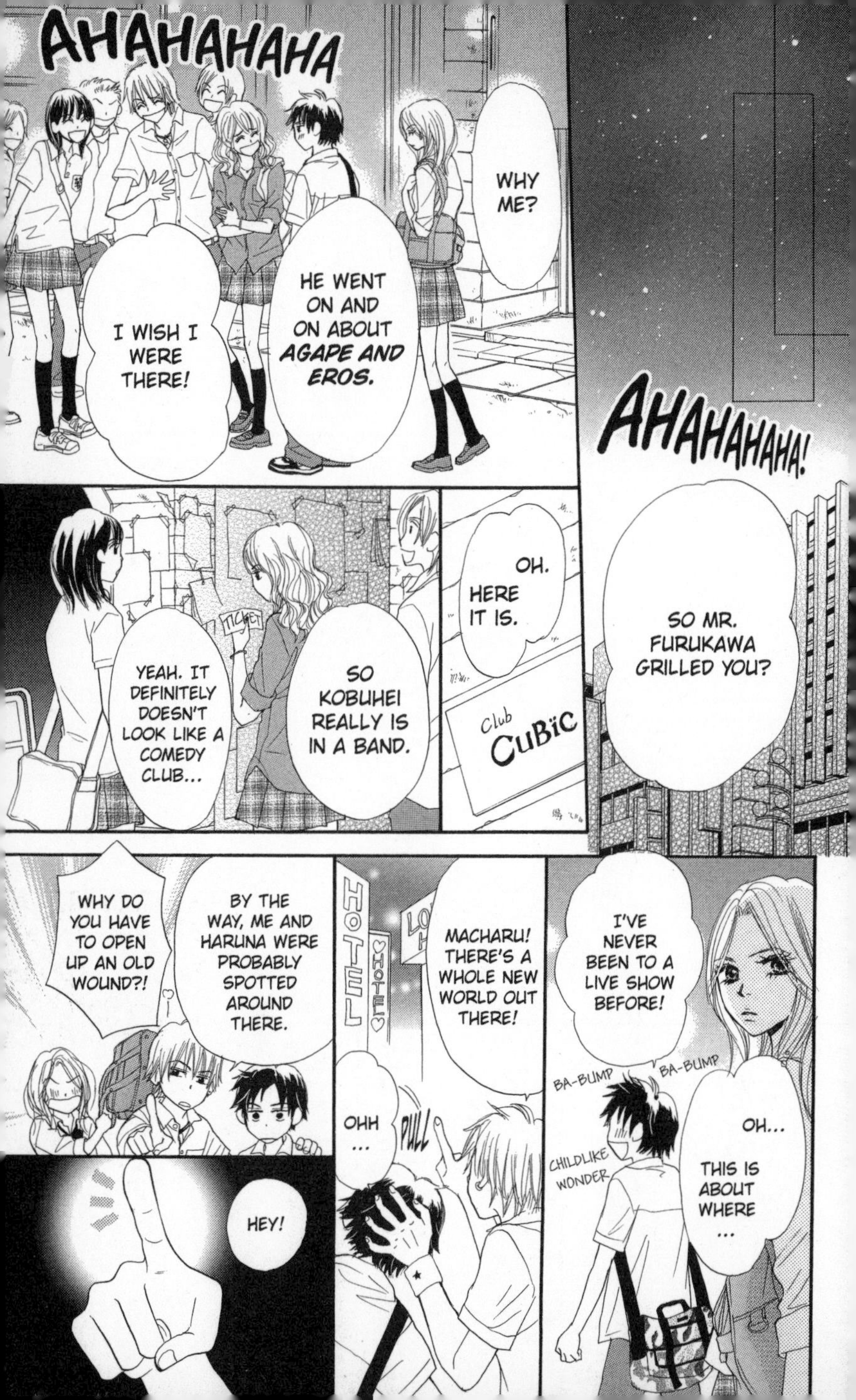
AHAHAHAHA!
SO MR. FURUKAWA GRILLED YOU?
WHY ME?
HE WENT ON AND ON ABOUT *AGAPE AND EROS.*
I WISH I WERE THERE!
AHAHAHAHA
OH. HERE IT IS.
Club CuBiC
SO KOBUHEI REALLY IS IN A BAND.
TICKET
YEAH. IT DEFINITELY DOESN'T LOOK LIKE A COMEDY CLUB...
I'VE NEVER BEEN TO A LIVE SHOW BEFORE!
BA-BUMP
BA-BUMP
CHILDLIKE WONDER
OH... THIS IS ABOUT WHERE ...
MACHARU! THERE'S A WHOLE NEW WORLD OUT THERE!
HOTEL
HOTEL
PULL
OHH ...
BY THE WAY, ME AND HARUNA WERE PROBABLY SPOTTED AROUND THERE.
WHY DO YOU HAVE TO OPEN UP AN OLD WOUND?!
HEY!

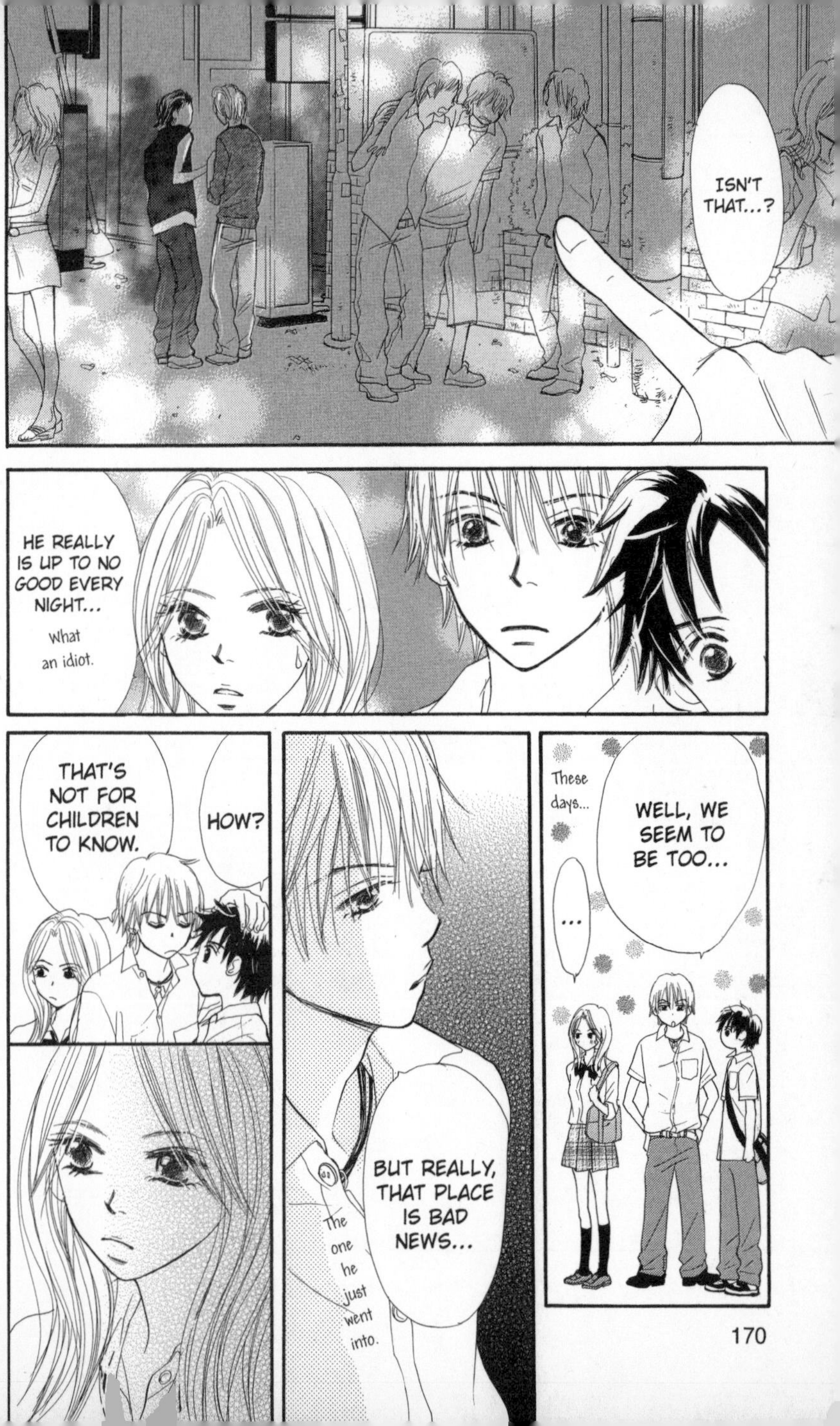
ISN'T THAT...?
HE REALLY IS UP TO NO GOOD EVERY NIGHT...
What an idiot.
These days...
WELL, WE SEEM TO BE TOO...
...
BUT REALLY, THAT PLACE IS BAD NEWS...
The one he just went into.
HOW?
THAT'S NOT FOR CHILDREN TO KNOW.

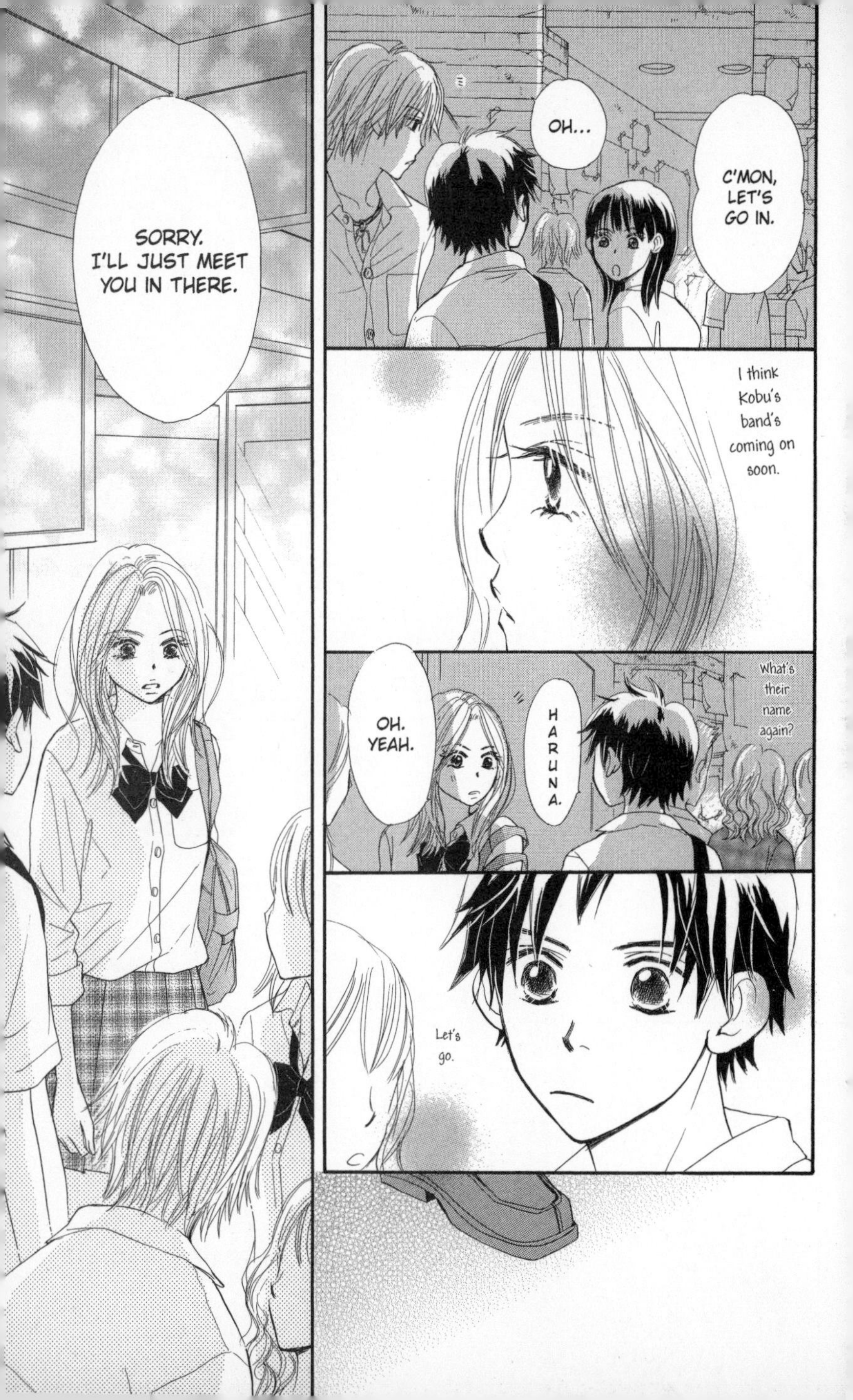
C'MON, LET'S GO IN.
OH...
I think Kobu's band's coming on soon.
What's their name again?
HARUNA.
OH. YEAH.
Let's go.
SORRY. I'LL JUST MEET YOU IN THERE.

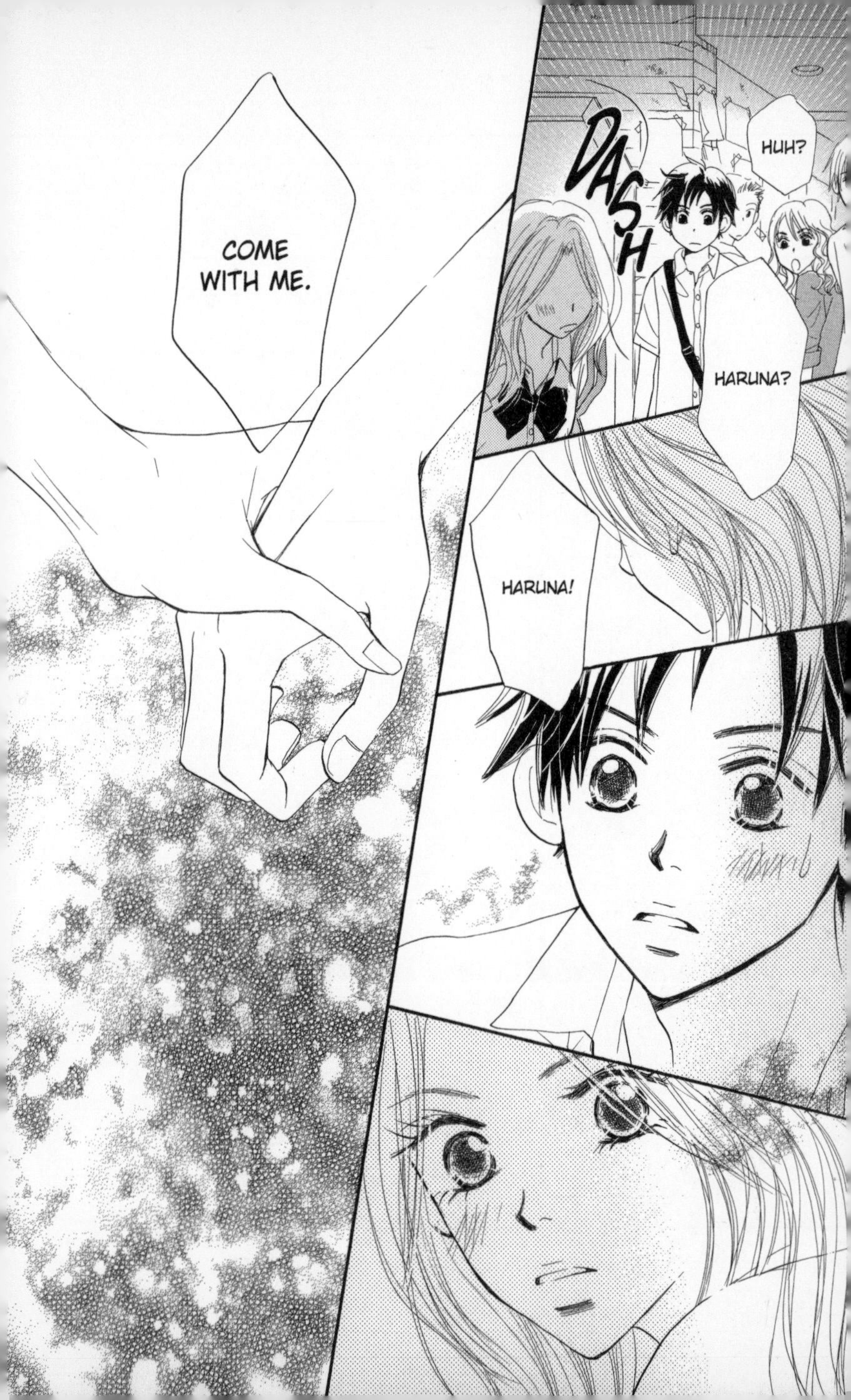
DASH
HUH?
HARUNA?
HARUNA!
COME WITH ME.

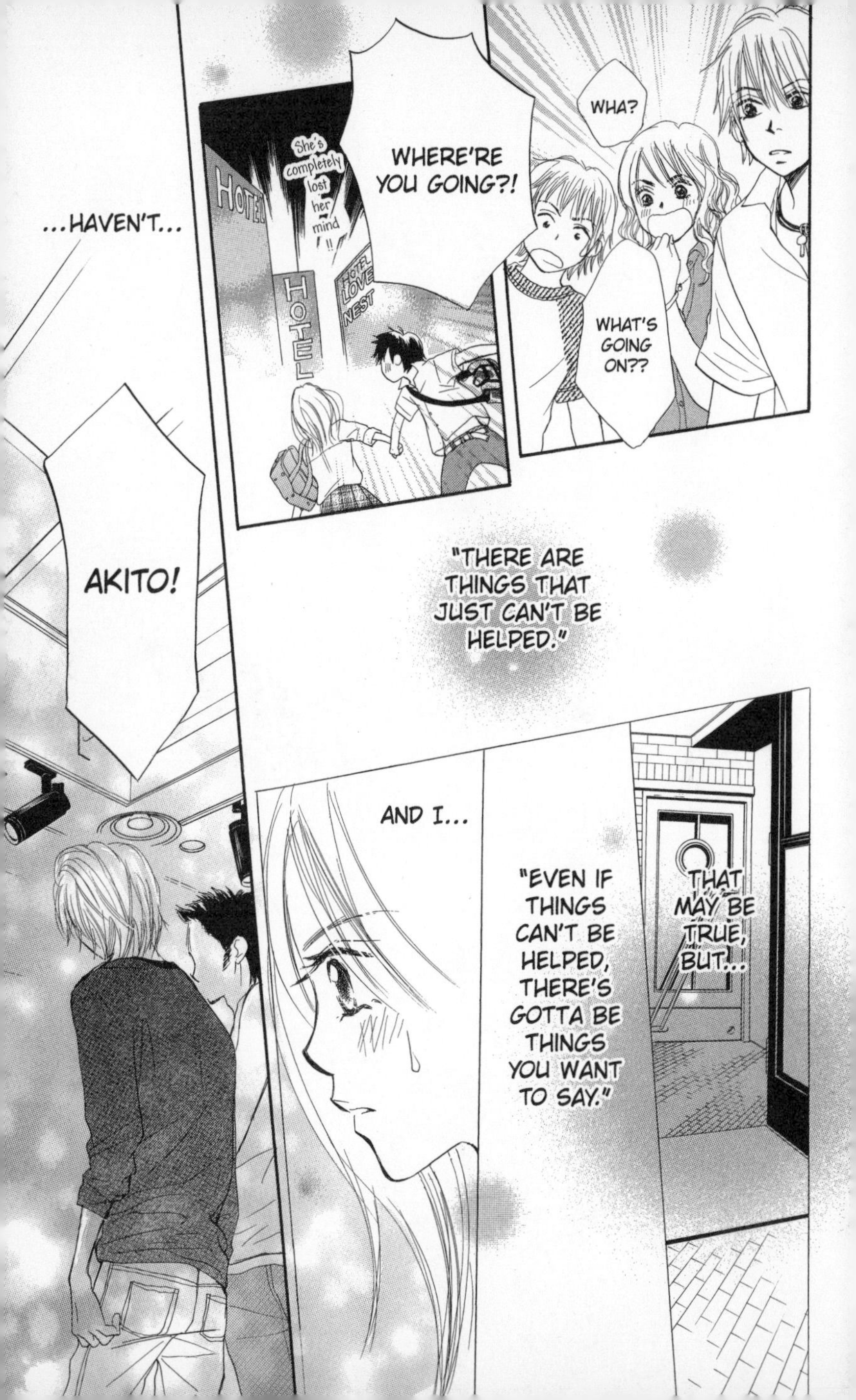
WHA?
WHAT'S GOING ON??
WHERE'RE YOU GOING?!
She's completely lost her mind!!
HOTEL
HOTEL
HOTEL LOVE NEST
"THERE ARE THINGS THAT JUST CAN'T BE HELPED."
THAT MAY BE TRUE, BUT...
"EVEN IF THINGS CAN'T BE HELPED, THERE'S GOTTA BE THINGS YOU WANT TO SAY."
AND I...
...HAVEN'T...
AKITO!

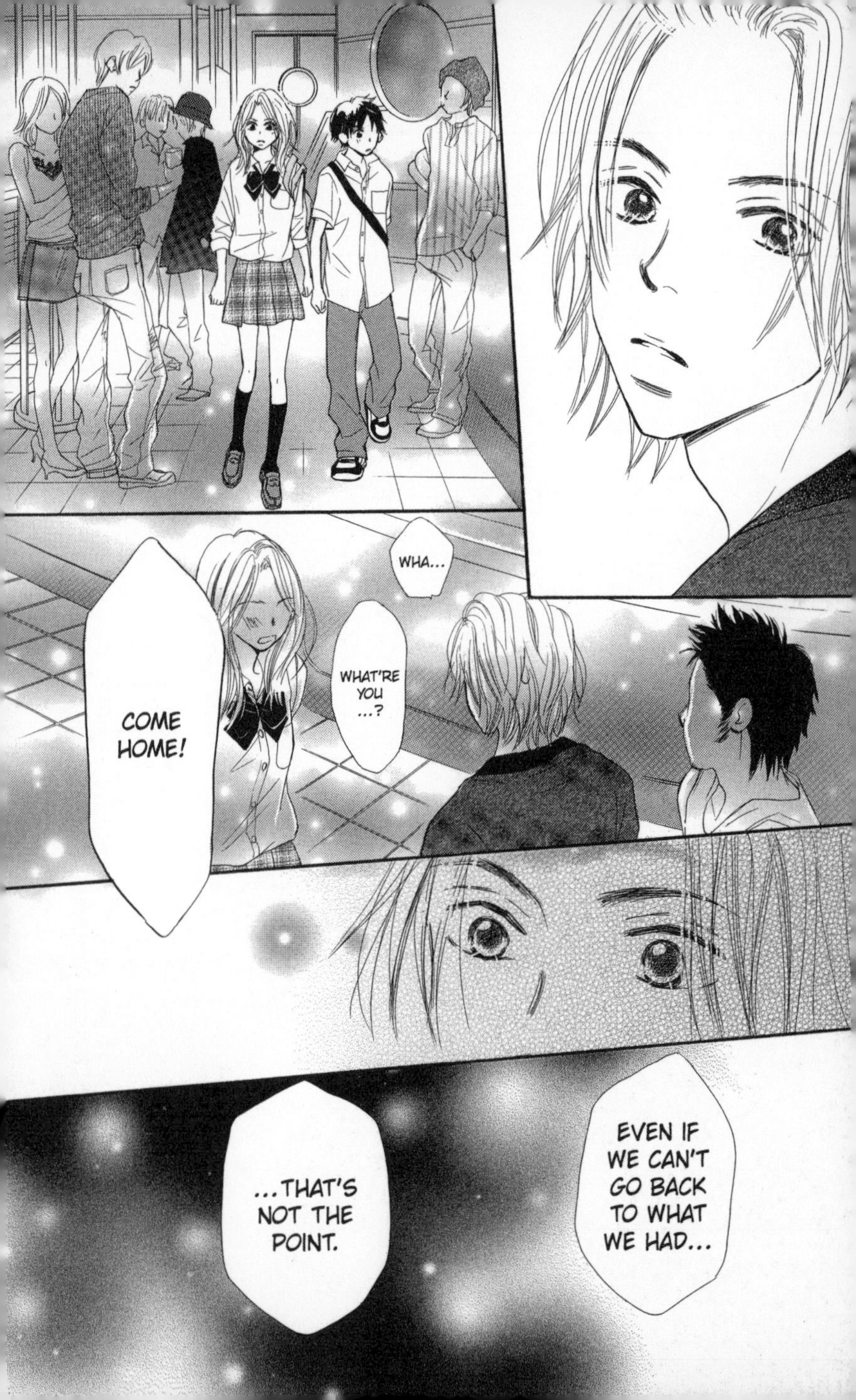
WHA...
WHAT'RE YOU ...?
COME HOME!
EVEN IF WE CAN'T GO BACK TO WHAT WE HAD...
...THAT'S NOT THE POINT.

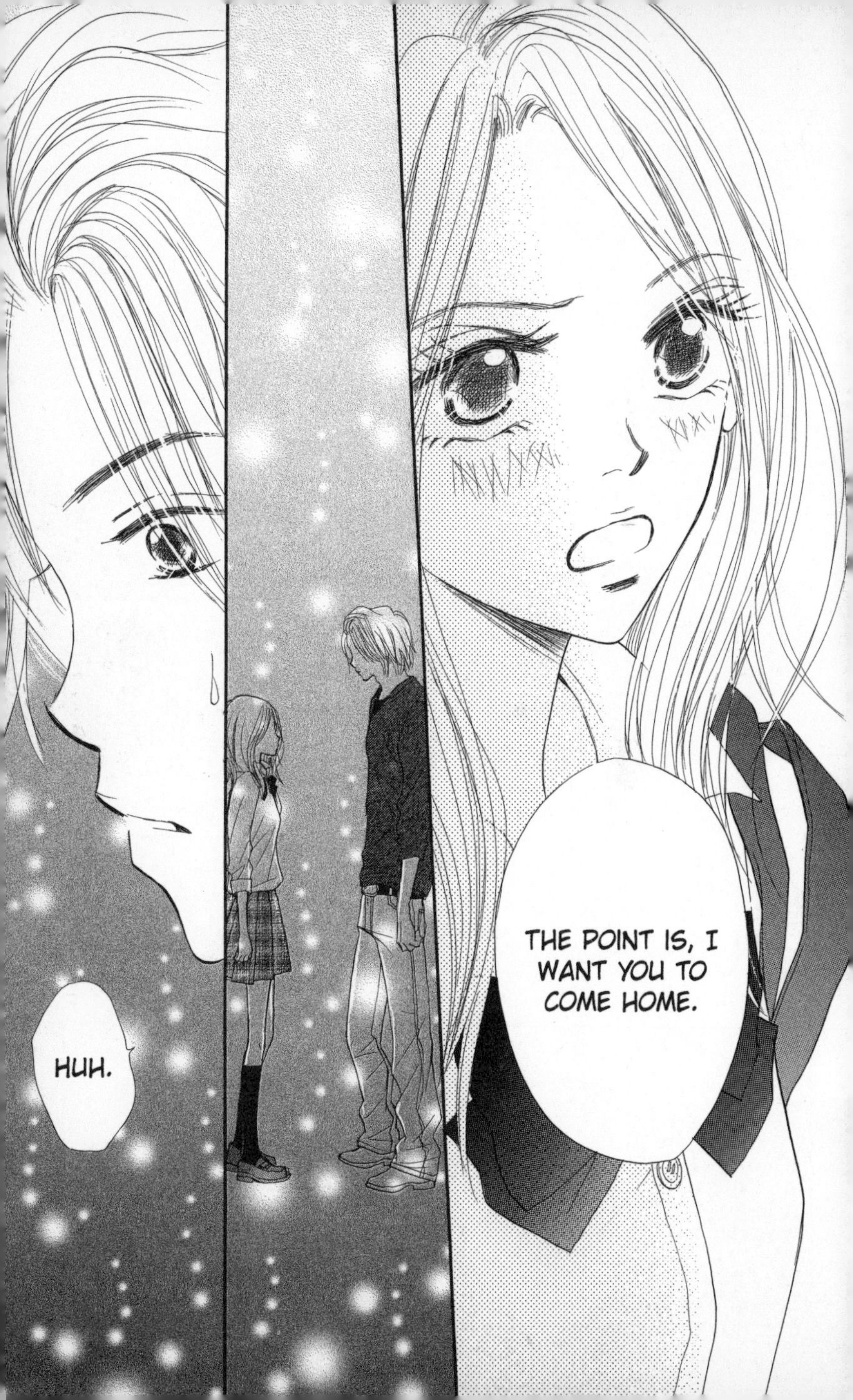
THE POINT IS, I WANT YOU TO COME HOME.
HUH.

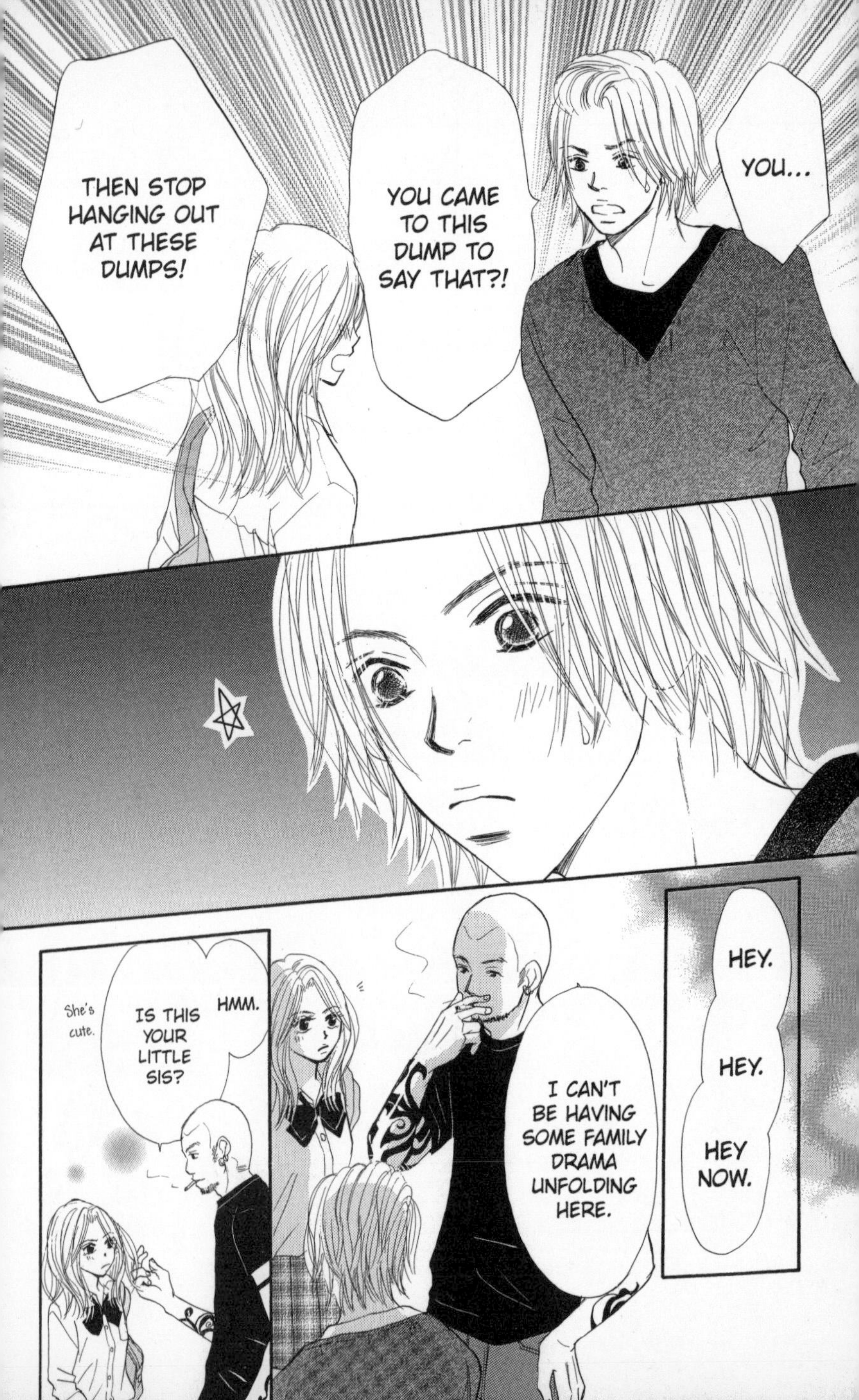
YOU...
YOU CAME TO THIS DUMP TO SAY THAT?!
THEN STOP HANGING OUT AT THESE DUMPS!
HEY.
HEY.
HEY NOW.
I CAN'T BE HAVING SOME FAMILY DRAMA UNFOLDING HERE.
HMM.
IS THIS YOUR LITTLE SIS?
She's cute.

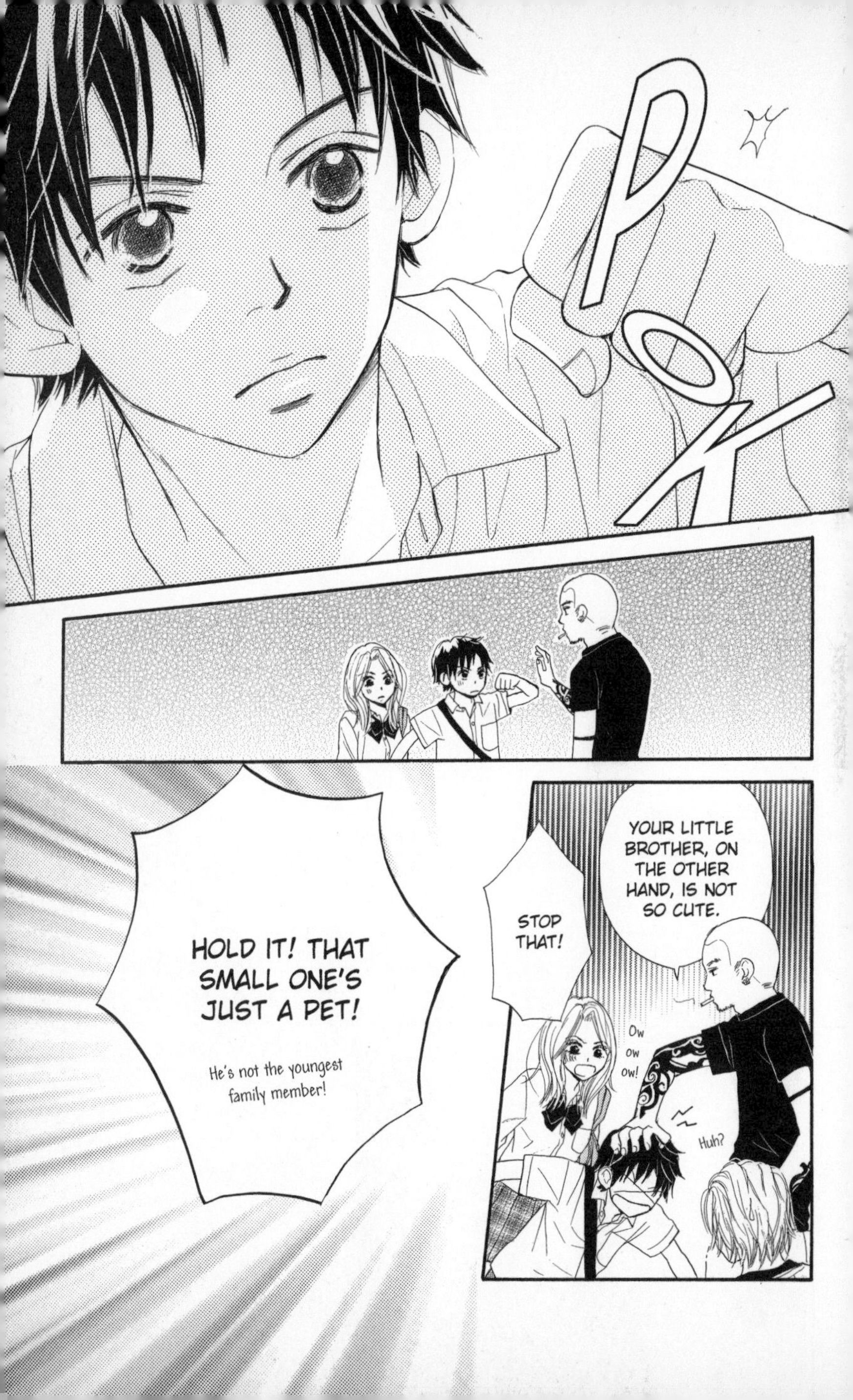
POK
YOUR LITTLE BROTHER, ON THE OTHER HAND, IS NOT SO CUTE.
STOP THAT!
Ow ow ow!
Huh?
HOLD IT! THAT SMALL ONE'S JUST A PET!
He's not the youngest family member!

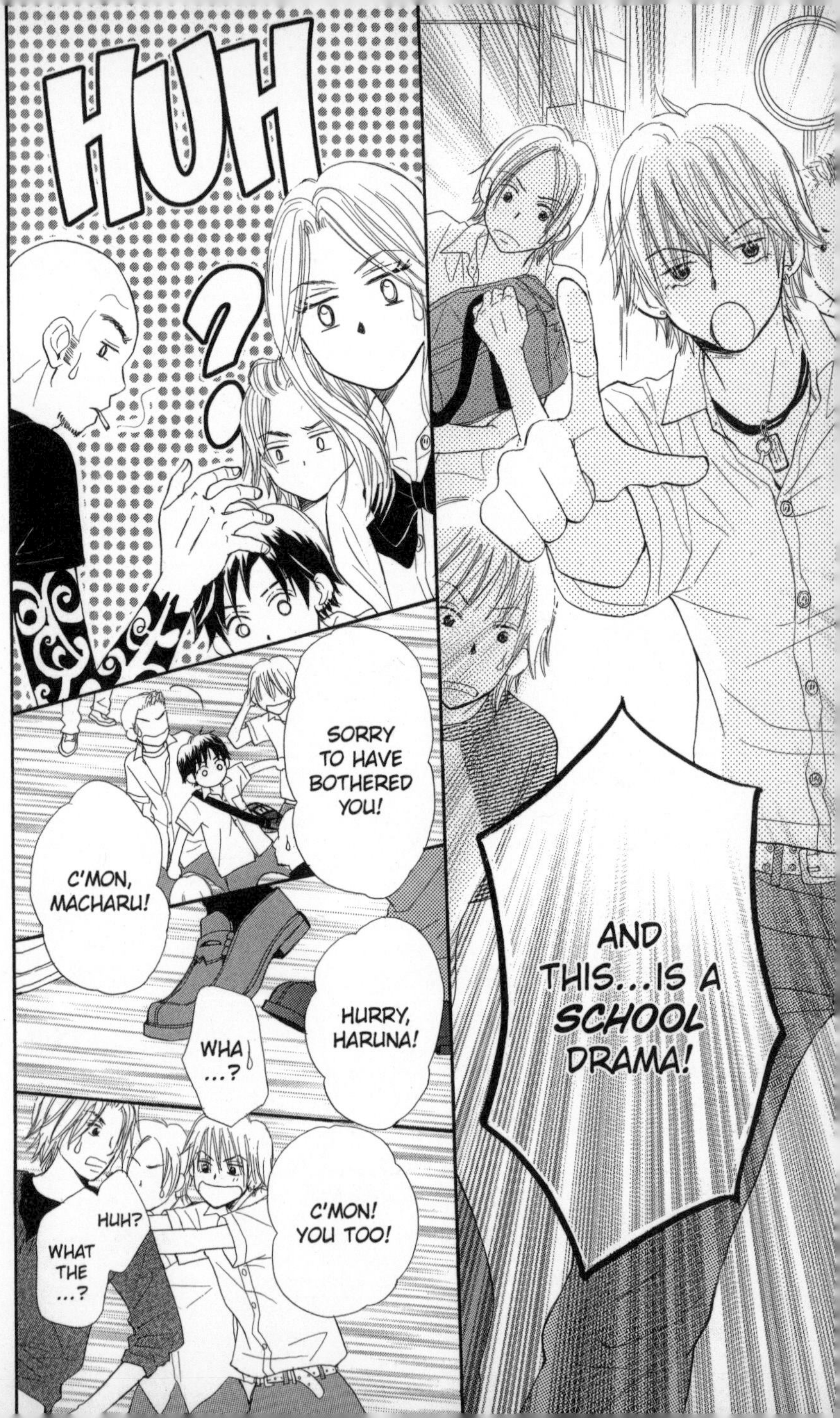
AND THIS...IS A SCHOOL DRAMA!
HUH
?
SORRY TO HAVE BOTHERED YOU!
C'MON, MACHARU!
HURRY, HARUNA!
WHA ...?
C'MON! YOU TOO!
HUH?
WHAT THE ...?

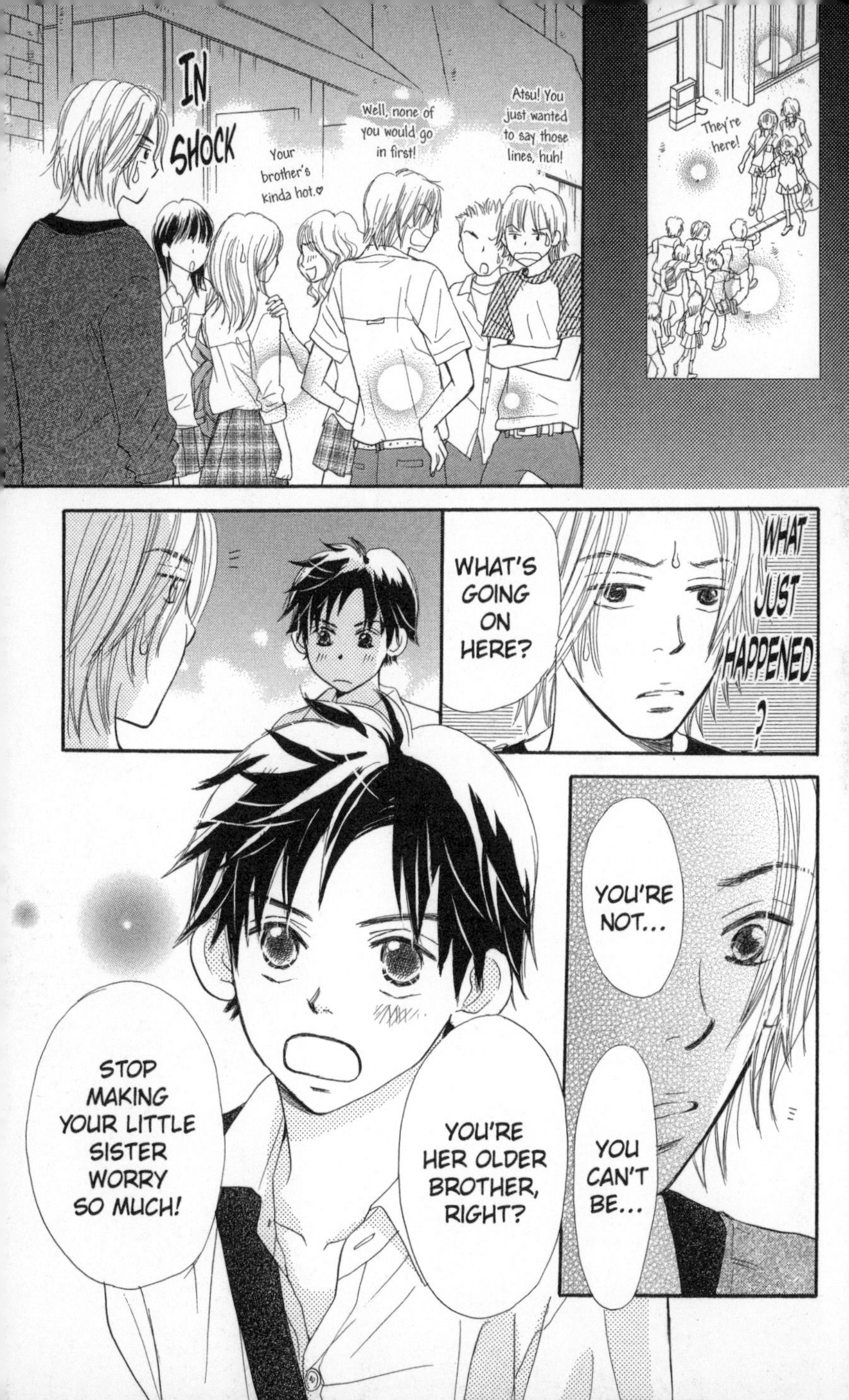
They're here!
Atsu! You just wanted to say those lines, huh!
Well, none of you would go in first!
Your brother's kinda hot.♡
IN SHOCK
WHAT JUST HAPPENED?
WHAT'S GOING ON HERE?
YOU'RE NOT...
YOU CAN'T BE...
YOU'RE HER OLDER BROTHER, RIGHT?
STOP MAKING YOUR LITTLE SISTER WORRY SO MUCH!

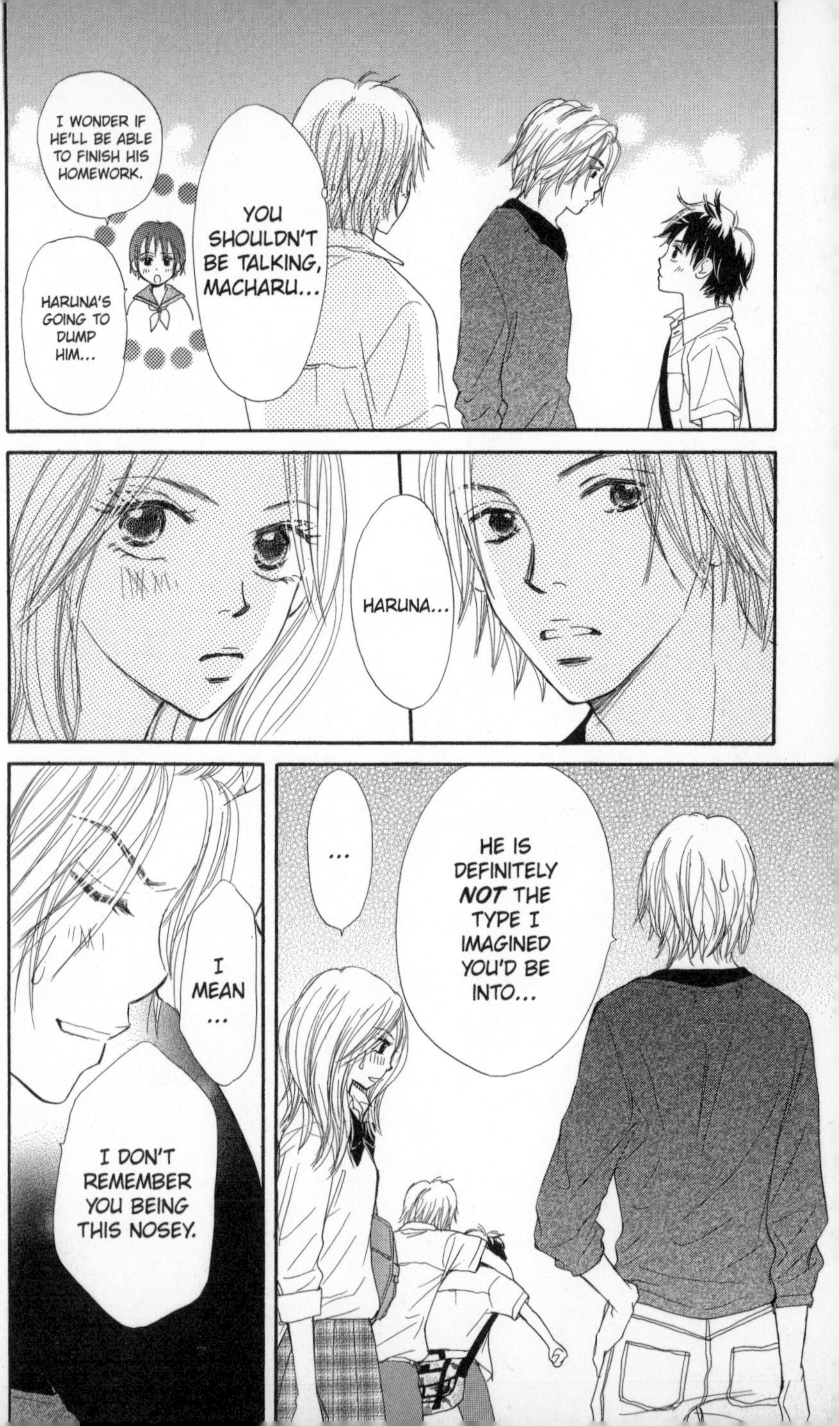
I WONDER IF HE'LL BE ABLE TO FINISH HIS HOMEWORK.
HARUNA'S GOING TO DUMP HIM...
YOU SHOULDN'T BE TALKING, MACHARU...
HARUNA...
HE IS DEFINITELY *NOT* THE TYPE I IMAGINED YOU'D BE INTO...
...
I MEAN ...
I DON'T REMEMBER YOU BEING THIS NOSEY.

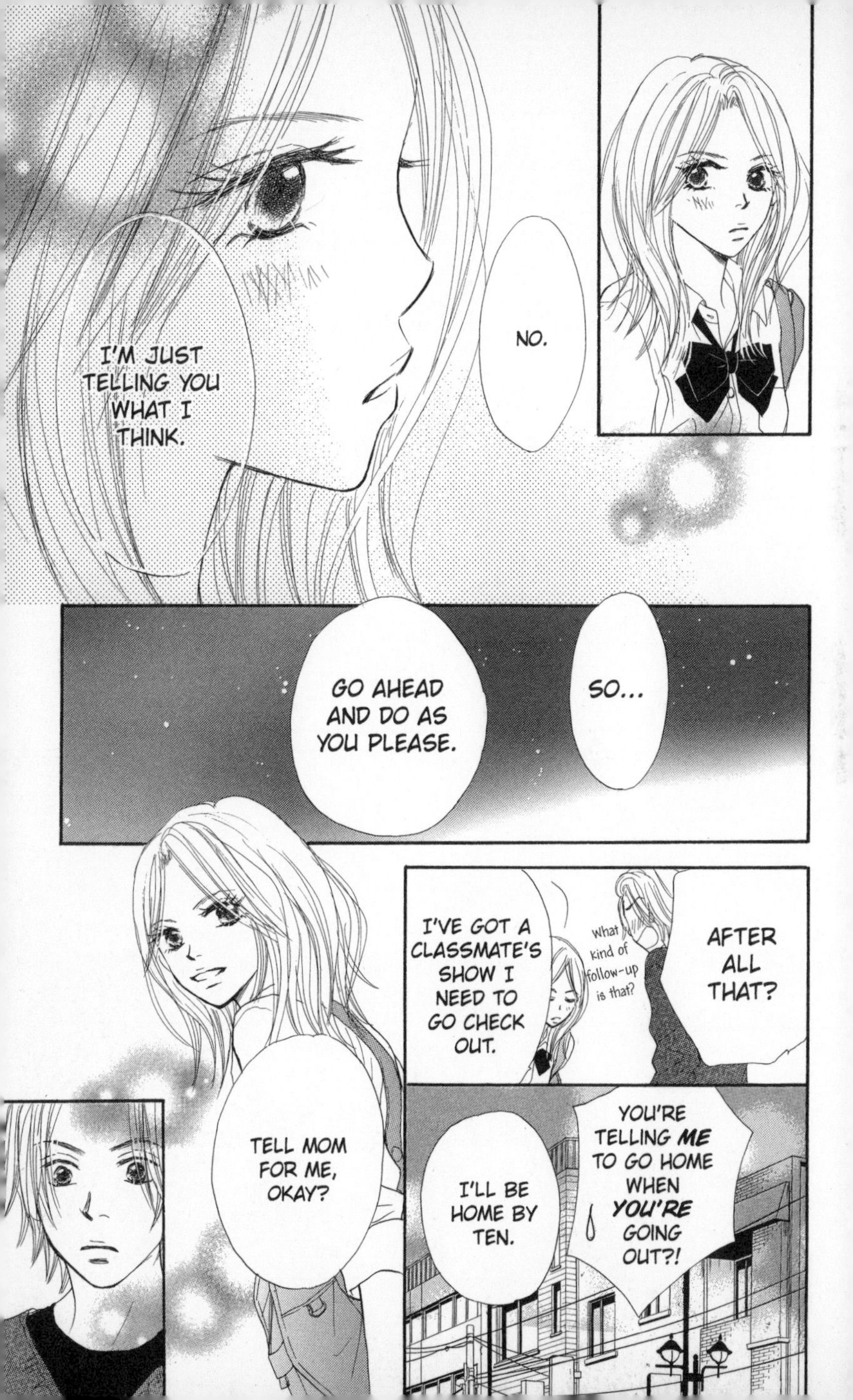

NO.
I'M JUST TELLING YOU WHAT I THINK.
SO...
GO AHEAD AND DO AS YOU PLEASE.
AFTER ALL THAT?
What kind of follow-up is that?
I'VE GOT A CLASSMATE'S SHOW I NEED TO GO CHECK OUT.
YOU'RE TELLING *ME* TO GO HOME WHEN *YOU'RE* GOING OUT?!
I'LL BE HOME BY TEN.
TELL MOM FOR ME, OKAY?

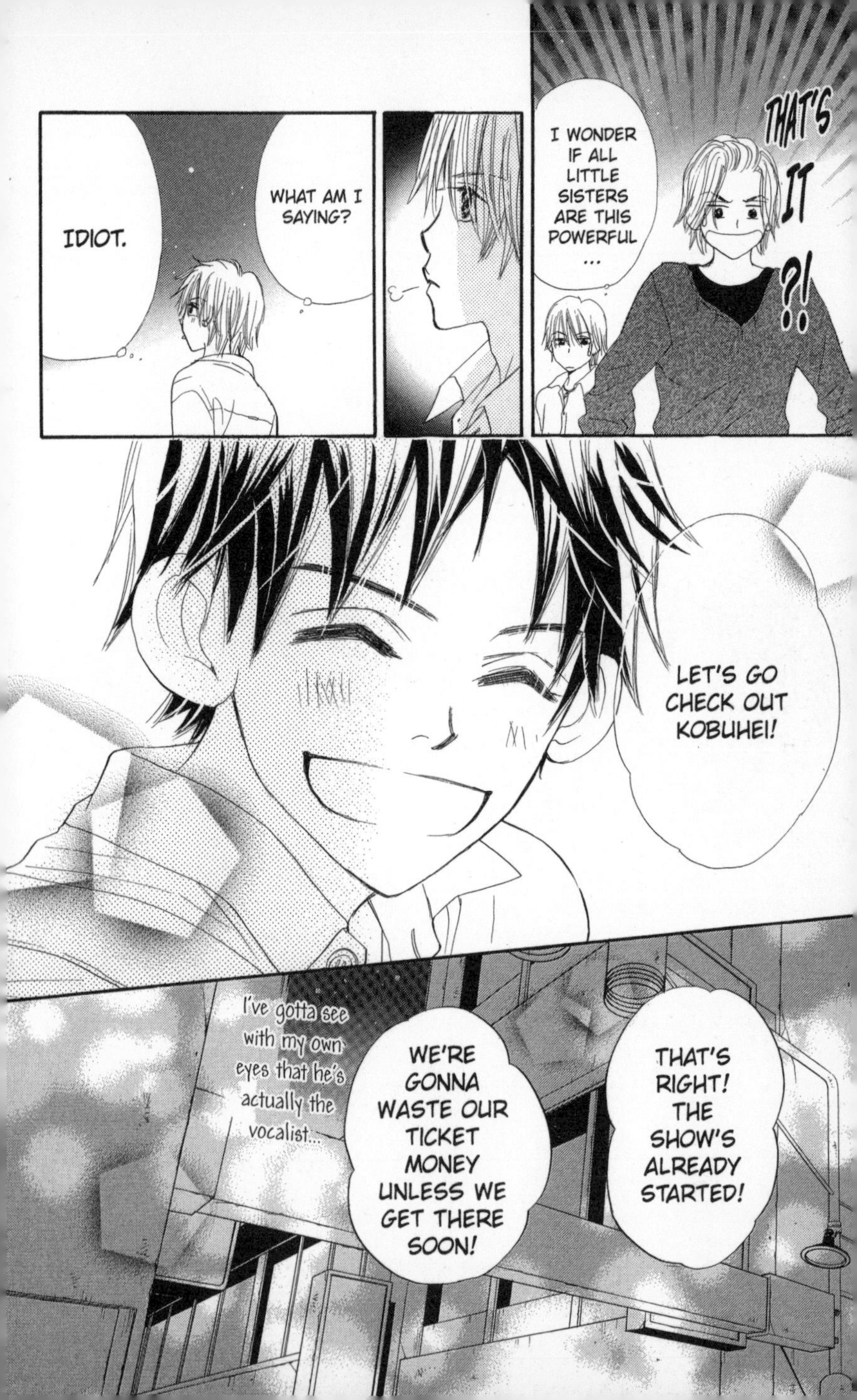
THAT'S IT ?!
I WONDER IF ALL LITTLE SISTERS ARE THIS POWERFUL ...
WHAT AM I SAYING?
IDIOT.
LET'S GO CHECK OUT KOBUHEI!
THAT'S RIGHT! THE SHOW'S ALREADY STARTED!
WE'RE GONNA WASTE OUR TICKET MONEY UNLESS WE GET THERE SOON!
I've gotta see with my own eyes that he's actually the vocalist...

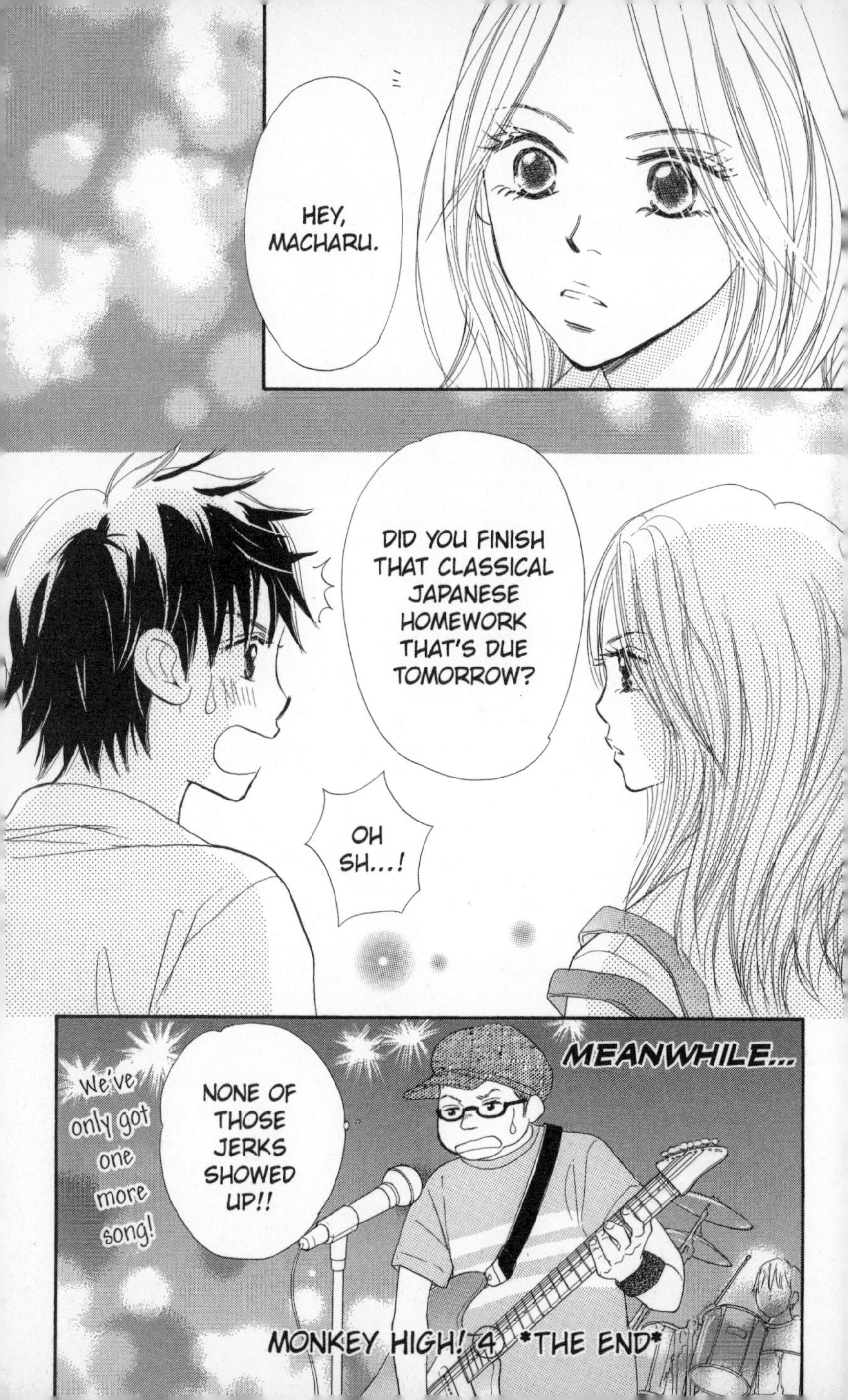
HEY, MACHARU.
DID YOU FINISH THAT CLASSICAL JAPANESE HOMEWORK THAT'S DUE TOMORROW?
OH SH...!
MEANWHILE...
NONE OF THOSE JERKS SHOWED UP!!
We've only got one more song!
MONKEY HIGH! 4 *THE END*

★ POSTSCRIPT ★

THANK YOU SO MUCH FOR READING! I'M SHOUKO AKIRA. CAN YOU BELIEVE IT'S ALREADY VOLUME 4? VOLUME 4!! I'M NOT SURE IF THIS IS ALL PART OF SOME KIND OF GREAT, BIG JOKE, BUT... IN ANY CASE, I WOULDN'T HAVE MADE IT WITHOUT THE SUPPORT OF MANY PEOPLE. THANK YOU SO MUCH. I'D LIKE TO WRITE A LITTLE BIT ABOUT THE DIFFERENT STORIES IN THIS BOOK NOW.

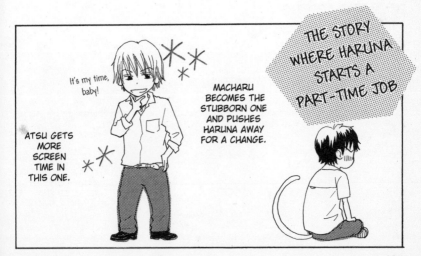

THE STORY WHERE HARUNA STARTS A PART-TIME JOB
MACHARU BECOMES THE STUBBORN ONE AND PUSHES HARUNA AWAY FOR A CHANGE.
It's my time, baby!
ATSU GETS MORE SCREEN TIME IN THIS ONE.

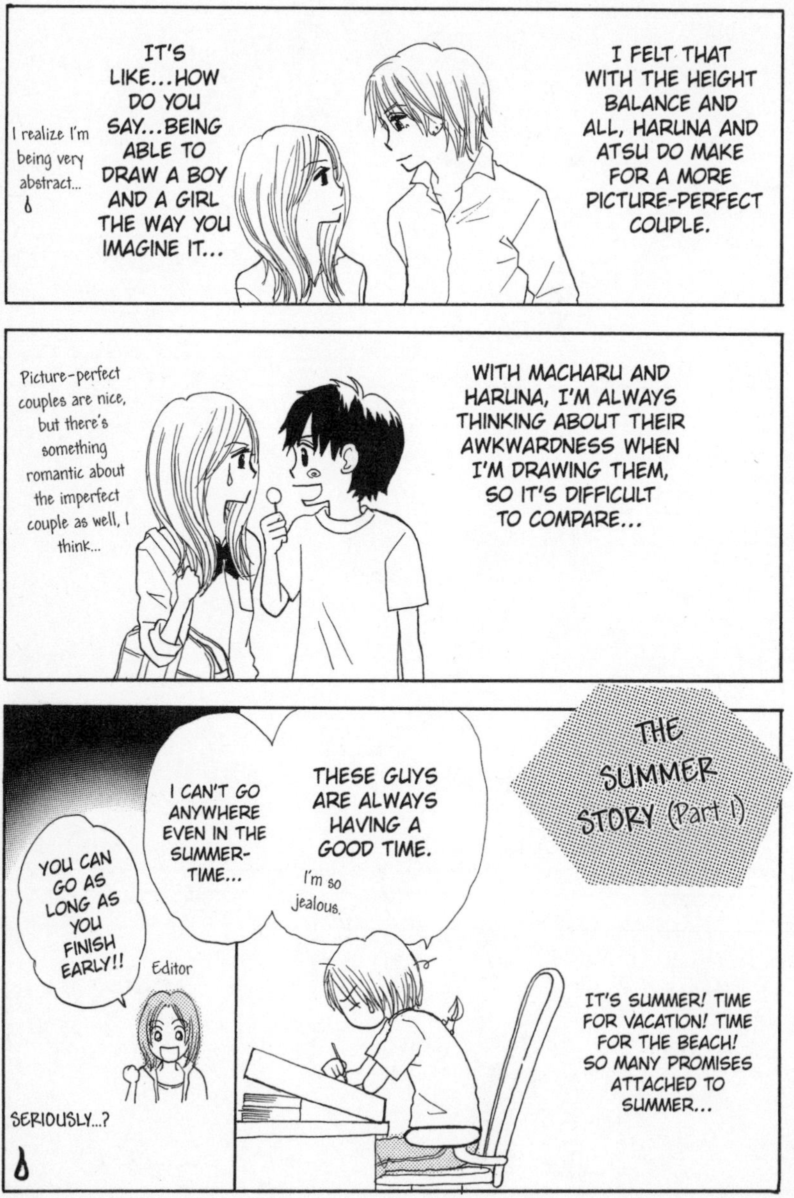
I FELT THAT WITH THE HEIGHT BALANCE AND ALL, HARUNA AND ATSU DO MAKE FOR A MORE PICTURE-PERFECT COUPLE.
IT'S LIKE...HOW DO YOU SAY...BEING ABLE TO DRAW A BOY AND A GIRL THE WAY YOU IMAGINE IT...
I realize I'm being very abstract...
WITH MACHARU AND HARUNA, I'M ALWAYS THINKING ABOUT THEIR AWKWARDNESS WHEN I'M DRAWING THEM, SO IT'S DIFFICULT TO COMPARE...
Picture-perfect couples are nice, but there's something romantic about the imperfect couple as well, I think...
THE SUMMER STORY (Part 1)
IT'S SUMMER! TIME FOR VACATION! TIME FOR THE BEACH! SO MANY PROMISES ATTACHED TO SUMMER...
THESE GUYS ARE ALWAYS HAVING A GOOD TIME.
I'm so jealous.
I CAN'T GO ANYWHERE EVEN IN THE SUMMER-TIME...
YOU CAN GO AS LONG AS YOU FINISH EARLY!!
Editor
SERIOUSLY...?

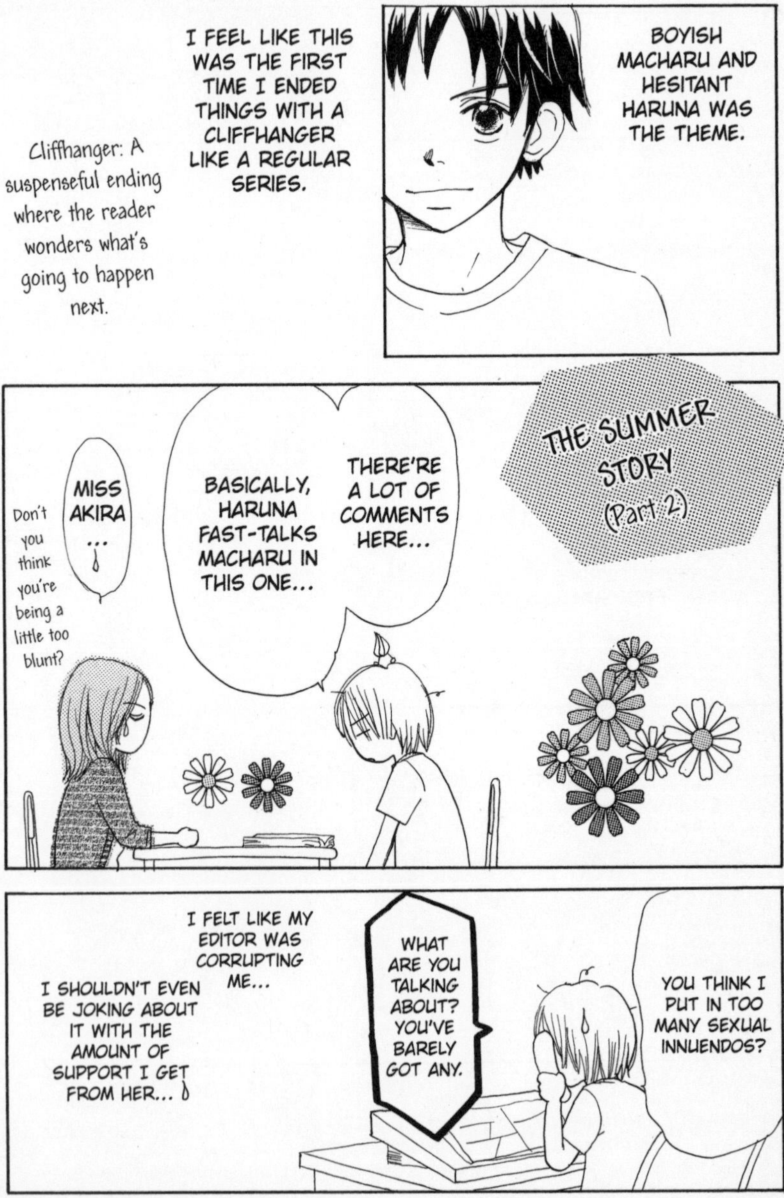
BOYISH MACHARU AND HESITANT HARUNA WAS THE THEME.
I FEEL LIKE THIS WAS THE FIRST TIME I ENDED THINGS WITH A CLIFFHANGER LIKE A REGULAR SERIES.
Cliffhanger: A suspenseful ending where the reader wonders what's going to happen next.
THE SUMMER STORY (Part 2)
THERE'RE A LOT OF COMMENTS HERE...
BASICALLY, HARUNA FAST-TALKS MACHARU IN THIS ONE...
MISS AKIRA...
Don't you think you're being a little too blunt?
YOU THINK I PUT IN TOO MANY SEXUAL INNUENDOS?
WHAT ARE YOU TALKING ABOUT? YOU'VE BARELY GOT ANY.
I FELT LIKE MY EDITOR WAS CORRUPTING ME...
I SHOULDN'T EVEN BE JOKING ABOUT IT WITH THE AMOUNT OF SUPPORT I GET FROM HER...

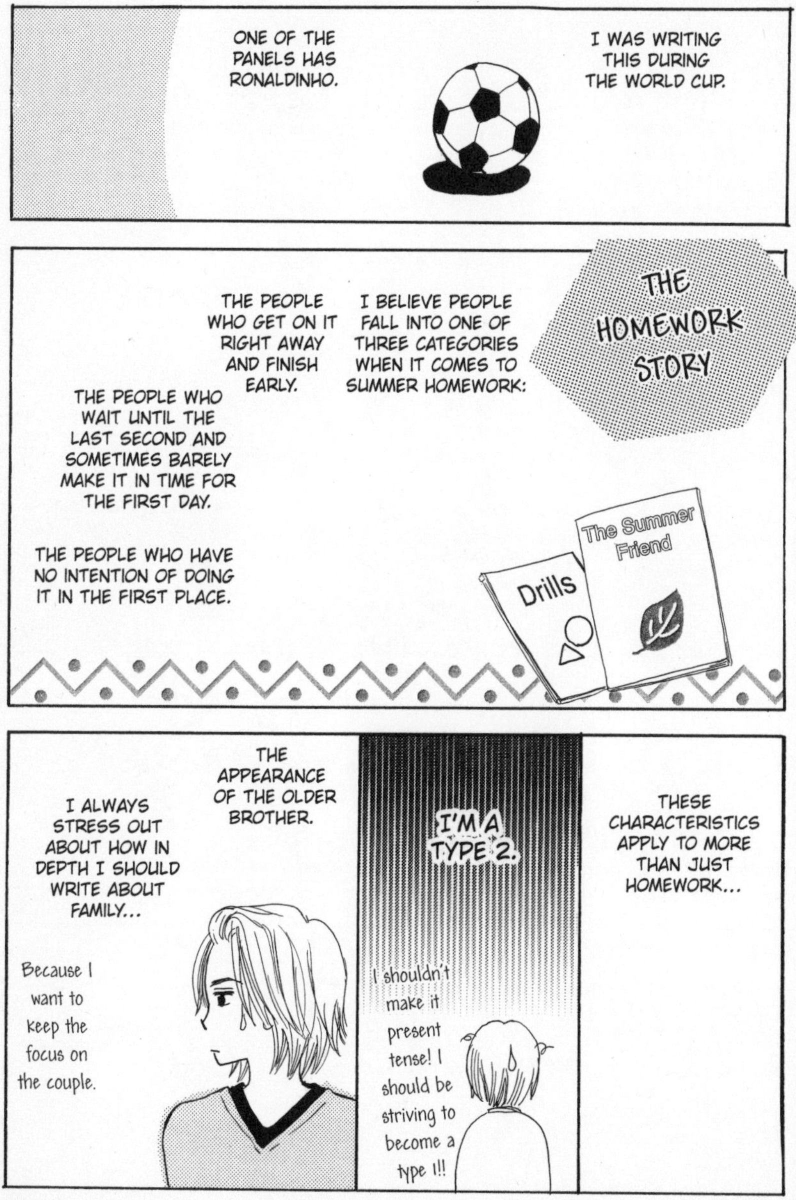
I WAS WRITING THIS DURING THE WORLD CUP.
ONE OF THE PANELS HAS RONALDINHO.
THE HOMEWORK STORY
I BELIEVE PEOPLE FALL INTO ONE OF THREE CATEGORIES WHEN IT COMES TO SUMMER HOMEWORK:
THE PEOPLE WHO GET ON IT RIGHT AWAY AND FINISH EARLY.
THE PEOPLE WHO WAIT UNTIL THE LAST SECOND AND SOMETIMES BARELY MAKE IT IN TIME FOR THE FIRST DAY.
THE PEOPLE WHO HAVE NO INTENTION OF DOING IT IN THE FIRST PLACE.
The Summer Friend
Drills
THESE CHARACTERISTICS APPLY TO MORE THAN JUST HOMEWORK...
I'M A TYPE 2.
I shouldn't make it present tense! I should be striving to become a type 1!!
THE APPEARANCE OF THE OLDER BROTHER.
I ALWAYS STRESS OUT ABOUT HOW IN DEPTH I SHOULD WRITE ABOUT FAMILY...
Because I want to keep the focus on the couple.

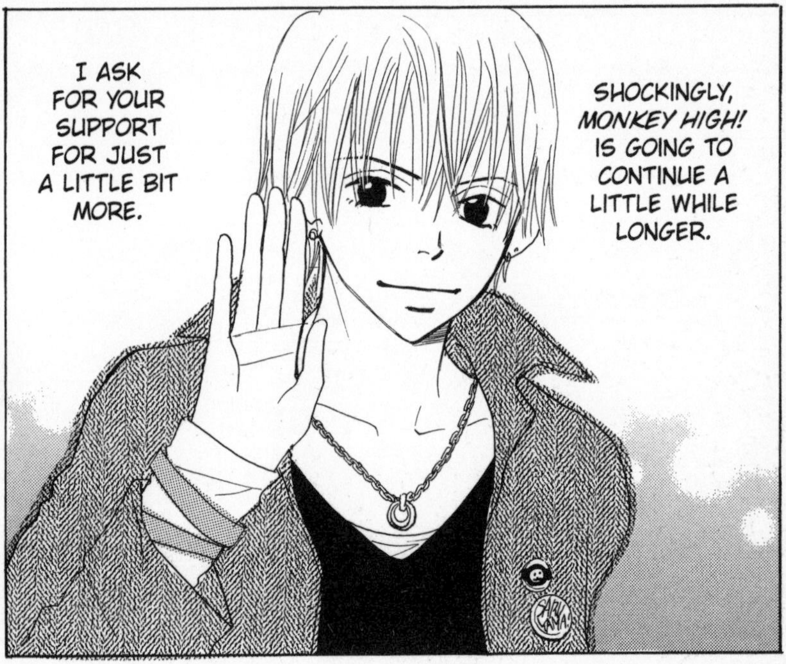
SHOCKINGLY, *MONKEY HIGH!* IS GOING TO CONTINUE A LITTLE WHILE LONGER.
I ASK FOR YOUR SUPPORT FOR JUST A LITTLE BIT MORE.
ZARU CANA!

I'D LIKE TO THANK EVERYBODY WHO HELPS ME—
MY EDITOR, MY COORDINATOR, MY DESIGNER,
MY FAMILY, FRIENDS AND ALL MY READERS.
THANK YOU SO MUCH AND I HOPE YOU'LL CONTINUE
SUPPORTING ME!

October 2006
Shouko Akira

Slightly confused by all the monkeying around?
Here are some notes to help you out!

Page 4: **Masaru**
Even though everyone refers to him by his nickname, Macharu's real name is "Masaru," which means "superior" in Japanese. Interestingly enough, *saru* by itself means "monkey."

Page 115, panel 3: **Yukata**
The *yukata* is a garment that is worn in the summertime in Japan, especially to outdoor festivals and events. Though it resembles the more formal kimono, yukata are made out of cotton rather than silk.

Page 123, panel 4: **Takoyaki and Ikayaki**
Both *takoyaki* and *ikayaki* are often sold at Japanese festivals. *Takoyaki* are dough balls with pieces of octopus in them. *Ikayaki* is grilled squid on a stick. *Tako* means "octopus" and *ika* means "squid" in Japanese.

Page 127, panel 2: **Obi**
Belt or sash used to tie kimono and yukata.

Page 140, panel 1: **Haiku**
Japanese poem that consists of three lines where the syllable count is five, seven, five.

Page 169, panel 2: *Agape and Eros*
Swedish theologian Anders Nygren wrote *Agape and Eros*, where eros (sexual love) and agape (unconditional love) are analyzed.

Volume 4 feels like a new personal record for me (with the exception of the manga I drew in my notebooks back in grade school). This is seriously uncharted territory. And it's all possible because of you, the readers. Thank you so much.

—Shouko Akira

Volume four!!

I'm trembling...

Shouko Akira was born on September 10th and grew up in Kyoto. She currently lives in Tokyo and loves soccer, cycling, and Yoshimoto Shin Kigeki (a comedy stage show based out of Osaka). Most of her works revolve around school life and love, including *Times Two*, a collection of five romantic short stories.

MONKEY HIGH!
VOL. 4
The Shojo Beat Manga Edition

STORY AND ART BY
SHOUKO AKIRA

Translation & Adaptation/Mai Ihara
Touch-up Art & Lettering/John Hunt
Design/Hidemi Dunn
Editor/Amy Yu

Editor in Chief, Books/Alvin Lu
Editor in Chief, Magazines/Marc Weidenbaum
VP, Publishing Licensing/Rika Inouye
VP, Sales & Product Marketing/Gonzalo Ferreyra
VP, Creative/Linda Espinosa
Publisher/Hyoe Narita

© 2006 Shouko AKIRA/Shogakukan Inc.
First published by Shogakukan Inc. in Japan as "Saruyama!"
All rights reserved.
The stories, characters and incidents mentioned in this publication
are entirely fictional.

Printed in Canada

Published by VIZ Media, LLC
P.O. Box 77010
San Francisco, CA 94107

Shojo Beat Manga Edition
10 9 8 7 6 5 4 3 2 1
First printing, December 2008

www.viz.com

store.viz.com

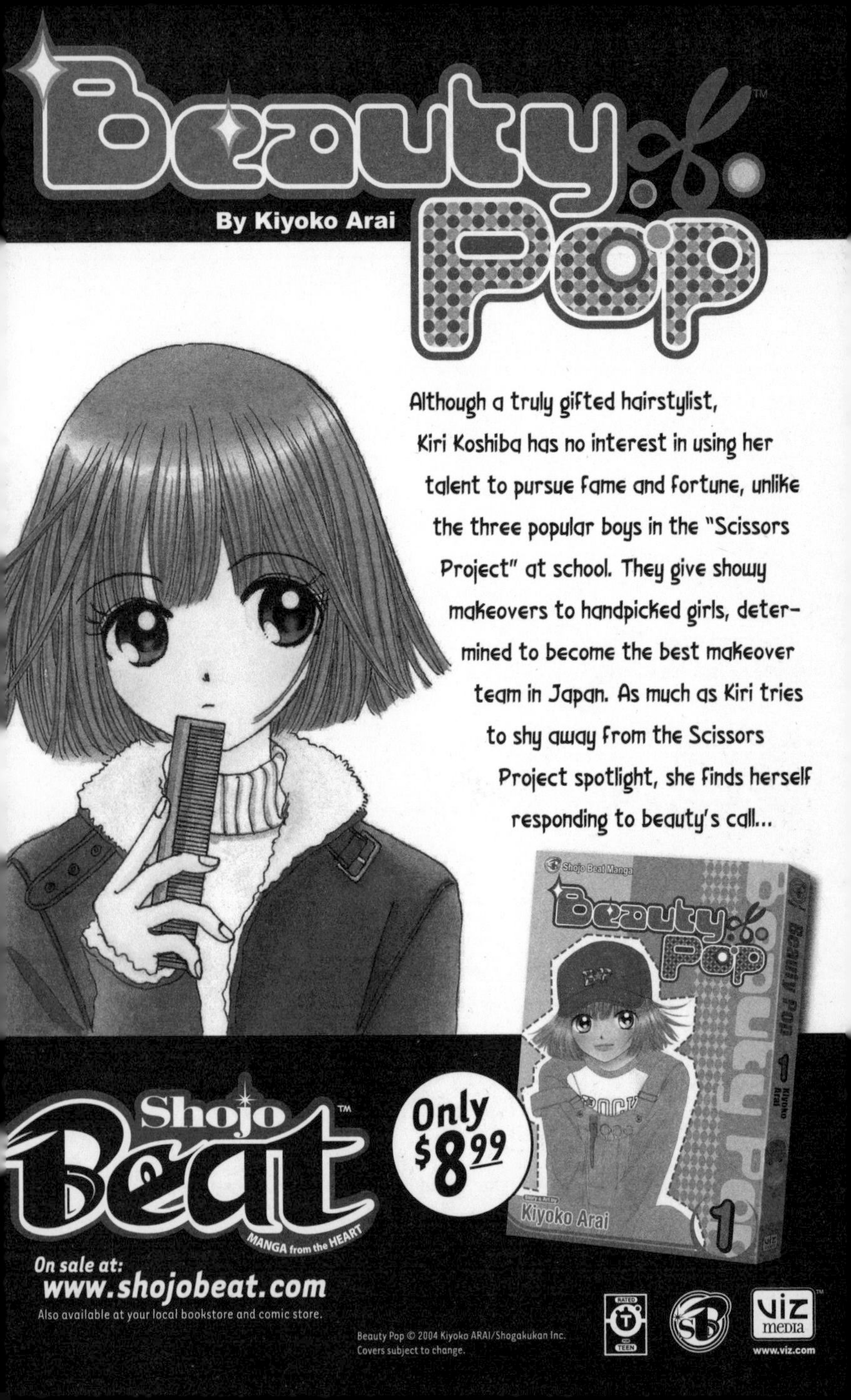
Beauty Pop™
By Kiyoko Arai
Although a truly gifted hairstylist, Kiri Koshiba has no interest in using her talent to pursue fame and fortune, unlike the three popular boys in the "Scissors Project" at school. They give showy makeovers to handpicked girls, determined to become the best makeover team in Japan. As much as Kiri tries to shy away from the Scissors Project spotlight, she finds herself responding to beauty's call...
Shojo Beat Manga
Beauty Pop
Kiyoko Arai
1
Shojo Beat™
MANGA from the HEART
Only $8.99
On sale at:
www.shojobeat.com
Also available at your local bookstore and comic store.
Beauty Pop © 2004 Kiyoko ARAI/Shogakukan Inc.
Covers subject to change.
RATED T FOR TEEN
VIZ MEDIA
www.viz.com

Kaze Hikaru™

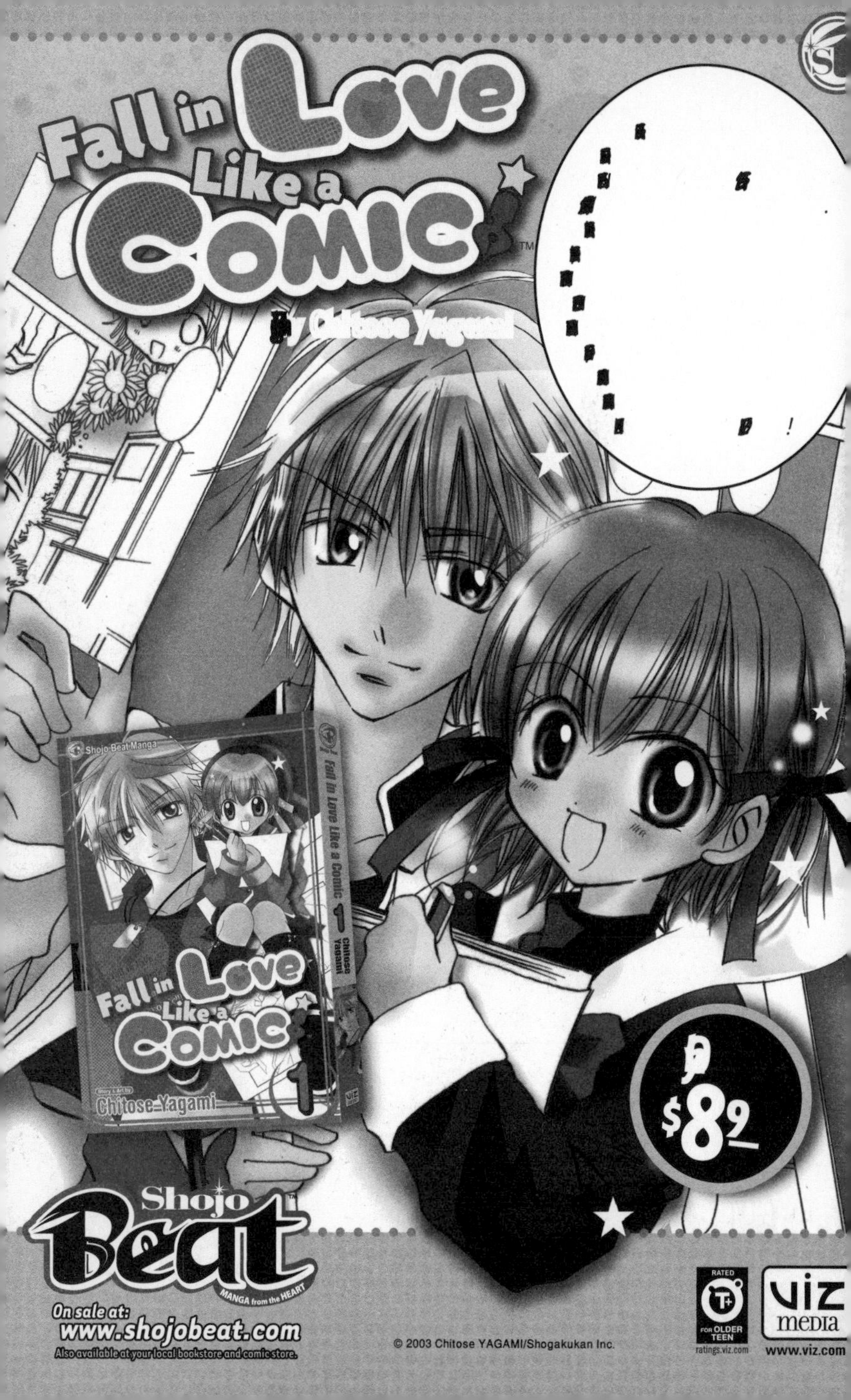

Fall in Love Like a Comic™
[redacted]y Chitose Yagami
[redacted]!
Shojo Beat Manga
Fall in Love Like a Comic 1
Chitose Yagami
Fall in Love Like a Comic
Story & Art by
Chitose Yagami
1
[redacted]
$8.9
Shojo Beat™
MANGA from the HEART
On sale at:
www.shojobeat.com
Also available at your local bookstore and comic store.
© 2003 Chitose YAGAMI/Shogakukan Inc.
RATED T+ FOR OLDER TEEN
ratings.viz.com
VIZ media
www.viz.com

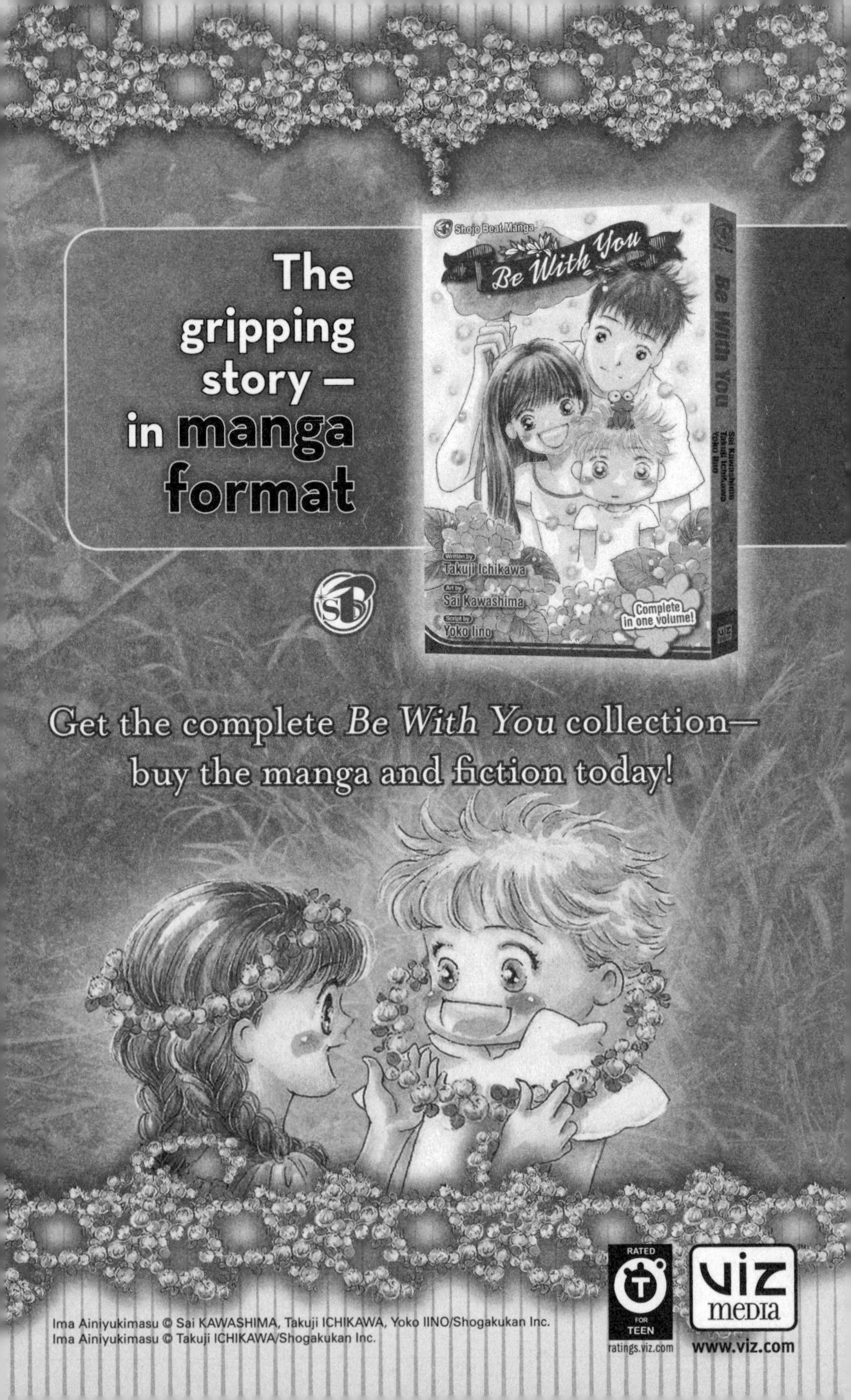
The gripping story — in manga format
Shojo Beat Manga
Be With You
Written by Takuji Ichikawa
Art by Sai Kawashima
Script by Yoko Iino
Complete in one volume!
Get the complete Be With You collection— buy the manga and fiction today!
Ima Ainiyukimasu © Sai KAWASHIMA, Takuji ICHIKAWA, Yoko IINO/Shogakukan Inc.
Ima Ainiyukimasu © Takuji ICHIKAWA/Shogakukan Inc.
RATED T FOR TEEN
ratings.viz.com
viz media
www.viz.com

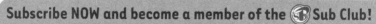

Shojo Beat
MANGA from the HEART

The Shojo Manga Authority

This monthly magazine is injected with the most **ADDICTIVE** shojo manga stories from Japan. PLUS, unique editorial coverage on the arts, music, culture, fashion, and much more!

✔ **YES!** Please enter my one-year subscription (12 GIANT issues) to **Shojo Beat** at the LOW SUBSCRIPTION RATE of **$34.99!**

Over **300 pages** per issue!

NAME

ADDRESS

CITY   STATE   ZIP

E-MAIL ADDRESS   P7GNC1

☐ MY CHECK IS ENCLOSED (PAYABLE TO Shojo Beat)   ☐ BILL ME LATER

CREDIT CARD: ☐ VISA   ☐ MASTERCARD

ACCOUNT #   EXP. DATE

SIGNATURE

CLIP AND MAIL TO →   SHOJO BEAT
Subscriptions Service Dept.
P.O. Box 438
Mount Morris, IL 61054-0438

Canada price for 12 issues: $46.99 USD, including GST, HST and QST. US/CAN orders only. Allow 6-8 weeks for delivery. Must be 16 or older to redeem offer. By redeeming this offer I represent that I am 16 or older.

Vampire Knight © Matsuri Hino 2004/HAKUSENSHA, Inc. Nana Kitade © Sony Music Entertainment (Japan), Inc.
CRIMSON HERO © 2002 by Mitsuba Takanashi/SHUEISHA Inc.

RATED
T+
FOR OLDER
TEEN
ratings.viz.com